11/13

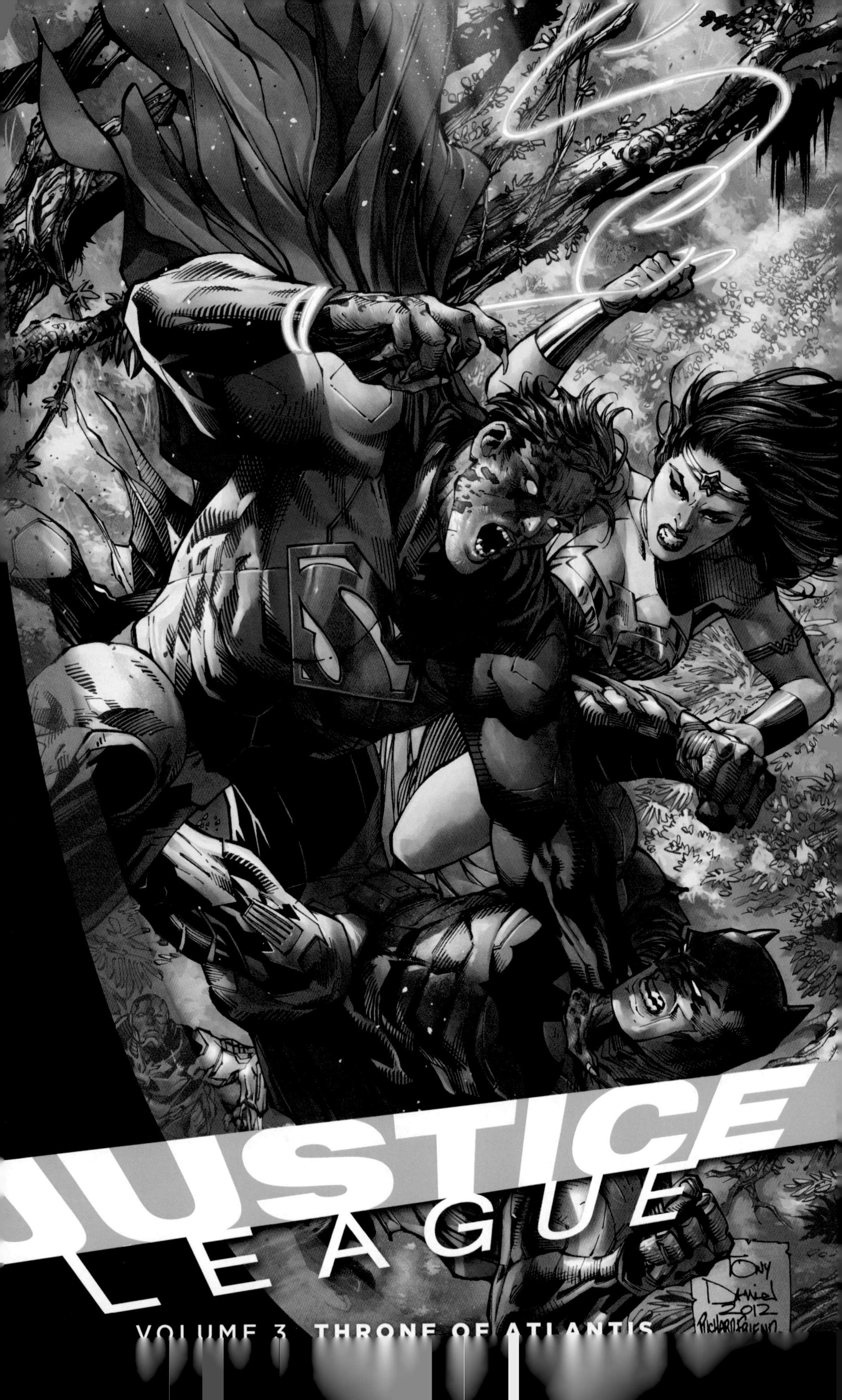

JUSTICE
LEAGUE
VOLUME 3 THRONE OF ATLANTIS
TONY DANIEL 2012
RICHARD FRIEND

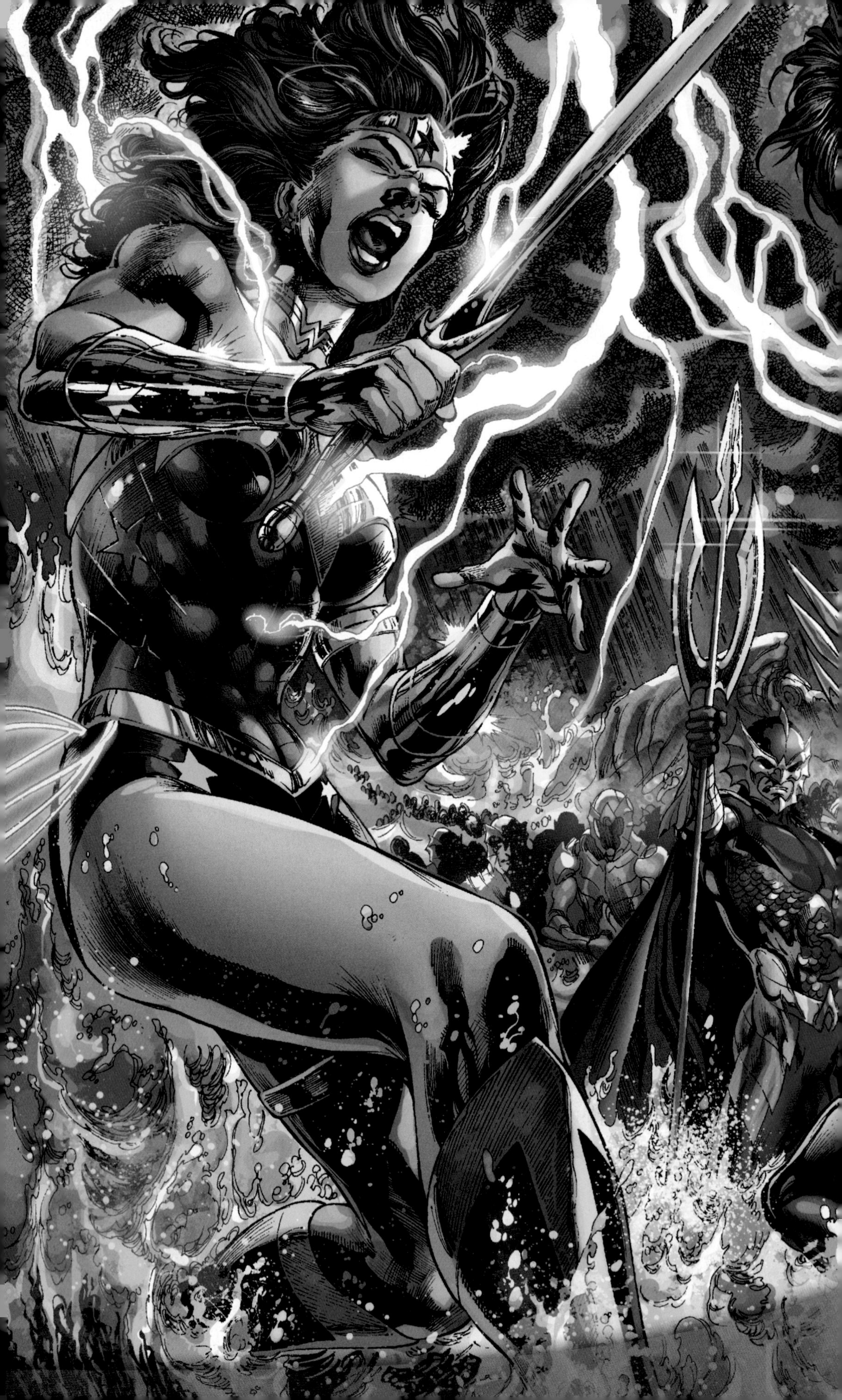

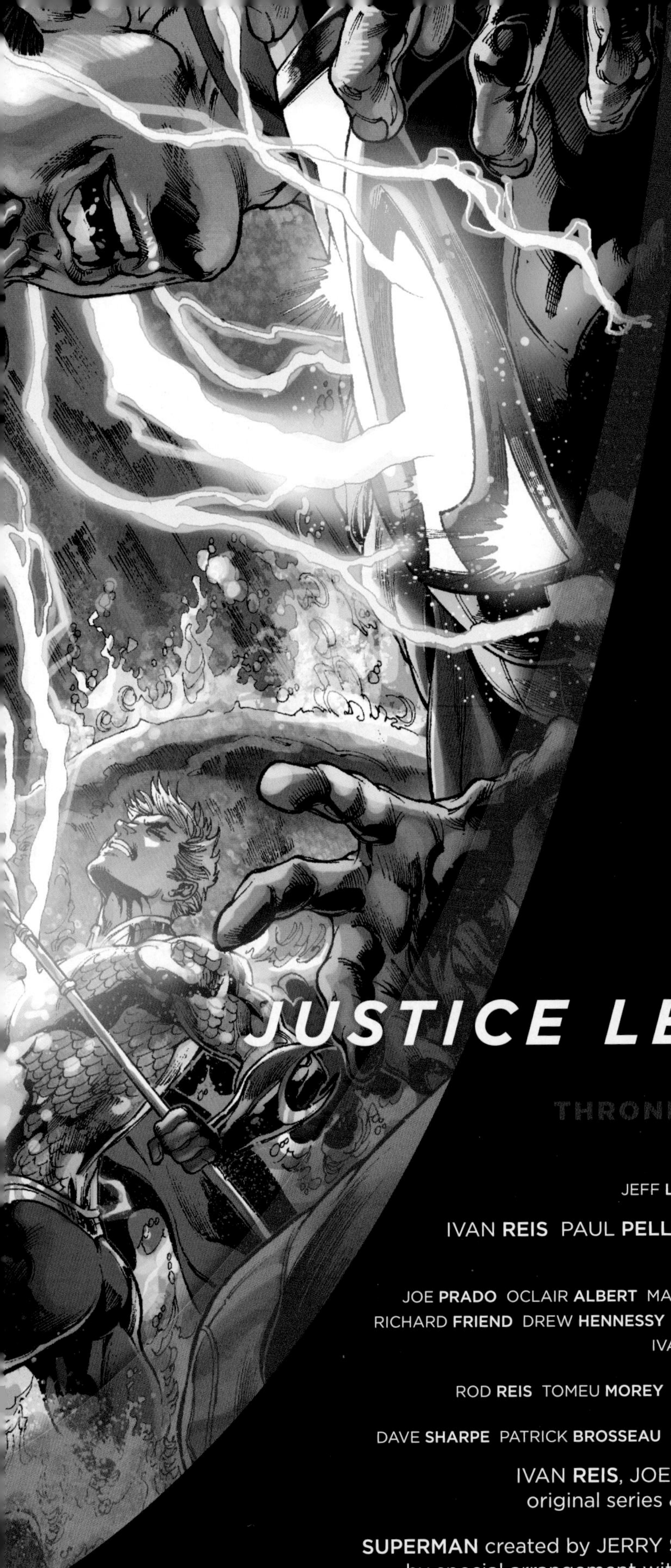

JUSTICE LEAGUE

VOLUME 3
THRONE OF ATLANTIS

GEOFF **JOHNS** writer
JEFF **LEMIRE** epilogue co-writer

IVAN **REIS** PAUL **PELLETIER** TONY S. **DANIEL**
BRAD **WALKER** pencillers

JOE **PRADO** OCLAIR **ALBERT** MATT **BANNING** SANDU **FLOREA**
RICHARD **FRIEND** DREW **HENNESSY** KARL **KESEL** SEAN **PARSONS**
IVAN **REIS** ART **THIBERT** inkers

ROD **REIS** TOMEU **MOREY** JAY DAVID **RAMOS** colorists

DAVE **SHARPE** PATRICK **BROSSEAU** NICK **NAPOLITANO** letterers

IVAN **REIS**, JOE **PRADO** AND ROD **REIS**
original series & collection cover artists

SUPERMAN created by JERRY **SIEGEL** & JOE **SHUSTER**
by special arrangement with the Jerry Siegel family

BRIAN CUNNINGHAM PAT McCALLUM Editors – Original Series KATIE KUBERT Assistant Editor – Original Series
PETER HAMBOUSSI Editor ROBIN WILDMAN Assistant Editor
ROBBIN BROSTERMAN Design Director – Books ROBBIE BIEDERMAN Publication Design

BOB HARRAS Senior VP – Editor-in-Chief, DC Comics

DIANE NELSON President DAN DIDIO and JIM LEE Co-Publishers
GEOFF JOHNS Chief Creative Officer
JOHN ROOD Executive VP – Sales, Marketing and Business Development
AMY GENKINS Senior VP – Business and Legal Affairs NAIRI GARDINER Senior VP – Finance
JEFF BOISON VP – Publishing Planning MARK CHIARELLO VP – Art Direction and Design
JOHN CUNNINGHAM VP – Marketing TERRI CUNNINGHAM VP – Editorial Administration
ALISON GILL Senior VP – Manufacturing and Operations HANK KANALZ Senior VP – Vertigo and Integrated Publishing
JAY KOGAN VP – Business and Legal Affairs, Publishing JACK MAHAN VP – Business Affairs, Talent
NICK NAPOLITANO VP – Manufacturing Administration SUE POHJA VP – Book Sales
COURTNEY SIMMONS Senior VP – Publicity BOB WAYNE Senior VP – Sales

JUSTICE LEAGUE VOLUME 3: THRONE OF ATLANTIS

DC Comics, 1700 Broadway, New York, NY 10019
A Warner Bros. Entertainment Company.
Printed by RR Donnelley, Salem, VA, USA. 8/23/13. First Printing.

HC ISBN: 978-1-4012-4240-4
SC ISBN: 978-1-4012-4698-3

Library of Congress Cataloging-in-Publication Data

Johns, Geoff, 1973-
Justice League. Volume 3, Throne of Atlantis / Geoff Johns, Ivan Reis.
pages cm
"Originally published in single magazine form as Justice League 13-17, Aquaman 15-16."
ISBN 978-1-4012-4240-4
1. Graphic novels. I. Reis, Ivan. II. Title. III. Title: Throne of Atlantis.
PN6728.J87J654 2013
741.5'973—dc23
2013020542

SUSTAINABLE FORESTRY INITIATIVE

Certified Chain of Custody
At Least 20% Certified Forest Content
www.sfiprogram.org
SFI-01042
APPLIES TO TEXT STOCK ONLY

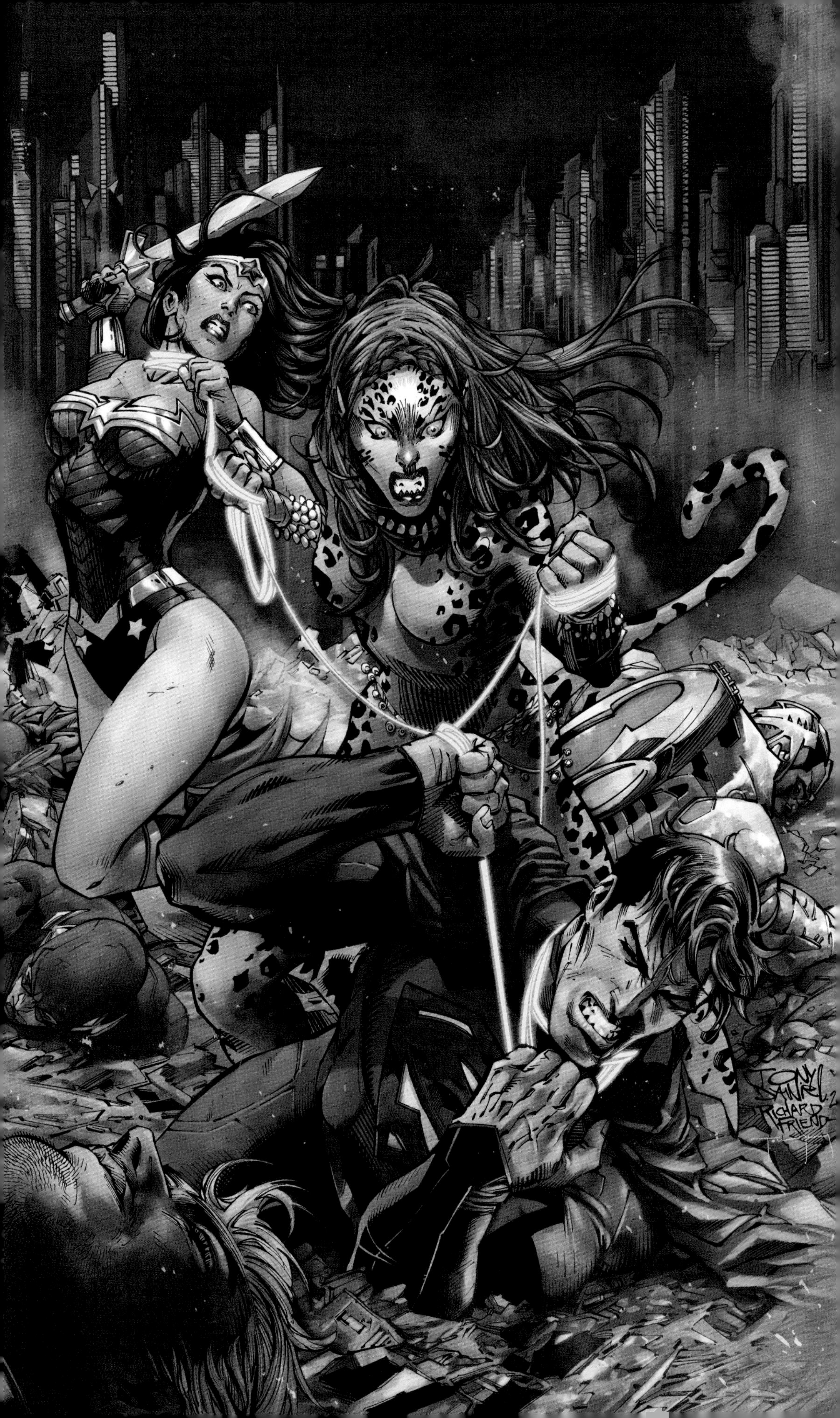

GEOFF JOHNS writer TONY S. DANIEL penciller RICHARD FRIEND & MATT BANNING inkers cover by TONY S. DANIEL, RICHARD FRIEND & TOMEU M

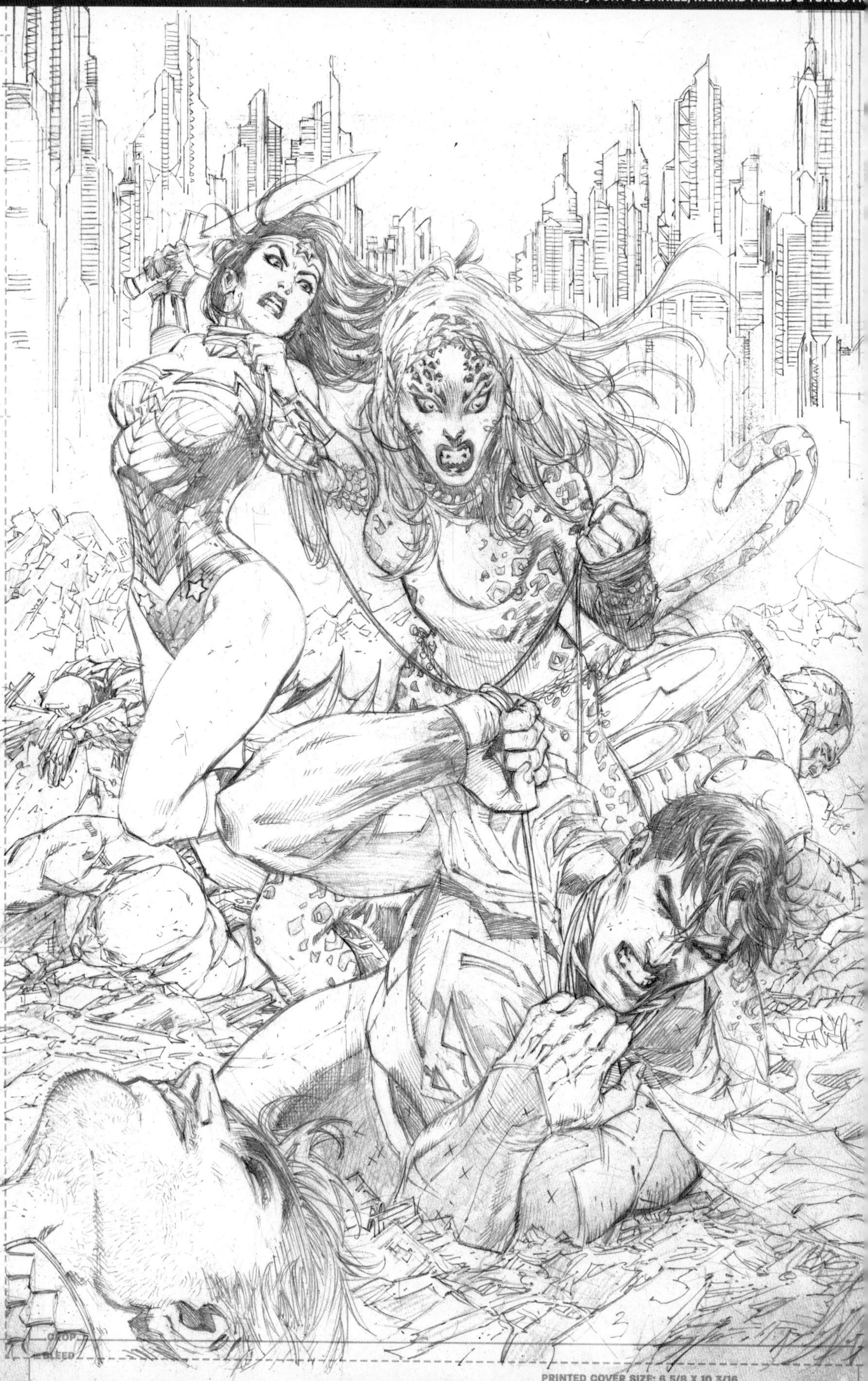
CROP
BLEED

PRINTED COVER SIZE: 6 5/8 X 10 3/16

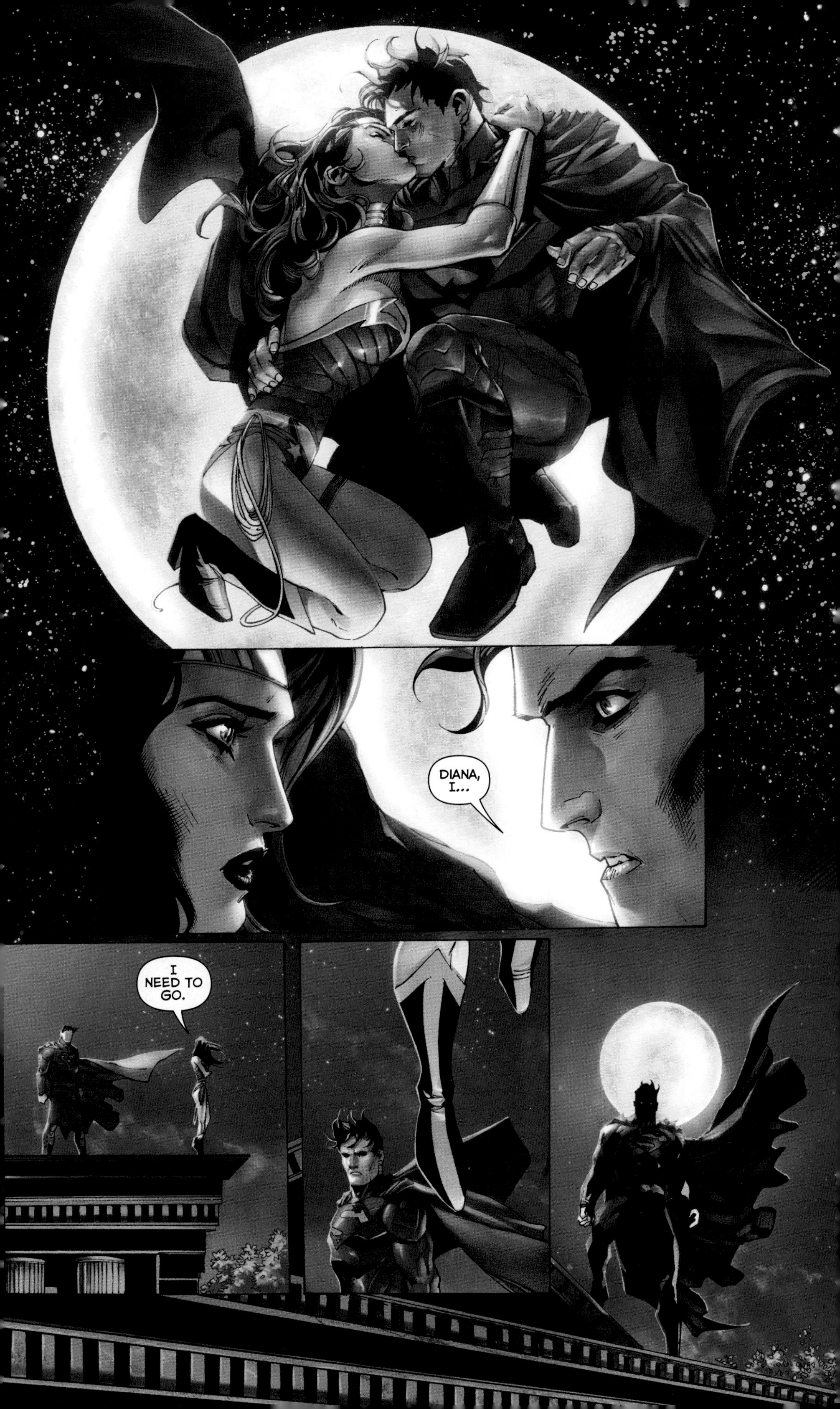
DIANA, I...
I NEED TO GO.

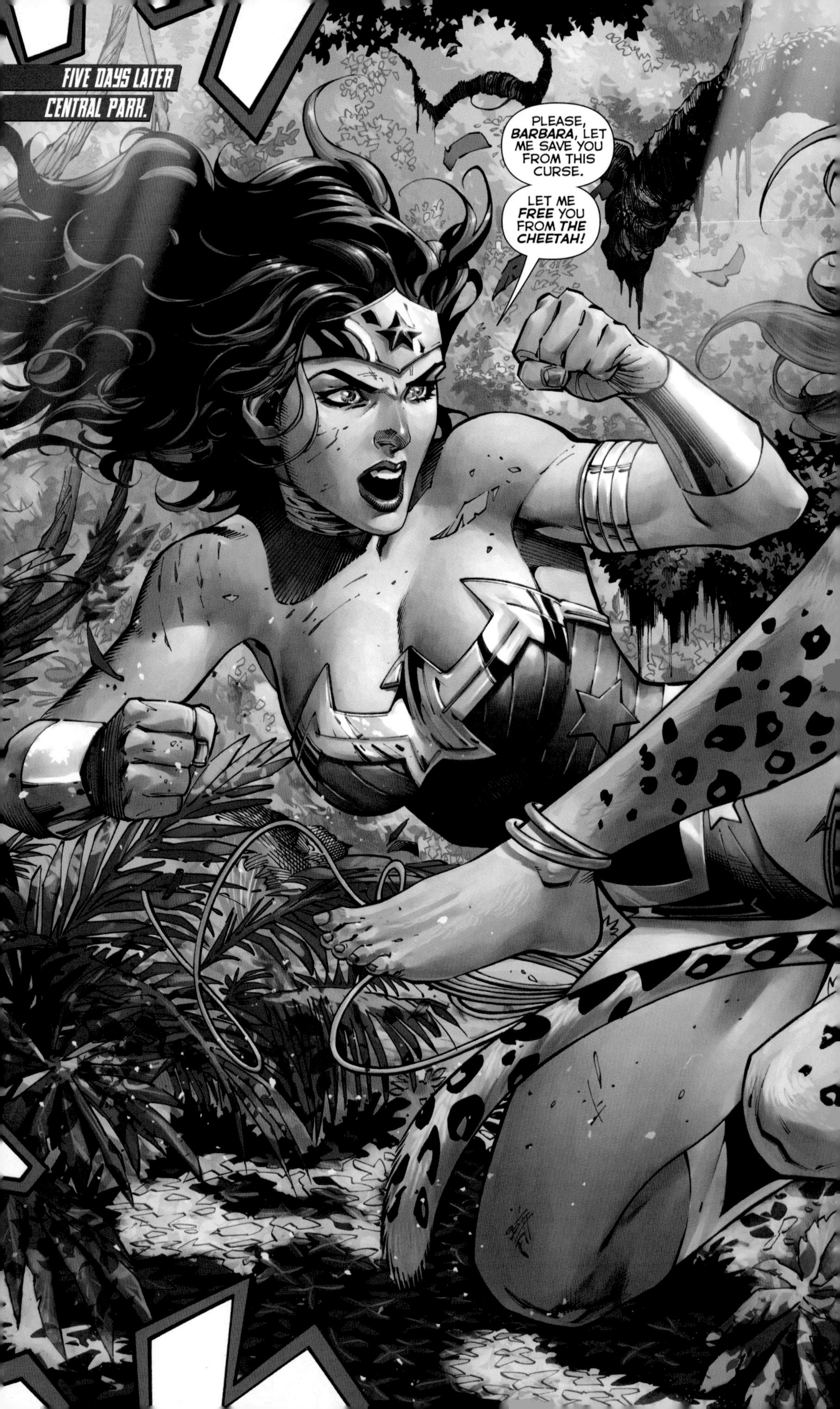
FIVE DAYS LATER
CENTRAL PARK.
PLEASE, BARBARA, LET ME SAVE YOU FROM THIS CURSE.
LET ME FREE YOU FROM THE CHEETAH!

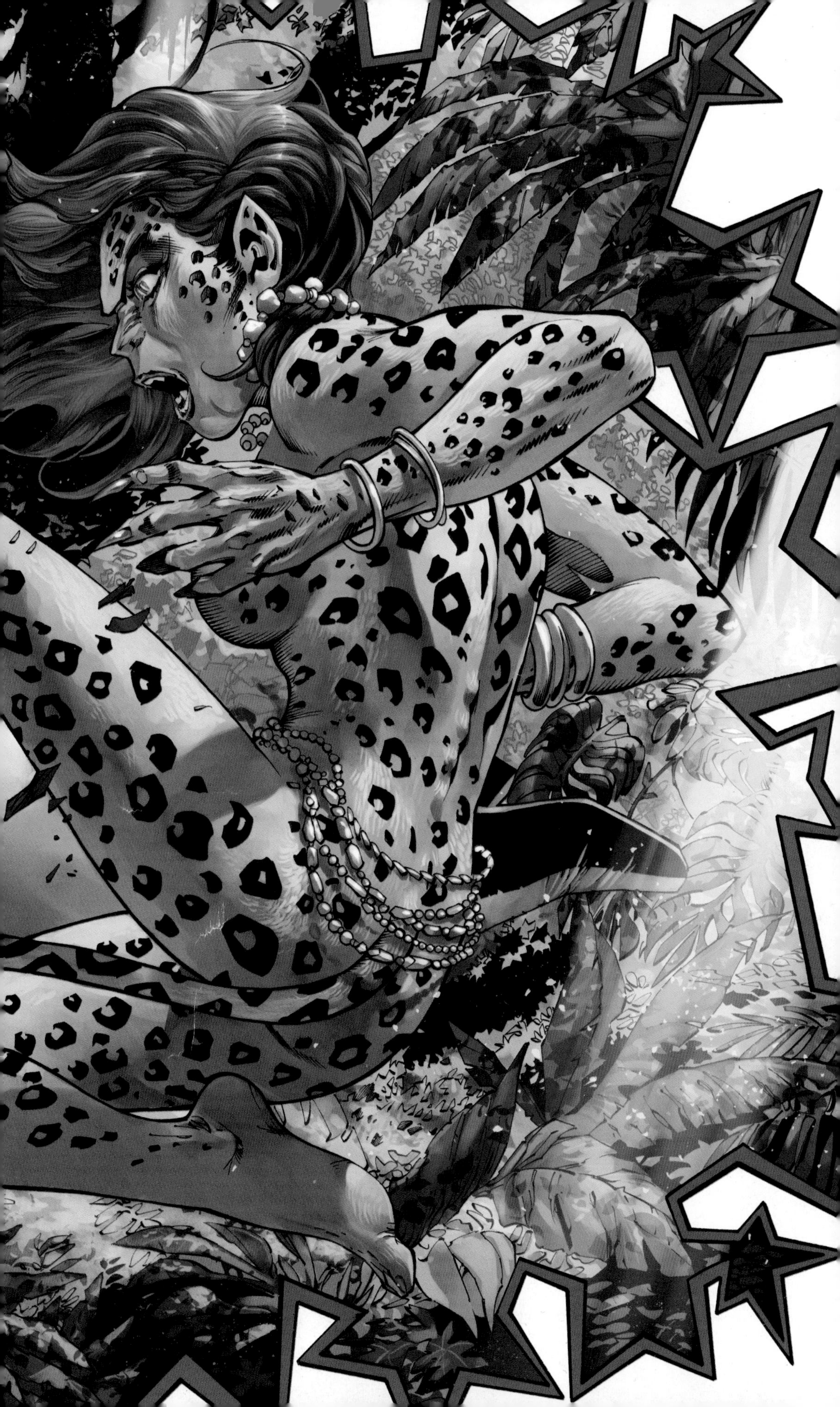

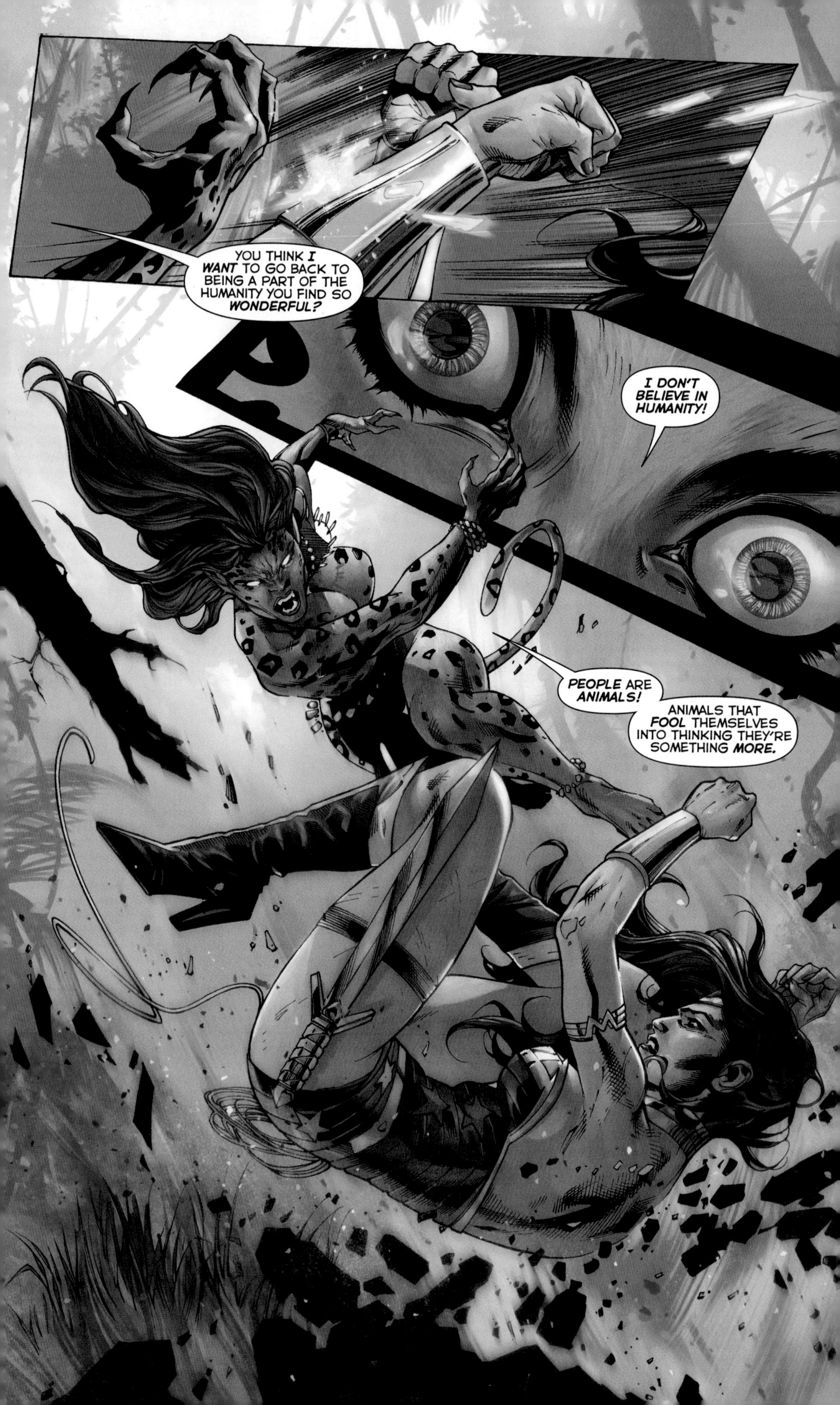

YOU THINK *I* *WANT* TO GO BACK TO BEING A PART OF THE HUMANITY YOU FIND SO *WONDERFUL?*
I DON'T BELIEVE IN HUMANITY!
PEOPLE ARE *ANIMALS!*
ANIMALS THAT *FOOL* THEMSELVES INTO THINKING THEY'RE SOMETHING *MORE.*

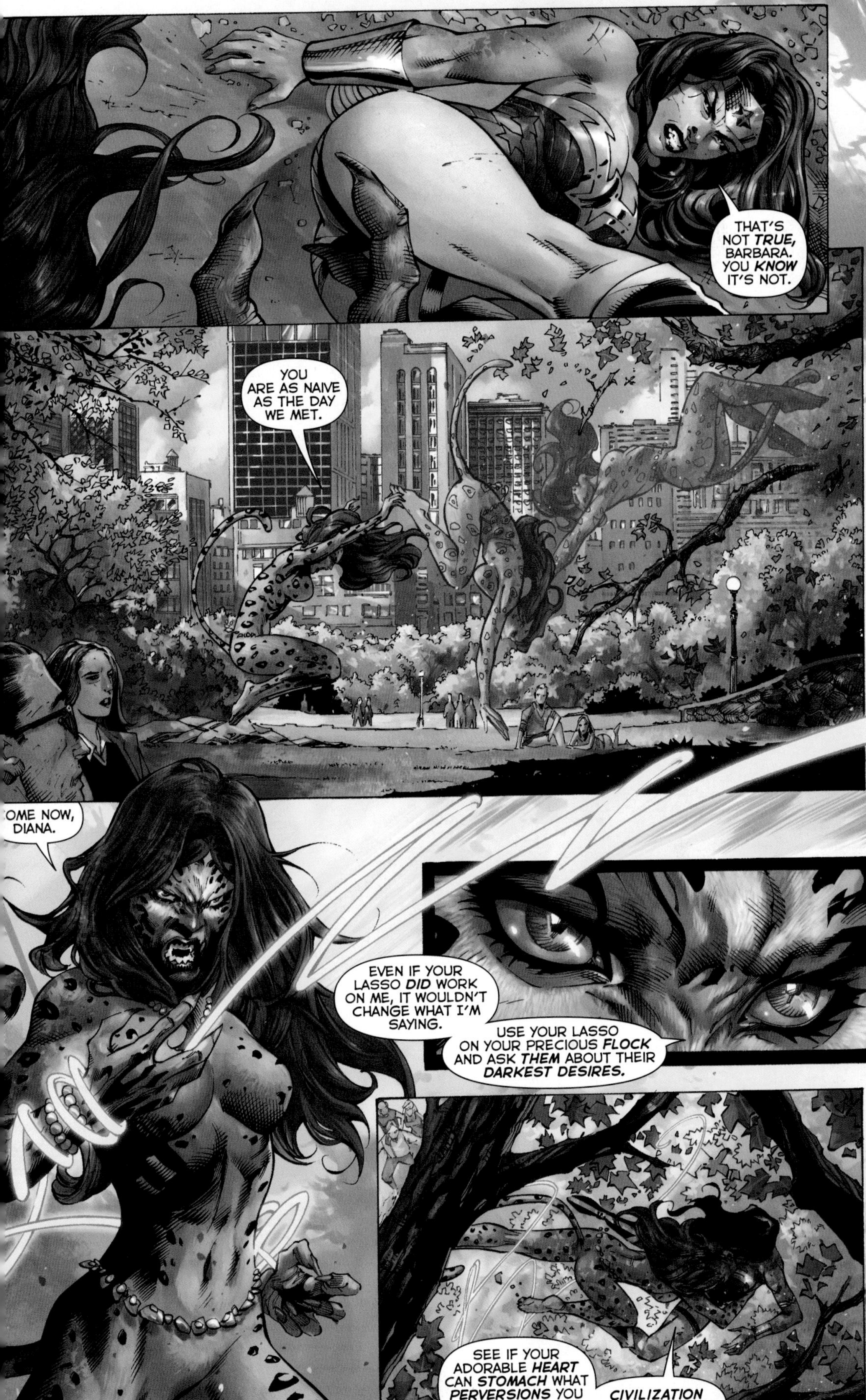
THAT'S NOT TRUE, BARBARA. YOU KNOW IT'S NOT.
YOU ARE AS NAIVE AS THE DAY WE MET.
OME NOW, DIANA.
EVEN IF YOUR LASSO DID WORK ON ME, IT WOULDN'T CHANGE WHAT I'M SAYING.
USE YOUR LASSO ON YOUR PRECIOUS FLOCK AND ASK THEM ABOUT THEIR DARKEST DESIRES.
SEE IF YOUR ADORABLE HEART CAN STOMACH WHAT PERVERSIONS YOU EXPOSE WITHIN THEM.
CIVILIZATION IS JUST A MASK THEY ALL WEAR.

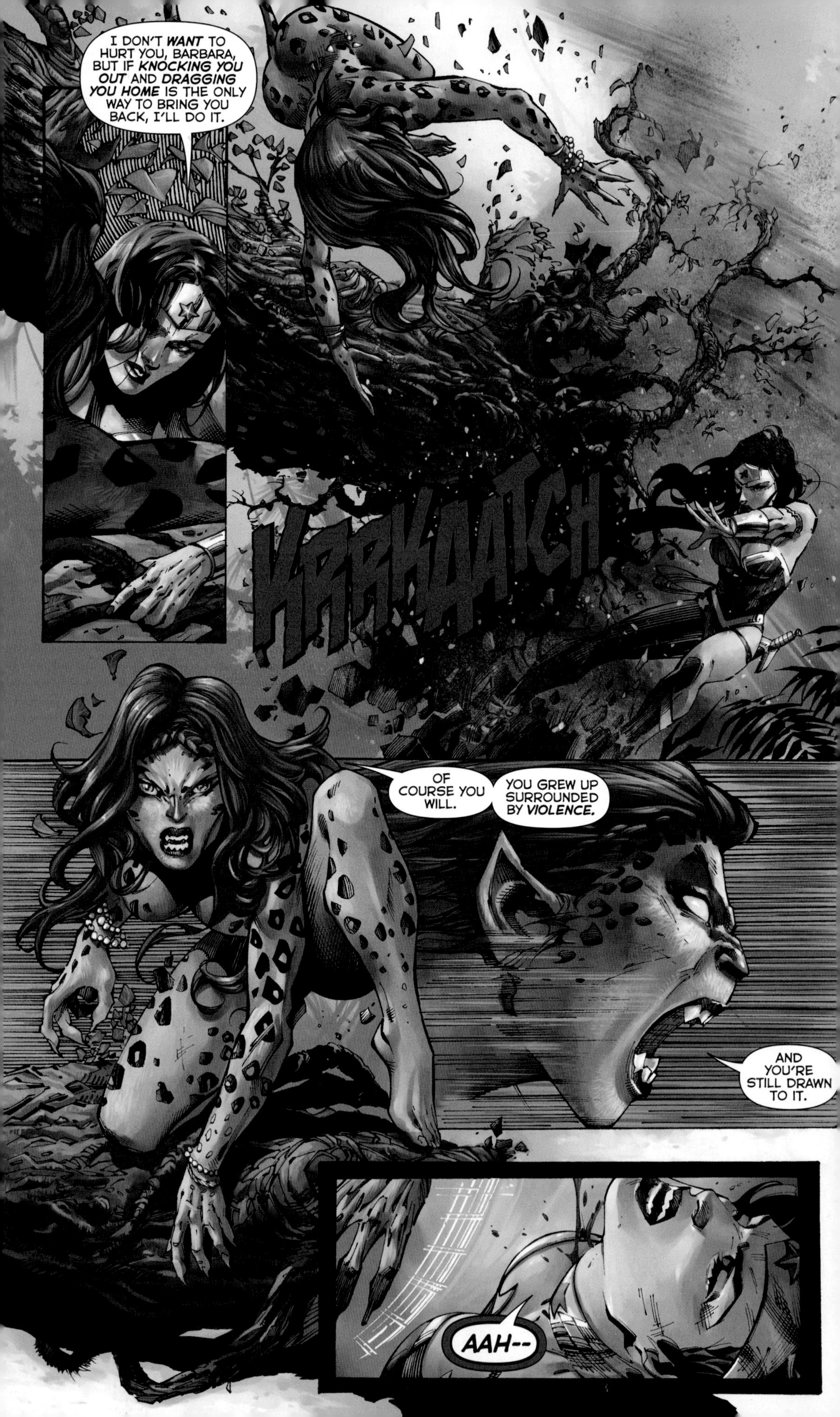

I DON'T WANT TO HURT YOU, BARBARA, BUT IF KNOCKING YOU OUT AND DRAGGING YOU HOME IS THE ONLY WAY TO BRING YOU BACK, I'LL DO IT.
KRRKAATCH
OF COURSE YOU WILL.
YOU GREW UP SURROUNDED BY VIOLENCE.
AND YOU'RE STILL DRAWN TO IT.
AAH--

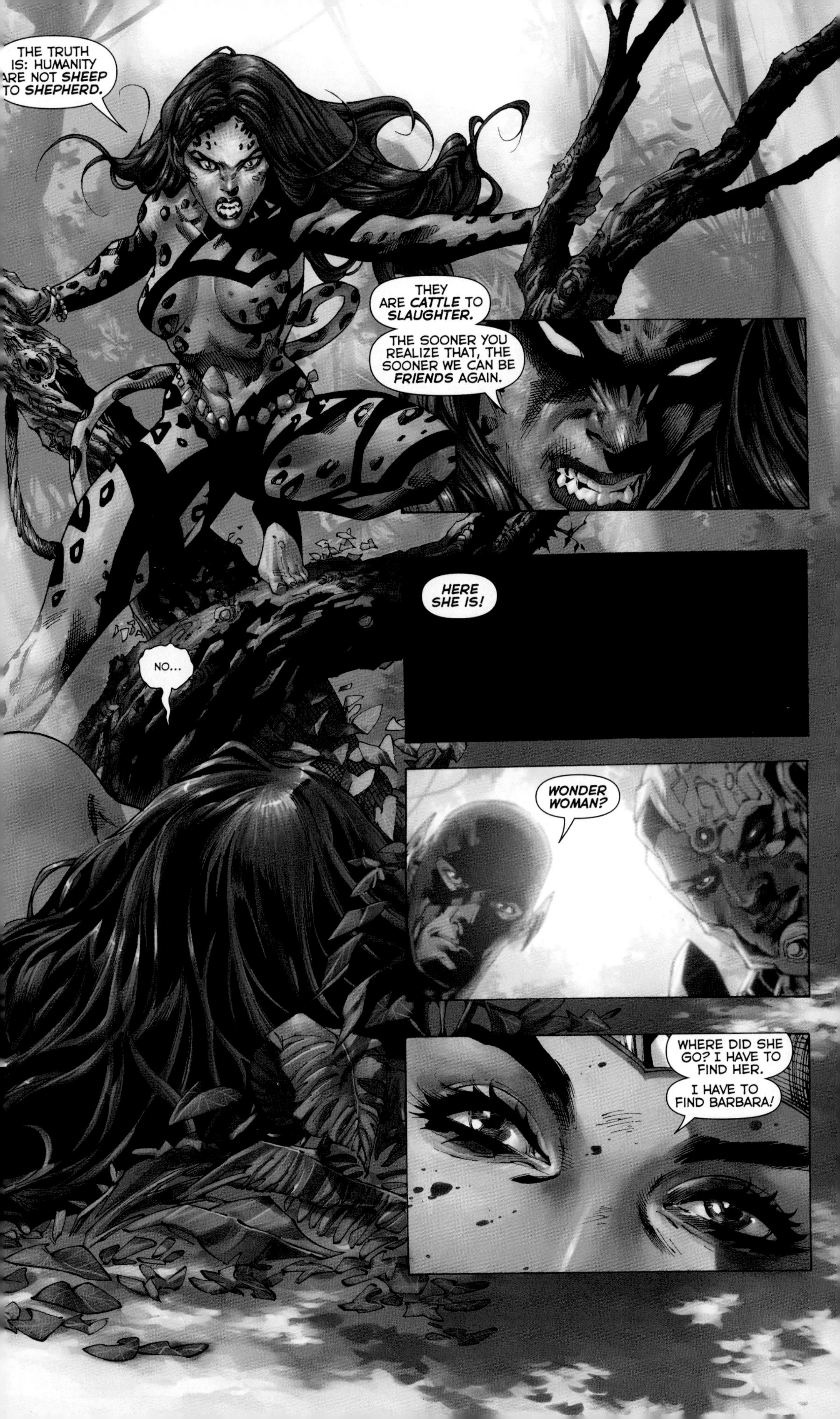
THE TRUTH IS: HUMANITY ARE NOT SHEEP TO SHEPHERD.
THEY ARE CATTLE TO SLAUGHTER.
THE SOONER YOU REALIZE THAT, THE SOONER WE CAN BE FRIENDS AGAIN.
HERE SHE IS!
NO...
WONDER WOMAN?
WHERE DID SHE GO? I HAVE TO FIND HER.
I HAVE TO FIND BARBARA!

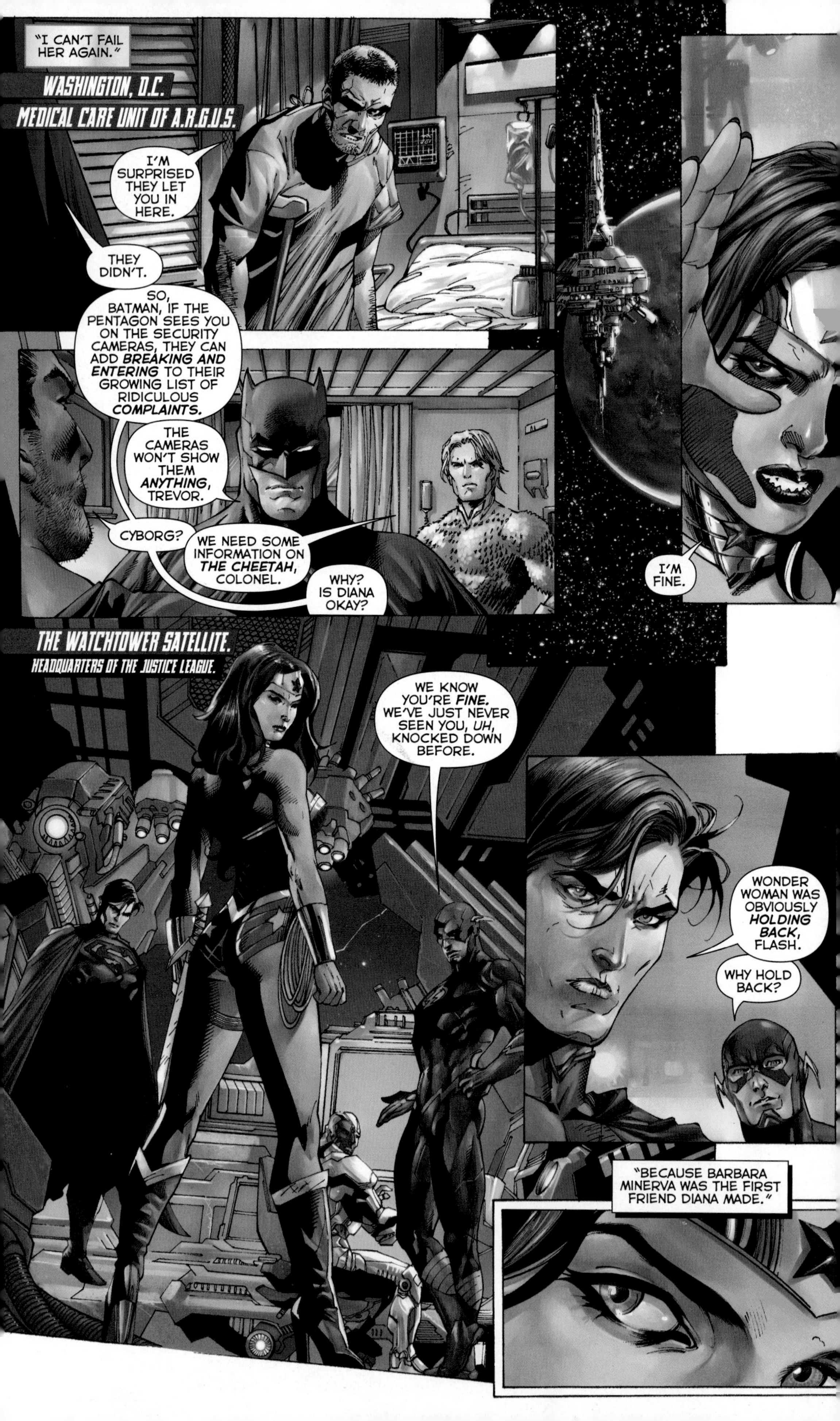

"I CAN'T FAIL HER AGAIN."
WASHINGTON, D.C.
MEDICAL CARE UNIT OF A.R.G.U.S.
I'M SURPRISED THEY LET YOU IN HERE.
THEY DIDN'T.
SO, BATMAN, IF THE PENTAGON SEES YOU ON THE SECURITY CAMERAS, THEY CAN ADD BREAKING AND ENTERING TO THEIR GROWING LIST OF RIDICULOUS COMPLAINTS.
THE CAMERAS WON'T SHOW THEM ANYTHING, TREVOR.
CYBORG?
WE NEED SOME INFORMATION ON THE CHEETAH, COLONEL.
WHY? IS DIANA OKAY?
I'M FINE.
THE WATCHTOWER SATELLITE.
HEADQUARTERS OF THE JUSTICE LEAGUE.
WE KNOW YOU'RE FINE. WE'VE JUST NEVER SEEN YOU, UH, KNOCKED DOWN BEFORE.
WONDER WOMAN WAS OBVIOUSLY HOLDING BACK, FLASH.
WHY HOLD BACK?
"BECAUSE BARBARA MINERVA WAS THE FIRST FRIEND DIANA MADE."

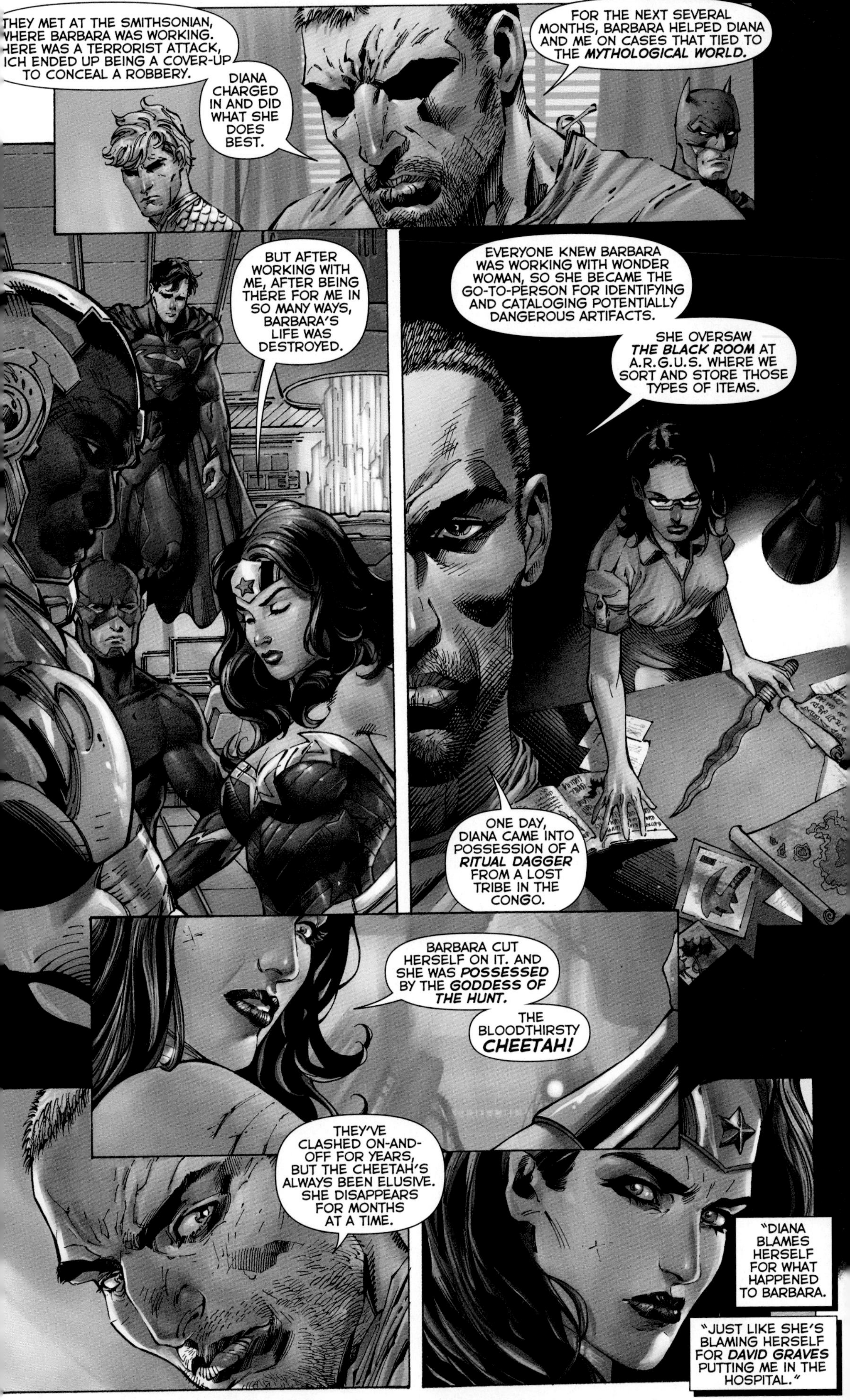
THEY MET AT THE SMITHSONIAN, WHERE BARBARA WAS WORKING. HERE WAS A TERRORIST ATTACK, ICH ENDED UP BEING A COVER-UP TO CONCEAL A ROBBERY.
DIANA CHARGED IN AND DID WHAT SHE DOES BEST.
FOR THE NEXT SEVERAL MONTHS, BARBARA HELPED DIANA AND ME ON CASES THAT TIED TO THE *MYTHOLOGICAL WORLD.*
BUT AFTER WORKING WITH ME, AFTER BEING THERE FOR ME IN SO MANY WAYS, BARBARA'S LIFE WAS DESTROYED.
EVERYONE KNEW BARBARA WAS WORKING WITH WONDER WOMAN, SO SHE BECAME THE GO-TO-PERSON FOR IDENTIFYING AND CATALOGING POTENTIALLY DANGEROUS ARTIFACTS.
SHE OVERSAW ***THE BLACK ROOM*** AT A.R.G.U.S. WHERE WE SORT AND STORE THOSE TYPES OF ITEMS.
ONE DAY, DIANA CAME INTO POSSESSION OF A ***RITUAL DAGGER*** FROM A LOST TRIBE IN THE CONGO.
BARBARA CUT HERSELF ON IT. AND SHE WAS *POSSESSED* BY THE ***GODDESS OF THE HUNT.***
THE BLOODTHIRSTY ***CHEETAH!***
THEY'VE CLASHED ON-AND-OFF FOR YEARS, BUT THE CHEETAH'S ALWAYS BEEN ELUSIVE. SHE DISAPPEARS FOR MONTHS AT A TIME.
"DIANA BLAMES HERSELF FOR WHAT HAPPENED TO BARBARA.
"JUST LIKE SHE'S BLAMING HERSELF FOR ***DAVID GRAVES*** PUTTING ME IN THE HOSPITAL."

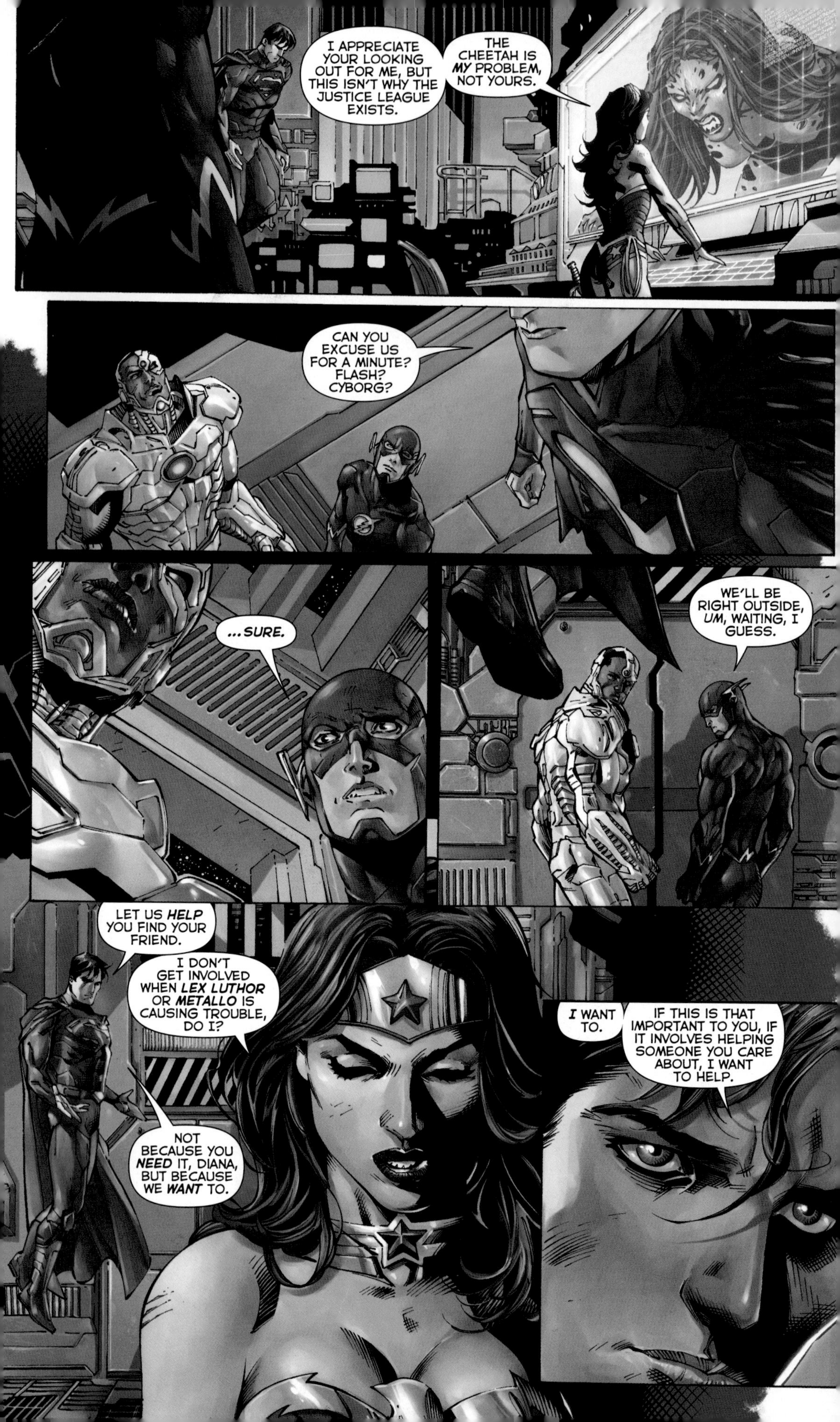
I APPRECIATE YOUR LOOKING OUT FOR ME, BUT THIS ISN'T WHY THE JUSTICE LEAGUE EXISTS.
THE CHEETAH IS *MY* PROBLEM, NOT YOURS.
CAN YOU EXCUSE US FOR A MINUTE? FLASH? CYBORG?
...SURE.
WE'LL BE RIGHT OUTSIDE, *UM*, WAITING, I GUESS.
LET US *HELP* YOU FIND YOUR FRIEND.
I DON'T GET INVOLVED WHEN *LEX LUTHOR* OR *METALLO* IS CAUSING TROUBLE, DO I?
NOT BECAUSE YOU *NEED* IT, DIANA, BUT BECAUSE WE *WANT* TO.
I WANT TO.
IF THIS IS THAT IMPORTANT TO YOU, IF IT INVOLVES HELPING SOMEONE YOU CARE ABOUT, I WANT TO HELP.

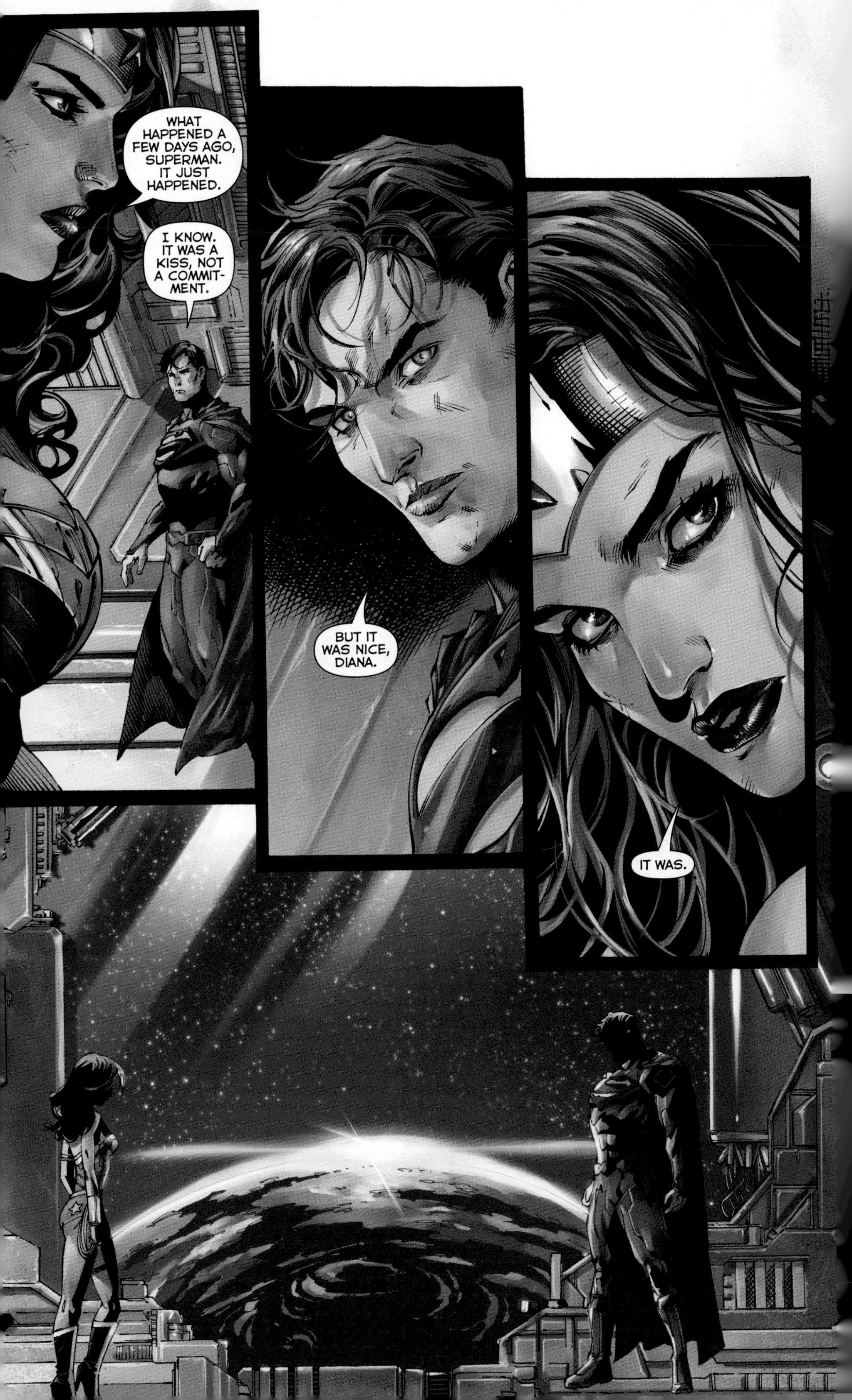
WHAT HAPPENED A FEW DAYS AGO, SUPERMAN. IT JUST HAPPENED.
I KNOW. IT WAS A KISS, NOT A COMMITMENT.
BUT IT WAS NICE, DIANA.
IT WAS.

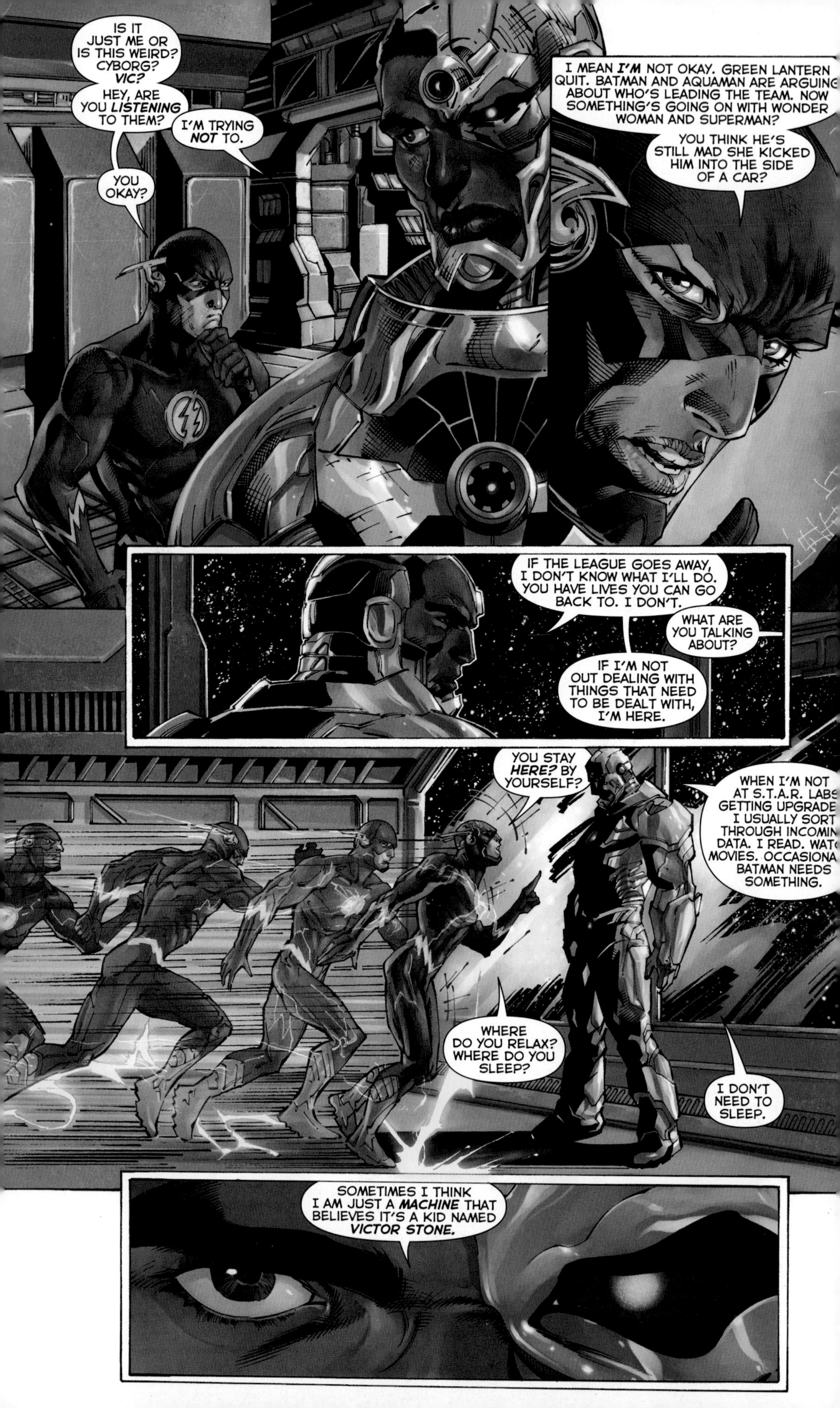

IS IT JUST ME OR IS THIS WEIRD? CYBORG? VIC?
HEY, ARE YOU LISTENING TO THEM?
I'M TRYING NOT TO.
YOU OKAY?
I MEAN I'M NOT OKAY. GREEN LANTERN QUIT. BATMAN AND AQUAMAN ARE ARGUING ABOUT WHO'S LEADING THE TEAM. NOW SOMETHING'S GOING ON WITH WONDER WOMAN AND SUPERMAN?
YOU THINK HE'S STILL MAD SHE KICKED HIM INTO THE SIDE OF A CAR?
IF THE LEAGUE GOES AWAY, I DON'T KNOW WHAT I'LL DO. YOU HAVE LIVES YOU CAN GO BACK TO. I DON'T.
WHAT ARE YOU TALKING ABOUT?
IF I'M NOT OUT DEALING WITH THINGS THAT NEED TO BE DEALT WITH, I'M HERE.
YOU STAY HERE? BY YOURSELF?
WHEN I'M NOT AT S.T.A.R. LABS GETTING UPGRADE I USUALLY SORT THROUGH INCOMIN DATA. I READ. WAT MOVIES. OCCASIONA BATMAN NEEDS SOMETHING.
WHERE DO YOU RELAX? WHERE DO YOU SLEEP?
I DON'T NEED TO SLEEP.
SOMETIMES I THINK I AM JUST A MACHINE THAT BELIEVES IT'S A KID NAMED VICTOR STONE.

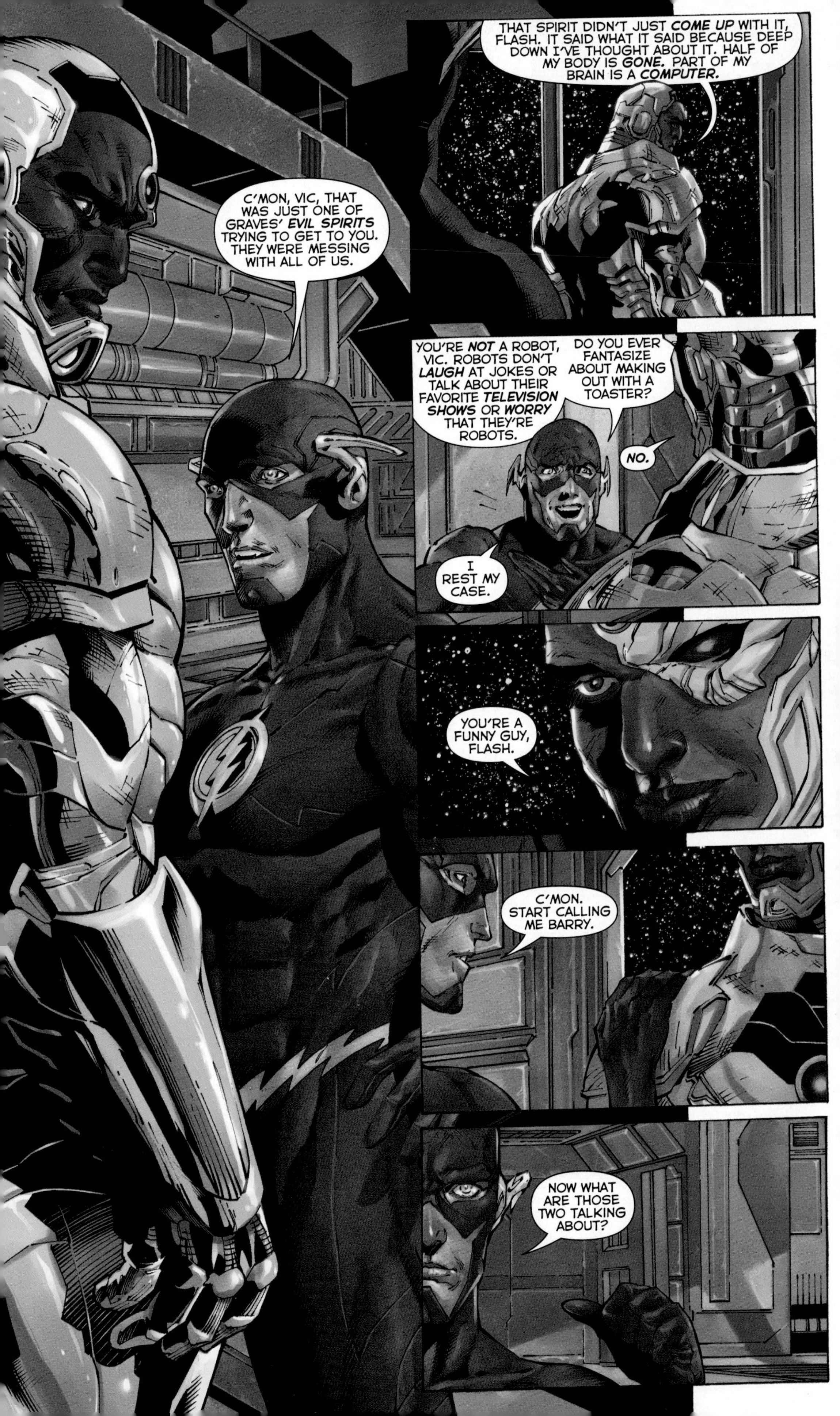

C'MON, VIC, THAT WAS JUST ONE OF GRAVES' EVIL SPIRITS TRYING TO GET TO YOU. THEY WERE MESSING WITH ALL OF US.
THAT SPIRIT DIDN'T JUST COME UP WITH IT, FLASH. IT SAID WHAT IT SAID BECAUSE DEEP DOWN I'VE THOUGHT ABOUT IT. HALF OF MY BODY IS GONE. PART OF MY BRAIN IS A COMPUTER.
YOU'RE NOT A ROBOT, VIC. ROBOTS DON'T LAUGH AT JOKES OR TALK ABOUT THEIR FAVORITE TELEVISION SHOWS OR WORRY THAT THEY'RE ROBOTS.
DO YOU EVER FANTASIZE ABOUT MAKING OUT WITH A TOASTER?
NO.
I REST MY CASE.
YOU'RE A FUNNY GUY, FLASH.
C'MON. START CALLING ME BARRY.
NOW WHAT ARE THOSE TWO TALKING ABOUT?

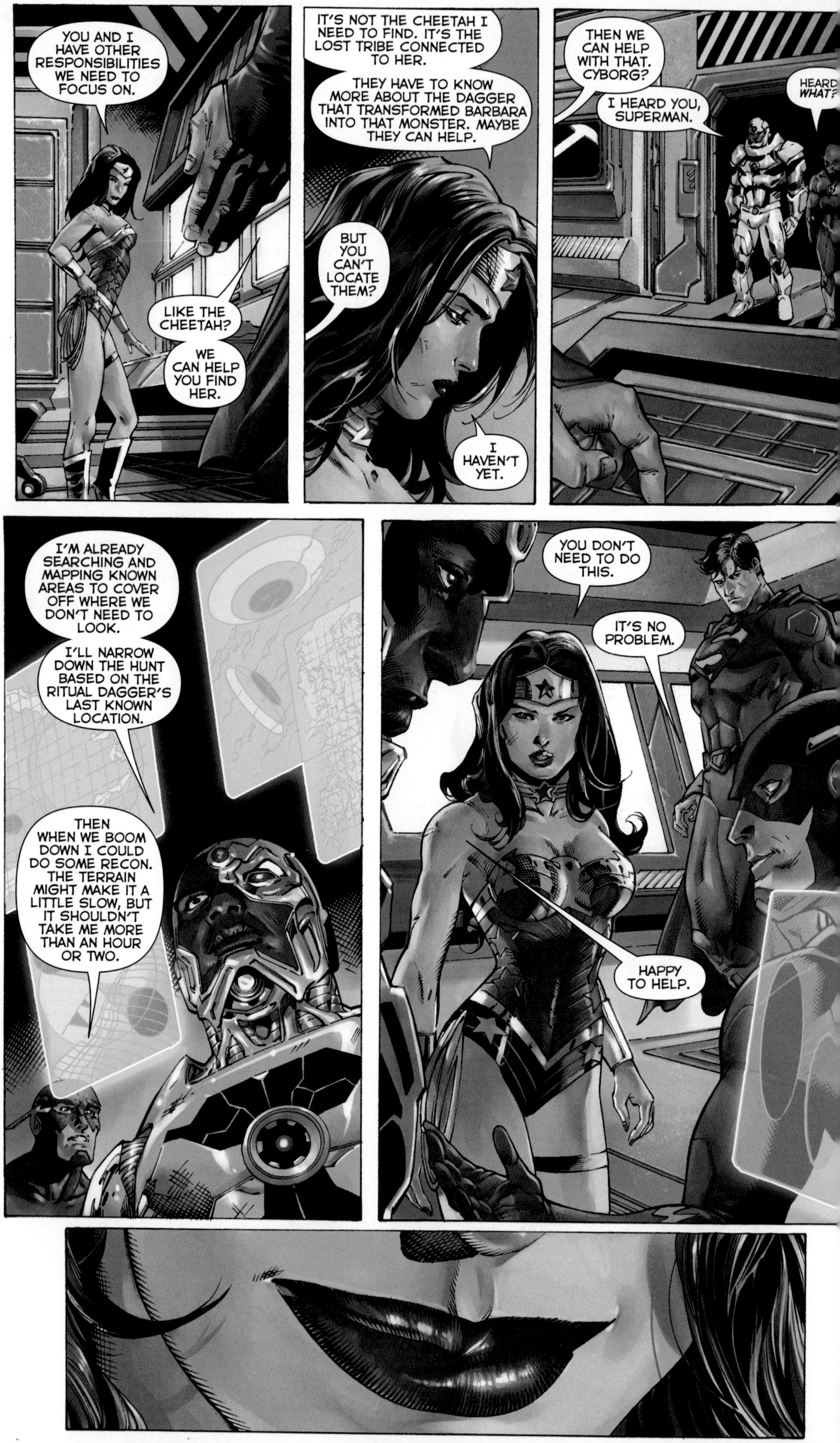
YOU AND I HAVE OTHER RESPONSIBILITIES WE NEED TO FOCUS ON.
LIKE THE CHEETAH?
WE CAN HELP YOU FIND HER.
IT'S NOT THE CHEETAH I NEED TO FIND. IT'S THE LOST TRIBE CONNECTED TO HER.
THEY HAVE TO KNOW MORE ABOUT THE DAGGER THAT TRANSFORMED BARBARA INTO THAT MONSTER. MAYBE THEY CAN HELP.
BUT YOU CAN'T LOCATE THEM?
I HAVEN'T YET.
THEN WE CAN HELP WITH THAT. CYBORG?
I HEARD YOU, SUPERMAN.
HEARD WHAT?
I'M ALREADY SEARCHING AND MAPPING KNOWN AREAS TO COVER OFF WHERE WE DON'T NEED TO LOOK.
I'LL NARROW DOWN THE HUNT BASED ON THE RITUAL DAGGER'S LAST KNOWN LOCATION.
THEN WHEN WE BOOM DOWN I COULD DO SOME RECON. THE TERRAIN MIGHT MAKE IT A LITTLE SLOW, BUT IT SHOULDN'T TAKE ME MORE THAN AN HOUR OR TWO.
YOU DON'T NEED TO DO THIS.
IT'S NO PROBLEM.
HAPPY TO HELP.

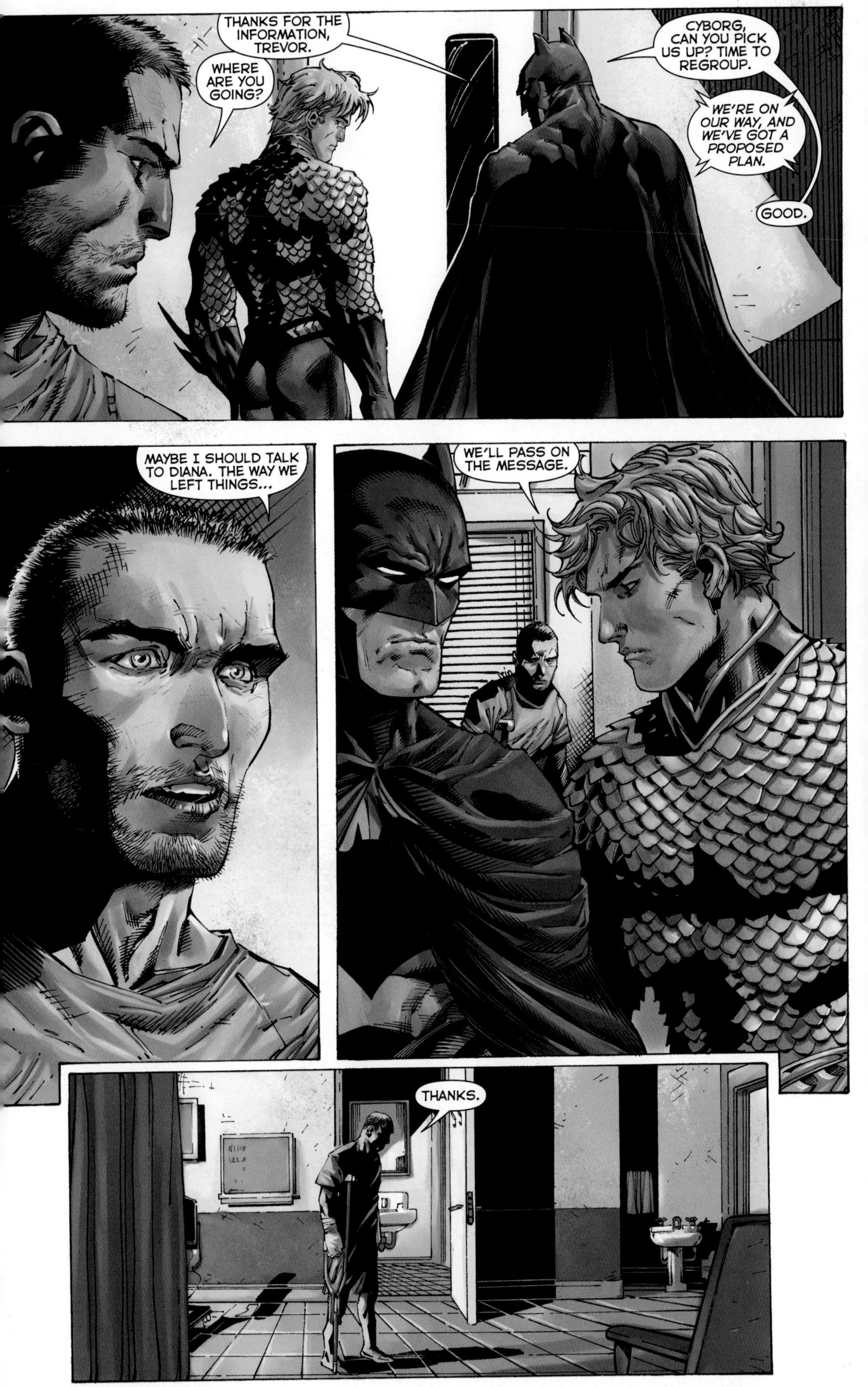

THANKS FOR THE INFORMATION, TREVOR.
WHERE ARE YOU GOING?
CYBORG, CAN YOU PICK US UP? TIME TO REGROUP.
WE'RE ON OUR WAY, AND WE'VE GOT A PROPOSED PLAN.
GOOD.
MAYBE I SHOULD TALK TO DIANA. THE WAY WE LEFT THINGS...
WE'LL PASS ON THE MESSAGE.
THANKS.

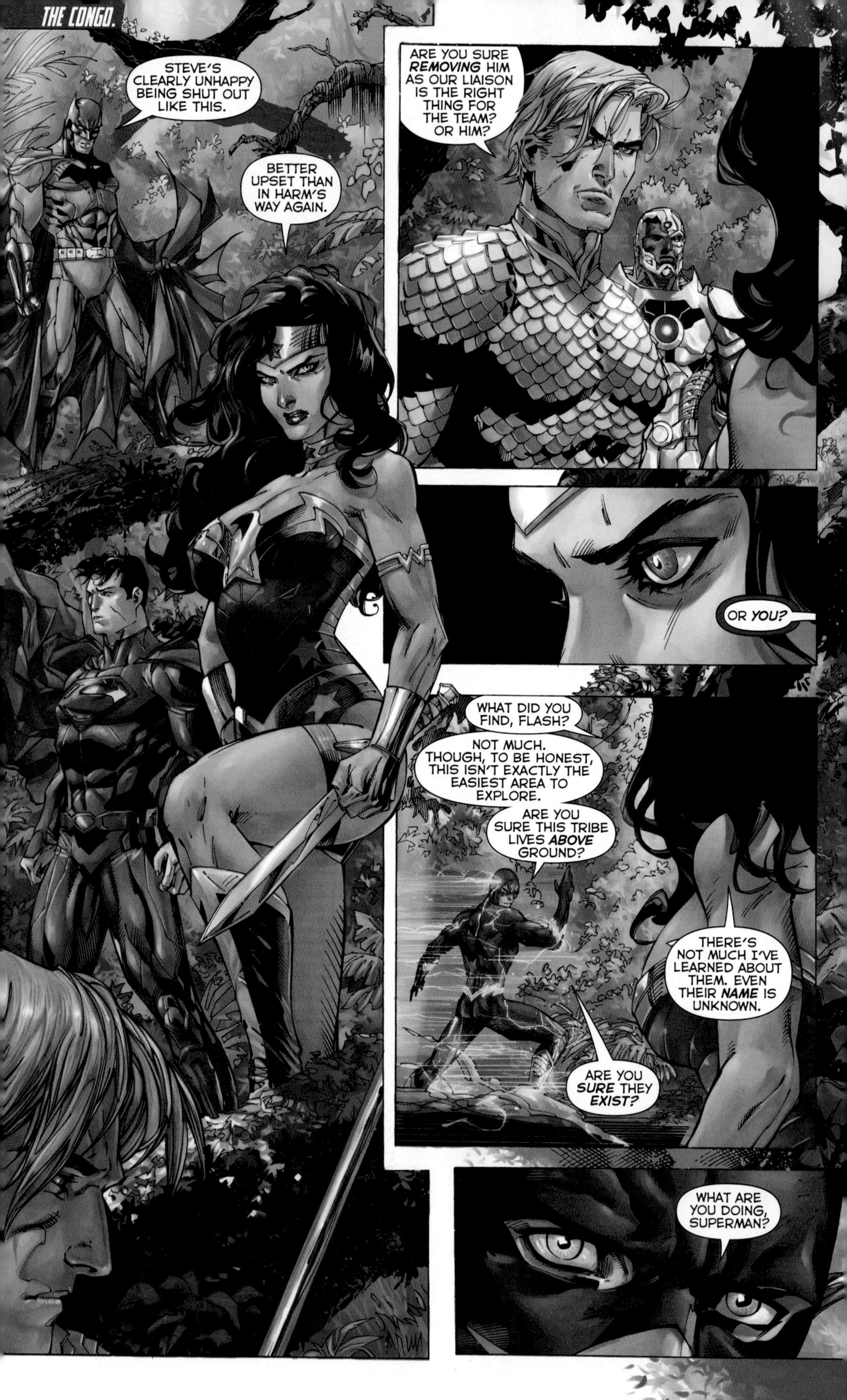
THE CONGO.
STEVE'S CLEARLY UNHAPPY BEING SHUT OUT LIKE THIS.
BETTER UPSET THAN IN HARM'S WAY AGAIN.
ARE YOU SURE REMOVING HIM AS OUR LIAISON IS THE RIGHT THING FOR THE TEAM? OR HIM?
OR YOU?
WHAT DID YOU FIND, FLASH?
NOT MUCH. THOUGH, TO BE HONEST, THIS ISN'T EXACTLY THE EASIEST AREA TO EXPLORE.
ARE YOU SURE THIS TRIBE LIVES ABOVE GROUND?
THERE'S NOT MUCH I'VE LEARNED ABOUT THEM. EVEN THEIR NAME IS UNKNOWN.
ARE YOU SURE THEY EXIST?
WHAT ARE YOU DOING, SUPERMAN?

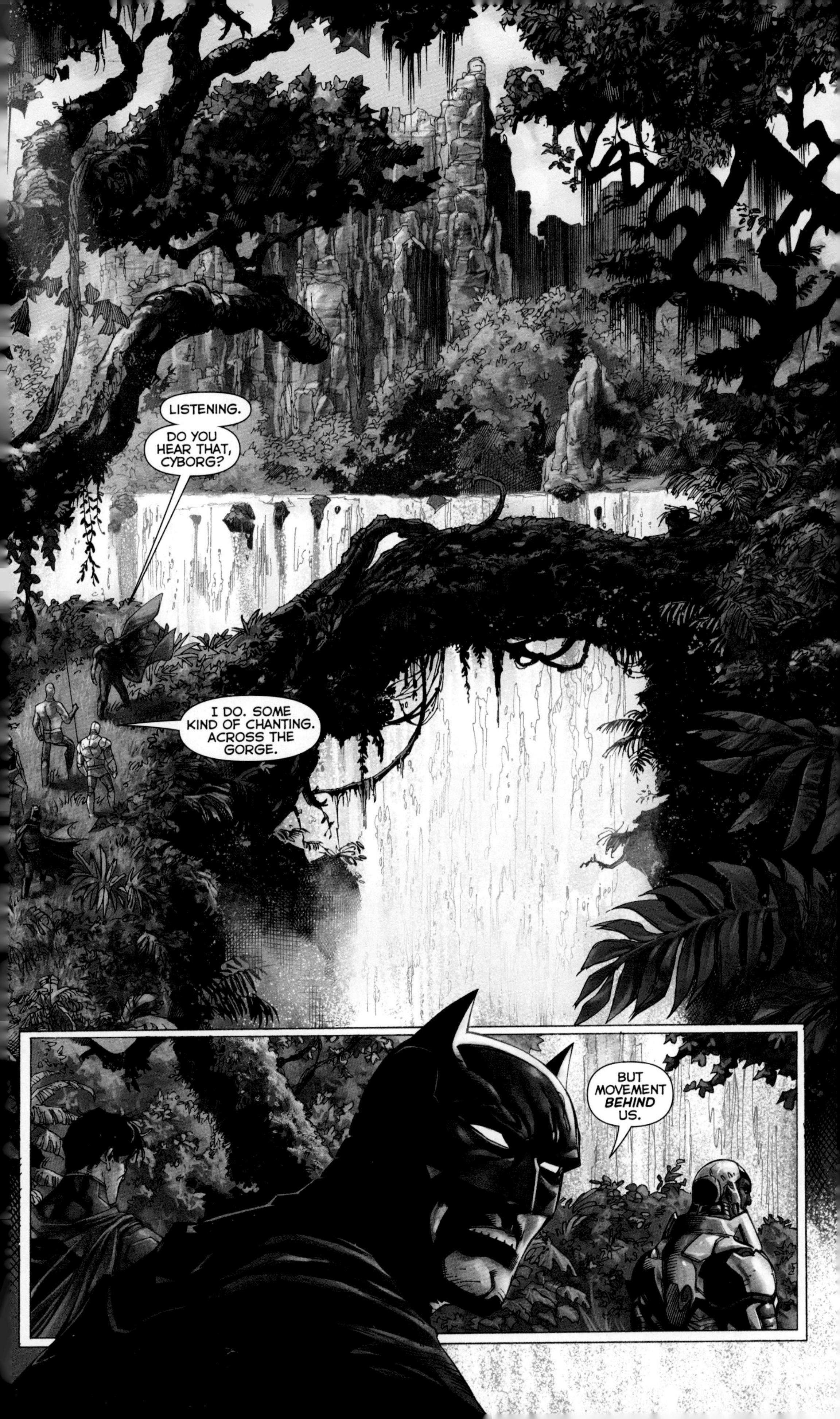
LISTENING.
DO YOU HEAR THAT, CYBORG?
I DO. SOME KIND OF CHANTING. ACROSS THE GORGE.
BUT MOVEMENT *BEHIND* US.

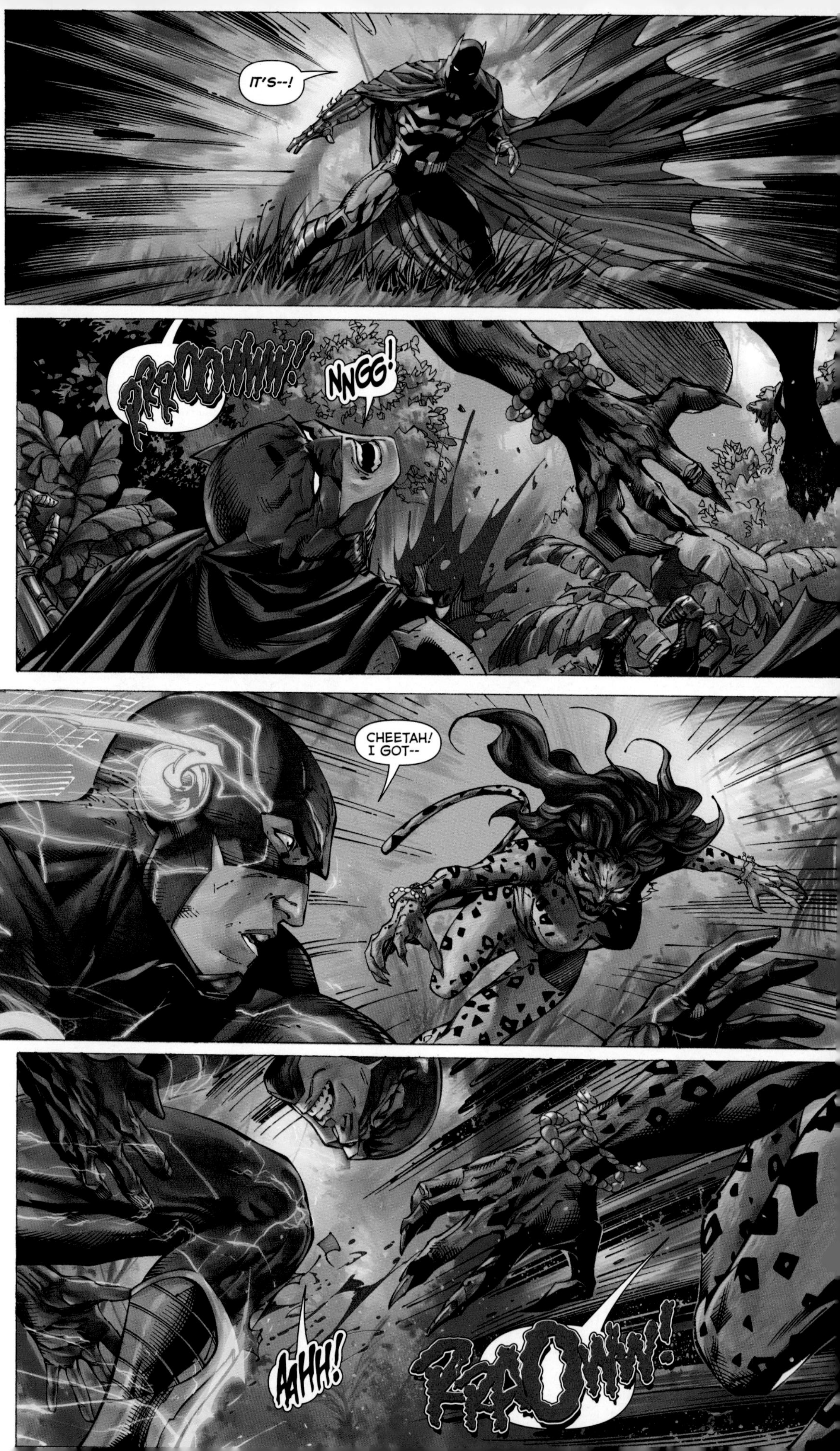
IT'S--!
NNGG!
CHEETAH! I GOT--
AAHH!

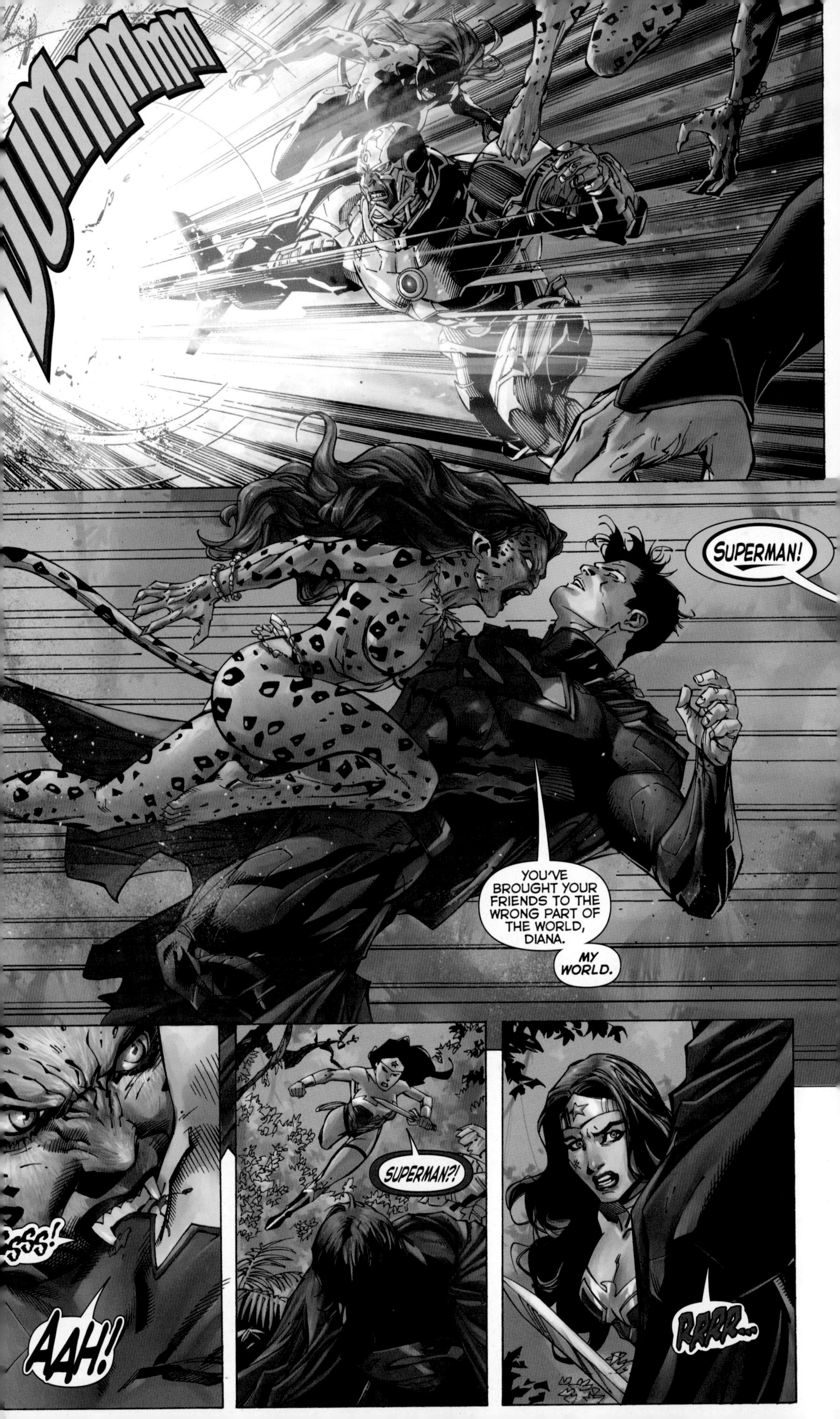
UMMMMM
SUPERMAN!
YOU'VE BROUGHT YOUR FRIENDS TO THE WRONG PART OF THE WORLD, DIANA.
MY WORLD.
SSS!
AAH!
SUPERMAN?!
RRRR...

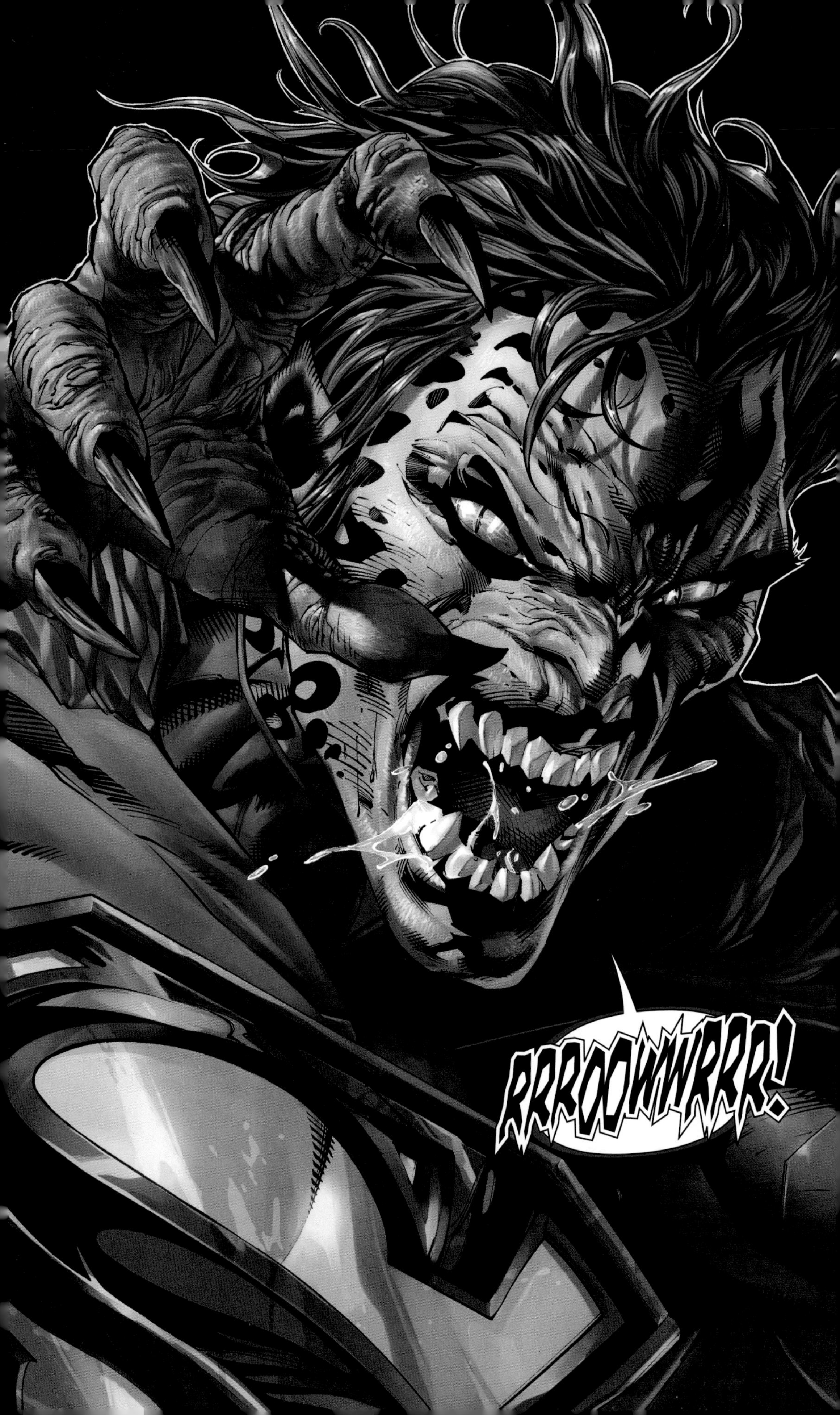
RRROOWWRRR!

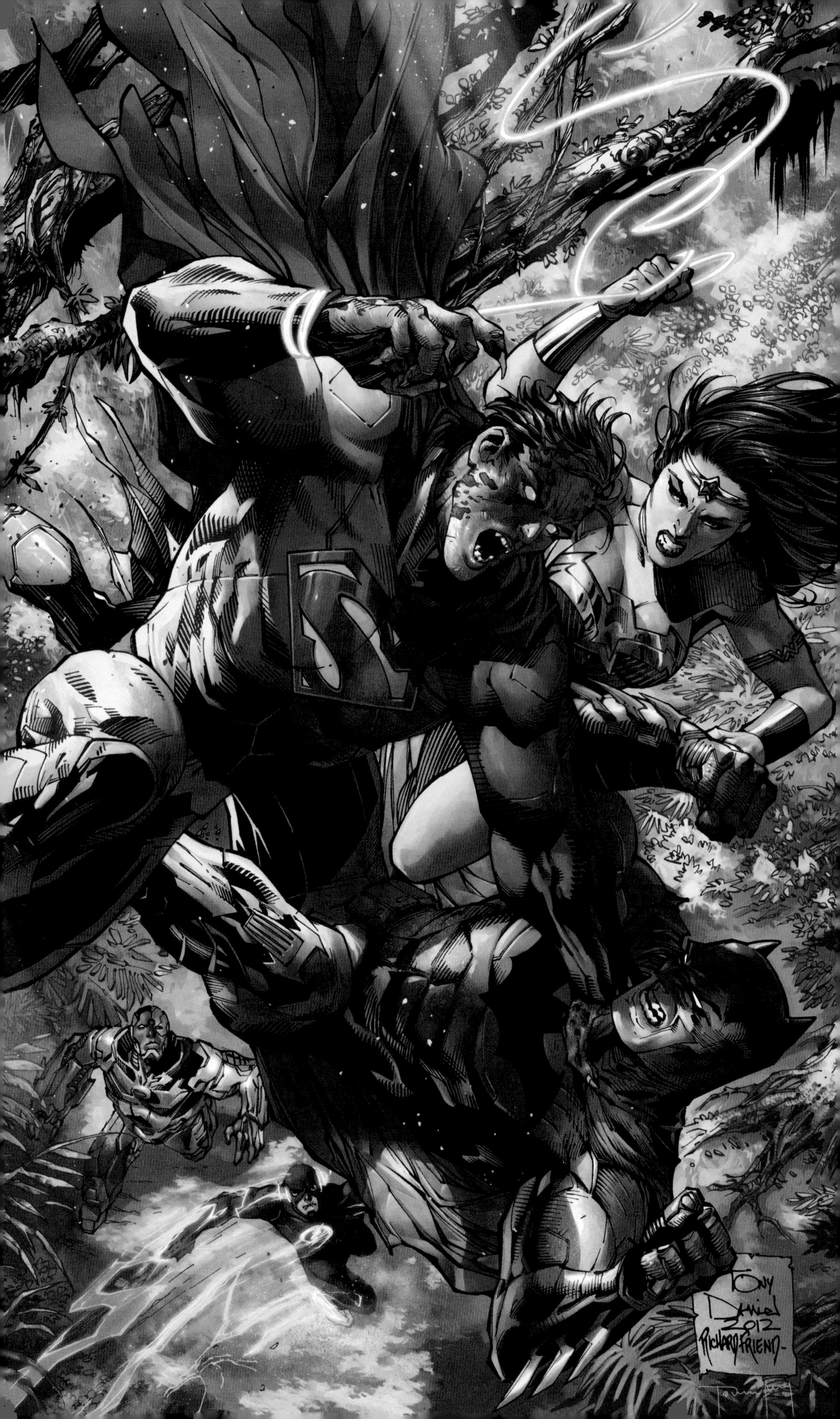
TONY DANIEL 2012
RICHARD FRIEND

GEOFF JOHNS writer TONY S. DANIEL penciller RICHARD FRIEND & SANDU FLOREA inkers cover by TONY S. DANIEL, RICHARD FRIEND & TOMEU M

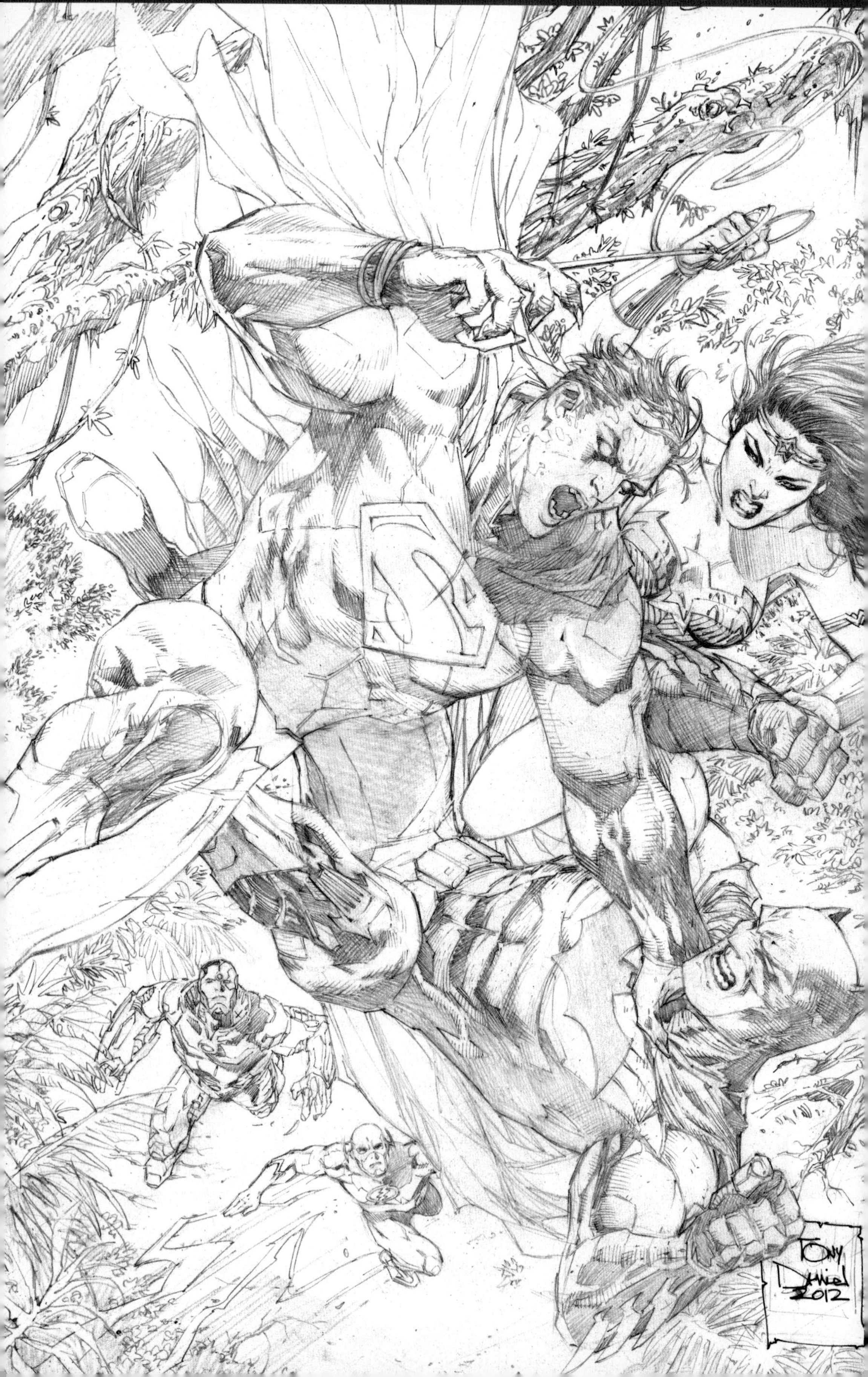
TONY DANIEL 2012

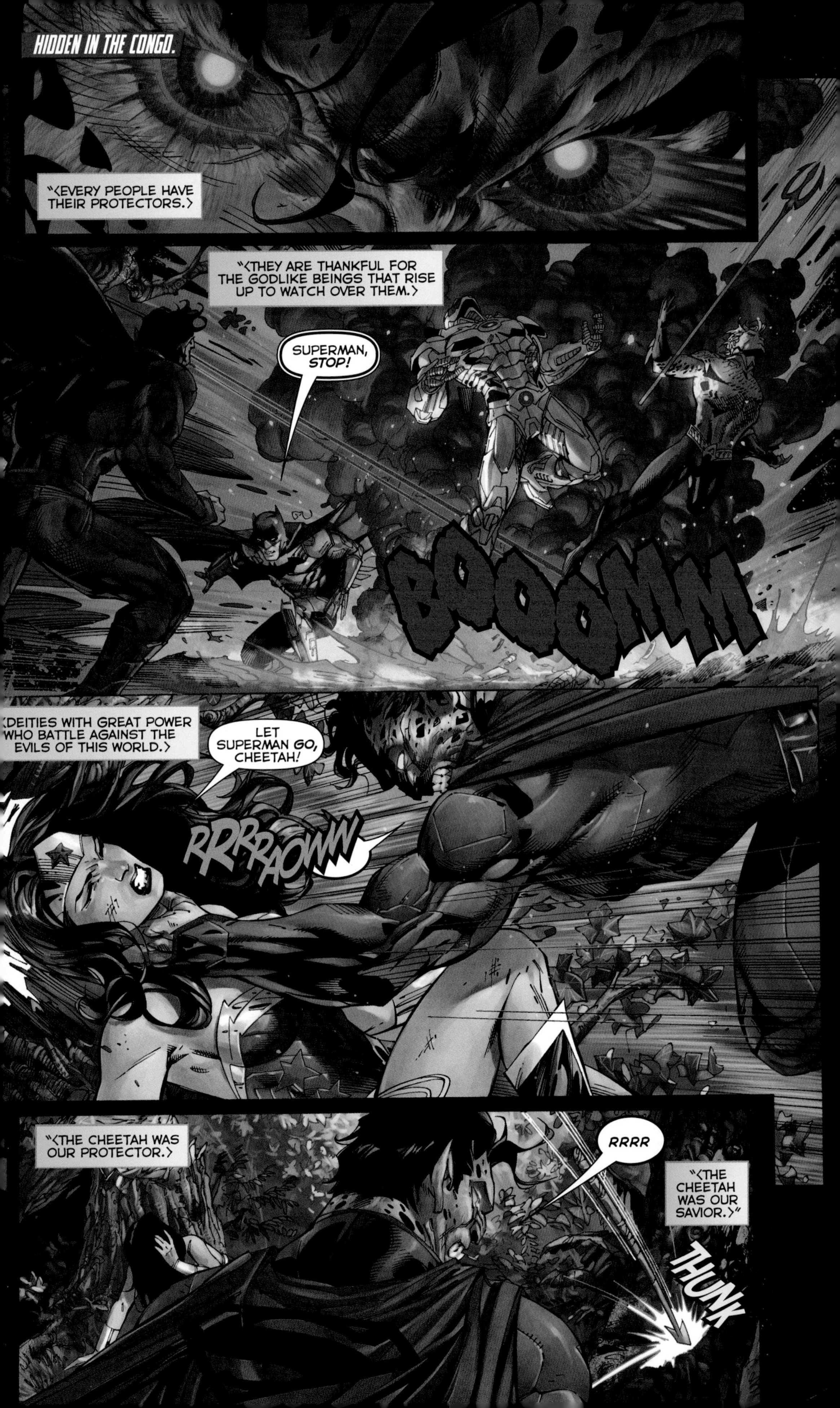
HIDDEN IN THE CONGO.
"<EVERY PEOPLE HAVE THEIR PROTECTORS.>
"<THEY ARE THANKFUL FOR THE GODLIKE BEINGS THAT RISE UP TO WATCH OVER THEM.>
SUPERMAN, STOP!
BOOOMM
<DEITIES WITH GREAT POWER WHO BATTLE AGAINST THE EVILS OF THIS WORLD.>
LET SUPERMAN GO, CHEETAH!
RRRRAOWWN
"<THE CHEETAH WAS OUR PROTECTOR.>
RRRR
"<THE CHEETAH WAS OUR SAVIOR.>"
THUNK

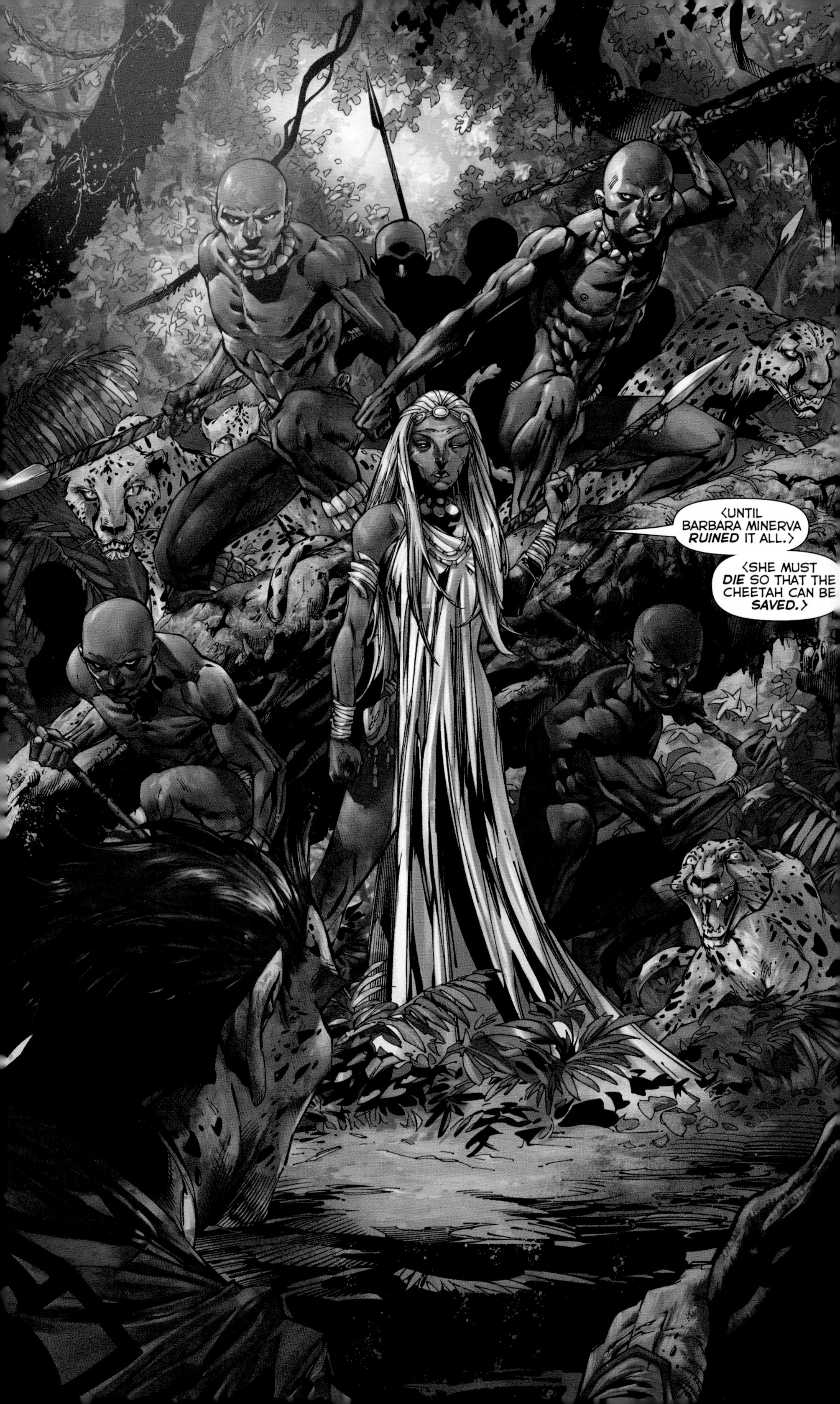
<UNTIL BARBARA MINERVA RUINED IT ALL.>
<SHE MUST DIE SO THAT THE CHEETAH CAN BE SAVED.>

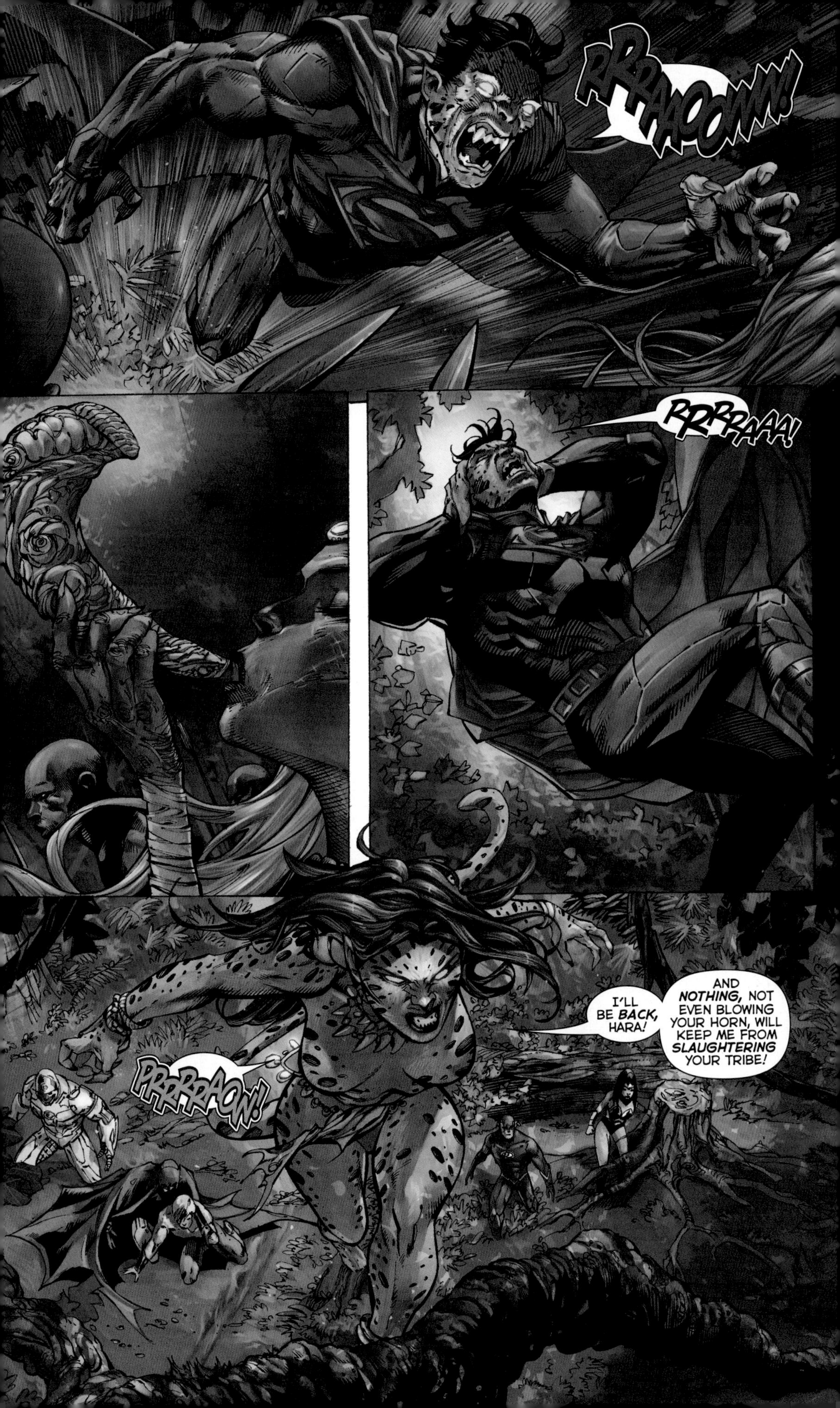
RRRAAOOWWW!
RRRRAAA!
I'LL BE BACK, HARA!
AND NOTHING, NOT EVEN BLOWING YOUR HORN, WILL KEEP ME FROM SLAUGHTERING YOUR TRIBE!
PRRRRAAON!

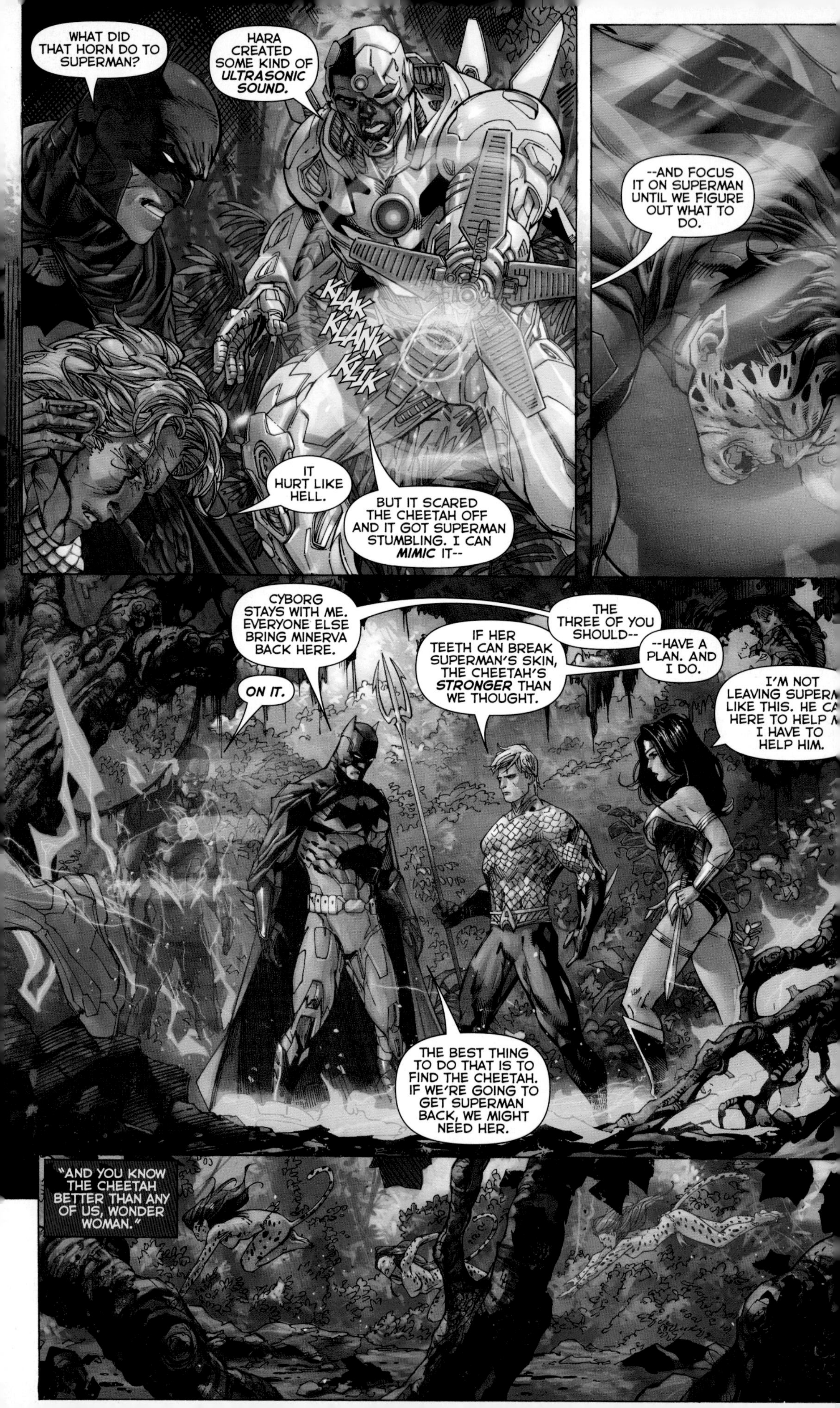
WHAT DID THAT HORN DO TO SUPERMAN?
HARA CREATED SOME KIND OF ULTRASONIC SOUND.
KLAK KLANK KLIK
IT HURT LIKE HELL.
BUT IT SCARED THE CHEETAH OFF AND IT GOT SUPERMAN STUMBLING. I CAN MIMIC IT--
--AND FOCUS IT ON SUPERMAN UNTIL WE FIGURE OUT WHAT TO DO.
CYBORG STAYS WITH ME. EVERYONE ELSE BRING MINERVA BACK HERE.
THE THREE OF YOU SHOULD--
ON IT.
IF HER TEETH CAN BREAK SUPERMAN'S SKIN, THE CHEETAH'S STRONGER THAN WE THOUGHT.
--HAVE A PLAN. AND I DO.
THE BEST THING TO DO THAT IS TO FIND THE CHEETAH. IF WE'RE GOING TO GET SUPERMAN BACK, WE MIGHT NEED HER.
"AND YOU KNOW THE CHEETAH BETTER THAN ANY OF US, WONDER WOMAN."

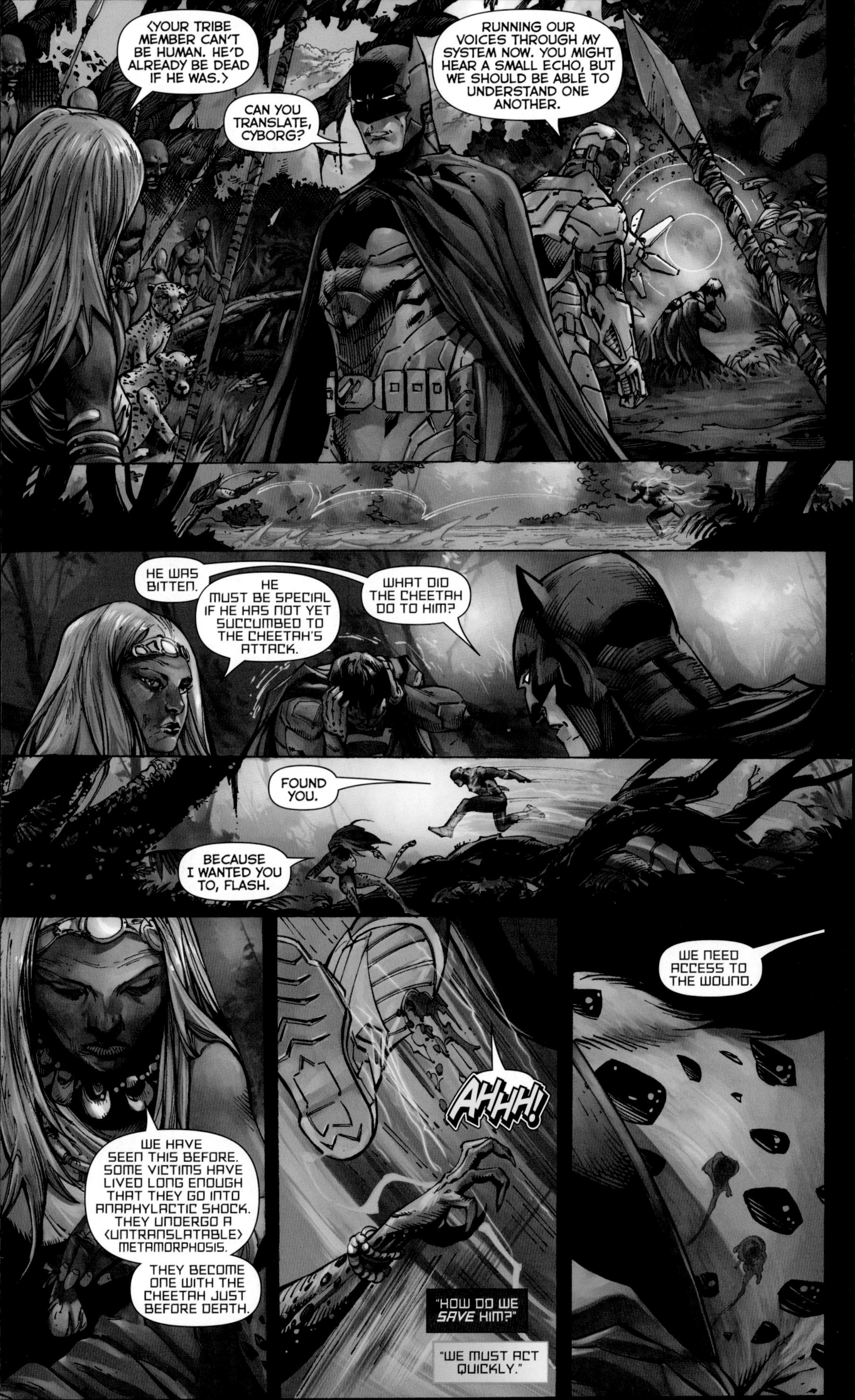

<YOUR TRIBE MEMBER CAN'T BE HUMAN. HE'D ALREADY BE DEAD IF HE WAS.>
CAN YOU TRANSLATE, CYBORG?
RUNNING OUR VOICES THROUGH MY SYSTEM NOW. YOU MIGHT HEAR A SMALL ECHO, BUT WE SHOULD BE ABLE TO UNDERSTAND ONE ANOTHER.
HE WAS BITTEN.
HE MUST BE SPECIAL IF HE HAS NOT YET SUCCUMBED TO THE CHEETAH'S ATTACK.
WHAT DID THE CHEETAH DO TO HIM?
FOUND YOU.
BECAUSE I WANTED YOU TO, FLASH.
WE HAVE SEEN THIS BEFORE. SOME VICTIMS HAVE LIVED LONG ENOUGH THAT THEY GO INTO ANAPHYLACTIC SHOCK. THEY UNDERGO A <UNTRANSLATABLE> METAMORPHOSIS.
THEY BECOME ONE WITH THE CHEETAH JUST BEFORE DEATH.
AHHH!
"HOW DO WE SAVE HIM?"
"WE MUST ACT QUICKLY."
WE NEED ACCESS TO THE WOUND.

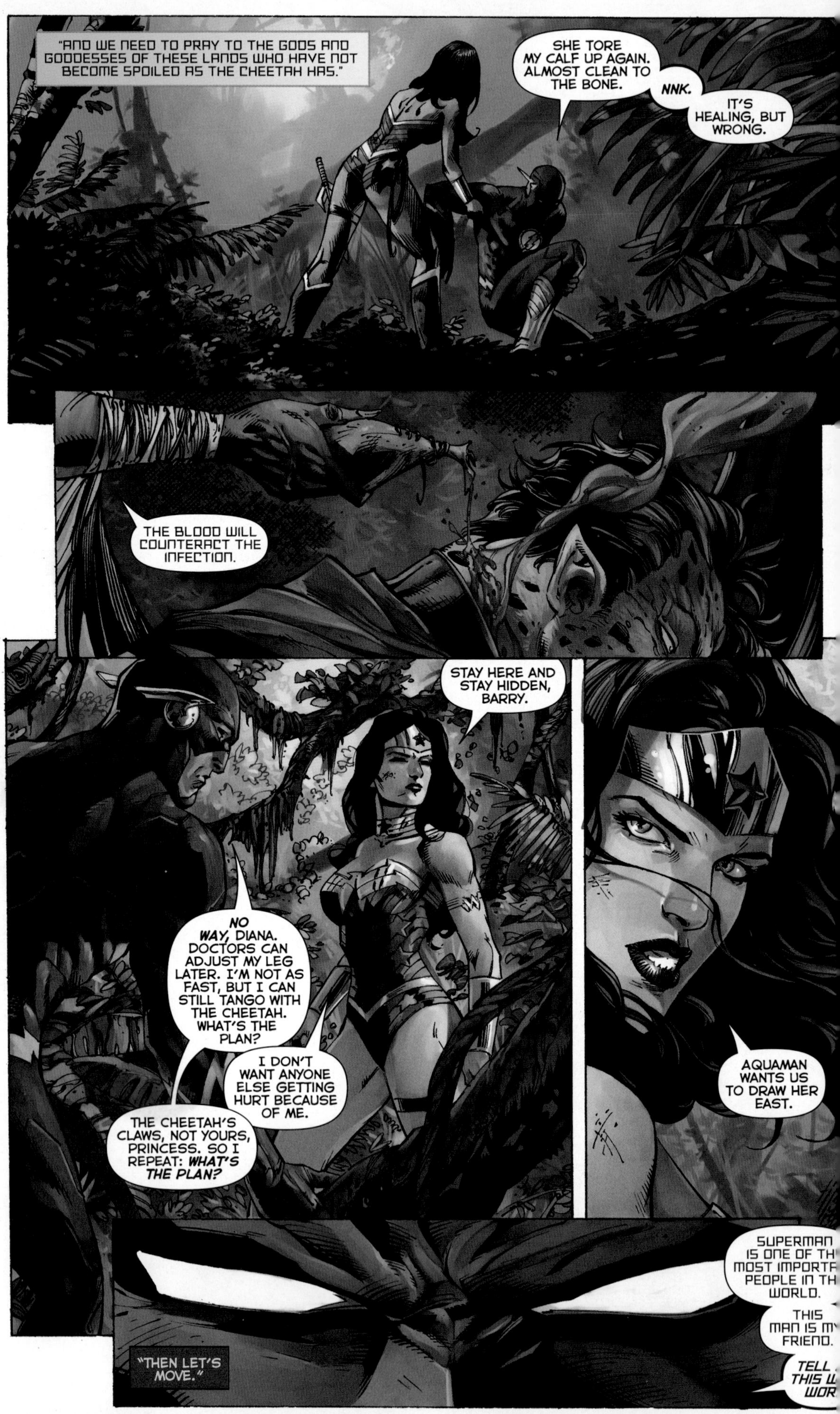
"AND WE NEED TO PRAY TO THE GODS AND GODDESSES OF THESE LANDS WHO HAVE NOT BECOME SPOILED AS THE CHEETAH HAS."
SHE TORE MY CALF UP AGAIN. ALMOST CLEAN TO THE BONE.
NNK.
IT'S HEALING, BUT WRONG.
THE BLOOD WILL COUNTERACT THE INFECTION.
STAY HERE AND STAY HIDDEN, BARRY.
NO WAY, DIANA. DOCTORS CAN ADJUST MY LEG LATER. I'M NOT AS FAST, BUT I CAN STILL TANGO WITH THE CHEETAH. WHAT'S THE PLAN?
I DON'T WANT ANYONE ELSE GETTING HURT BECAUSE OF ME.
THE CHEETAH'S CLAWS, NOT YOURS, PRINCESS. SO I REPEAT: WHAT'S THE PLAN?
AQUAMAN WANTS US TO DRAW HER EAST.
"THEN LET'S MOVE."

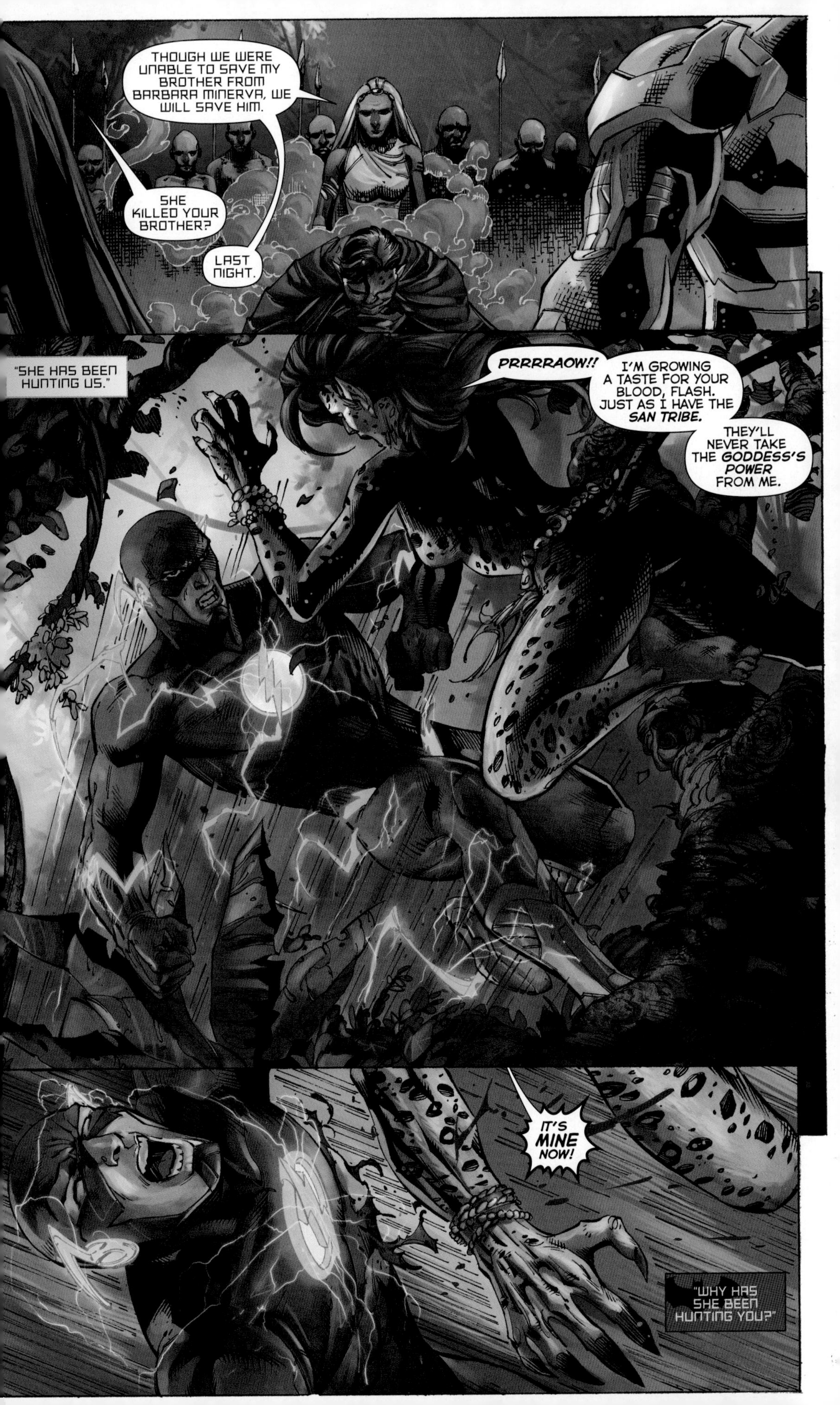
THOUGH WE WERE UNABLE TO SAVE MY BROTHER FROM BARBARA MINERVA, WE WILL SAVE HIM.
SHE KILLED YOUR BROTHER?
LAST NIGHT.
"SHE HAS BEEN HUNTING US."
PRRRRAOW!!
I'M GROWING A TASTE FOR YOUR BLOOD, FLASH. JUST AS I HAVE THE SAN TRIBE.
THEY'LL NEVER TAKE THE GODDESS'S POWER FROM ME.
IT'S MINE NOW!
"WHY HAS SHE BEEN HUNTING YOU?"

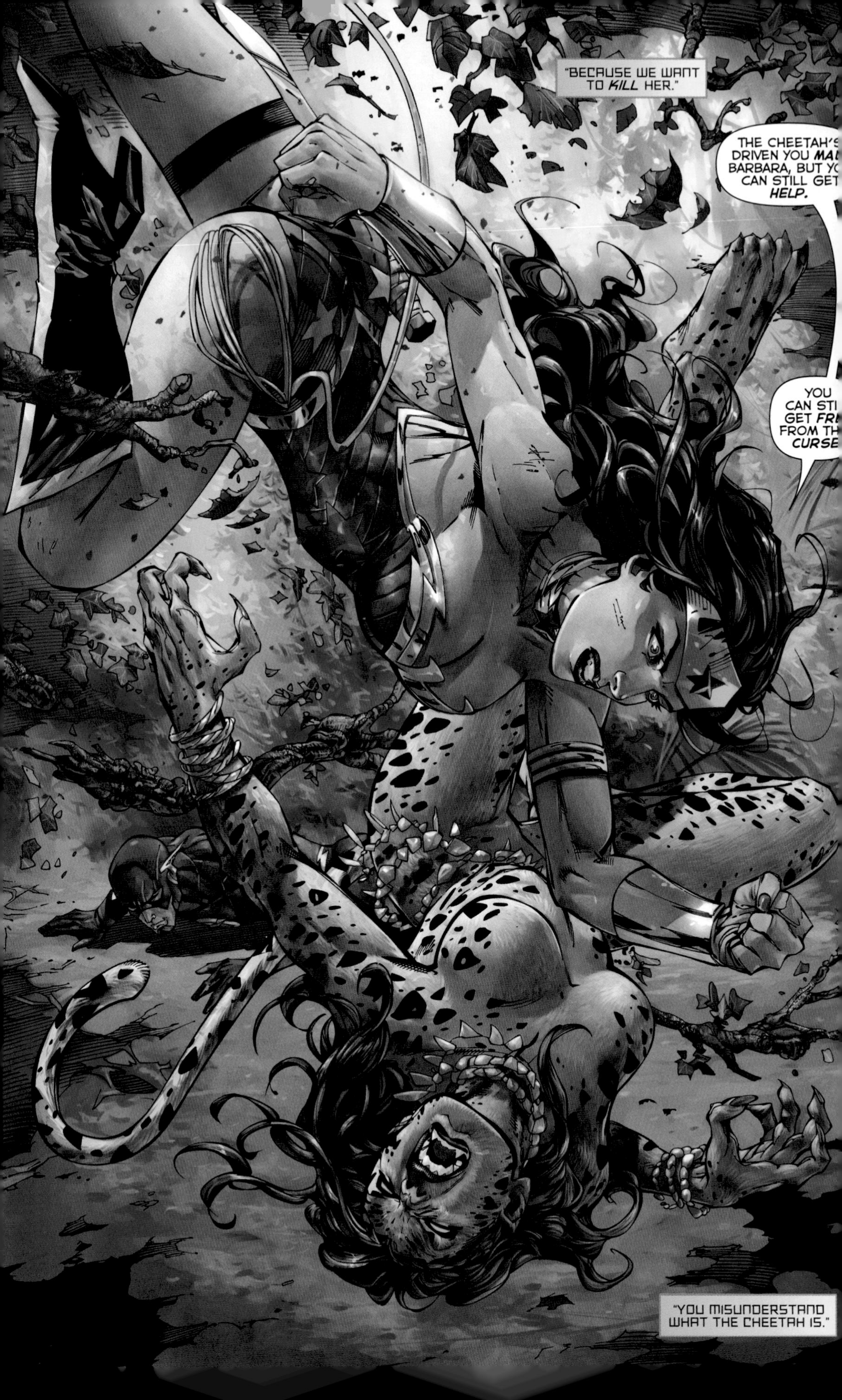
"BECAUSE WE WANT TO KILL HER."
THE CHEETAH'S DRIVEN YOU MA BARBARA, BUT YO CAN STILL GET HELP.
YOU CAN STI GET FR FROM TH CURSE
"YOU MISUNDERSTAND WHAT THE CHEETAH IS."

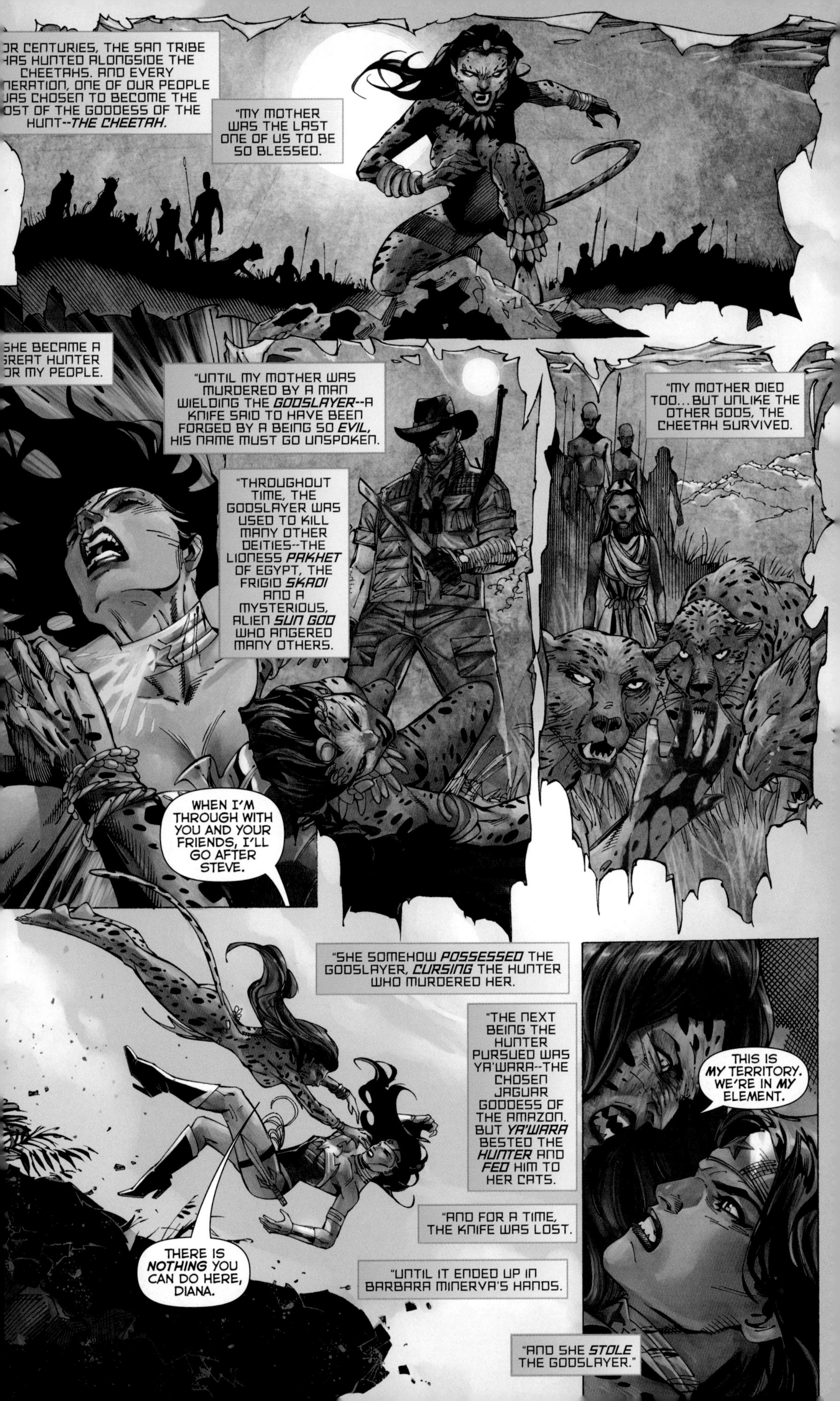

OR CENTURIES, THE SAN TRIBE HAS HUNTED ALONGSIDE THE CHEETAHS. AND EVERY GENERATION, ONE OF OUR PEOPLE WAS CHOSEN TO BECOME THE HOST OF THE GODDESS OF THE HUNT--THE CHEETAH.
"MY MOTHER WAS THE LAST ONE OF US TO BE SO BLESSED.
SHE BECAME A GREAT HUNTER FOR MY PEOPLE.
"UNTIL MY MOTHER WAS MURDERED BY A MAN WIELDING THE GODSLAYER--A KNIFE SAID TO HAVE BEEN FORGED BY A BEING SO EVIL, HIS NAME MUST GO UNSPOKEN.
"THROUGHOUT TIME, THE GODSLAYER WAS USED TO KILL MANY OTHER DEITIES--THE LIONESS PAKHET OF EGYPT, THE FRIGID SKADI AND A MYSTERIOUS, ALIEN SUN GOD WHO ANGERED MANY OTHERS.
"MY MOTHER DIED TOO...BUT UNLIKE THE OTHER GODS, THE CHEETAH SURVIVED.
WHEN I'M THROUGH WITH YOU AND YOUR FRIENDS, I'LL GO AFTER STEVE.
"SHE SOMEHOW POSSESSED THE GODSLAYER, CURSING THE HUNTER WHO MURDERED HER.
"THE NEXT BEING THE HUNTER PURSUED WAS YA'WARA--THE CHOSEN JAGUAR GODDESS OF THE AMAZON. BUT YA'WARA BESTED THE HUNTER AND FED HIM TO HER CATS.
THIS IS MY TERRITORY. WE'RE IN MY ELEMENT.
"AND FOR A TIME, THE KNIFE WAS LOST.
THERE IS NOTHING YOU CAN DO HERE, DIANA.
"UNTIL IT ENDED UP IN BARBARA MINERVA'S HANDS.
"AND SHE STOLE THE GODSLAYER."

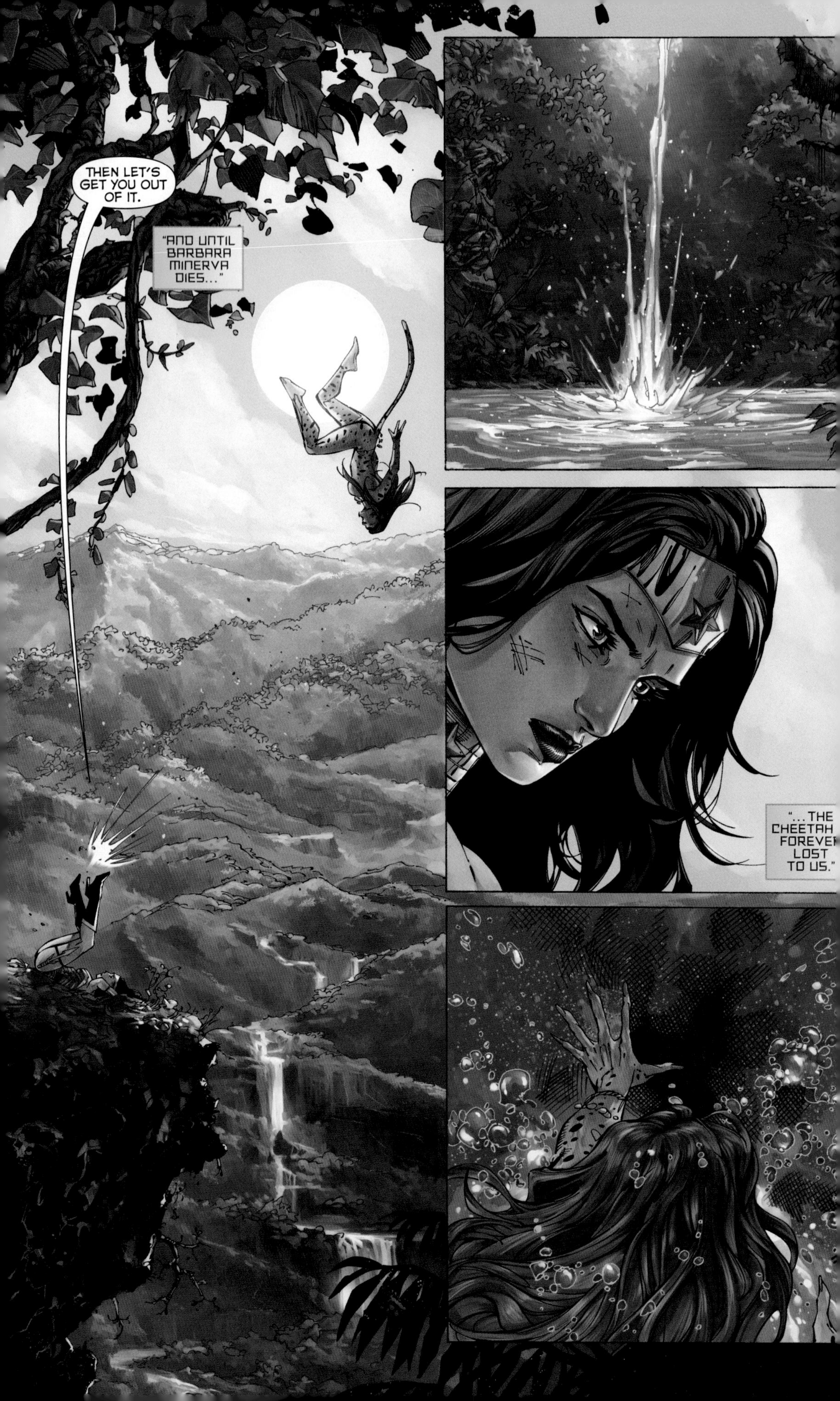
THEN LET'S GET YOU OUT OF IT.
"AND UNTIL BARBARA MINERVA DIES..."
"...THE CHEETAH FOREVER LOST TO US."

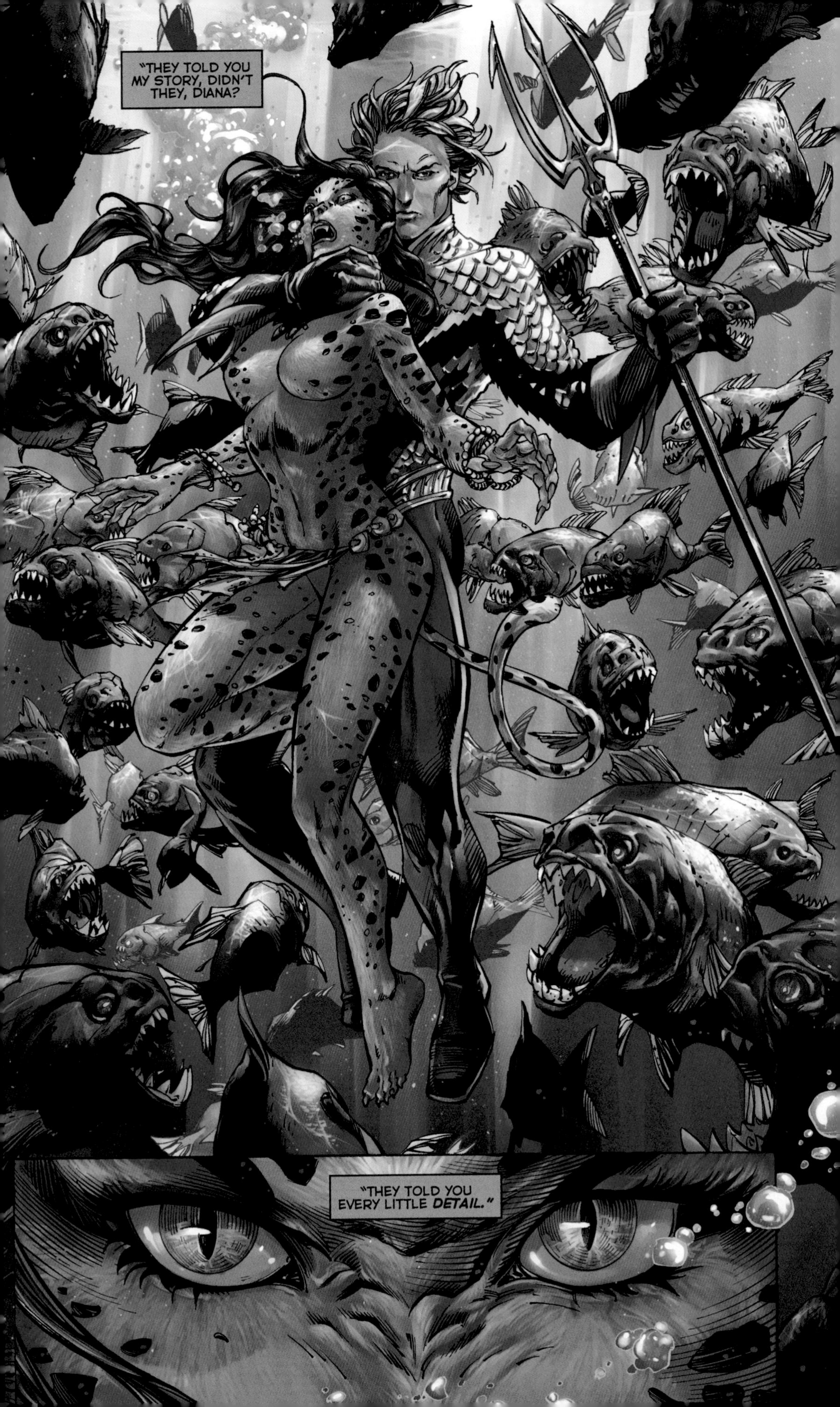
"THEY TOLD YOU MY STORY, DIDN'T THEY, DIANA?
"THEY TOLD YOU EVERY LITTLE DETAIL."

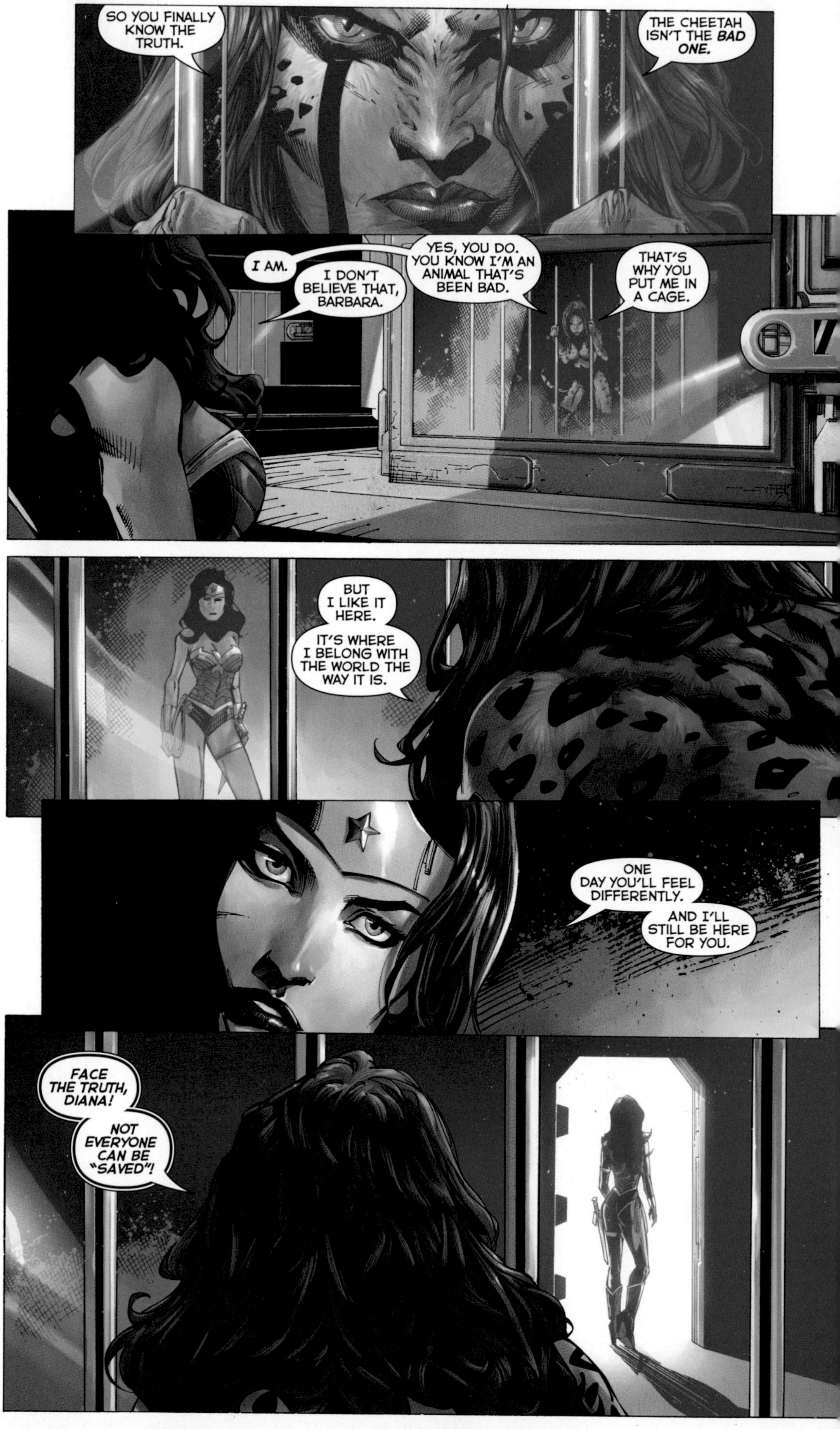
SO YOU FINALLY KNOW THE TRUTH.
THE CHEETAH ISN'T THE *BAD ONE.*
I AM.
I DON'T BELIEVE THAT, BARBARA.
YES, YOU DO. YOU KNOW I'M AN ANIMAL THAT'S BEEN BAD.
THAT'S WHY YOU PUT ME IN A CAGE.
BUT I LIKE IT HERE.
IT'S WHERE I BELONG WITH THE WORLD THE WAY IT IS.
ONE DAY YOU'LL FEEL DIFFERENTLY.
AND I'LL STILL BE HERE FOR YOU.
FACE THE TRUTH, DIANA!
NOT EVERYONE CAN BE "SAVED"!

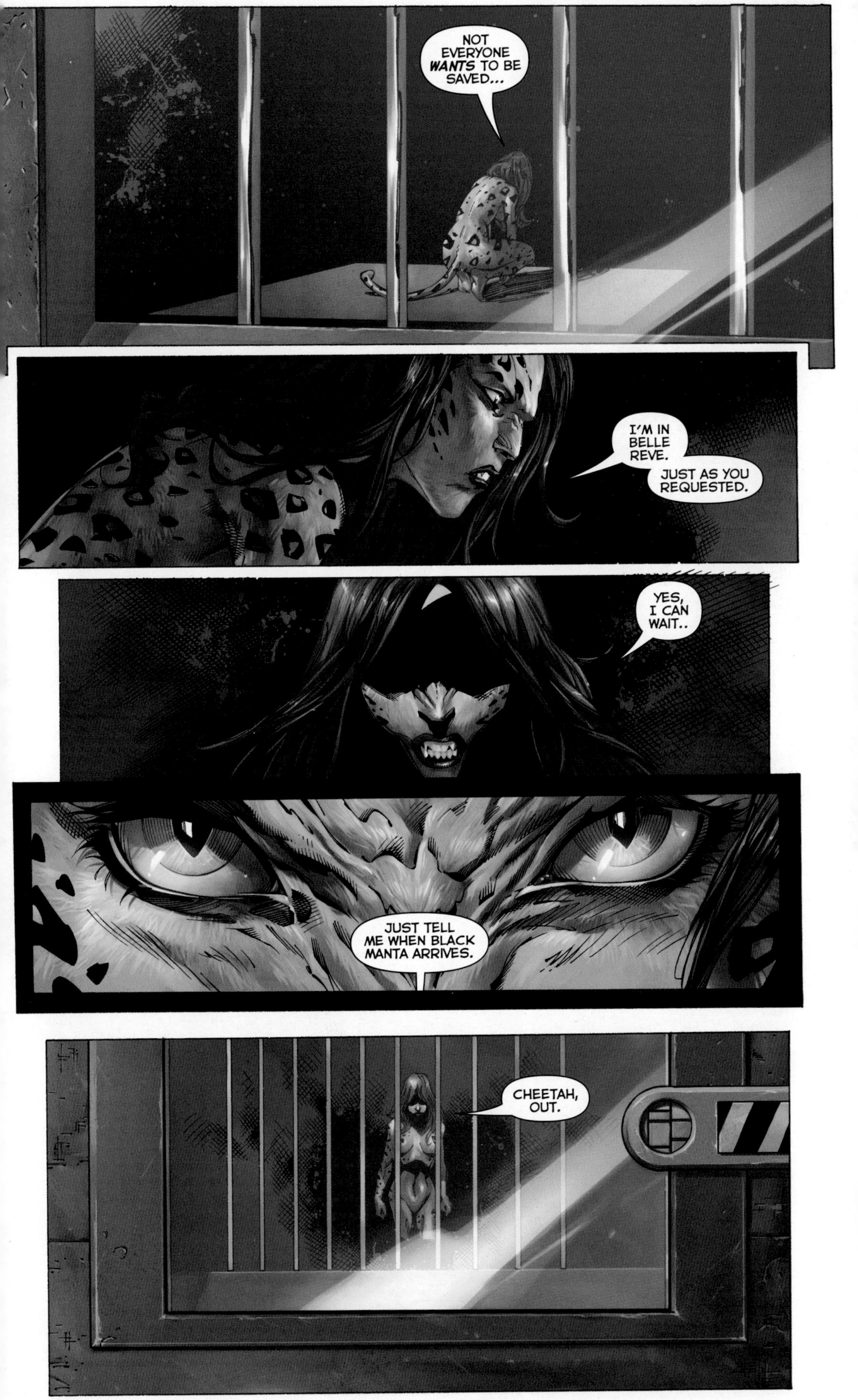

NOT EVERYONE WANTS TO BE SAVED...
I'M IN BELLE REVE.
JUST AS YOU REQUESTED.
YES, I CAN WAIT..
JUST TELL ME WHEN BLACK MANTA ARRIVES.
CHEETAH, OUT.

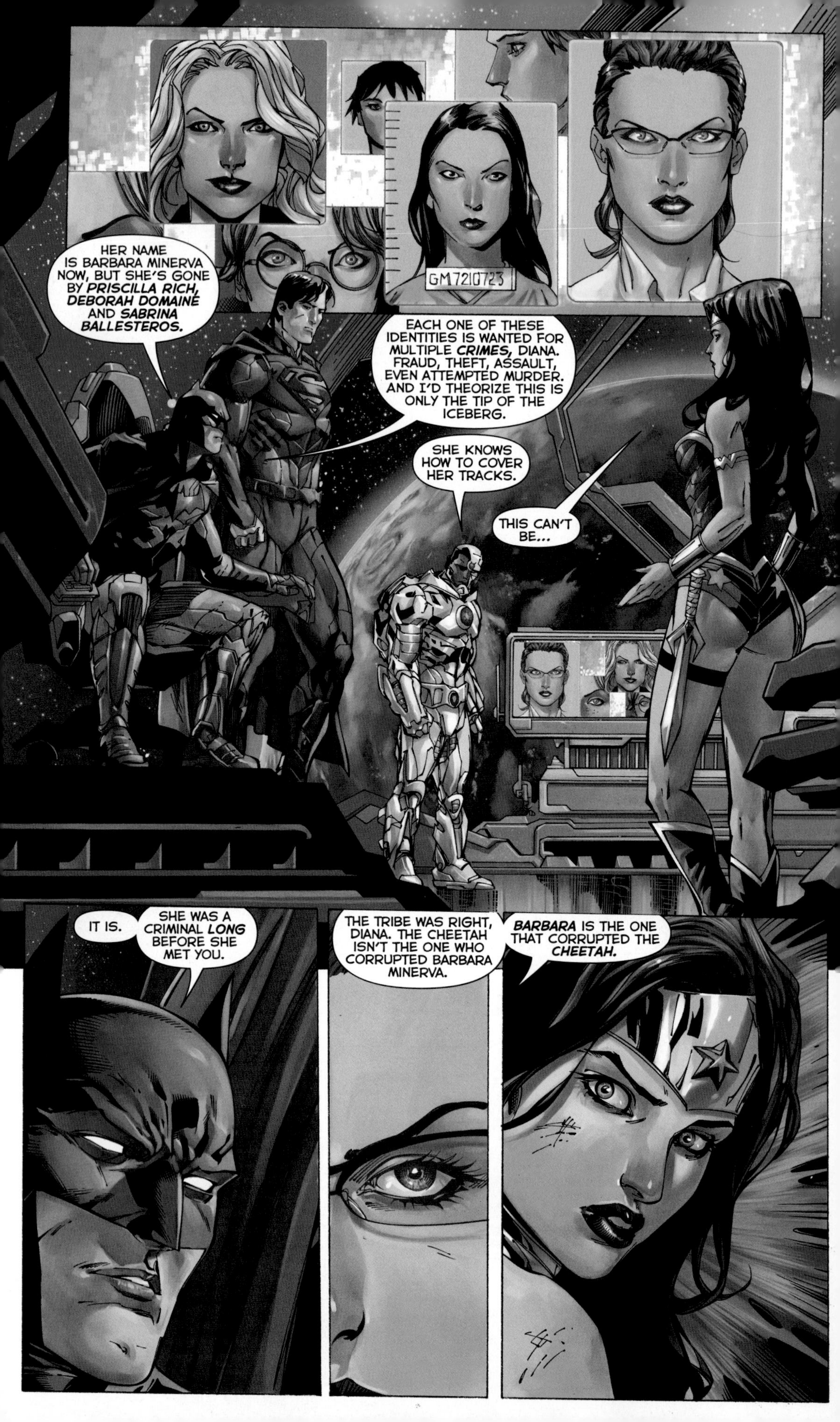
HER NAME IS BARBARA MINERVA NOW, BUT SHE'S GONE BY PRISCILLA RICH, DEBORAH DOMAINE AND SABRINA BALLESTEROS.
GM7210723
EACH ONE OF THESE IDENTITIES IS WANTED FOR MULTIPLE CRIMES, DIANA. FRAUD, THEFT, ASSAULT, EVEN ATTEMPTED MURDER. AND I'D THEORIZE THIS IS ONLY THE TIP OF THE ICEBERG.
SHE KNOWS HOW TO COVER HER TRACKS.
THIS CAN'T BE...
IT IS.
SHE WAS A CRIMINAL LONG BEFORE SHE MET YOU.
THE TRIBE WAS RIGHT, DIANA. THE CHEETAH ISN'T THE ONE WHO CORRUPTED BARBARA MINERVA.
BARBARA IS THE ONE THAT CORRUPTED THE CHEETAH.

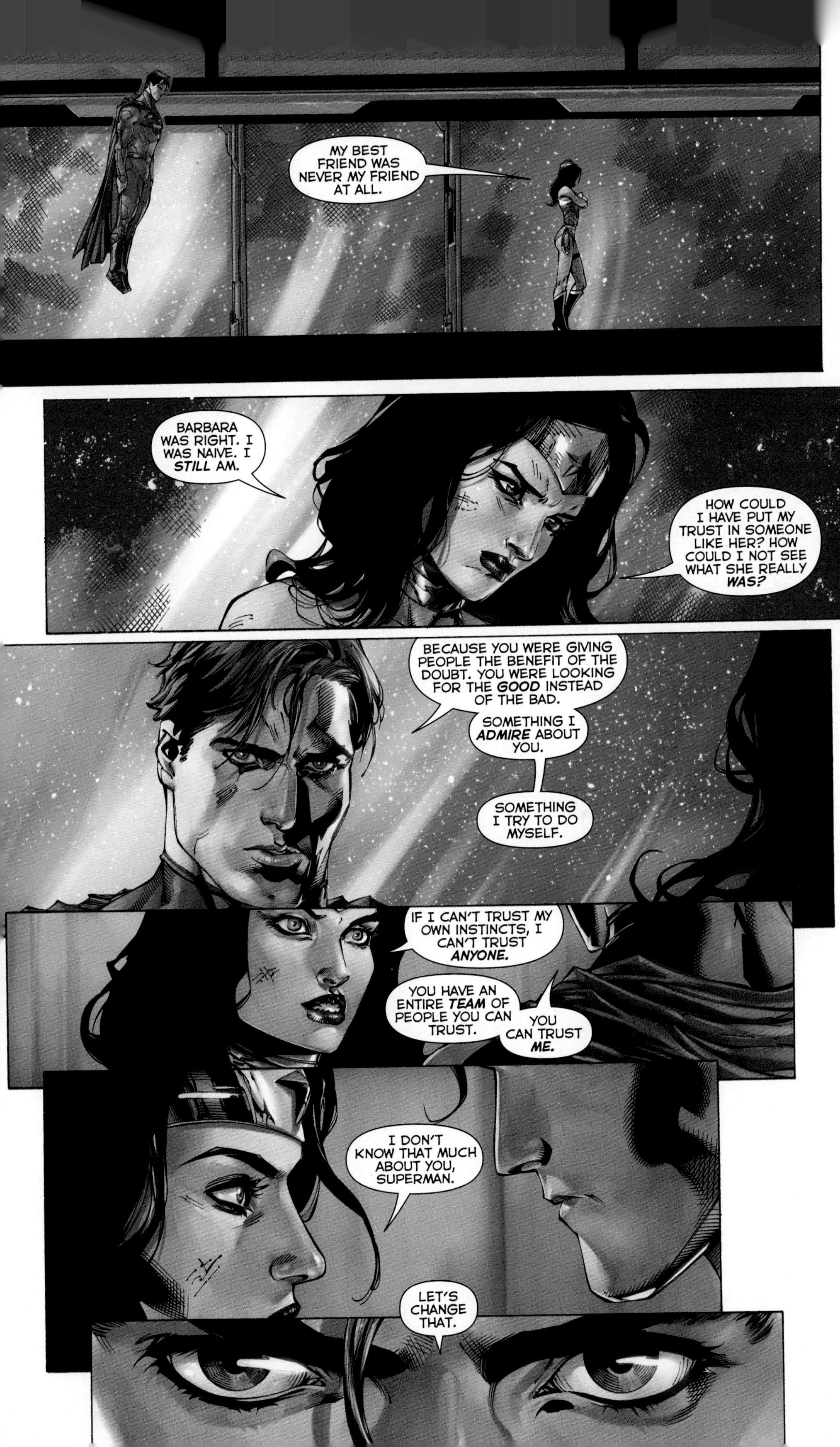
MY BEST FRIEND WAS NEVER MY FRIEND AT ALL.
BARBARA WAS RIGHT. I WAS NAIVE. I *STILL* AM.
HOW COULD I HAVE PUT MY TRUST IN SOMEONE LIKE HER? HOW COULD I NOT SEE WHAT SHE REALLY *WAS?*
BECAUSE YOU WERE GIVING PEOPLE THE BENEFIT OF THE DOUBT. YOU WERE LOOKING FOR THE *GOOD* INSTEAD OF THE BAD.
SOMETHING I *ADMIRE* ABOUT YOU.
SOMETHING I TRY TO DO MYSELF.
IF I CAN'T TRUST MY OWN INSTINCTS, I CAN'T TRUST *ANYONE.*
YOU HAVE AN ENTIRE *TEAM* OF PEOPLE YOU CAN TRUST.
YOU CAN TRUST *ME.*
I DON'T KNOW THAT MUCH ABOUT YOU, SUPERMAN.
LET'S CHANGE THAT.

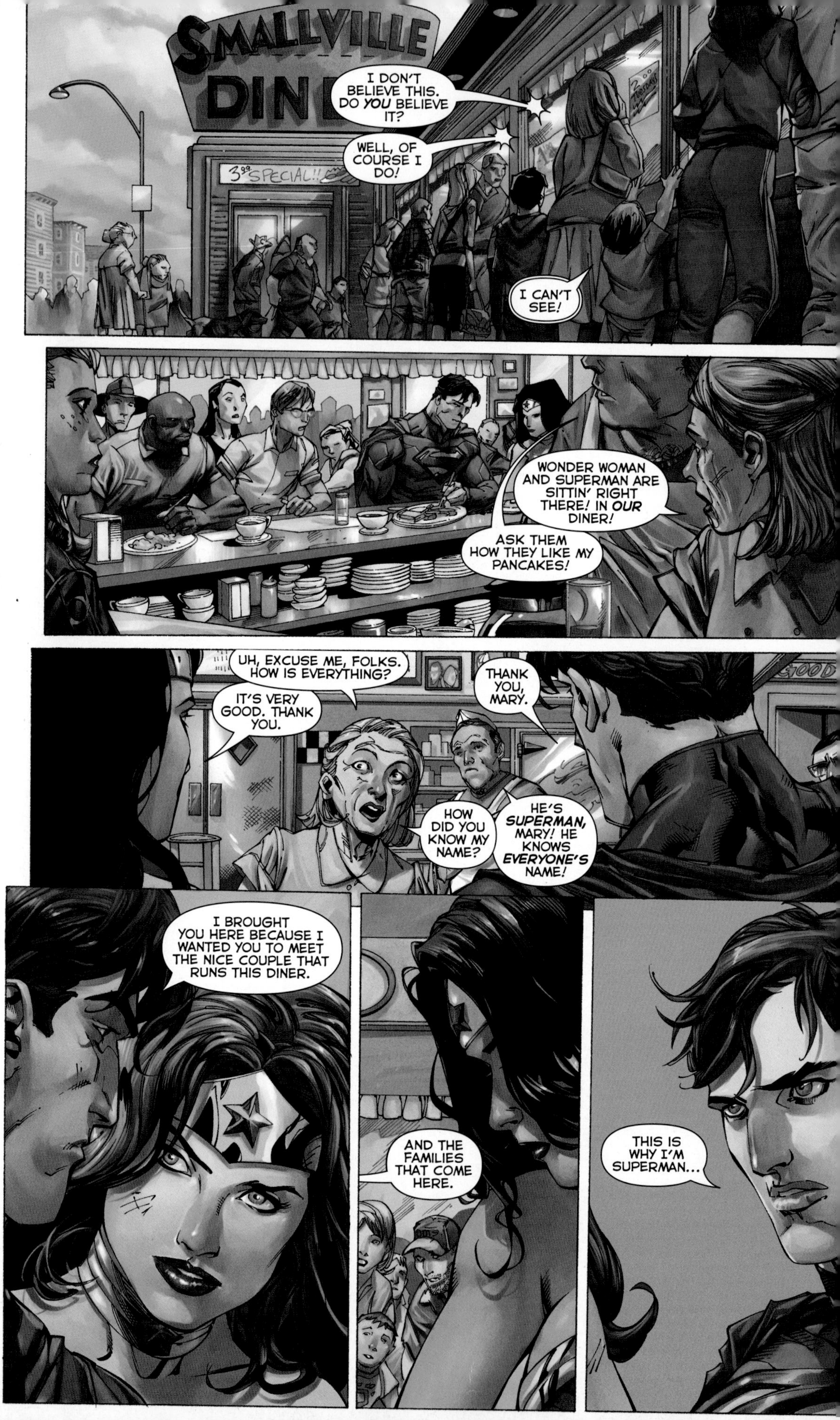
SMALLVILLE
DIN
I DON'T BELIEVE THIS. DO YOU BELIEVE IT?
WELL, OF COURSE I DO!
3.99 SPECIAL!!
I CAN'T SEE!
WONDER WOMAN AND SUPERMAN ARE SITTIN' RIGHT THERE! IN OUR DINER!
ASK THEM HOW THEY LIKE MY PANCAKES!
UH, EXCUSE ME, FOLKS. HOW IS EVERYTHING?
IT'S VERY GOOD. THANK YOU.
THANK YOU, MARY.
HOW DID YOU KNOW MY NAME?
HE'S SUPERMAN, MARY! HE KNOWS EVERYONE'S NAME!
I BROUGHT YOU HERE BECAUSE I WANTED YOU TO MEET THE NICE COUPLE THAT RUNS THIS DINER.
AND THE FAMILIES THAT COME HERE.
THIS IS WHY I'M SUPERMAN...

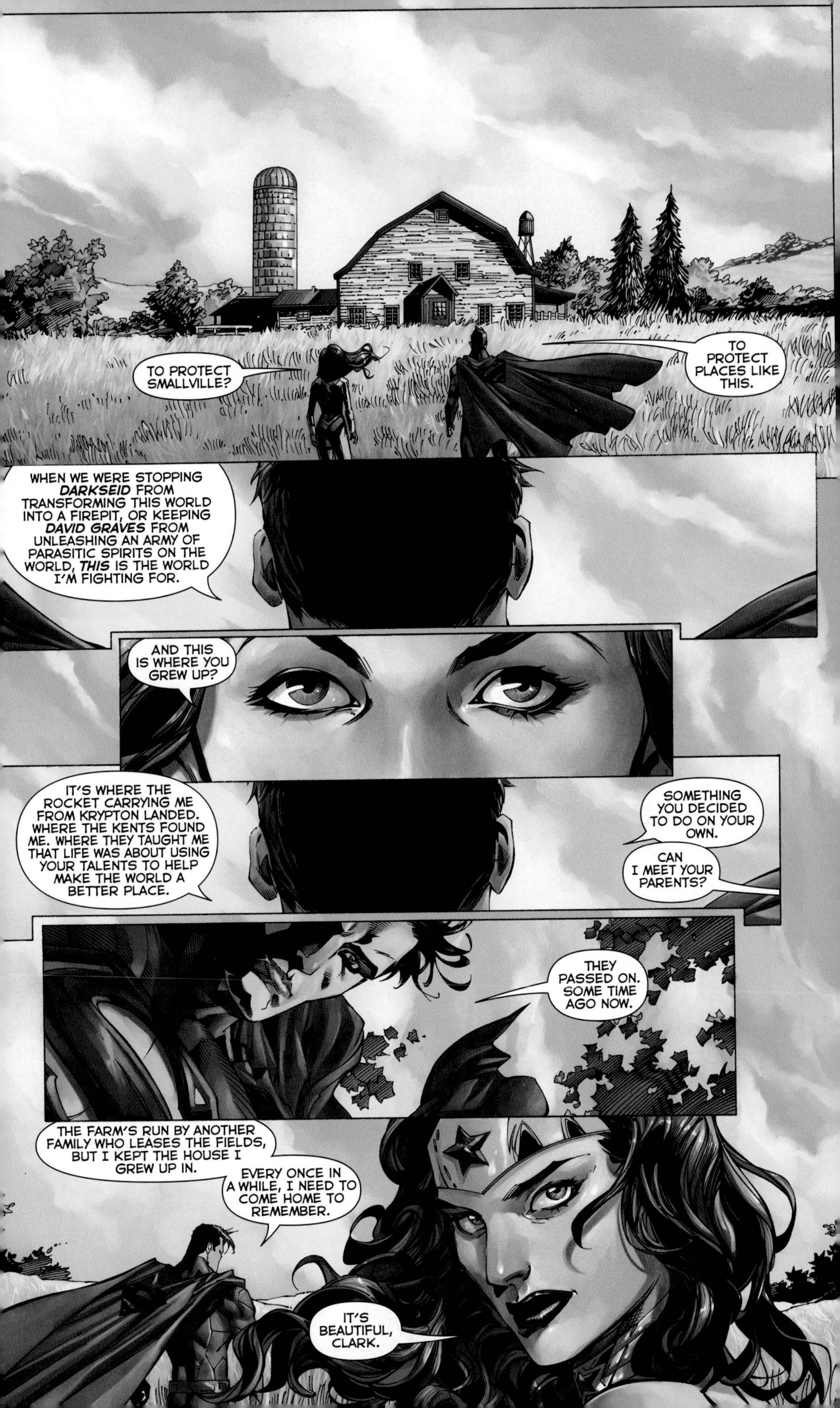

TO PROTECT SMALLVILLE?
TO PROTECT PLACES LIKE THIS.
WHEN WE WERE STOPPING DARKSEID FROM TRANSFORMING THIS WORLD INTO A FIREPIT, OR KEEPING DAVID GRAVES FROM UNLEASHING AN ARMY OF PARASITIC SPIRITS ON THE WORLD, THIS IS THE WORLD I'M FIGHTING FOR.
AND THIS IS WHERE YOU GREW UP?
IT'S WHERE THE ROCKET CARRYING ME FROM KRYPTON LANDED. WHERE THE KENTS FOUND ME. WHERE THEY TAUGHT ME THAT LIFE WAS ABOUT USING YOUR TALENTS TO HELP MAKE THE WORLD A BETTER PLACE.
SOMETHING YOU DECIDED TO DO ON YOUR OWN.
CAN I MEET YOUR PARENTS?
THEY PASSED ON. SOME TIME AGO NOW.
THE FARM'S RUN BY ANOTHER FAMILY WHO LEASES THE FIELDS, BUT I KEPT THE HOUSE I GREW UP IN.
EVERY ONCE IN A WHILE, I NEED TO COME HOME TO REMEMBER.
IT'S BEAUTIFUL, CLARK.

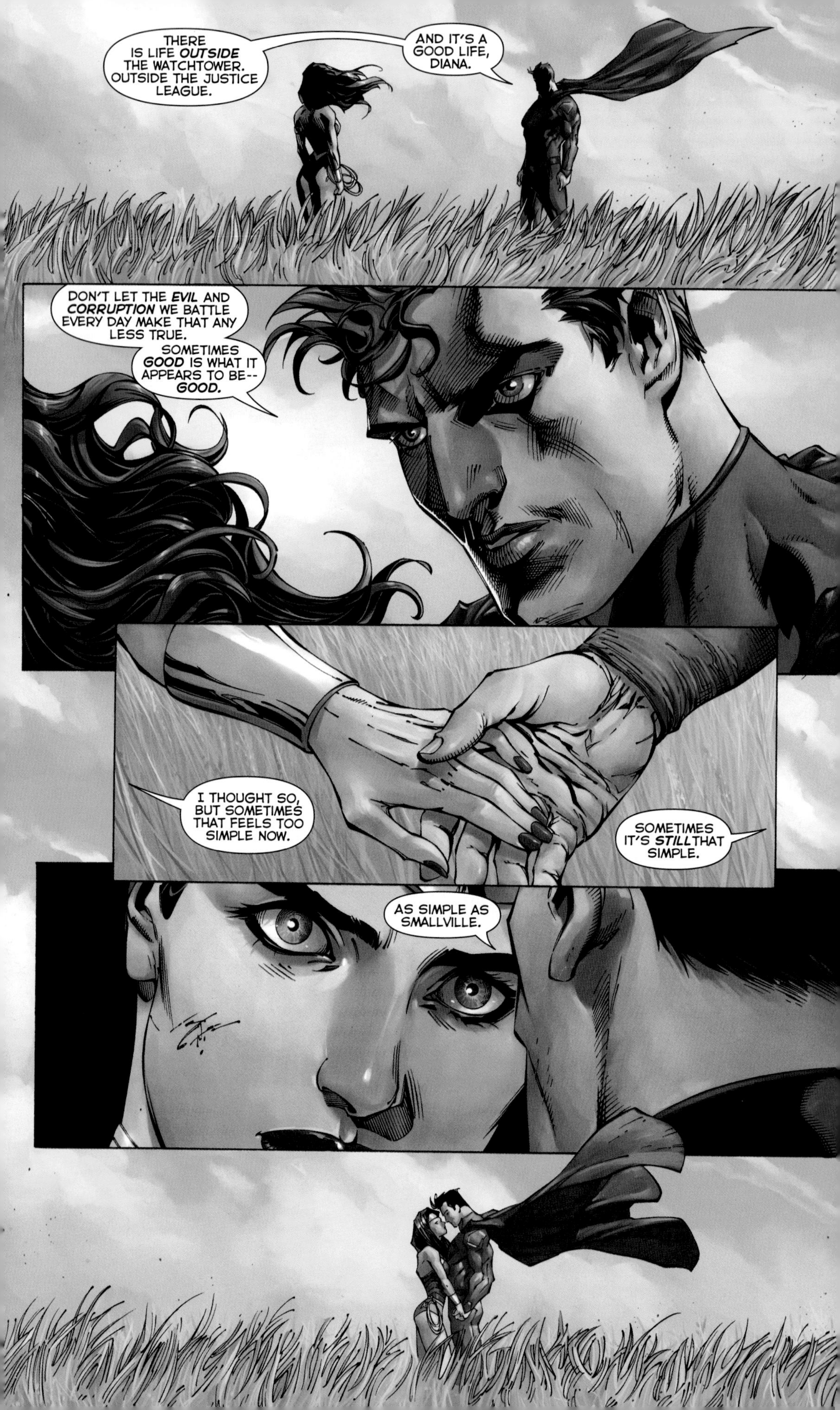
THERE IS LIFE OUTSIDE THE WATCHTOWER. OUTSIDE THE JUSTICE LEAGUE.
AND IT'S A GOOD LIFE, DIANA.
DON'T LET THE EVIL AND CORRUPTION WE BATTLE EVERY DAY MAKE THAT ANY LESS TRUE.
SOMETIMES GOOD IS WHAT IT APPEARS TO BE-- GOOD.
I THOUGHT SO, BUT SOMETIMES THAT FEELS TOO SIMPLE NOW.
SOMETIMES IT'S STILL THAT SIMPLE.
AS SIMPLE AS SMALLVILLE.

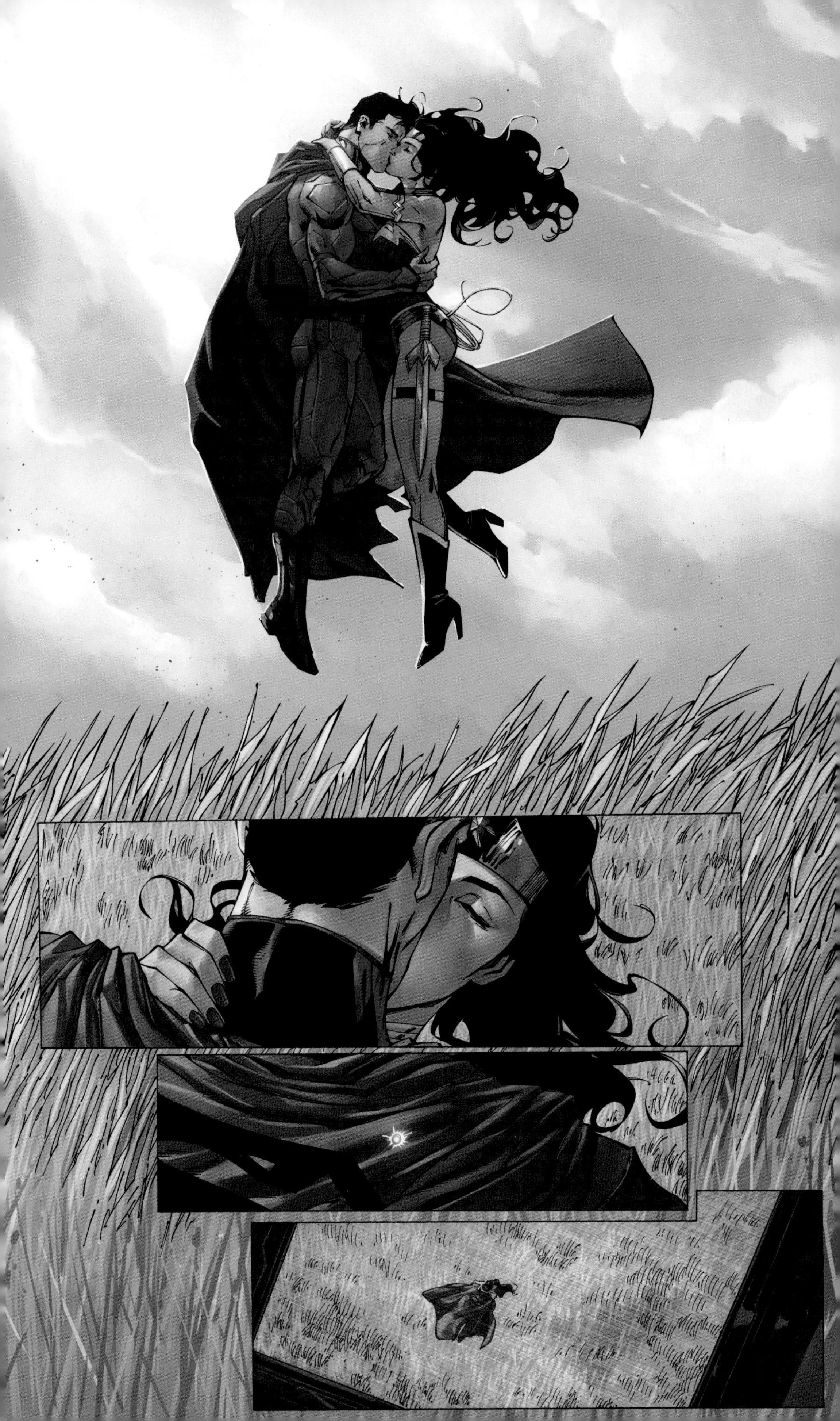

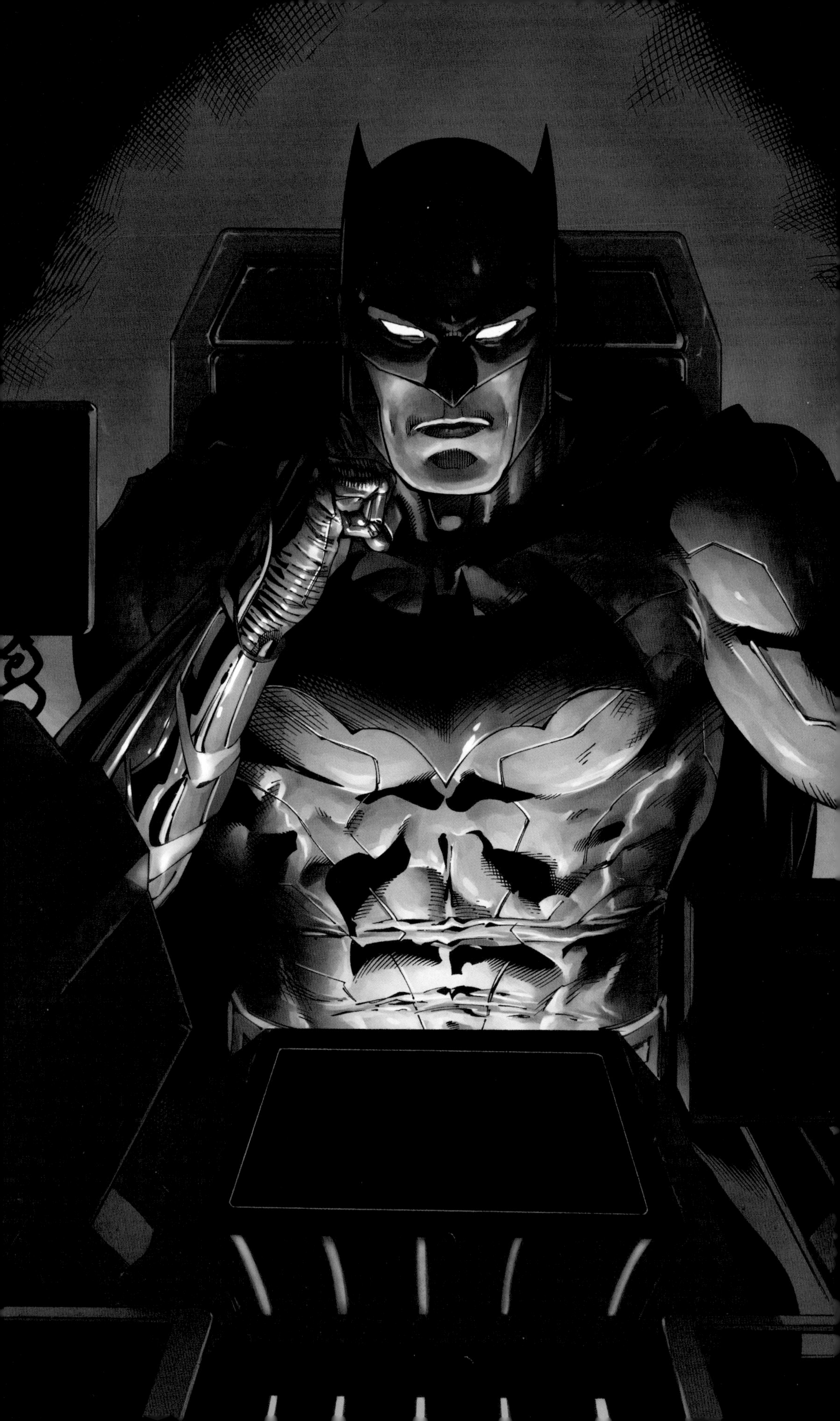

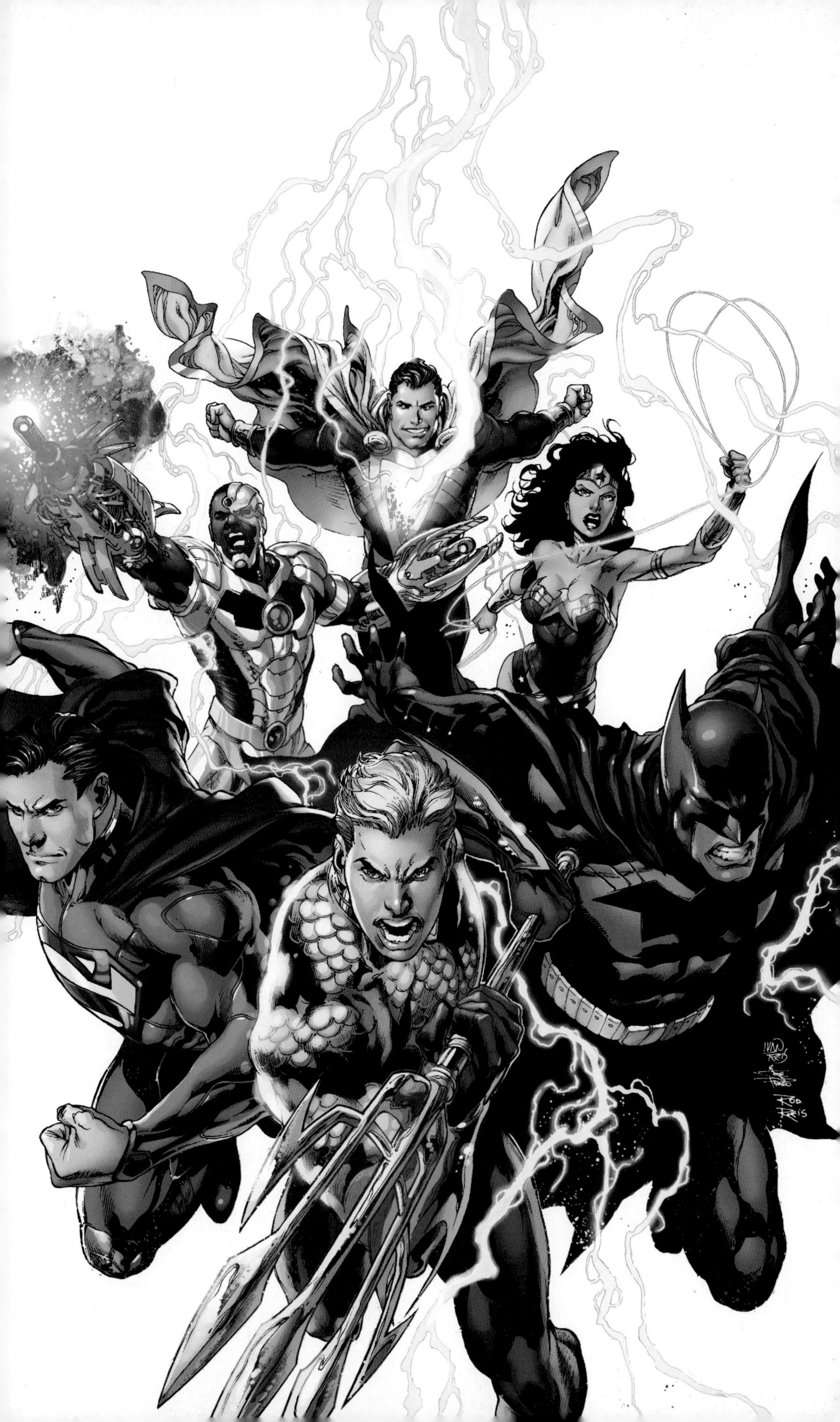

GEOFF JOHNS writer IVAN REIS penciller JOE PRADO inker cover by IVAN REIS, JOE PRADO & ROD REIS

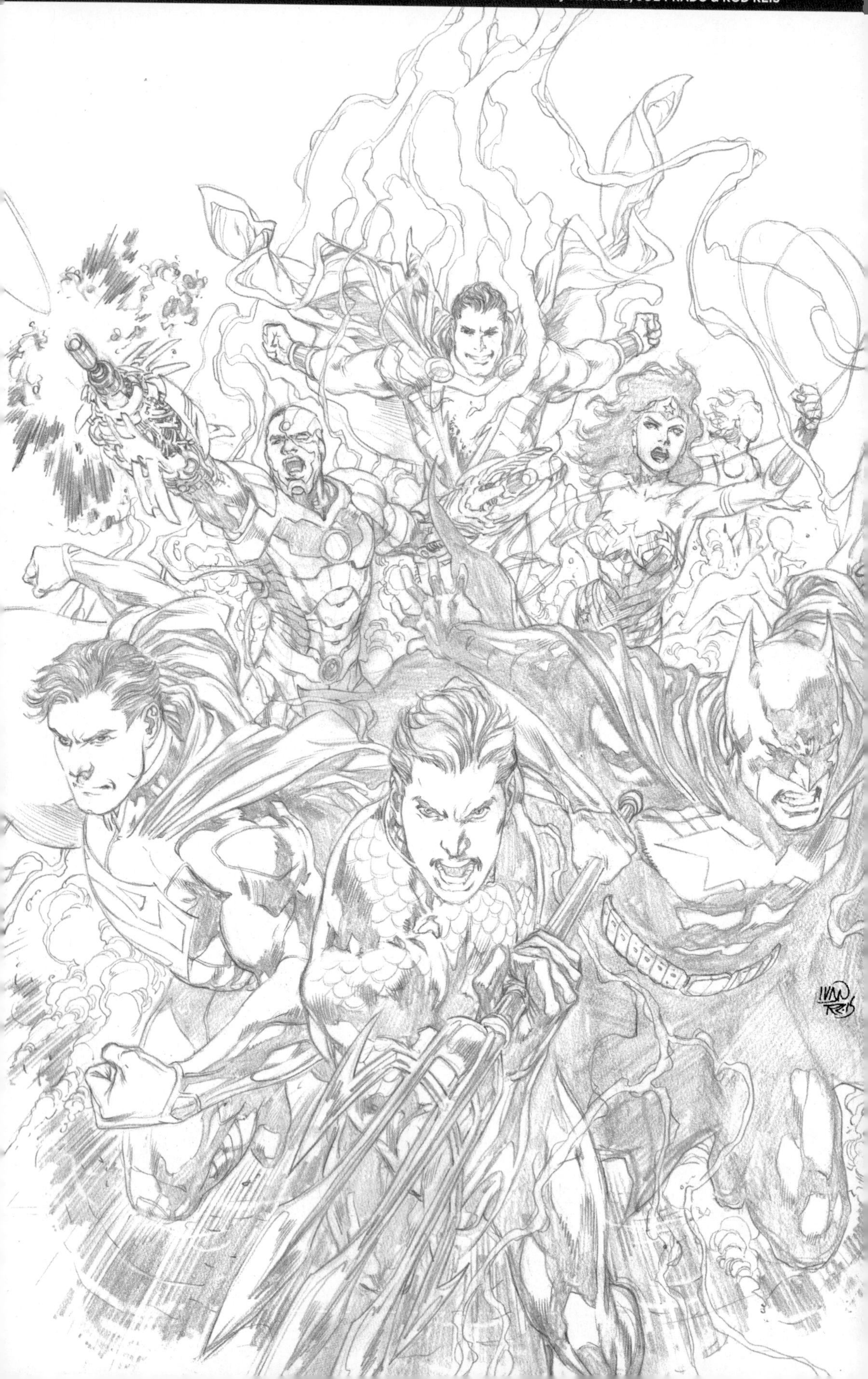
IVAN REIS

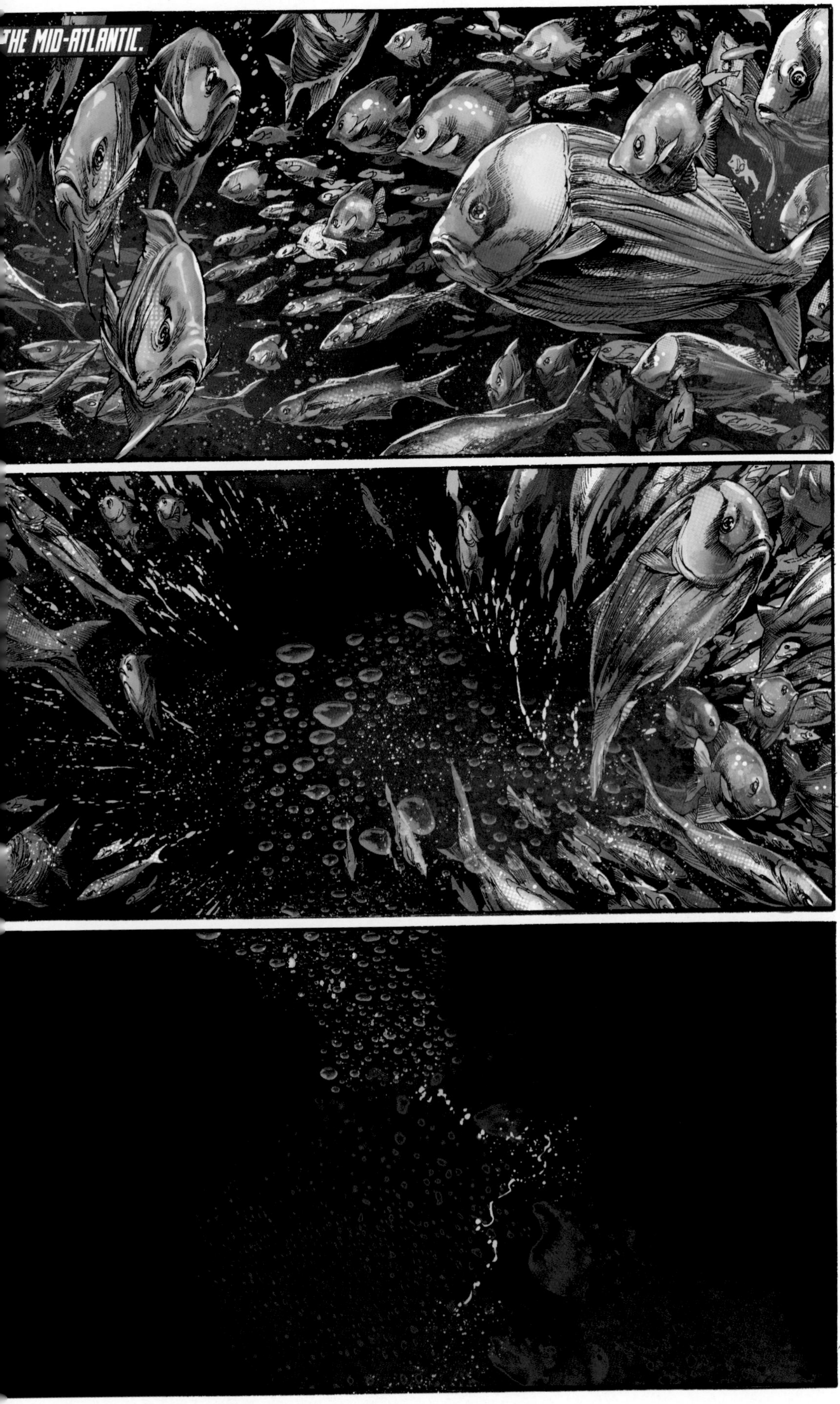
THE MID-ATLANTIC.

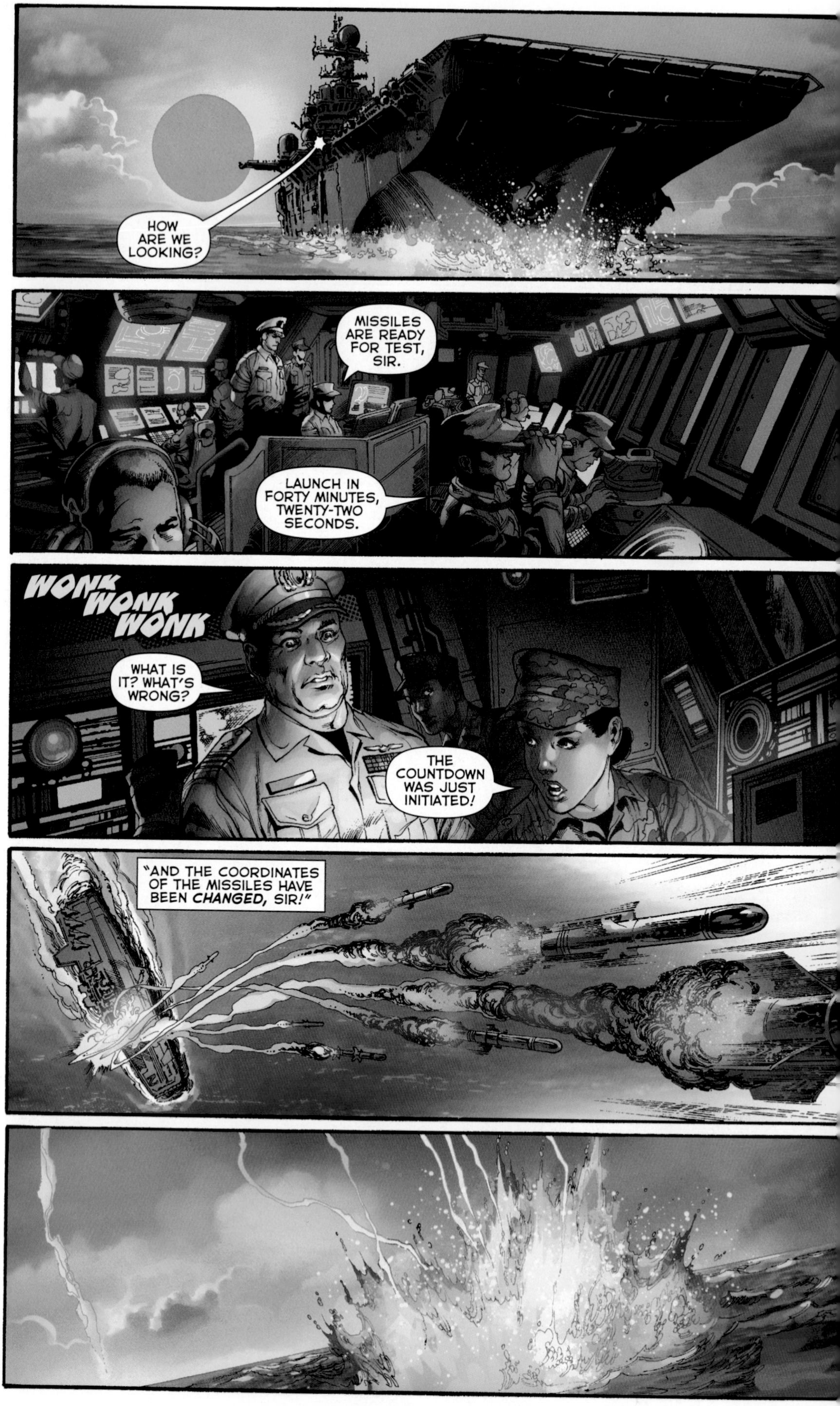
HOW ARE WE LOOKING?
MISSILES ARE READY FOR TEST, SIR.
LAUNCH IN FORTY MINUTES, TWENTY-TWO SECONDS.
WONK WONK WONK
WHAT IS IT? WHAT'S WRONG?
THE COUNTDOWN WAS JUST INITIATED!
"AND THE COORDINATES OF THE MISSILES HAVE BEEN CHANGED, SIR!"

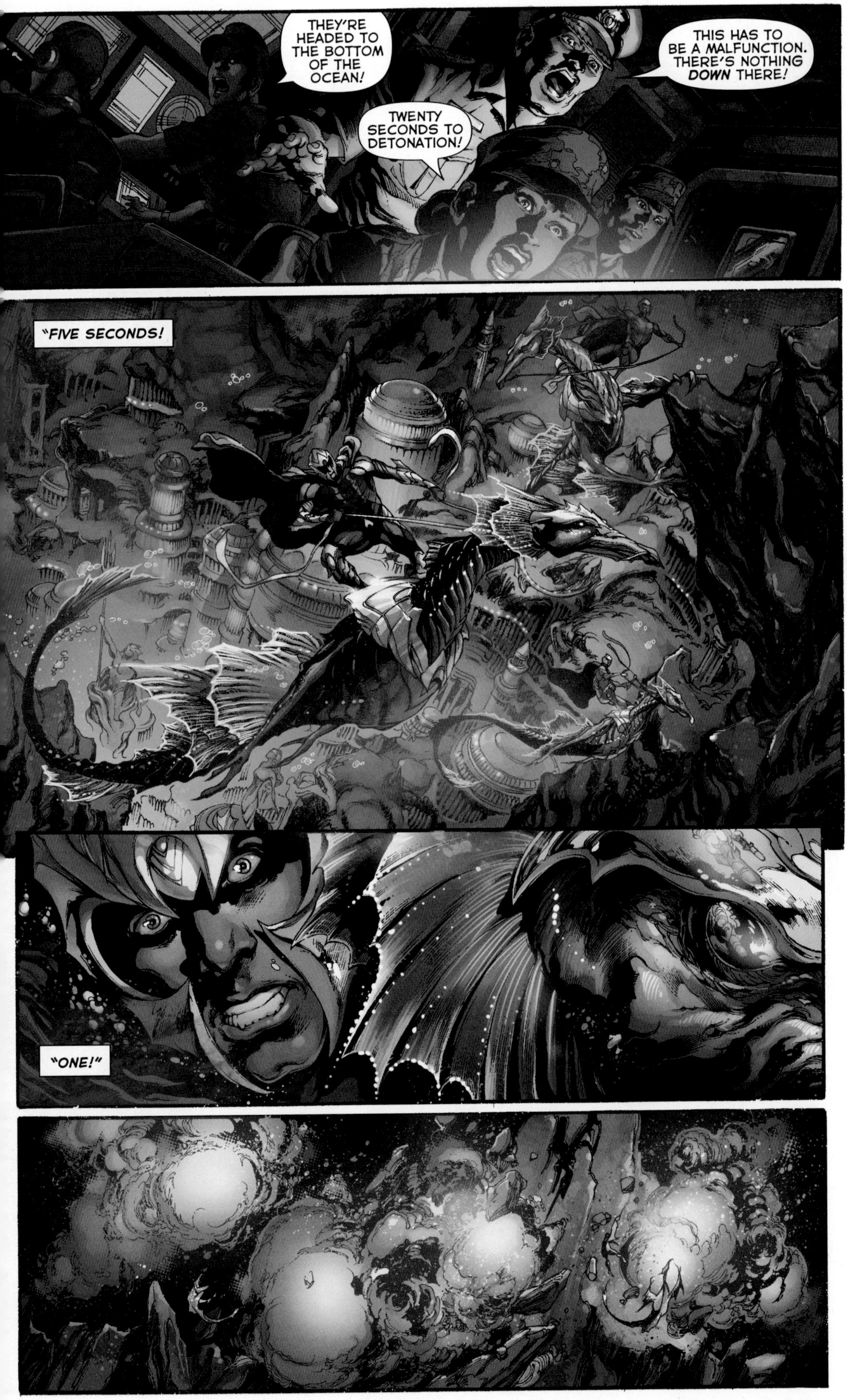
THEY'RE HEADED TO THE BOTTOM OF THE OCEAN!
THIS HAS TO BE A MALFUNCTION. THERE'S NOTHING *DOWN* THERE!
TWENTY SECONDS TO DETONATION!
"FIVE SECONDS!
"ONE!"

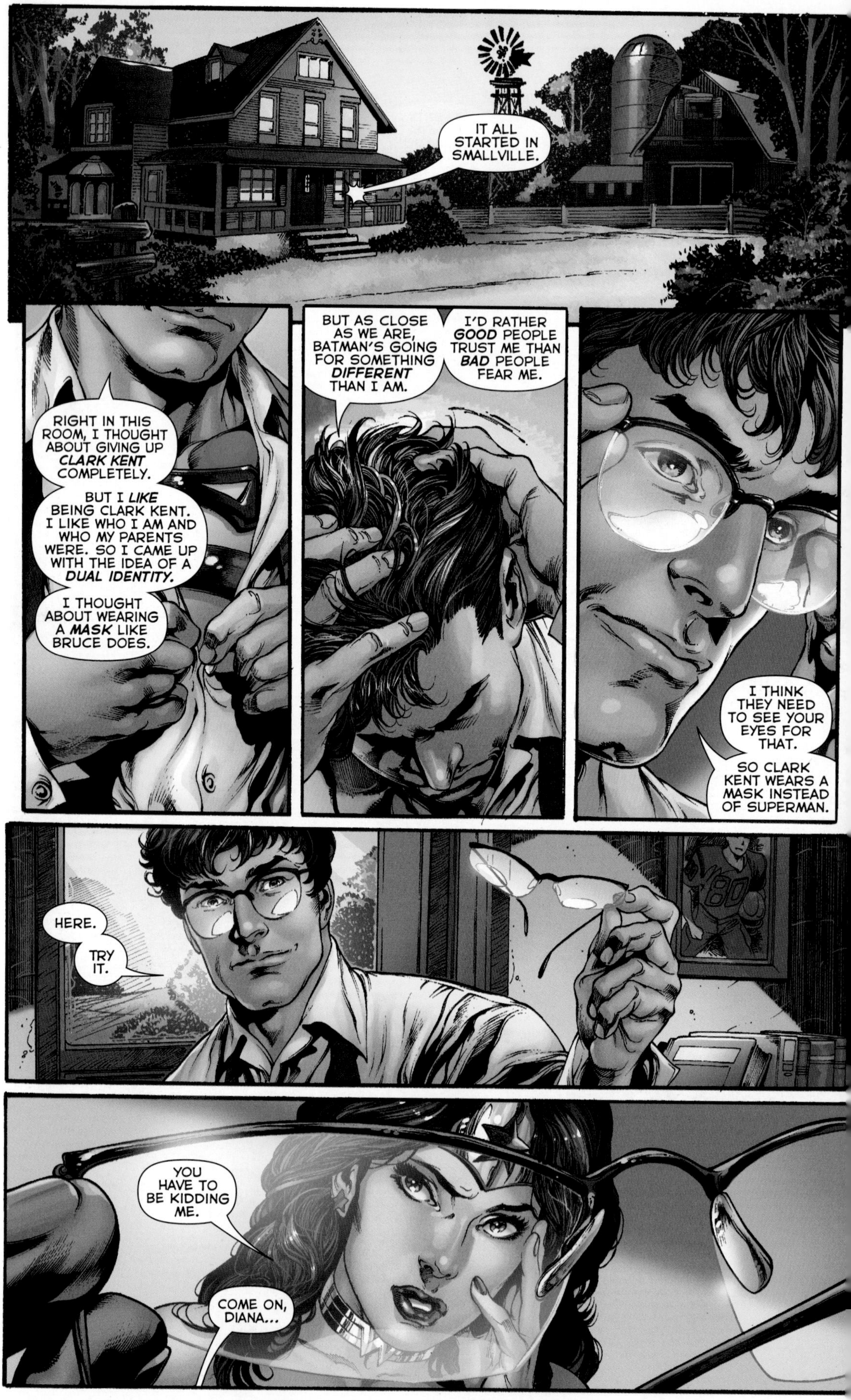
IT ALL STARTED IN SMALLVILLE.
RIGHT IN THIS ROOM, I THOUGHT ABOUT GIVING UP CLARK KENT COMPLETELY.
BUT I LIKE BEING CLARK KENT. I LIKE WHO I AM AND WHO MY PARENTS WERE. SO I CAME UP WITH THE IDEA OF A DUAL IDENTITY.
I THOUGHT ABOUT WEARING A MASK LIKE BRUCE DOES.
BUT AS CLOSE AS WE ARE, BATMAN'S GOING FOR SOMETHING DIFFERENT THAN I AM.
I'D RATHER GOOD PEOPLE TRUST ME THAN BAD PEOPLE FEAR ME.
I THINK THEY NEED TO SEE YOUR EYES FOR THAT.
SO CLARK KENT WEARS A MASK INSTEAD OF SUPERMAN.
HERE.
TRY IT.
YOU HAVE TO BE KIDDING ME.
COME ON, DIANA...

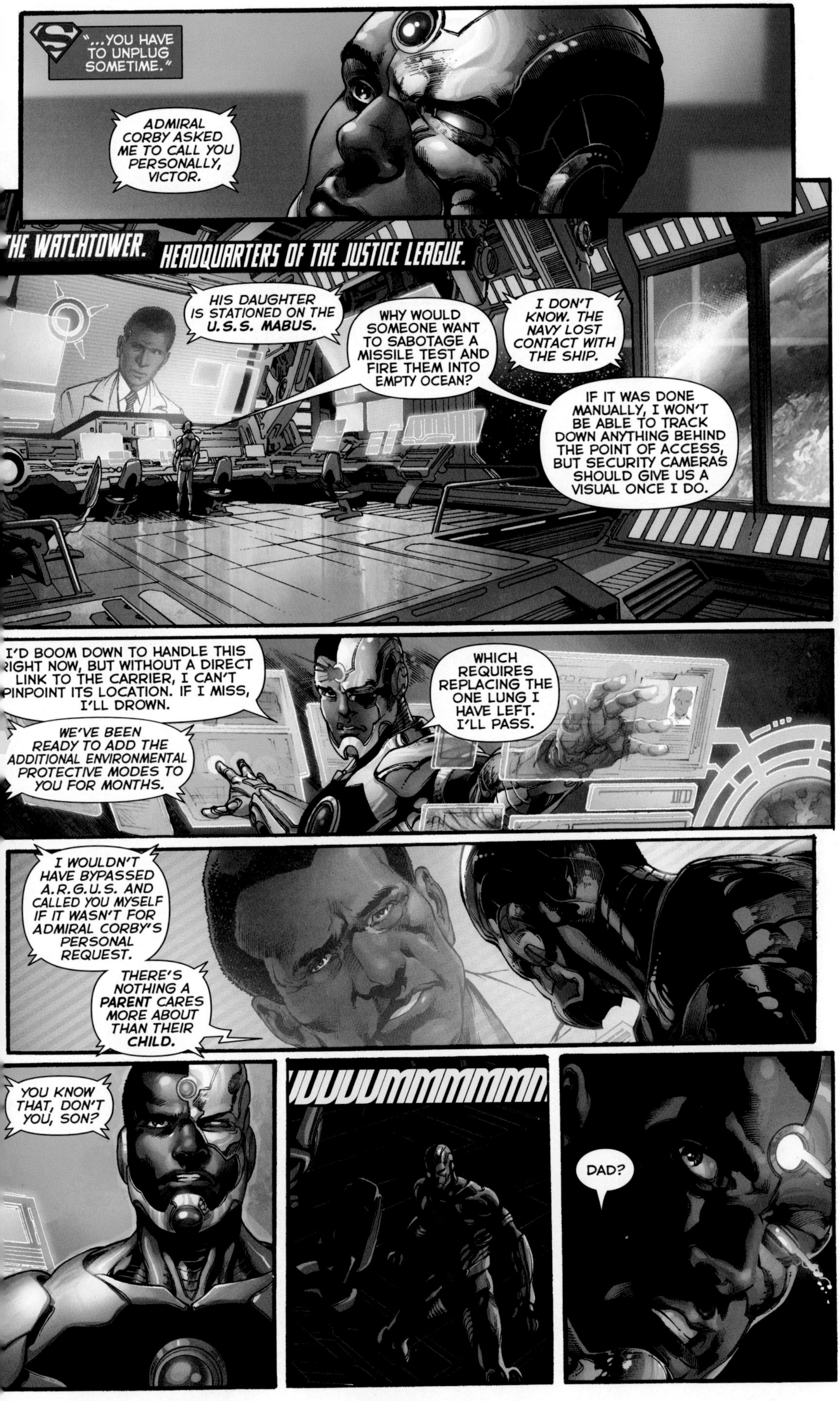
"...YOU HAVE TO UNPLUG SOMETIME."
ADMIRAL CORBY ASKED ME TO CALL YOU PERSONALLY, VICTOR.
THE WATCHTOWER.
HEADQUARTERS OF THE JUSTICE LEAGUE.
HIS DAUGHTER IS STATIONED ON THE U.S.S. MABUS.
WHY WOULD SOMEONE WANT TO SABOTAGE A MISSILE TEST AND FIRE THEM INTO EMPTY OCEAN?
I DON'T KNOW. THE NAVY LOST CONTACT WITH THE SHIP.
IF IT WAS DONE MANUALLY, I WON'T BE ABLE TO TRACK DOWN ANYTHING BEHIND THE POINT OF ACCESS, BUT SECURITY CAMERAS SHOULD GIVE US A VISUAL ONCE I DO.
I'D BOOM DOWN TO HANDLE THIS RIGHT NOW, BUT WITHOUT A DIRECT LINK TO THE CARRIER, I CAN'T PINPOINT ITS LOCATION. IF I MISS, I'LL DROWN.
WE'VE BEEN READY TO ADD THE ADDITIONAL ENVIRONMENTAL PROTECTIVE MODES TO YOU FOR MONTHS.
WHICH REQUIRES REPLACING THE ONE LUNG I HAVE LEFT. I'LL PASS.
I WOULDN'T HAVE BYPASSED A.R.G.U.S. AND CALLED YOU MYSELF IF IT WASN'T FOR ADMIRAL CORBY'S PERSONAL REQUEST.
THERE'S NOTHING A PARENT CARES MORE ABOUT THAN THEIR CHILD.
YOU KNOW THAT, DON'T YOU, SON?
VVVVVMMMMMMMM
DAD?

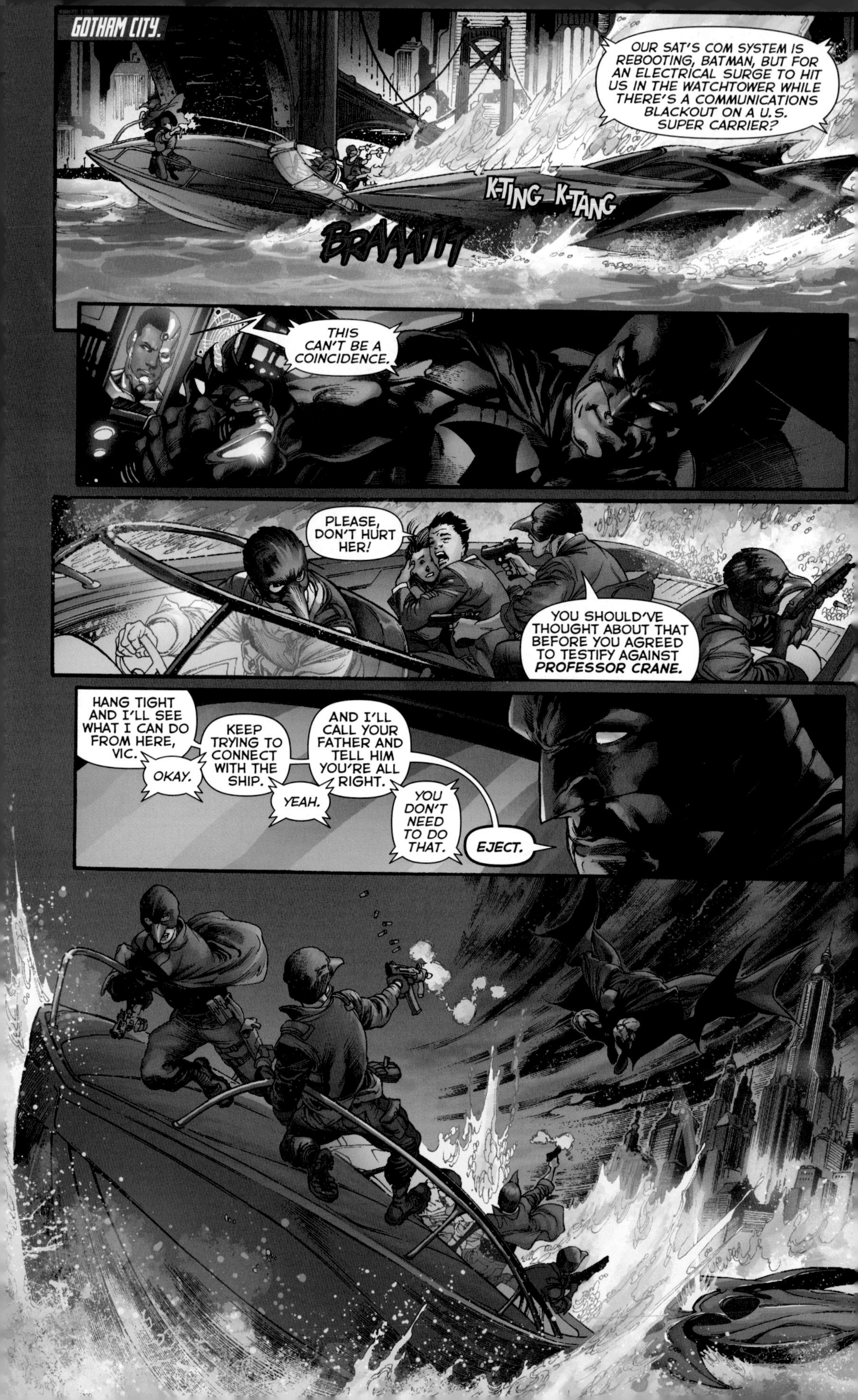
GOTHAM CITY.
OUR SAT'S COM SYSTEM IS REBOOTING, BATMAN, BUT FOR AN ELECTRICAL SURGE TO HIT US IN THE WATCHTOWER WHILE THERE'S A COMMUNICATIONS BLACKOUT ON A U.S. SUPER CARRIER?
K-TING K-TANG
BRAAAMTT
THIS CAN'T BE A COINCIDENCE.
PLEASE, DON'T HURT HER!
YOU SHOULD'VE THOUGHT ABOUT THAT BEFORE YOU AGREED TO TESTIFY AGAINST PROFESSOR CRANE.
HANG TIGHT AND I'LL SEE WHAT I CAN DO FROM HERE, VIC.
OKAY.
KEEP TRYING TO CONNECT WITH THE SHIP.
YEAH.
AND I'LL CALL YOUR FATHER AND TELL HIM YOU'RE ALL RIGHT.
YOU DON'T NEED TO DO THAT.
EJECT.

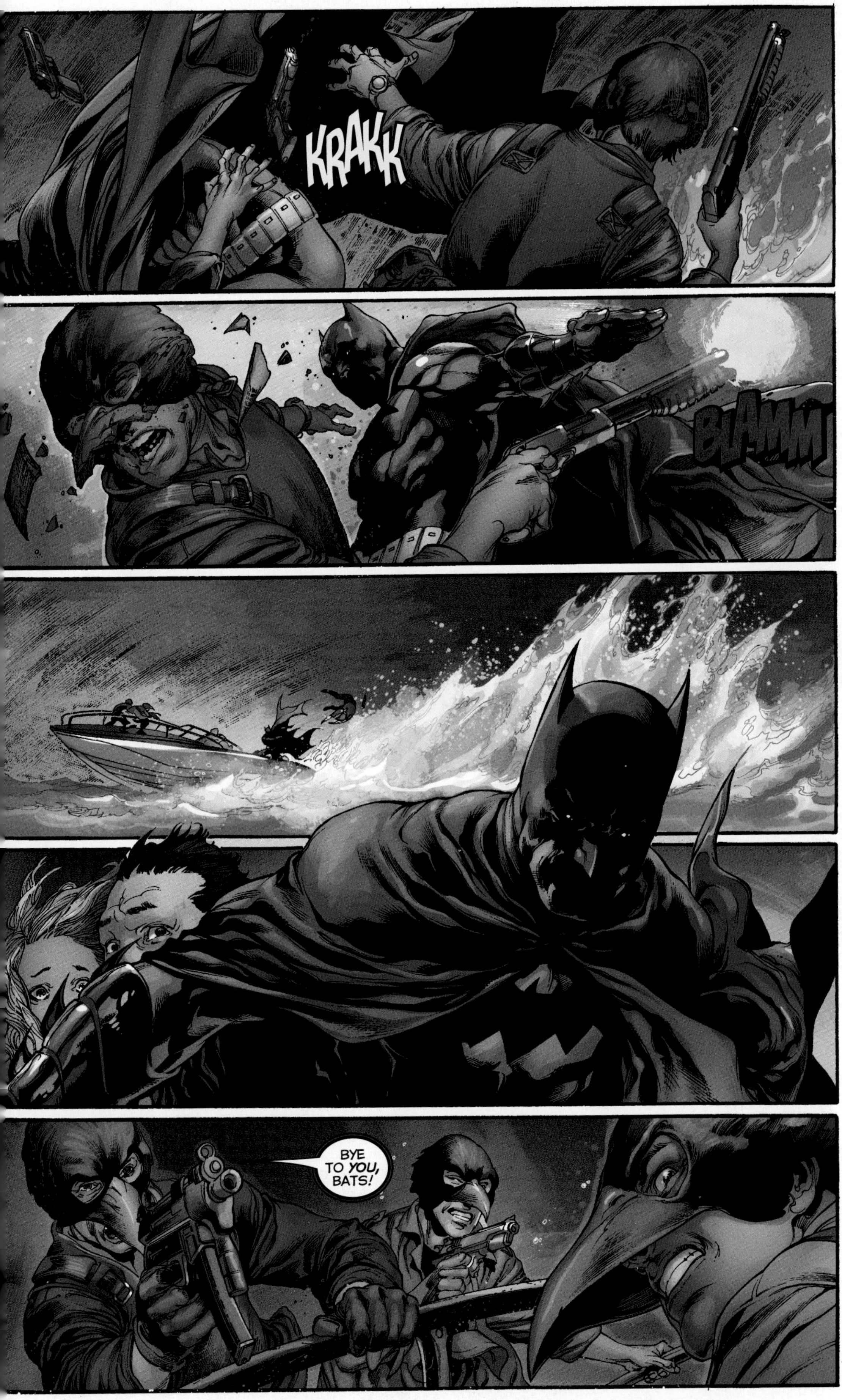
KRAKK
BLAMM
BYE TO YOU, BATS!

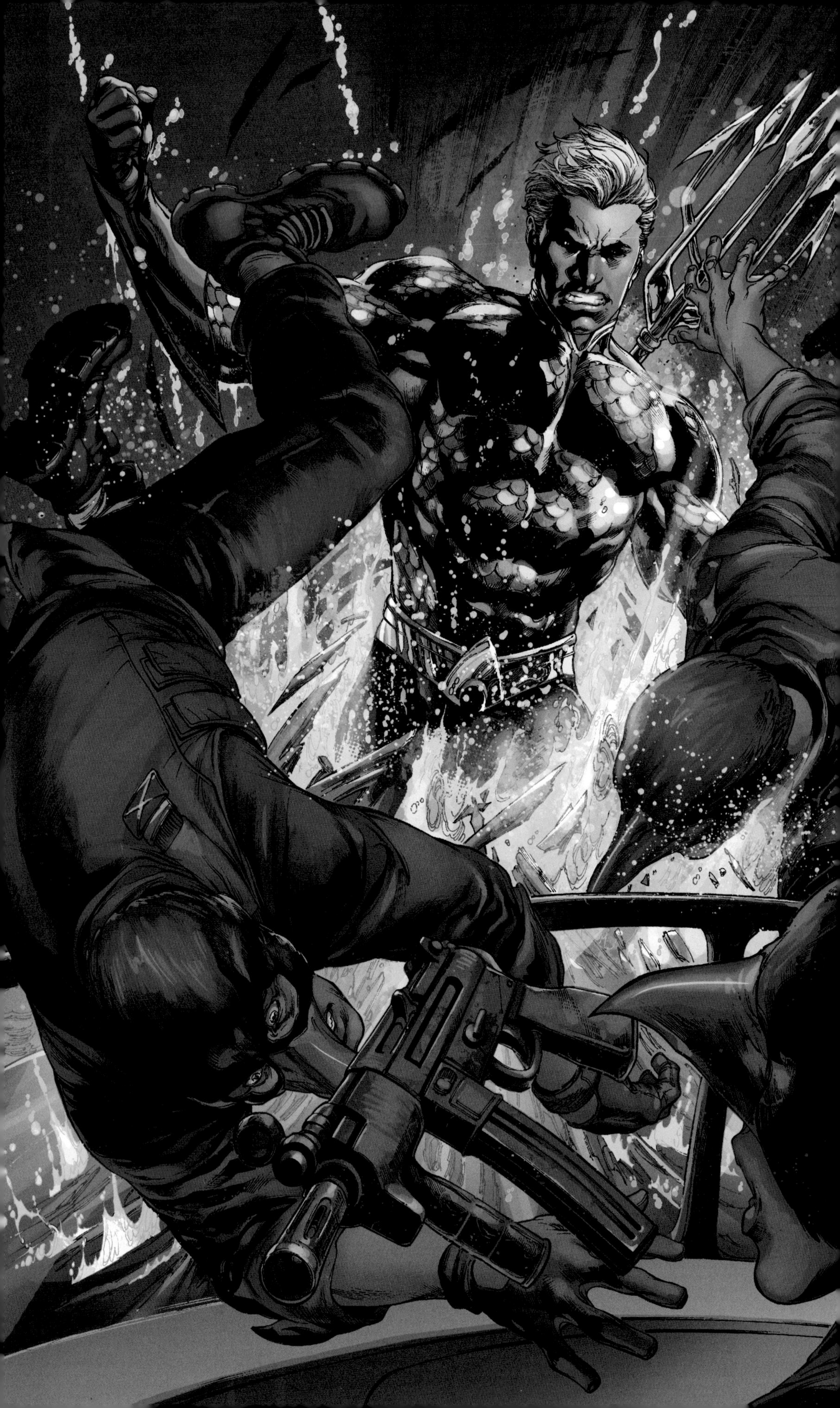

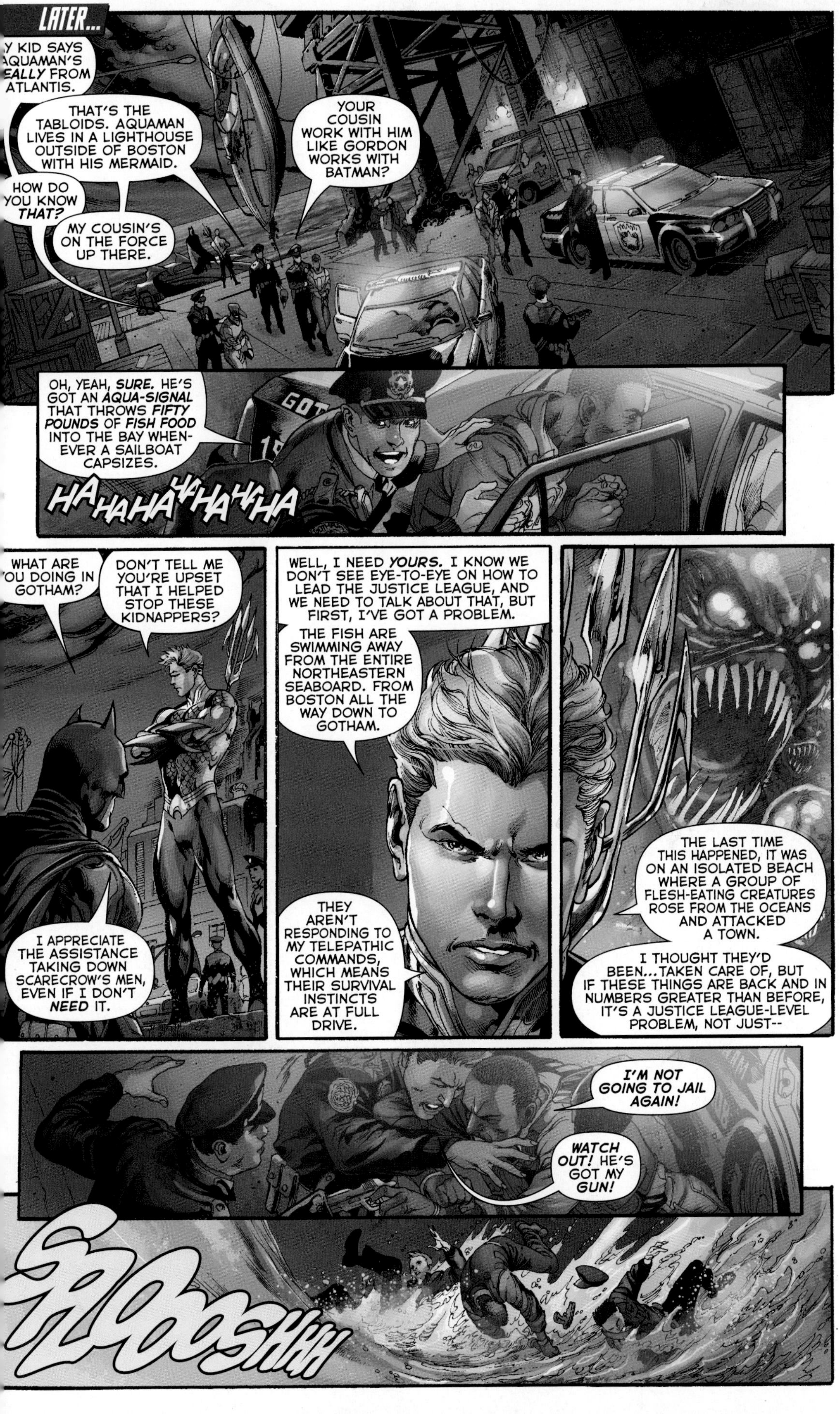
LATER...
Y KID SAYS AQUAMAN'S EALLY FROM ATLANTIS.
THAT'S THE TABLOIDS. AQUAMAN LIVES IN A LIGHTHOUSE OUTSIDE OF BOSTON WITH HIS MERMAID.
HOW DO YOU KNOW THAT?
MY COUSIN'S ON THE FORCE UP THERE.
YOUR COUSIN WORK WITH HIM LIKE GORDON WORKS WITH BATMAN?
OH, YEAH, SURE. HE'S GOT AN AQUA-SIGNAL THAT THROWS FIFTY POUNDS OF FISH FOOD INTO THE BAY WHEN-EVER A SAILBOAT CAPSIZES.
HAHAHAHAHAHAHA
WHAT ARE OU DOING IN GOTHAM?
DON'T TELL ME YOU'RE UPSET THAT I HELPED STOP THESE KIDNAPPERS?
I APPRECIATE THE ASSISTANCE TAKING DOWN SCARECROW'S MEN, EVEN IF I DON'T NEED IT.
WELL, I NEED YOURS. I KNOW WE DON'T SEE EYE-TO-EYE ON HOW TO LEAD THE JUSTICE LEAGUE, AND WE NEED TO TALK ABOUT THAT, BUT FIRST, I'VE GOT A PROBLEM.
THE FISH ARE SWIMMING AWAY FROM THE ENTIRE NORTHEASTERN SEABOARD. FROM BOSTON ALL THE WAY DOWN TO GOTHAM.
THEY AREN'T RESPONDING TO MY TELEPATHIC COMMANDS, WHICH MEANS THEIR SURVIVAL INSTINCTS ARE AT FULL DRIVE.
THE LAST TIME THIS HAPPENED, IT WAS ON AN ISOLATED BEACH WHERE A GROUP OF FLESH-EATING CREATURES ROSE FROM THE OCEANS AND ATTACKED A TOWN.
I THOUGHT THEY'D BEEN...TAKEN CARE OF, BUT IF THESE THINGS ARE BACK AND IN NUMBERS GREATER THAN BEFORE, IT'S A JUSTICE LEAGUE-LEVEL PROBLEM, NOT JUST--
I'M NOT GOING TO JAIL AGAIN!
WATCH OUT! HE'S GOT MY GUN!
SPLOOSHHH

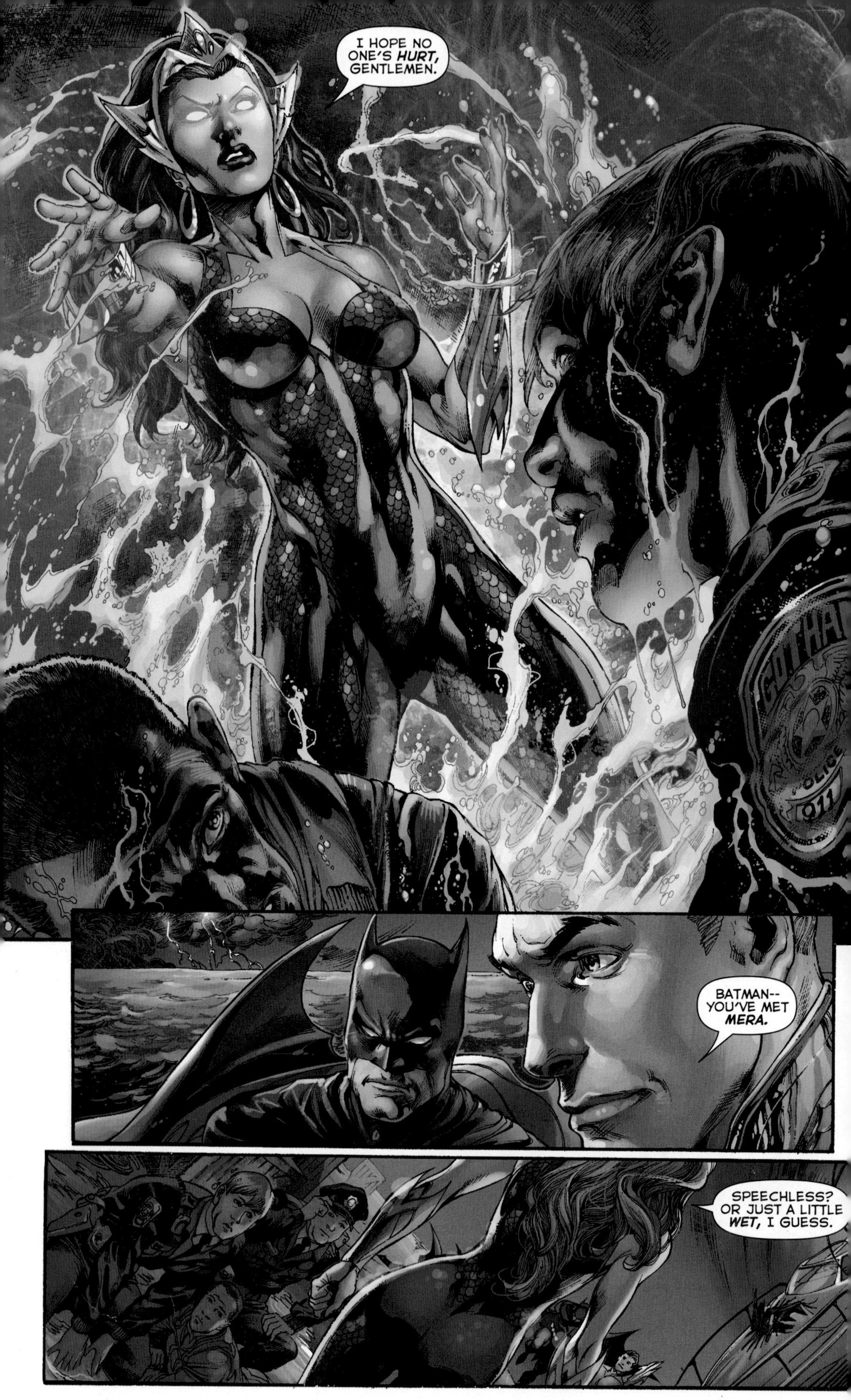
I HOPE NO ONE'S HURT, GENTLEMEN.
BATMAN-- YOU'VE MET MERA.
SPEECHLESS? OR JUST A LITTLE WET, I GUESS.

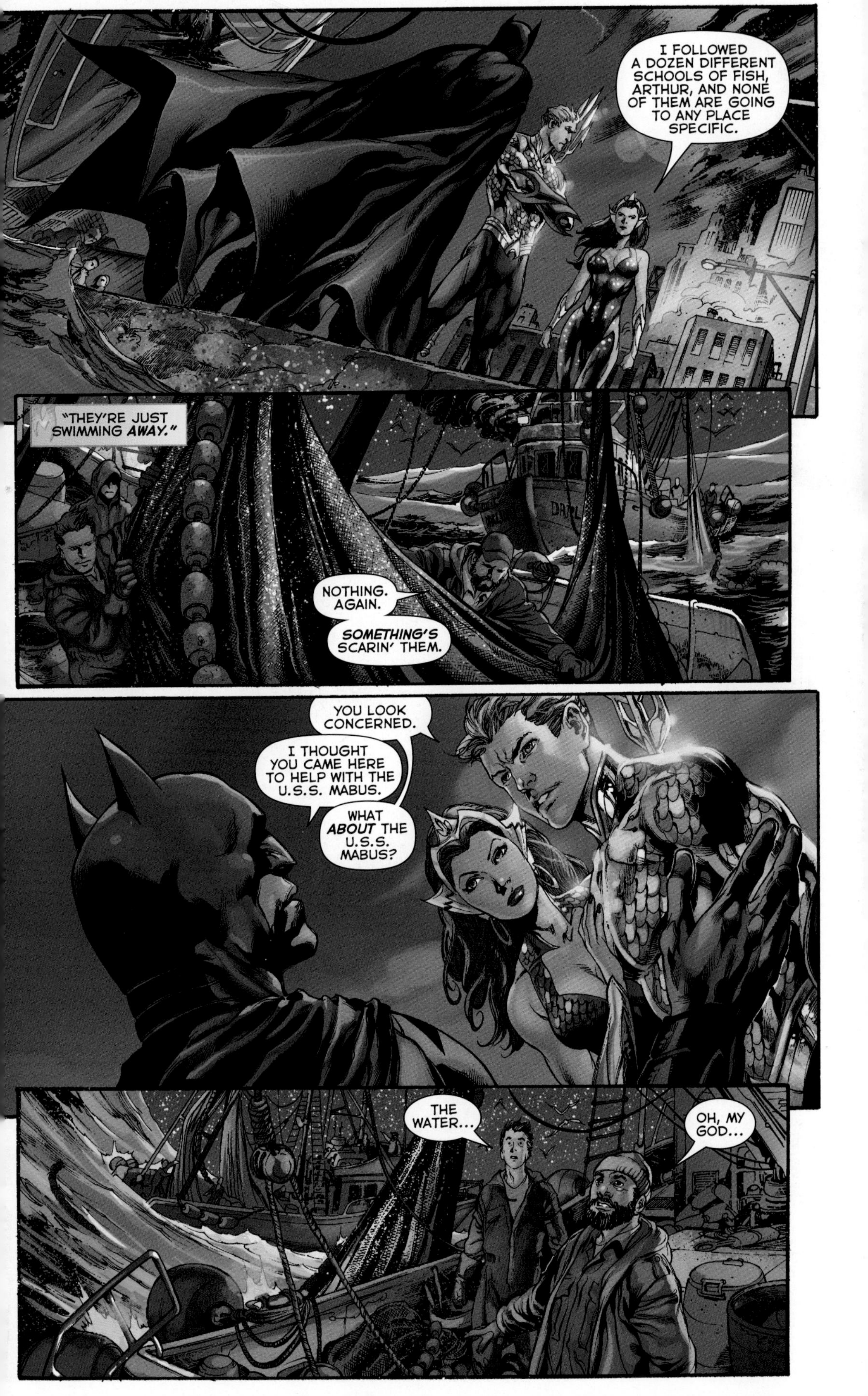
I FOLLOWED A DOZEN DIFFERENT SCHOOLS OF FISH, ARTHUR, AND NONE OF THEM ARE GOING TO ANY PLACE SPECIFIC.
"THEY'RE JUST SWIMMING AWAY."
NOTHING. AGAIN.
SOMETHING'S SCARIN' THEM.
YOU LOOK CONCERNED.
I THOUGHT YOU CAME HERE TO HELP WITH THE U.S.S. MABUS.
WHAT ABOUT THE U.S.S. MABUS?
THE WATER...
OH, MY GOD...

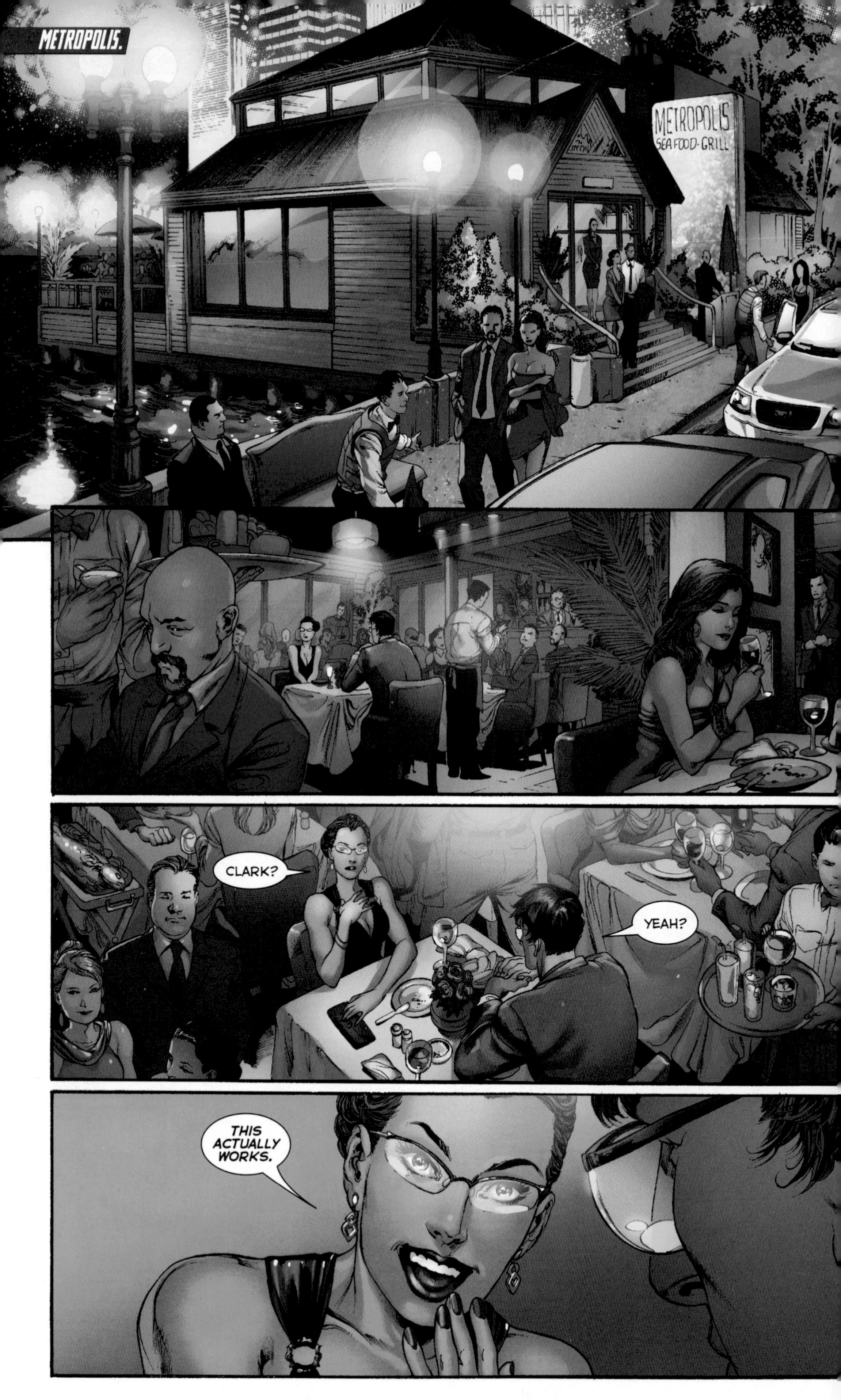
METROPOLIS.
METROPOLIS SEA FOOD-GRILL
CLARK?
YEAH?
THIS ACTUALLY WORKS.

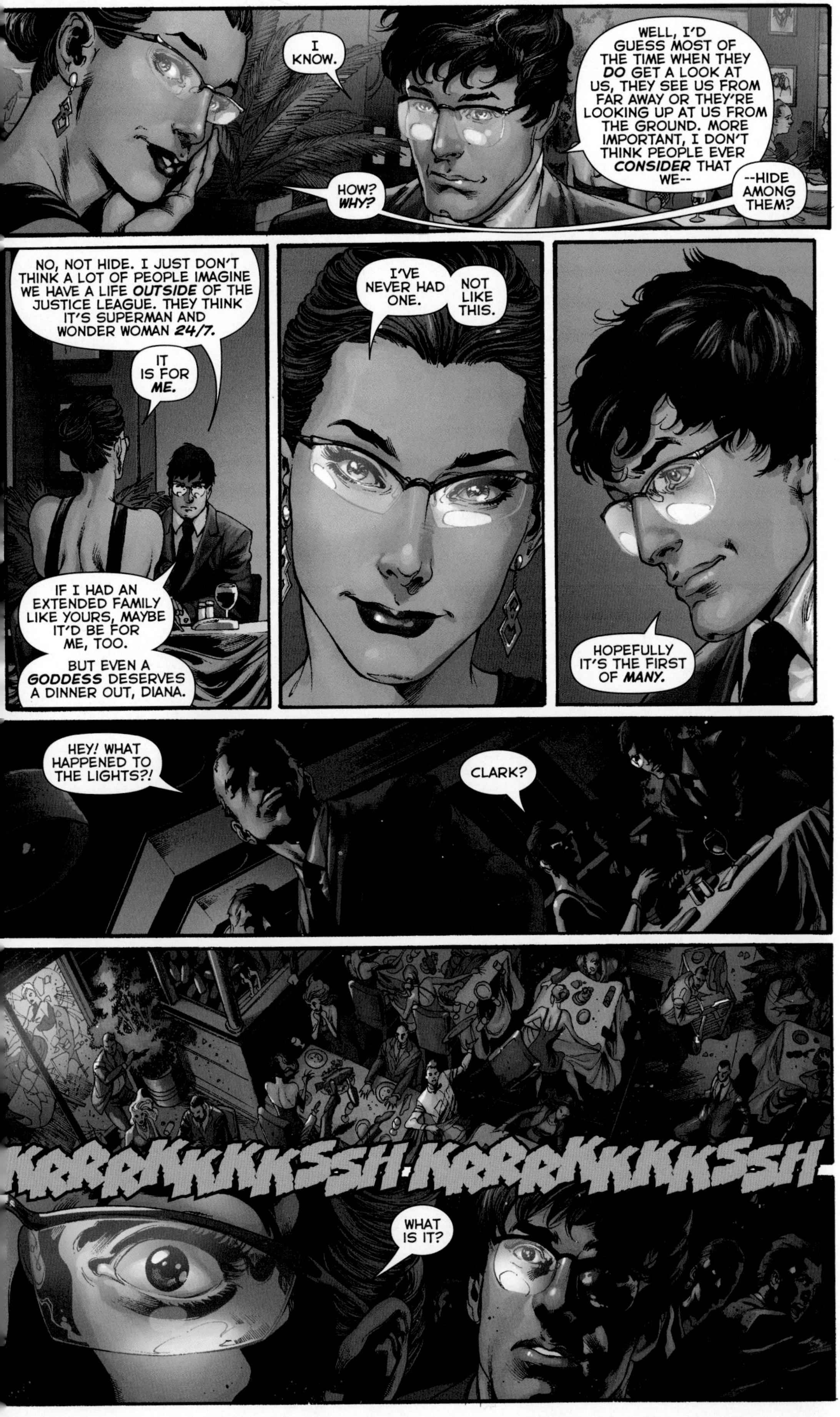
I KNOW.
WELL, I'D GUESS MOST OF THE TIME WHEN THEY DO GET A LOOK AT US, THEY SEE US FROM FAR AWAY OR THEY'RE LOOKING UP AT US FROM THE GROUND. MORE IMPORTANT, I DON'T THINK PEOPLE EVER CONSIDER THAT WE--
HOW? WHY?
--HIDE AMONG THEM?
NO, NOT HIDE. I JUST DON'T THINK A LOT OF PEOPLE IMAGINE WE HAVE A LIFE OUTSIDE OF THE JUSTICE LEAGUE. THEY THINK IT'S SUPERMAN AND WONDER WOMAN 24/7.
IT IS FOR ME.
IF I HAD AN EXTENDED FAMILY LIKE YOURS, MAYBE IT'D BE FOR ME, TOO.
BUT EVEN A GODDESS DESERVES A DINNER OUT, DIANA.
I'VE NEVER HAD ONE.
NOT LIKE THIS.
HOPEFULLY IT'S THE FIRST OF MANY.
HEY! WHAT HAPPENED TO THE LIGHTS?!
CLARK?
KRRRKKKKSSH KRRRKKKKSSH
WHAT IS IT?

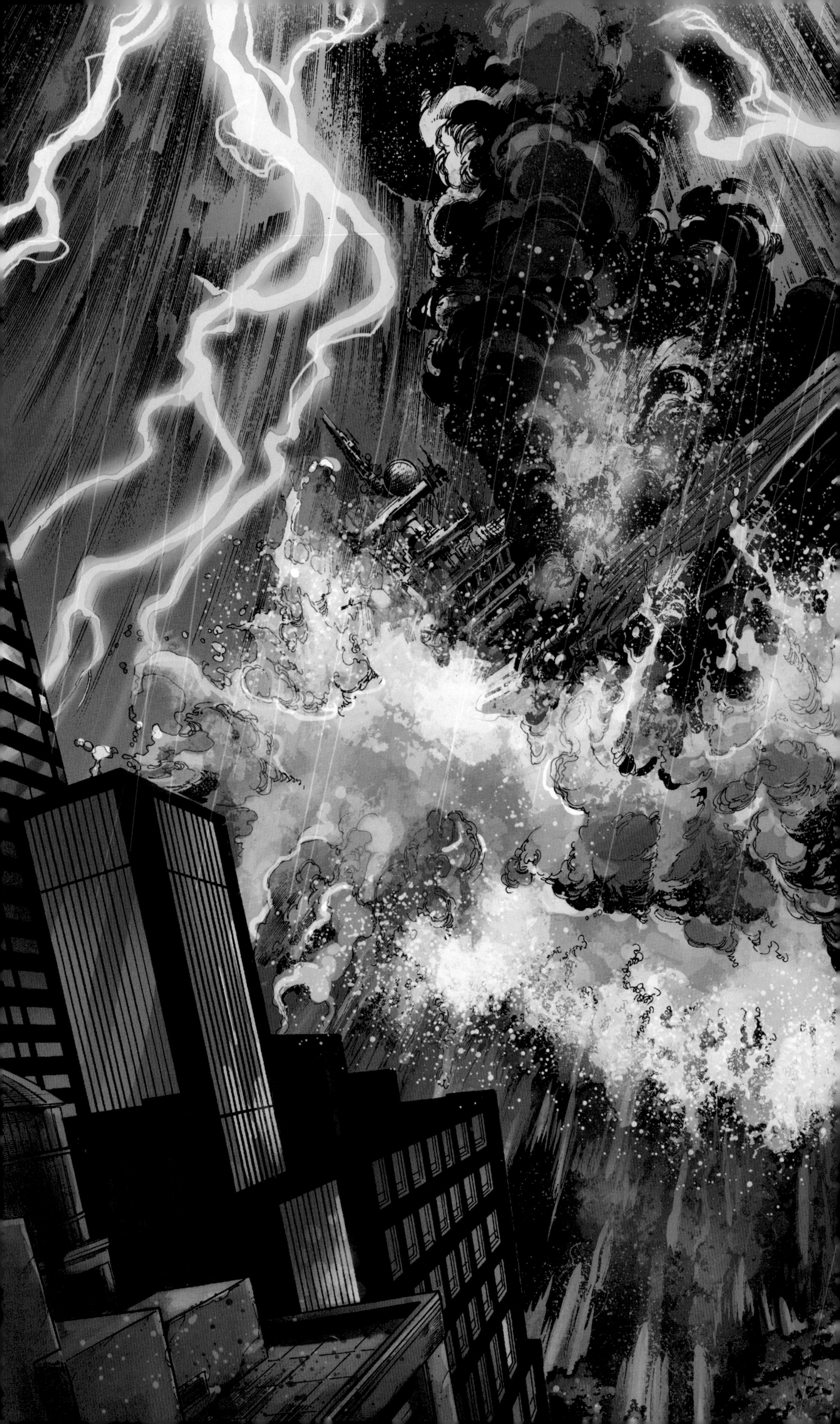

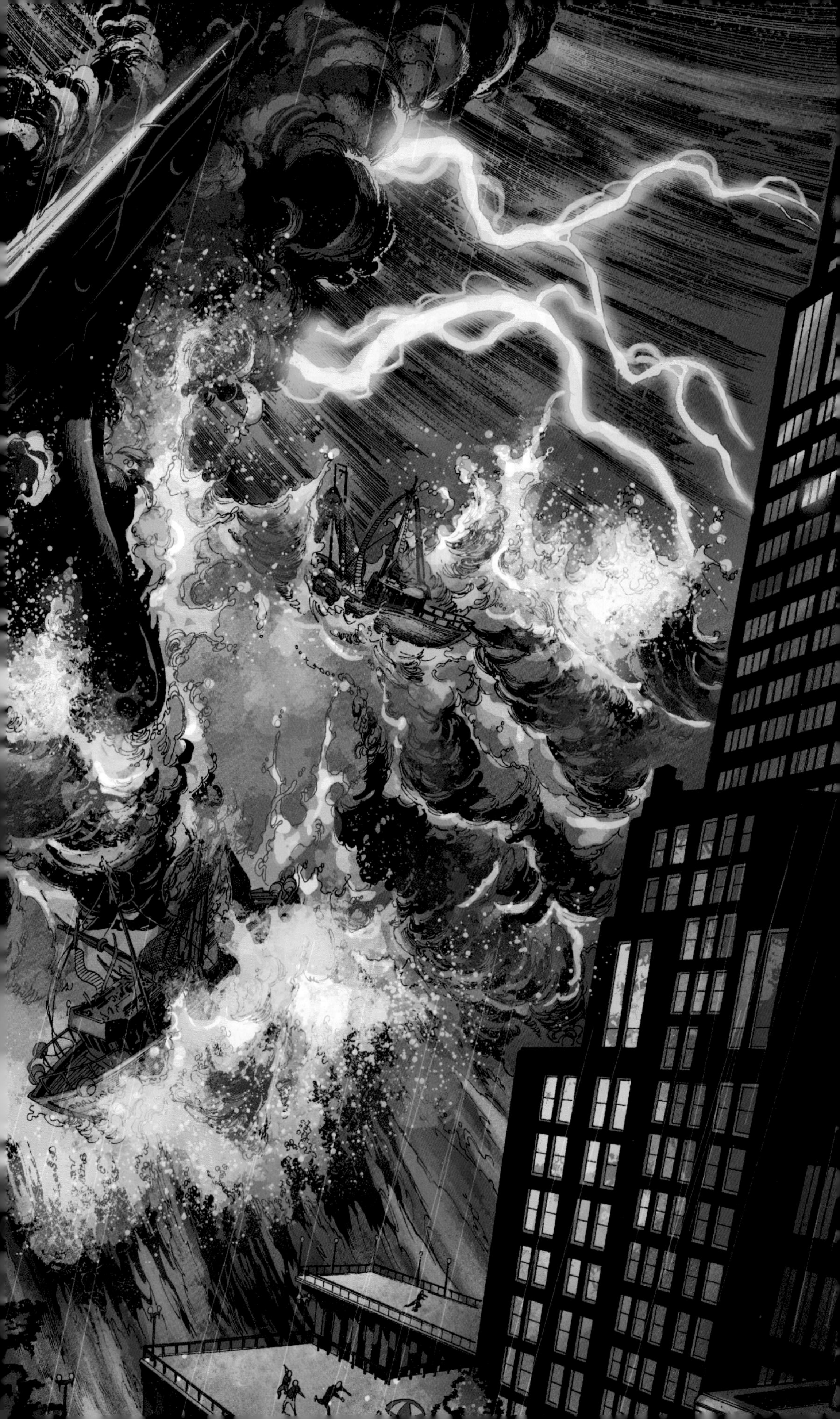

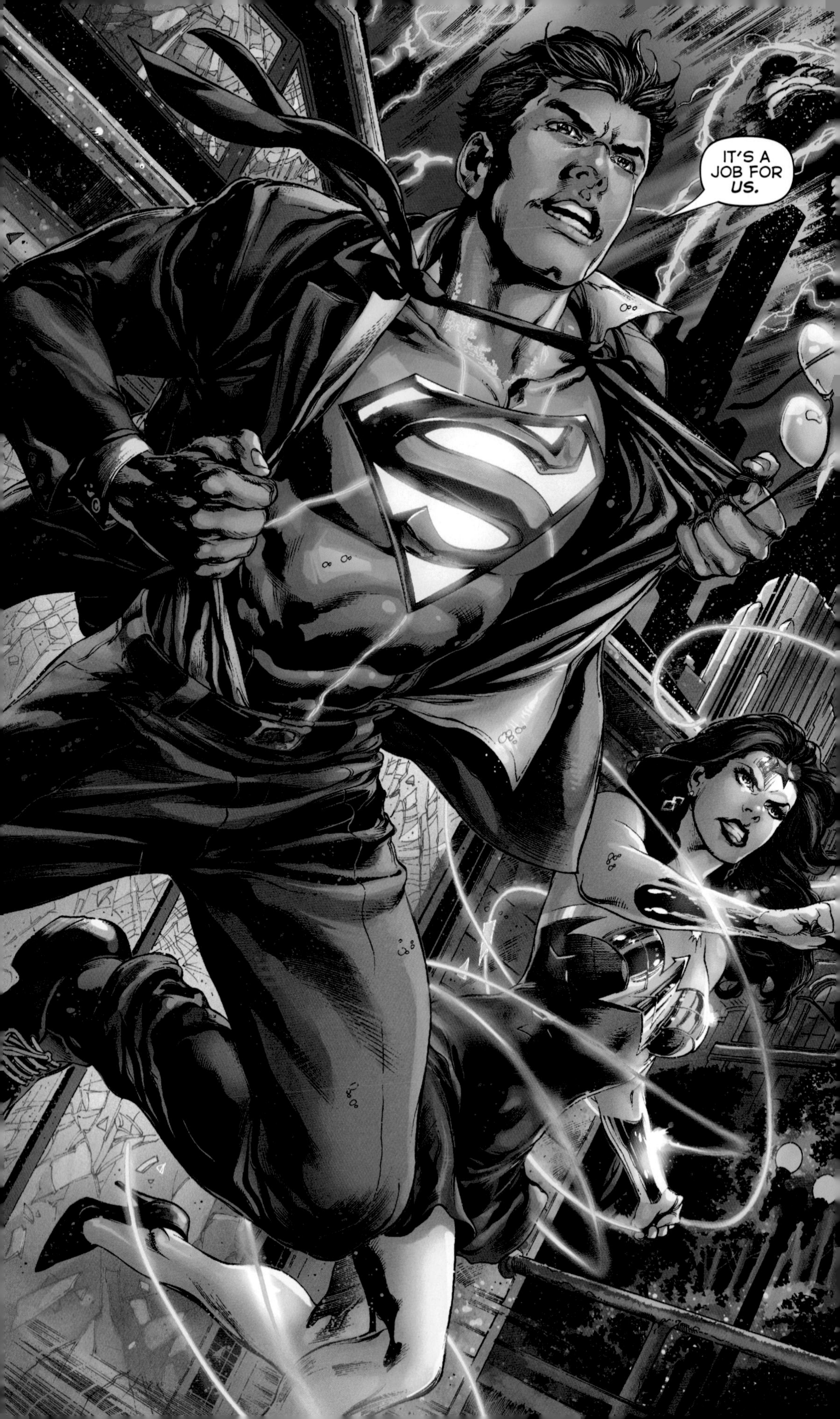
IT'S A JOB FOR US.

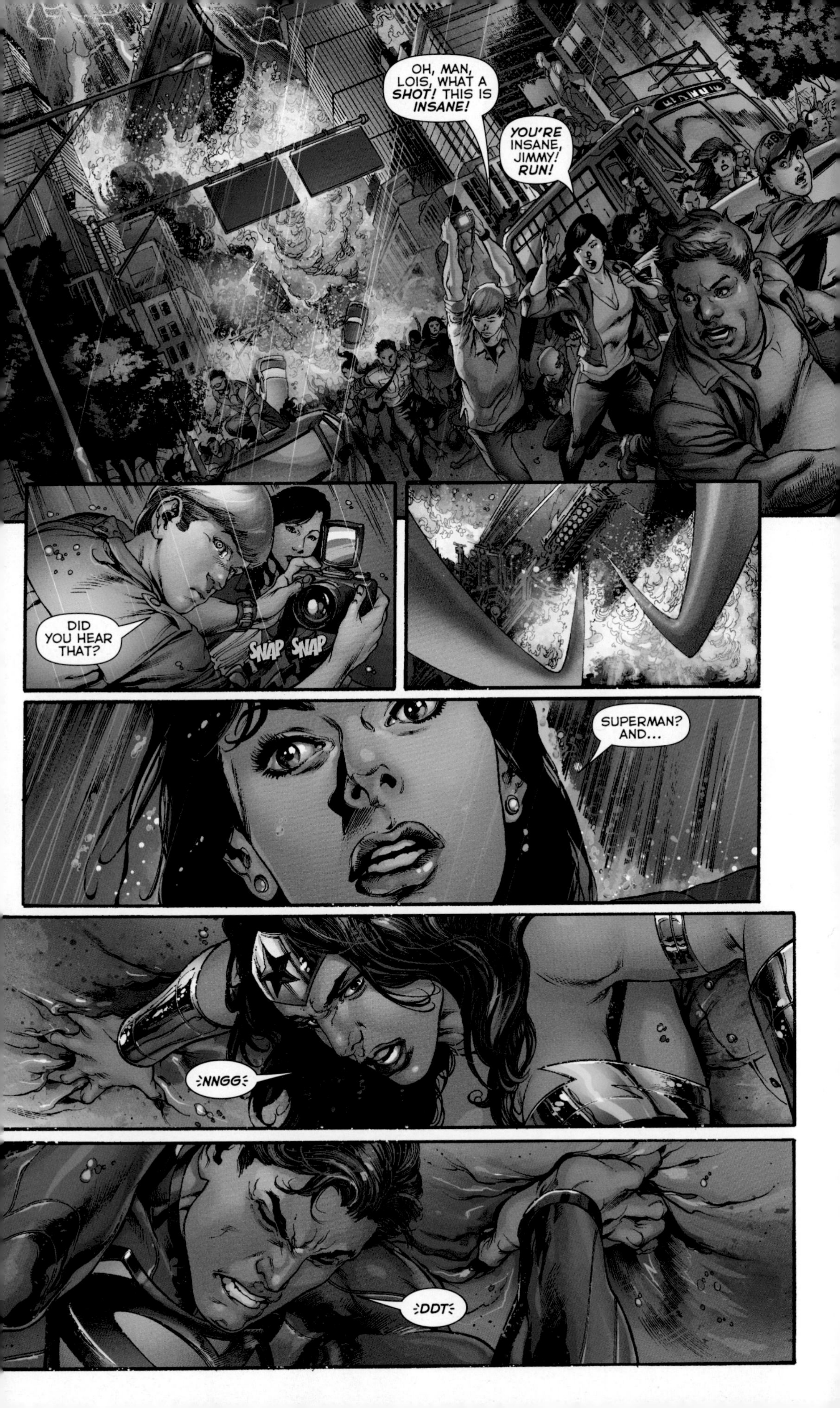

OH, MAN, LOIS, WHAT A SHOT! THIS IS INSANE!
YOU'RE INSANE, JIMMY! RUN!
DID YOU HEAR THAT?
SNAP SNAP
SUPERMAN? AND...
NNGG
DDT

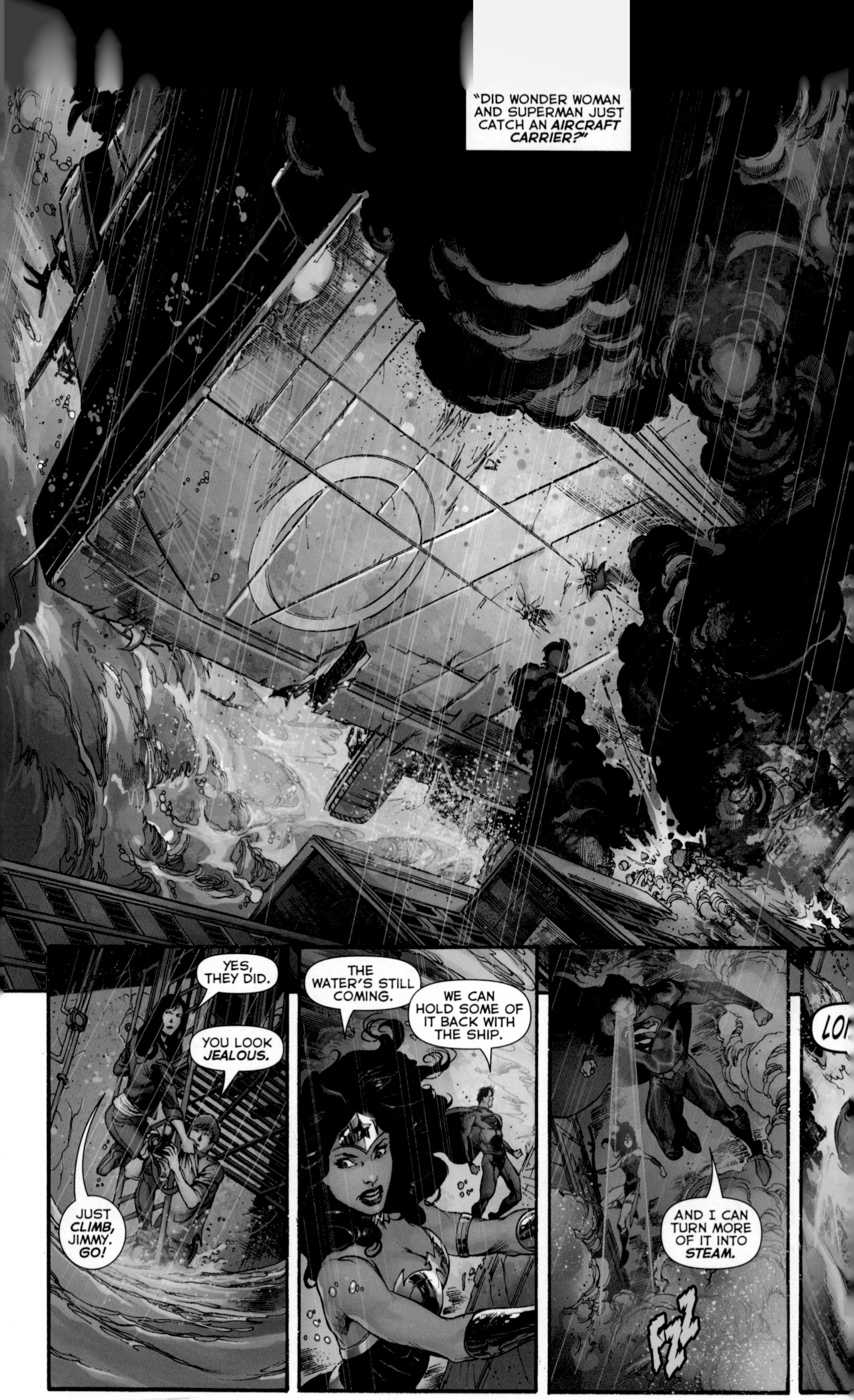
"DID WONDER WOMAN AND SUPERMAN JUST CATCH AN AIRCRAFT CARRIER?"
YES, THEY DID.
YOU LOOK JEALOUS.
JUST CLIMB, JIMMY. GO!
THE WATER'S STILL COMING.
WE CAN HOLD SOME OF IT BACK WITH THE SHIP.
AND I CAN TURN MORE OF IT INTO STEAM.
FZZ

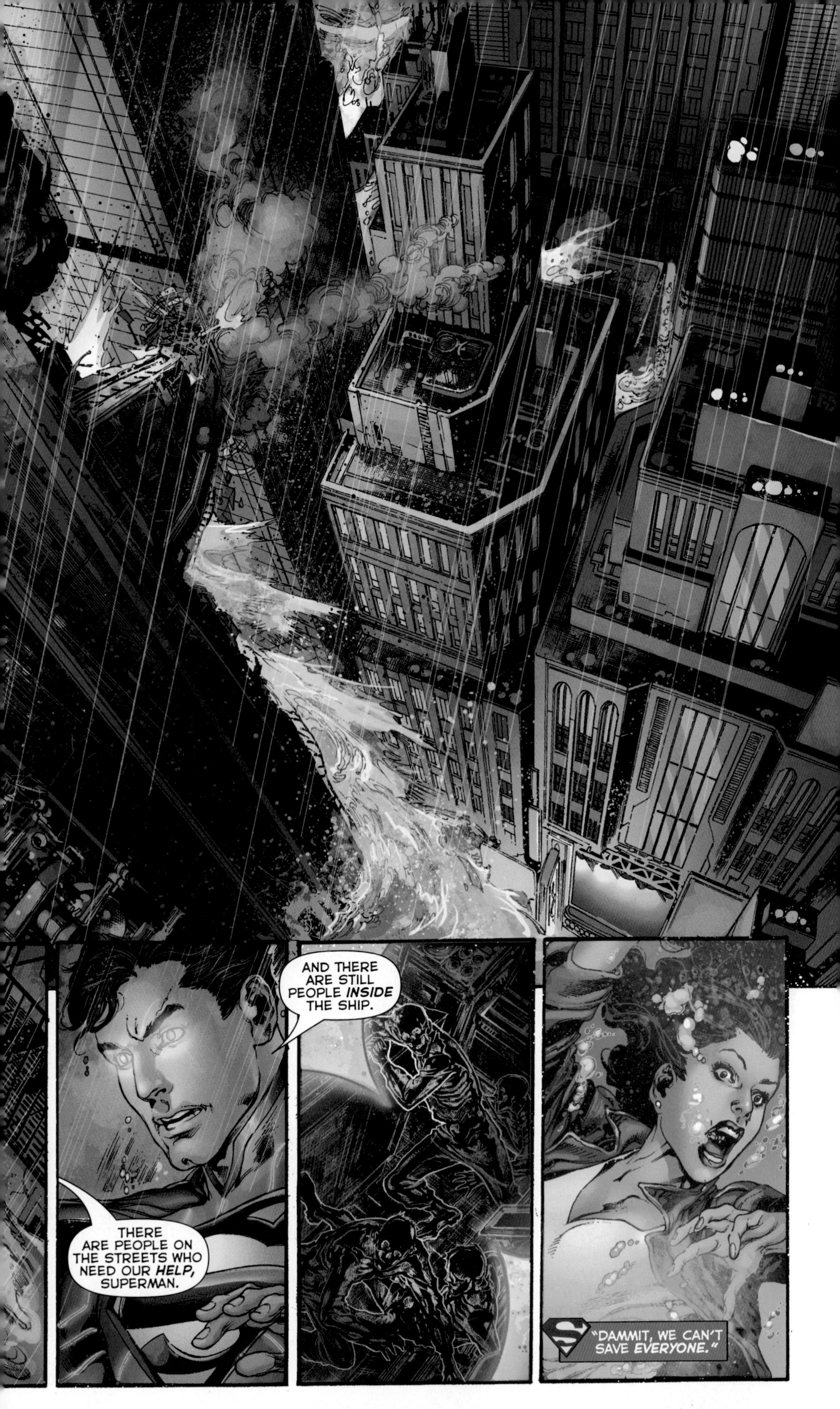
AND THERE ARE STILL PEOPLE INSIDE THE SHIP.
THERE ARE PEOPLE ON THE STREETS WHO NEED OUR HELP, SUPERMAN.
"DAMMIT, WE CAN'T SAVE EVERYONE."

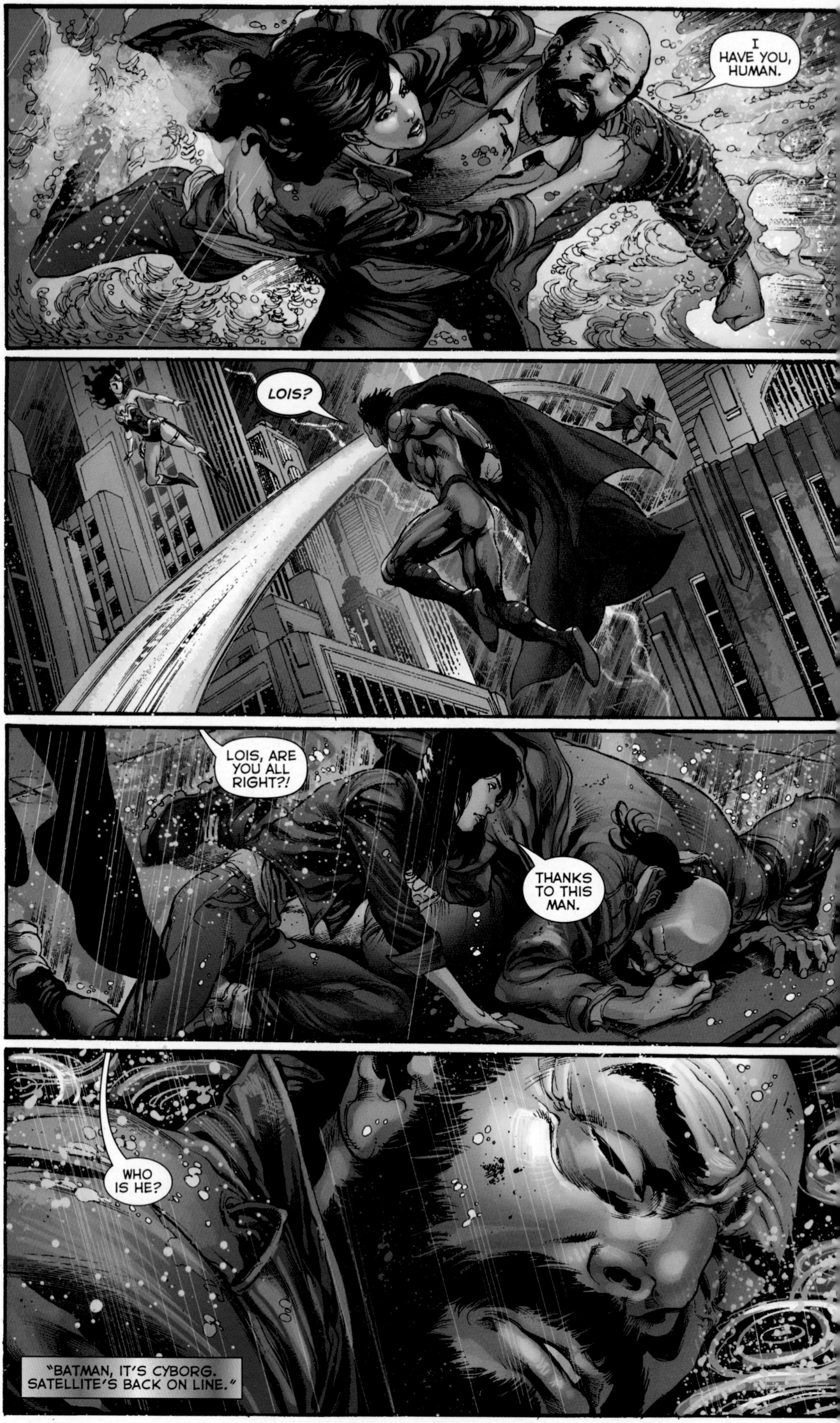
I HAVE YOU, HUMAN.
LOIS?
LOIS, ARE YOU ALL RIGHT?!
THANKS TO THIS MAN.
WHO IS HE?
"BATMAN, IT'S CYBORG. SATELLITE'S BACK ON LINE."

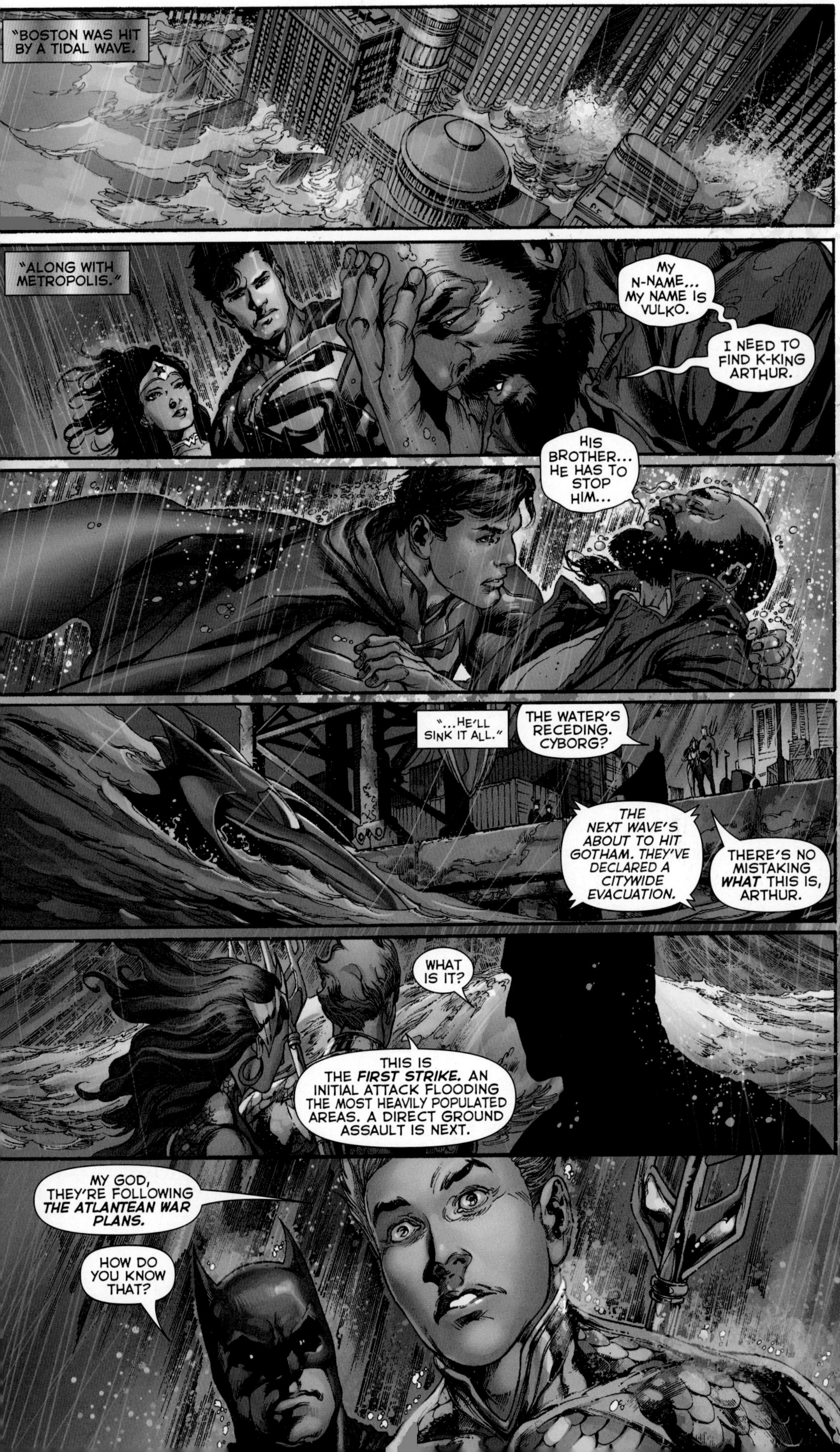
"BOSTON WAS HIT BY A TIDAL WAVE.
"ALONG WITH METROPOLIS."
MY N-NAME... MY NAME IS VULKO.
I NEED TO FIND K-KING ARTHUR.
HIS BROTHER... HE HAS TO STOP HIM...
"...HE'LL SINK IT ALL."
THE WATER'S RECEDING. CYBORG?
THE NEXT WAVE'S ABOUT TO HIT GOTHAM. THEY'VE DECLARED A CITYWIDE EVACUATION.
THERE'S NO MISTAKING WHAT THIS IS, ARTHUR.
WHAT IS IT?
THIS IS THE FIRST STRIKE. AN INITIAL ATTACK FLOODING THE MOST HEAVILY POPULATED AREAS. A DIRECT GROUND ASSAULT IS NEXT.
MY GOD, THEY'RE FOLLOWING THE ATLANTEAN WAR PLANS.
HOW DO YOU KNOW THAT?

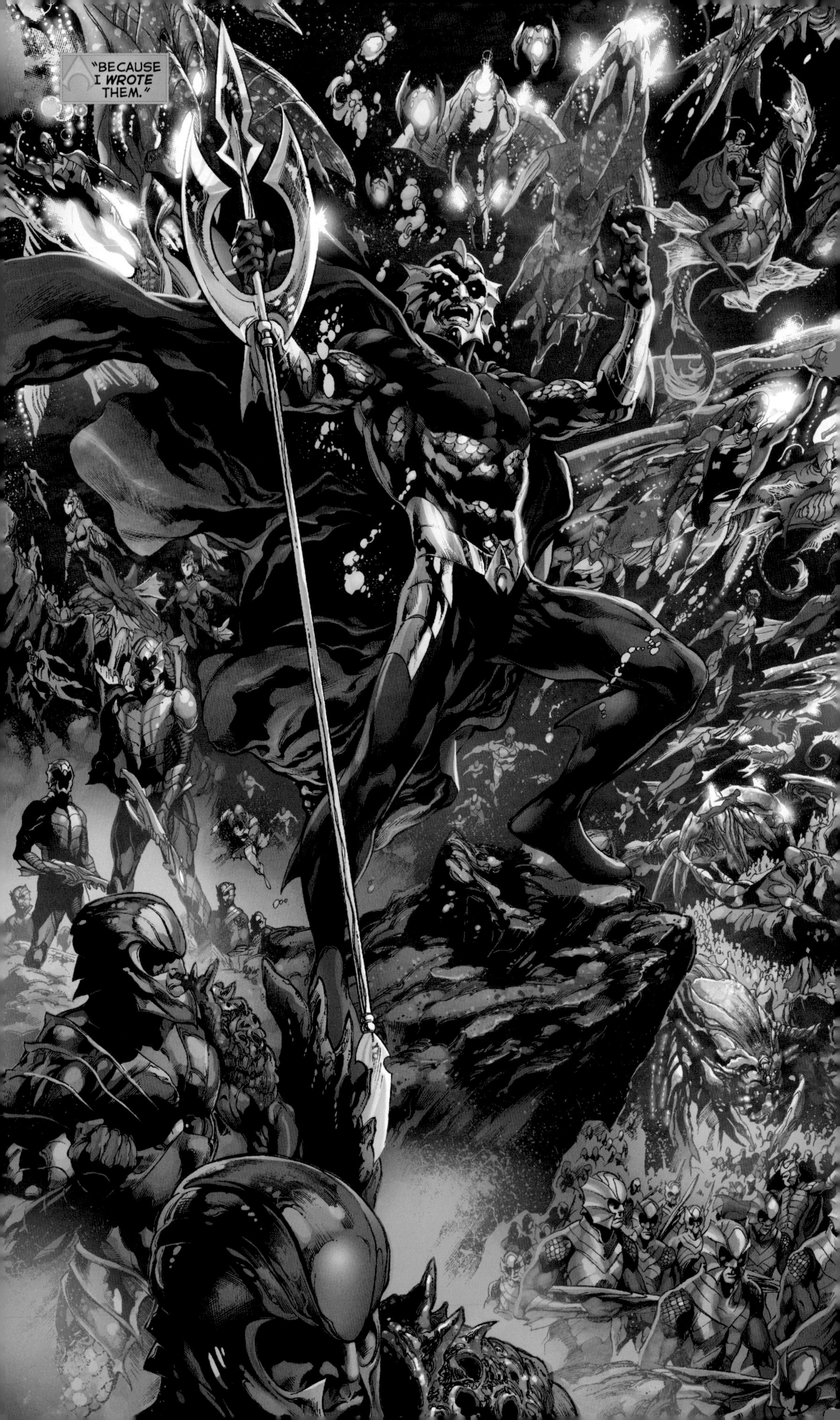
"BECAUSE I WROTE THEM."

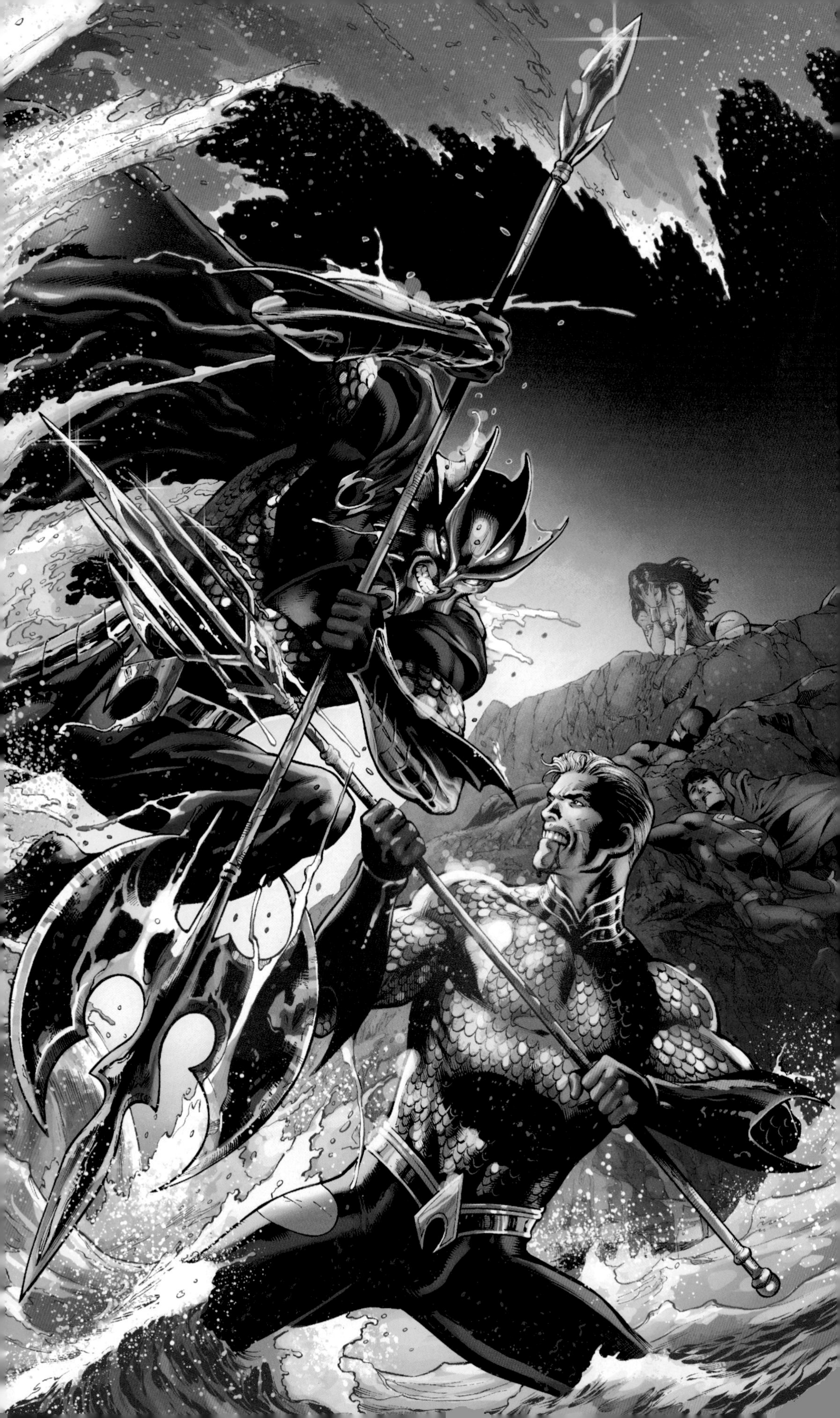

GEOFF JOHNS writer PAUL PELLETIER penciller ART THIBERT with KARL KESEL inkers cover by EDDY BARROWS, EBER FERREIRA & ROD REIS

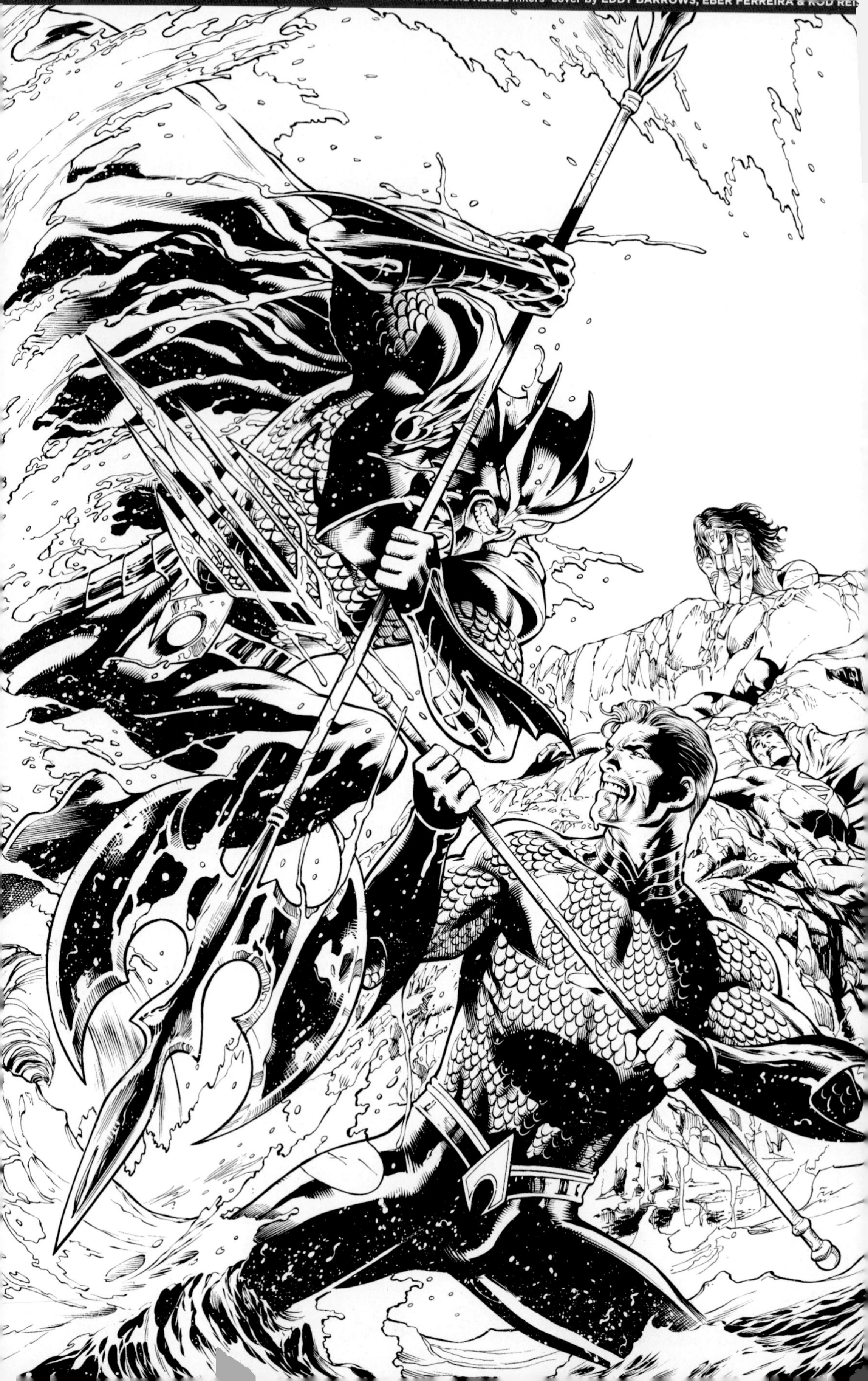

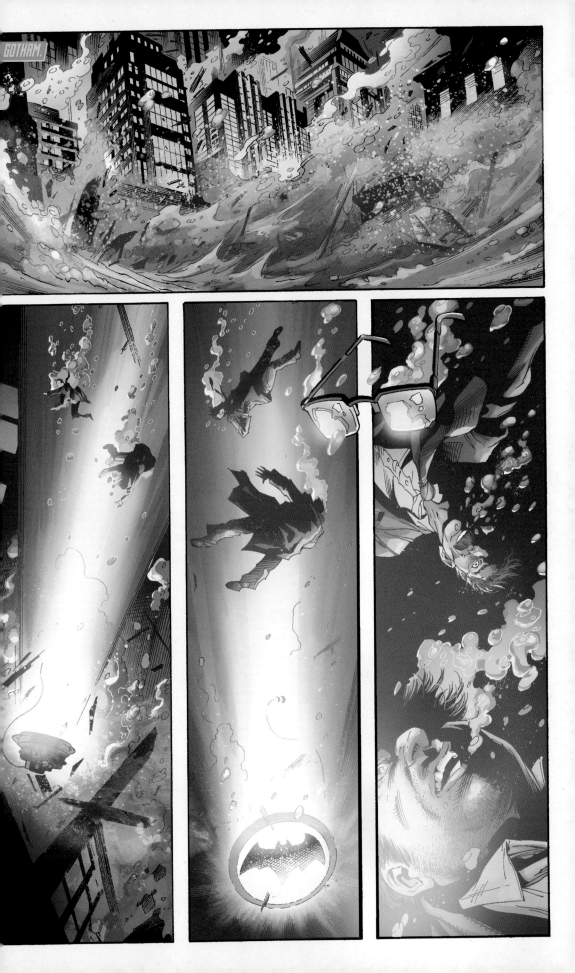

GOTHAM.

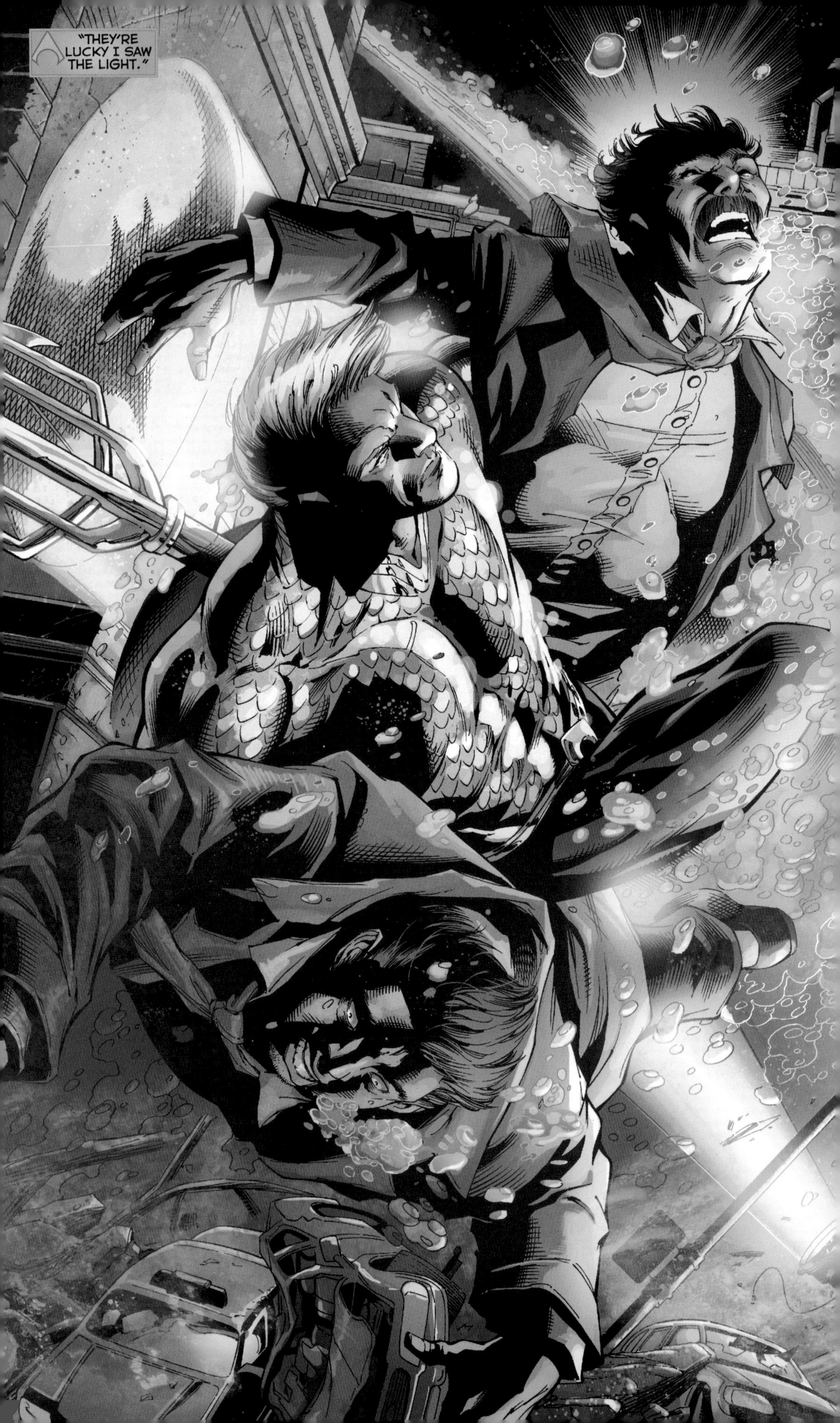
"THEY'RE LUCKY I SAW THE LIGHT."

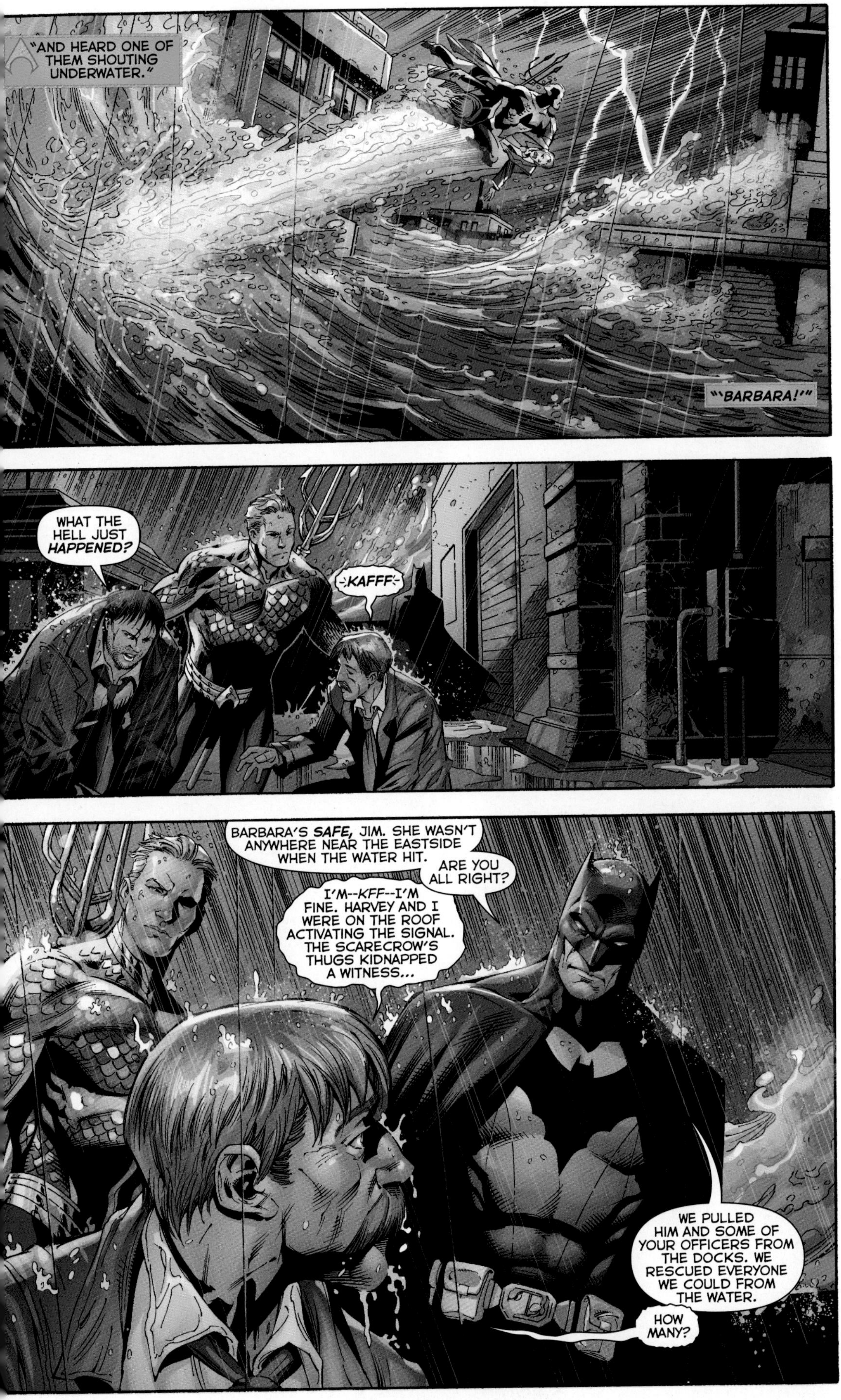
"AND HEARD ONE OF THEM SHOUTING UNDERWATER."
"'BARBARA!'"
WHAT THE HELL JUST HAPPENED?
-KAFFF-
BARBARA'S SAFE, JIM. SHE WASN'T ANYWHERE NEAR THE EASTSIDE WHEN THE WATER HIT.
ARE YOU ALL RIGHT?
I'M--KFF--I'M FINE. HARVEY AND I WERE ON THE ROOF ACTIVATING THE SIGNAL. THE SCARECROW'S THUGS KIDNAPPED A WITNESS...
WE PULLED HIM AND SOME OF YOUR OFFICERS FROM THE DOCKS. WE RESCUED EVERYONE WE COULD FROM THE WATER.
HOW MANY?

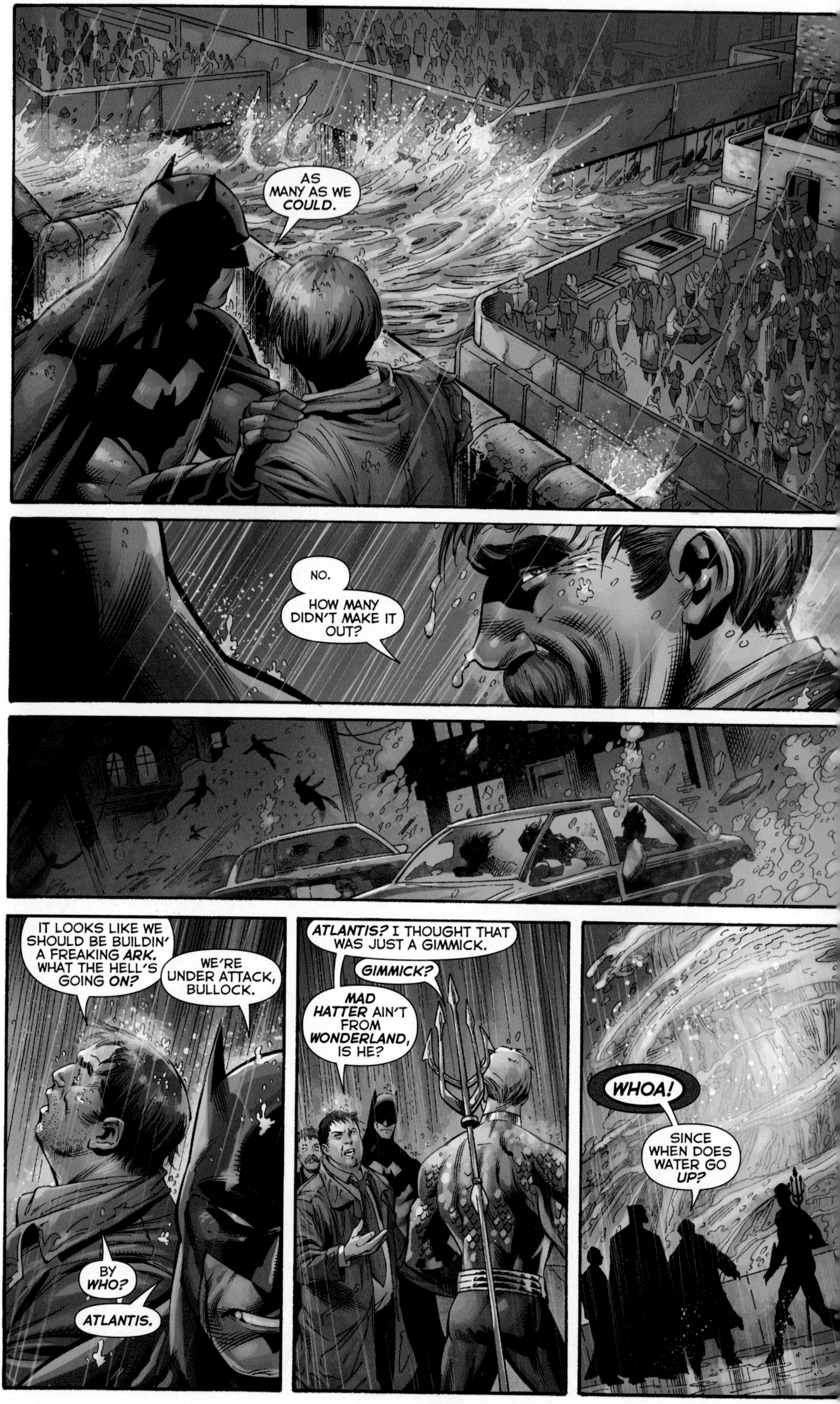
AS MANY AS WE COULD.
NO.
HOW MANY DIDN'T MAKE IT OUT?
IT LOOKS LIKE WE SHOULD BE BUILDIN' A FREAKING ARK. WHAT THE HELL'S GOING ON?
WE'RE UNDER ATTACK, BULLOCK.
BY WHO?
ATLANTIS.
ATLANTIS? I THOUGHT THAT WAS JUST A GIMMICK.
GIMMICK?
MAD HATTER AIN'T FROM WONDERLAND, IS HE?
WHOA!
SINCE WHEN DOES WATER GO UP?

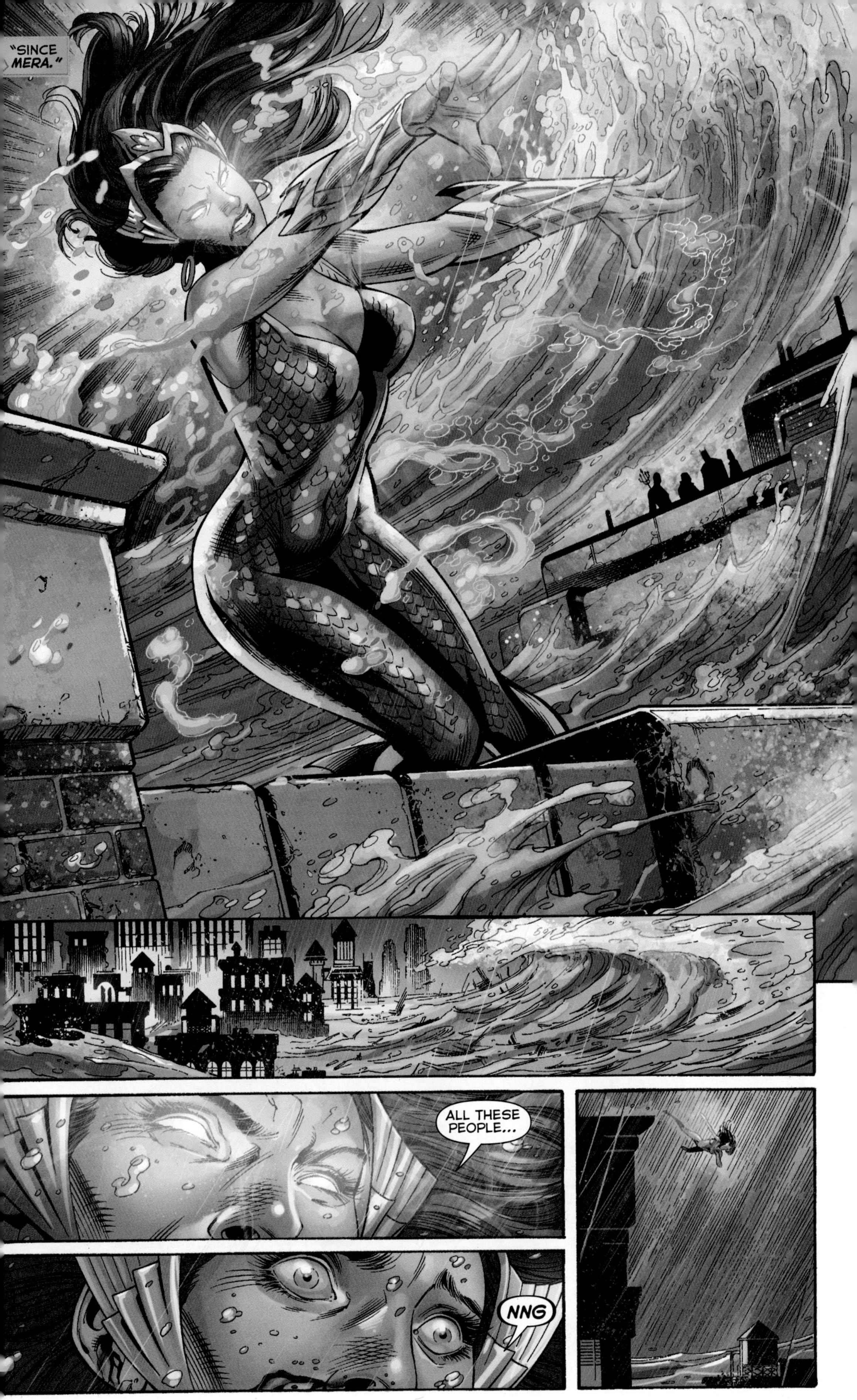
"SINCE MERA."
ALL THESE PEOPLE...
NNG

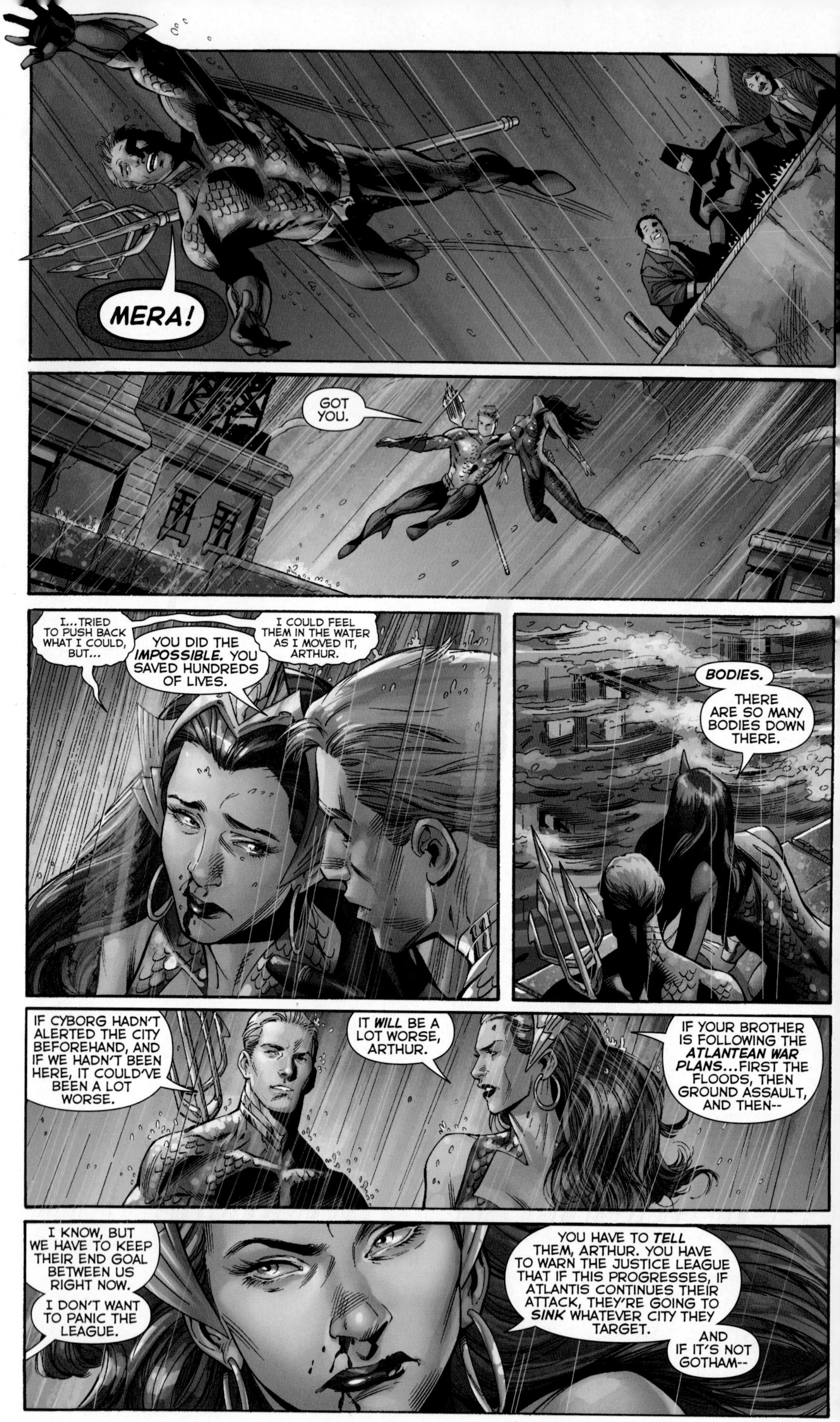
MERA!
GOT YOU.
I...TRIED TO PUSH BACK WHAT I COULD, BUT...
YOU DID THE IMPOSSIBLE. YOU SAVED HUNDREDS OF LIVES.
I COULD FEEL THEM IN THE WATER AS I MOVED IT, ARTHUR.
BODIES.
THERE ARE SO MANY BODIES DOWN THERE.
IF CYBORG HADN'T ALERTED THE CITY BEFOREHAND, AND IF WE HADN'T BEEN HERE, IT COULD'VE BEEN A LOT WORSE.
IT WILL BE A LOT WORSE, ARTHUR.
IF YOUR BROTHER IS FOLLOWING THE ATLANTEAN WAR PLANS...FIRST THE FLOODS, THEN GROUND ASSAULT, AND THEN--
YOU HAVE TO TELL THEM, ARTHUR. YOU HAVE TO WARN THE JUSTICE LEAGUE THAT IF THIS PROGRESSES, IF ATLANTIS CONTINUES THEIR ATTACK, THEY'RE GOING TO SINK WHATEVER CITY THEY TARGET.
AND IF IT'S NOT GOTHAM--
I KNOW, BUT WE HAVE TO KEEP THEIR END GOAL BETWEEN US RIGHT NOW.
I DON'T WANT TO PANIC THE LEAGUE.

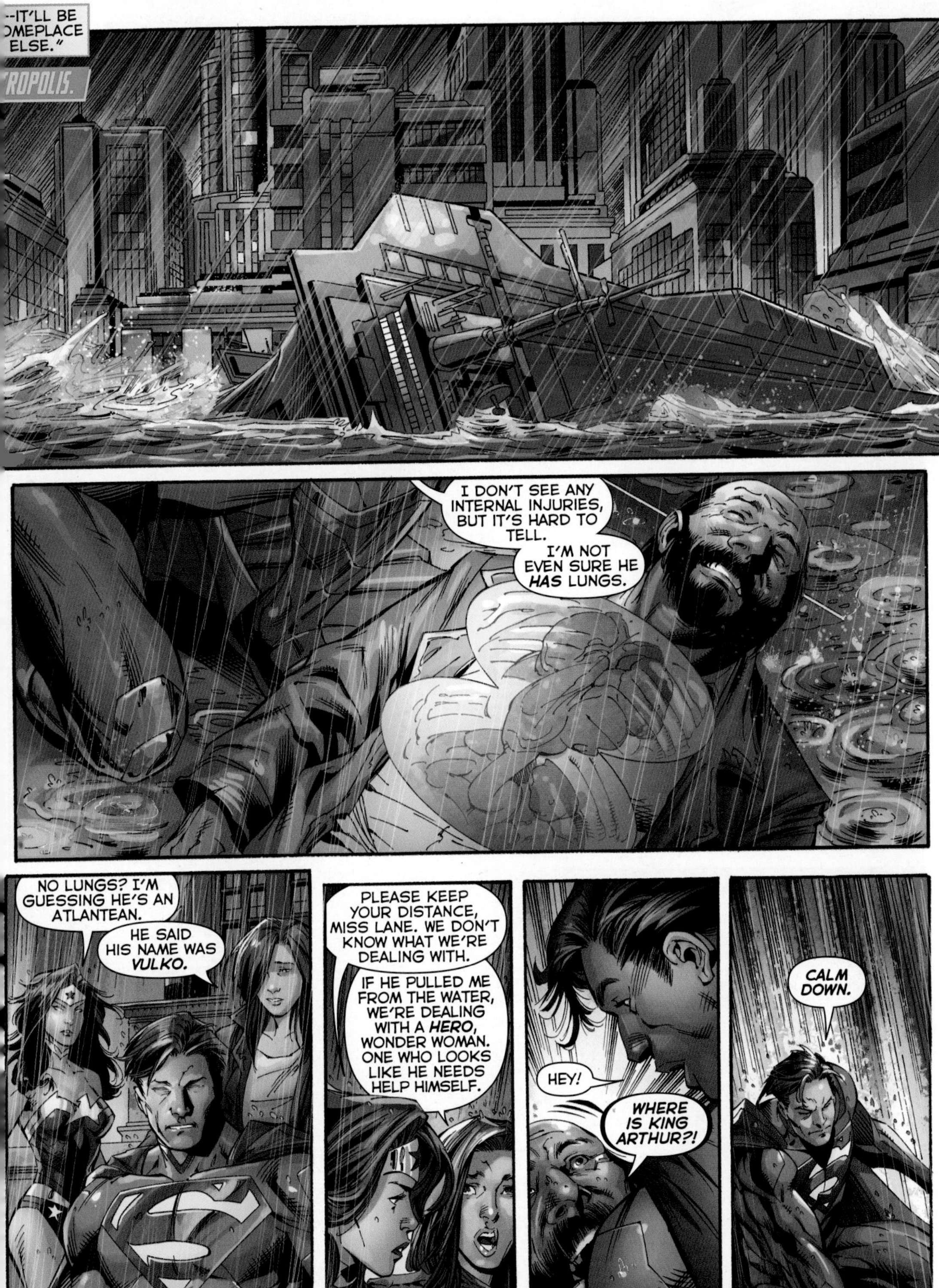

--IT'LL BE OMEPLACE ELSE."
ROPOLIS.
I DON'T SEE ANY INTERNAL INJURIES, BUT IT'S HARD TO TELL.
I'M NOT EVEN SURE HE HAS LUNGS.
NO LUNGS? I'M GUESSING HE'S AN ATLANTEAN.
HE SAID HIS NAME WAS VULKO.
PLEASE KEEP YOUR DISTANCE, MISS LANE. WE DON'T KNOW WHAT WE'RE DEALING WITH.
IF HE PULLED ME FROM THE WATER, WE'RE DEALING WITH A HERO, WONDER WOMAN. ONE WHO LOOKS LIKE HE NEEDS HELP HIMSELF.
HEY!
WHERE IS KING ARTHUR?!
CALM DOWN.

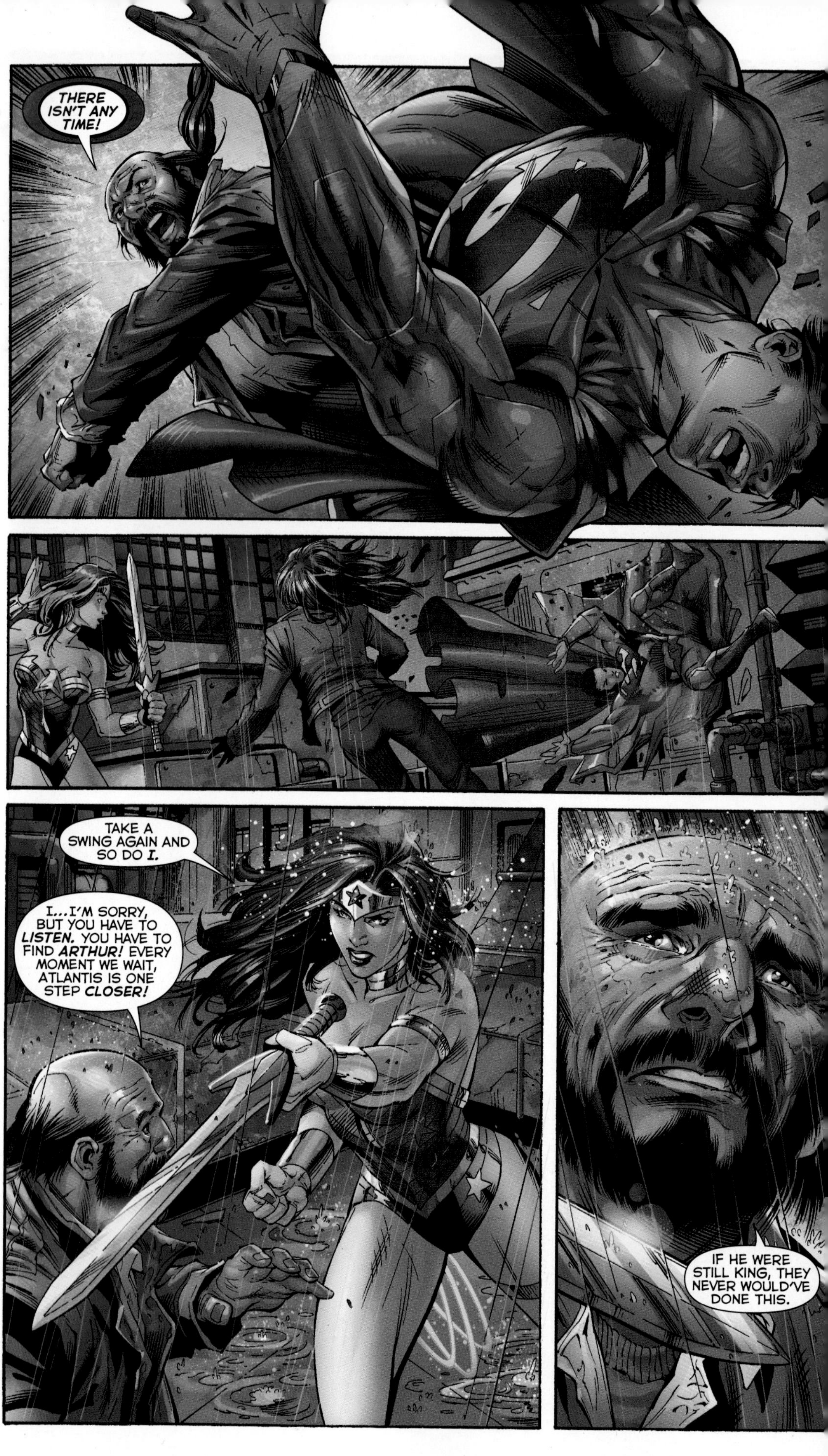
THERE ISN'T ANY TIME!
TAKE A SWING AGAIN AND SO DO I.
I...I'M SORRY, BUT YOU HAVE TO LISTEN. YOU HAVE TO FIND ARTHUR! EVERY MOMENT WE WAIT, ATLANTIS IS ONE STEP CLOSER!
IF HE WERE STILL KING, THEY NEVER WOULD'VE DONE THIS.

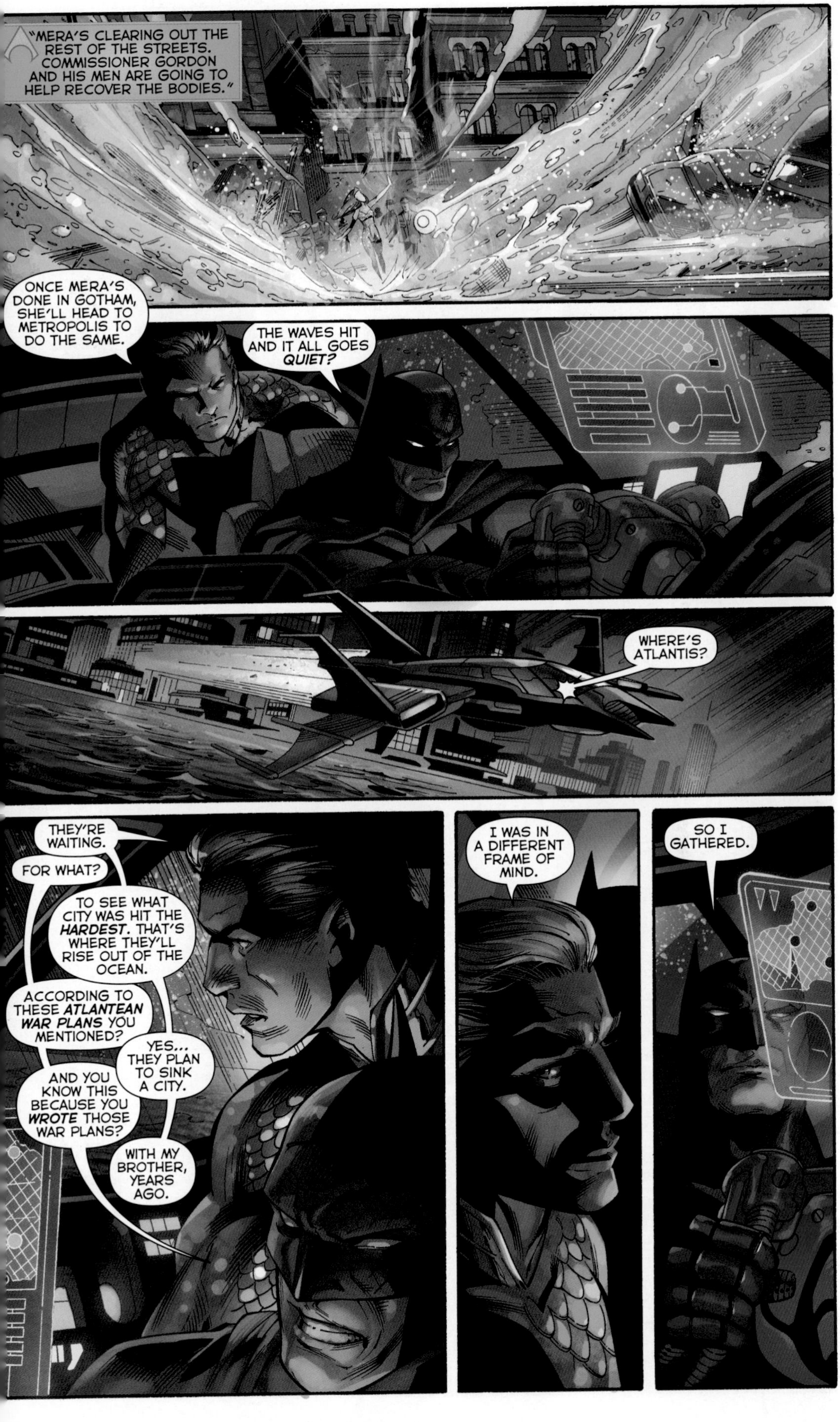
"MERA'S CLEARING OUT THE REST OF THE STREETS. COMMISSIONER GORDON AND HIS MEN ARE GOING TO HELP RECOVER THE BODIES."
ONCE MERA'S DONE IN GOTHAM, SHE'LL HEAD TO METROPOLIS TO DO THE SAME.
THE WAVES HIT AND IT ALL GOES QUIET?
WHERE'S ATLANTIS?
THEY'RE WAITING.
FOR WHAT?
TO SEE WHAT CITY WAS HIT THE HARDEST. THAT'S WHERE THEY'LL RISE OUT OF THE OCEAN.
ACCORDING TO THESE ATLANTEAN WAR PLANS YOU MENTIONED?
YES... THEY PLAN TO SINK A CITY.
AND YOU KNOW THIS BECAUSE YOU WROTE THOSE WAR PLANS?
WITH MY BROTHER, YEARS AGO.
I WAS IN A DIFFERENT FRAME OF MIND.
SO I GATHERED.

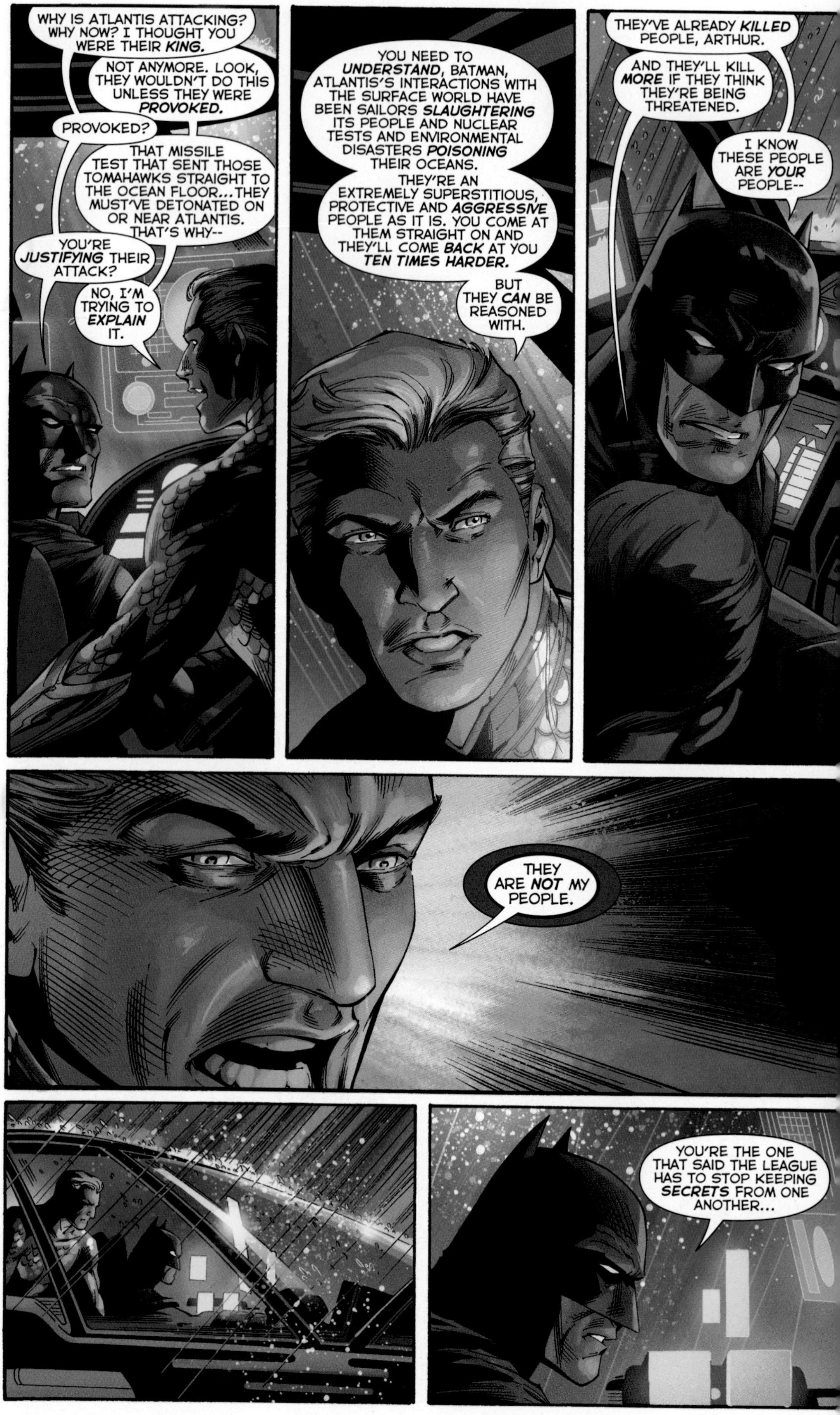

WHY IS ATLANTIS ATTACKING? WHY NOW? I THOUGHT YOU WERE THEIR **KING.**
NOT ANYMORE. LOOK, THEY WOULDN'T DO THIS UNLESS THEY WERE **PROVOKED.**
PROVOKED?
THAT MISSILE TEST THAT SENT THOSE TOMAHAWKS STRAIGHT TO THE OCEAN FLOOR... THEY MUST'VE DETONATED ON OR NEAR ATLANTIS. THAT'S WHY--
YOU'RE **JUSTIFYING** THEIR ATTACK?
NO, I'M TRYING TO **EXPLAIN** IT.
YOU NEED TO **UNDERSTAND**, BATMAN, ATLANTIS'S INTERACTIONS WITH THE SURFACE WORLD HAVE BEEN SAILORS **SLAUGHTERING** ITS PEOPLE AND NUCLEAR TESTS AND ENVIRONMENTAL DISASTERS **POISONING** THEIR OCEANS.
THEY'RE AN EXTREMELY SUPERSTITIOUS, PROTECTIVE AND **AGGRESSIVE** PEOPLE AS IT IS. YOU COME AT THEM STRAIGHT ON AND THEY'LL COME **BACK** AT YOU **TEN TIMES HARDER.**
BUT THEY **CAN** BE REASONED WITH.
THEY'VE ALREADY **KILLED** PEOPLE, ARTHUR.
AND THEY'LL KILL **MORE** IF THEY THINK THEY'RE BEING THREATENED.
I KNOW THESE PEOPLE ARE **YOUR** PEOPLE--
THEY ARE **NOT** MY PEOPLE.
YOU'RE THE ONE THAT SAID THE LEAGUE HAS TO STOP KEEPING **SECRETS** FROM ONE ANOTHER...

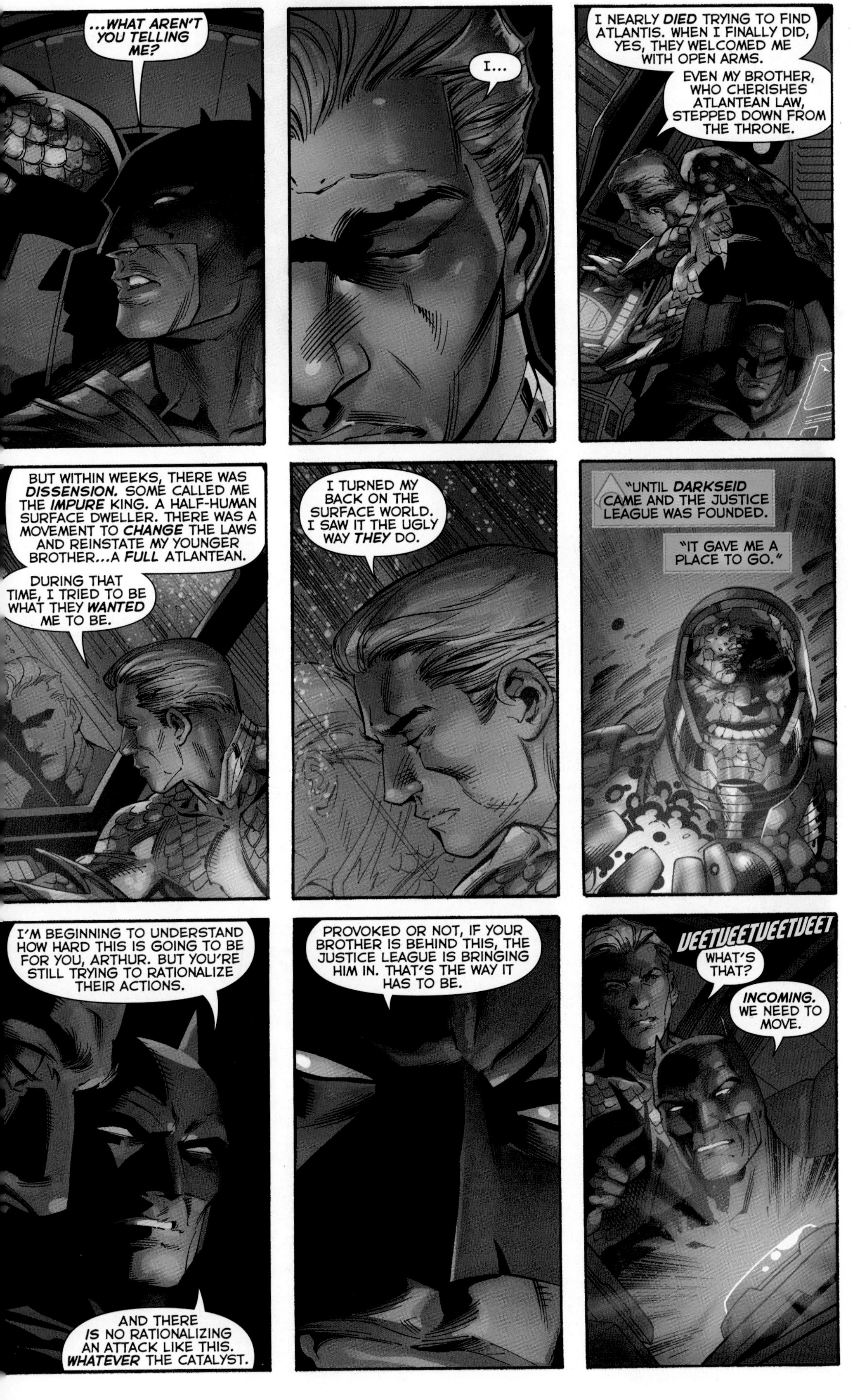
...WHAT AREN'T YOU TELLING ME?
I...
I NEARLY DIED TRYING TO FIND ATLANTIS. WHEN I FINALLY DID, YES, THEY WELCOMED ME WITH OPEN ARMS.
EVEN MY BROTHER, WHO CHERISHES ATLANTEAN LAW, STEPPED DOWN FROM THE THRONE.
BUT WITHIN WEEKS, THERE WAS DISSENSION. SOME CALLED ME THE IMPURE KING. A HALF-HUMAN SURFACE DWELLER. THERE WAS A MOVEMENT TO CHANGE THE LAWS AND REINSTATE MY YOUNGER BROTHER...A FULL ATLANTEAN.
DURING THAT TIME, I TRIED TO BE WHAT THEY WANTED ME TO BE.
I TURNED MY BACK ON THE SURFACE WORLD. I SAW IT THE UGLY WAY THEY DO.
"UNTIL DARKSEID CAME AND THE JUSTICE LEAGUE WAS FOUNDED.
"IT GAVE ME A PLACE TO GO."
I'M BEGINNING TO UNDERSTAND HOW HARD THIS IS GOING TO BE FOR YOU, ARTHUR. BUT YOU'RE STILL TRYING TO RATIONALIZE THEIR ACTIONS.
AND THERE IS NO RATIONALIZING AN ATTACK LIKE THIS. WHATEVER THE CATALYST.
PROVOKED OR NOT, IF YOUR BROTHER IS BEHIND THIS, THE JUSTICE LEAGUE IS BRINGING HIM IN. THAT'S THE WAY IT HAS TO BE.
VEETVEETVEETVEET
WHAT'S THAT?
INCOMING. WE NEED TO MOVE.

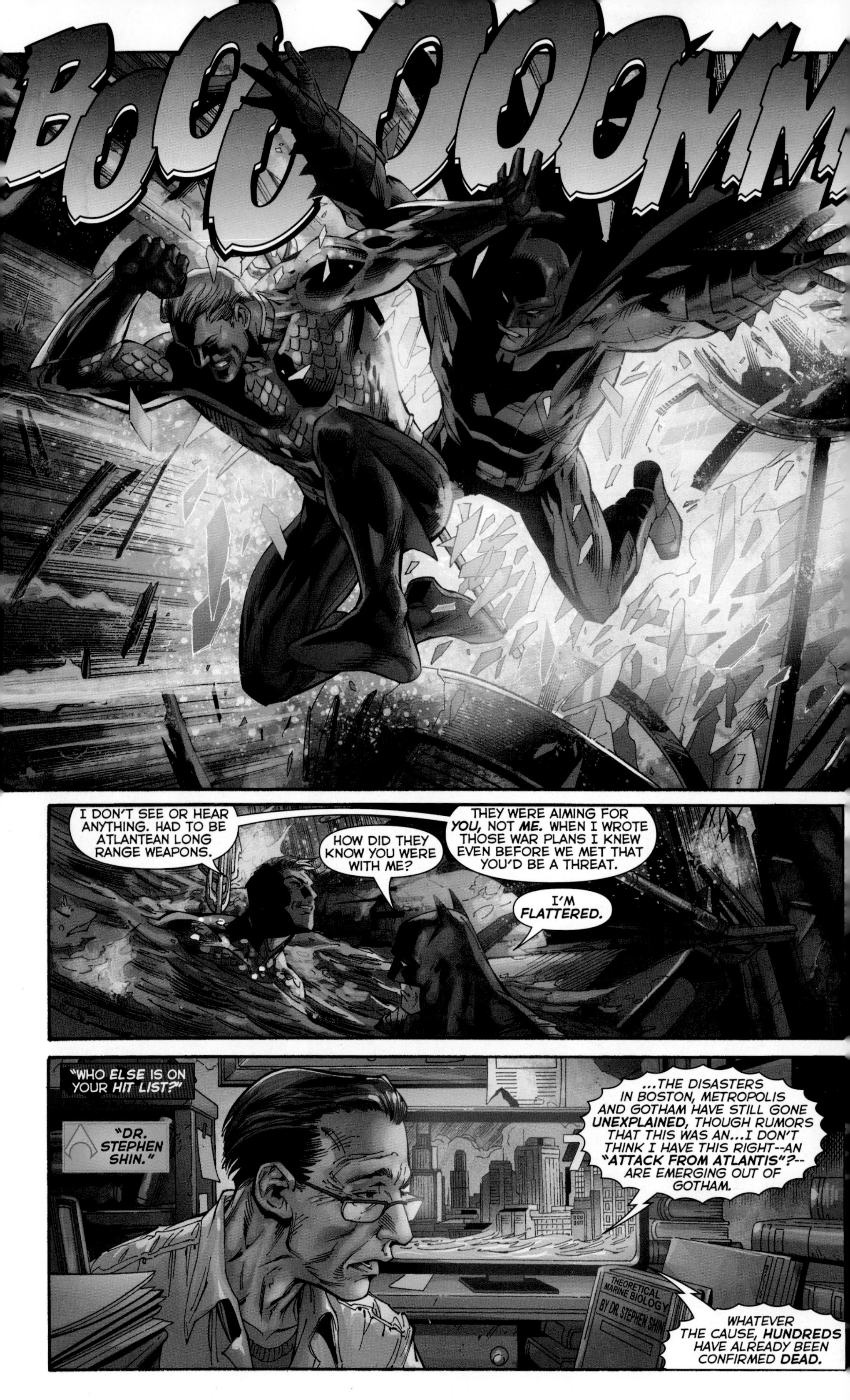
BOOOOOMM
I DON'T SEE OR HEAR ANYTHING. HAD TO BE ATLANTEAN LONG RANGE WEAPONS.
HOW DID THEY KNOW YOU WERE WITH ME?
THEY WERE AIMING FOR *YOU,* NOT *ME.* WHEN I WROTE THOSE WAR PLANS I KNEW EVEN BEFORE WE MET THAT YOU'D BE A THREAT.
I'M *FLATTERED.*
"WHO *ELSE* IS ON YOUR *HIT LIST?*"
"DR. STEPHEN SHIN."
...THE DISASTERS IN BOSTON, METROPOLIS AND GOTHAM HAVE STILL GONE *UNEXPLAINED,* THOUGH RUMORS THAT THIS WAS AN...I DON'T THINK I HAVE THIS RIGHT--AN *"ATTACK FROM ATLANTIS"?*-- ARE EMERGING OUT OF GOTHAM.
THEORETICAL MARINE BIOLOGY BY DR. STEPHEN SHIN
WHATEVER THE CAUSE, *HUNDREDS* HAVE ALREADY BEEN CONFIRMED *DEAD.*

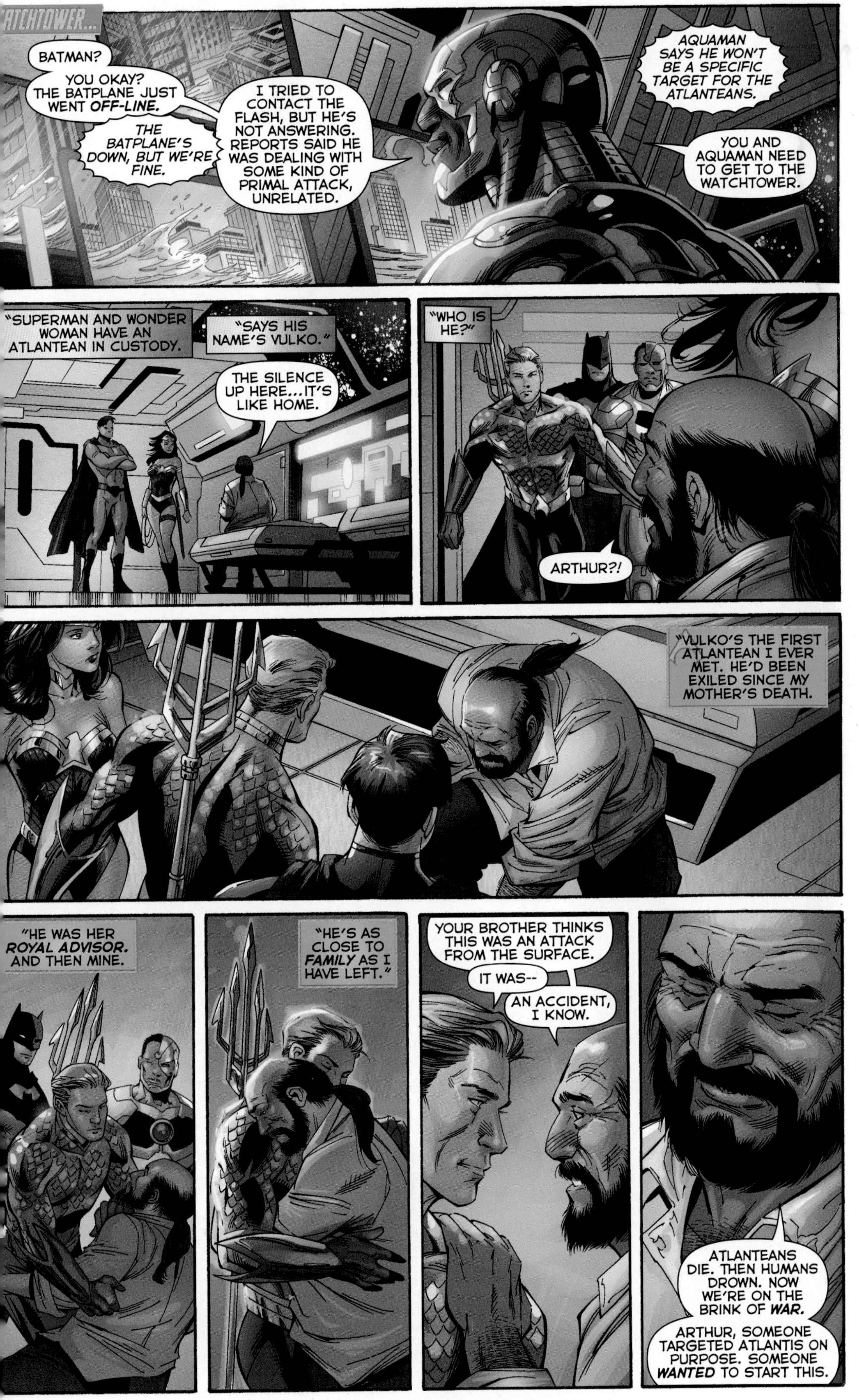
ATCHTOWER...
BATMAN?
YOU OKAY? THE BATPLANE JUST WENT OFF-LINE.
THE BATPLANE'S DOWN, BUT WE'RE FINE.
I TRIED TO CONTACT THE FLASH, BUT HE'S NOT ANSWERING. REPORTS SAID HE WAS DEALING WITH SOME KIND OF PRIMAL ATTACK, UNRELATED.
AQUAMAN SAYS HE WON'T BE A SPECIFIC TARGET FOR THE ATLANTEANS.
YOU AND AQUAMAN NEED TO GET TO THE WATCHTOWER.
"SUPERMAN AND WONDER WOMAN HAVE AN ATLANTEAN IN CUSTODY.
"SAYS HIS NAME'S VULKO."
THE SILENCE UP HERE...IT'S LIKE HOME.
"WHO IS HE?"
ARTHUR?!
"VULKO'S THE FIRST ATLANTEAN I EVER MET. HE'D BEEN EXILED SINCE MY MOTHER'S DEATH.
"HE WAS HER ROYAL ADVISOR. AND THEN MINE.
"HE'S AS CLOSE TO FAMILY AS I HAVE LEFT."
YOUR BROTHER THINKS THIS WAS AN ATTACK FROM THE SURFACE.
IT WAS--
AN ACCIDENT, I KNOW.
ATLANTEANS DIE. THEN HUMANS DROWN. NOW WE'RE ON THE BRINK OF WAR.
ARTHUR, SOMEONE TARGETED ATLANTIS ON PURPOSE. SOMEONE WANTED TO START THIS.

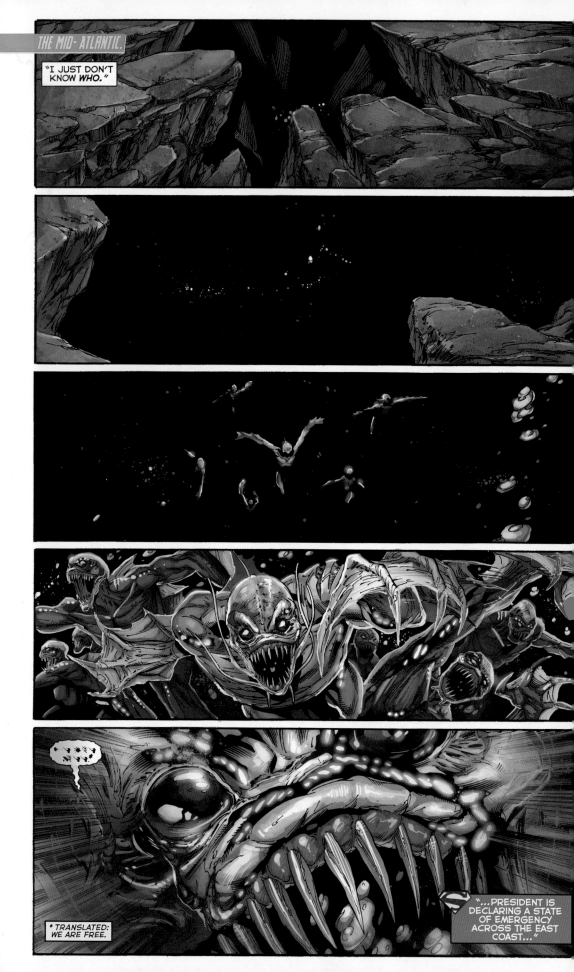

"I JUST DON'T KNOW *WHO*."

****

* TRANSLATED: WE ARE FREE.

"...PRESIDENT IS DECLARING A STATE OF EMERGENCY ACROSS THE EAST COAST..."

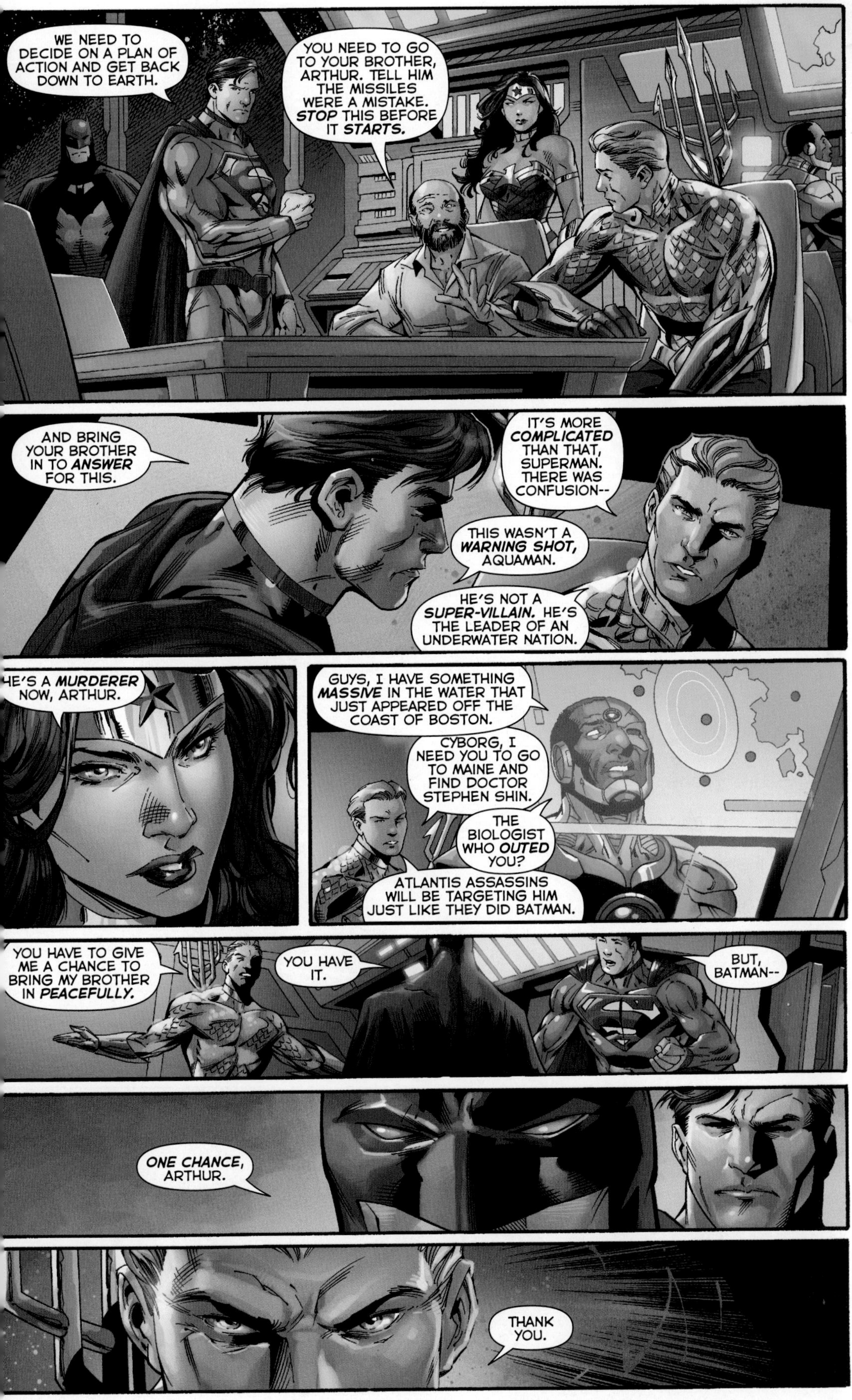
WE NEED TO DECIDE ON A PLAN OF ACTION AND GET BACK DOWN TO EARTH.
YOU NEED TO GO TO YOUR BROTHER, ARTHUR. TELL HIM THE MISSILES WERE A MISTAKE. STOP THIS BEFORE IT STARTS.
AND BRING YOUR BROTHER IN TO ANSWER FOR THIS.
IT'S MORE COMPLICATED THAN THAT, SUPERMAN. THERE WAS CONFUSION--
THIS WASN'T A WARNING SHOT, AQUAMAN.
HE'S NOT A SUPER-VILLAIN. HE'S THE LEADER OF AN UNDERWATER NATION.
HE'S A MURDERER NOW, ARTHUR.
GUYS, I HAVE SOMETHING MASSIVE IN THE WATER THAT JUST APPEARED OFF THE COAST OF BOSTON.
CYBORG, I NEED YOU TO GO TO MAINE AND FIND DOCTOR STEPHEN SHIN.
THE BIOLOGIST WHO OUTED YOU?
ATLANTIS ASSASSINS WILL BE TARGETING HIM JUST LIKE THEY DID BATMAN.
YOU HAVE TO GIVE ME A CHANCE TO BRING MY BROTHER IN PEACEFULLY.
YOU HAVE IT.
BUT, BATMAN--
ONE CHANCE, ARTHUR.
THANK YOU.

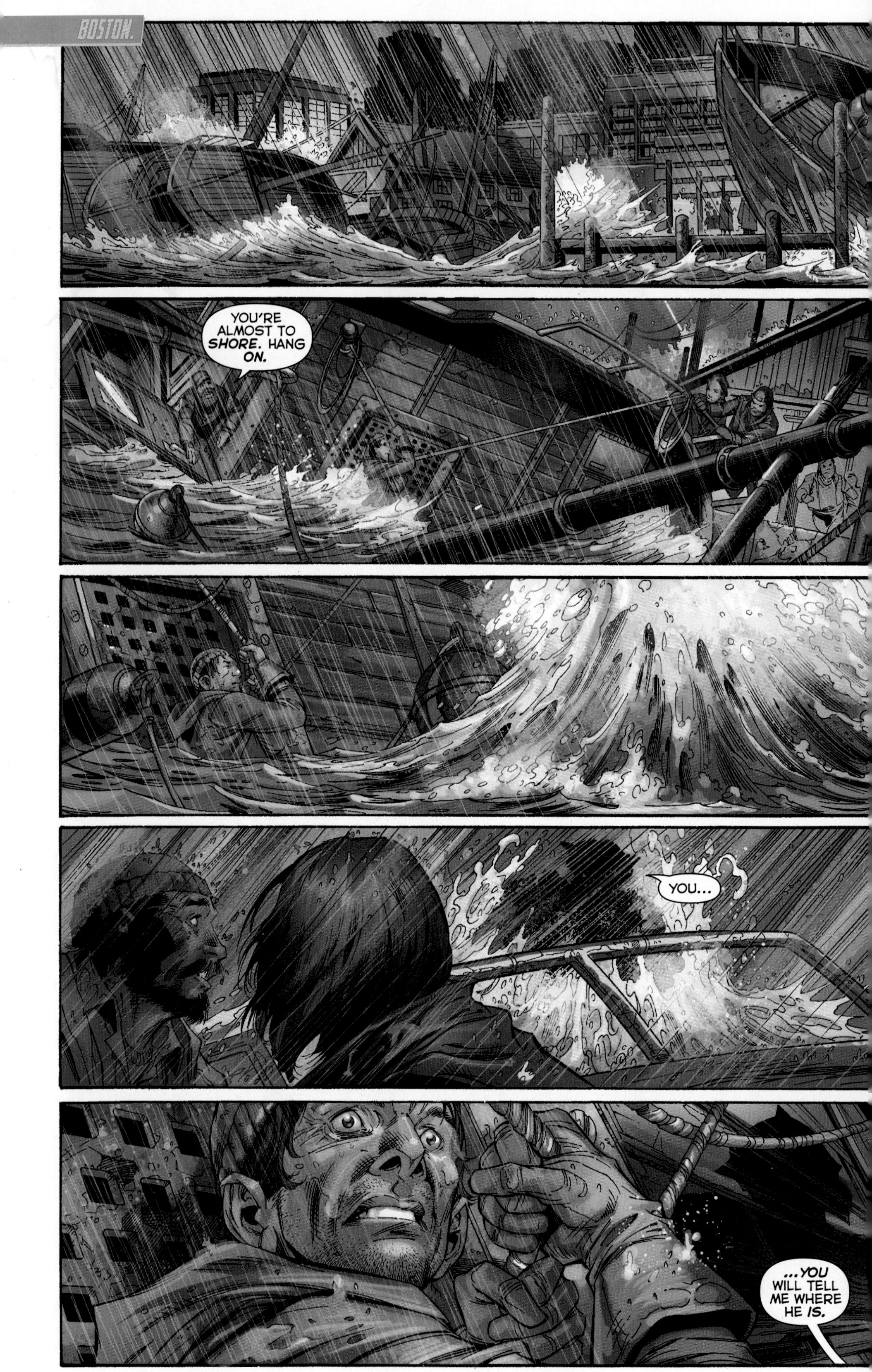
BOSTON.
YOU'RE ALMOST TO SHORE. HANG ON.
YOU...
...YOU WILL TELL ME WHERE HE IS.

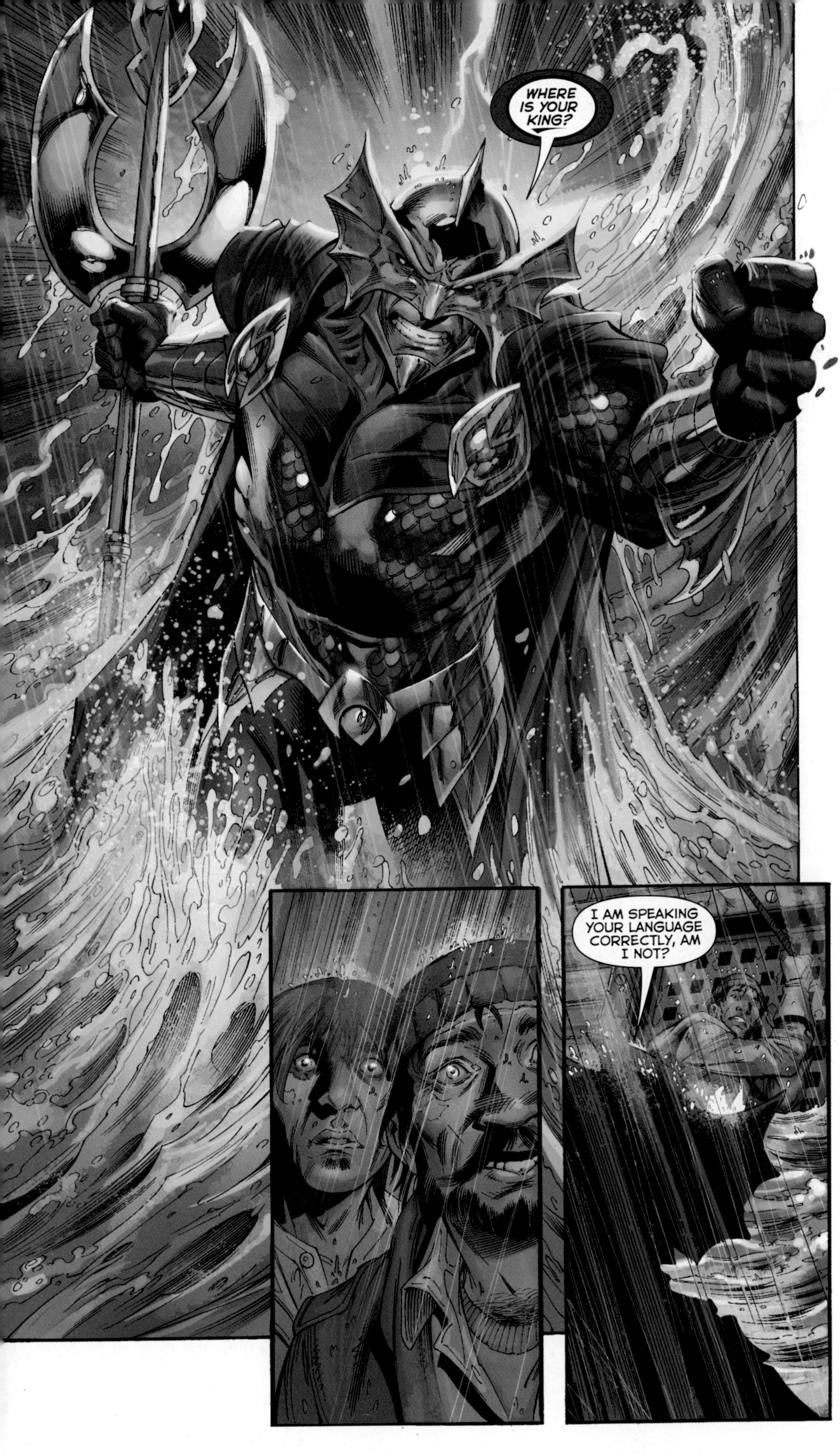
WHERE IS YOUR KING?
I AM SPEAKING YOUR LANGUAGE CORRECTLY, AM I NOT?

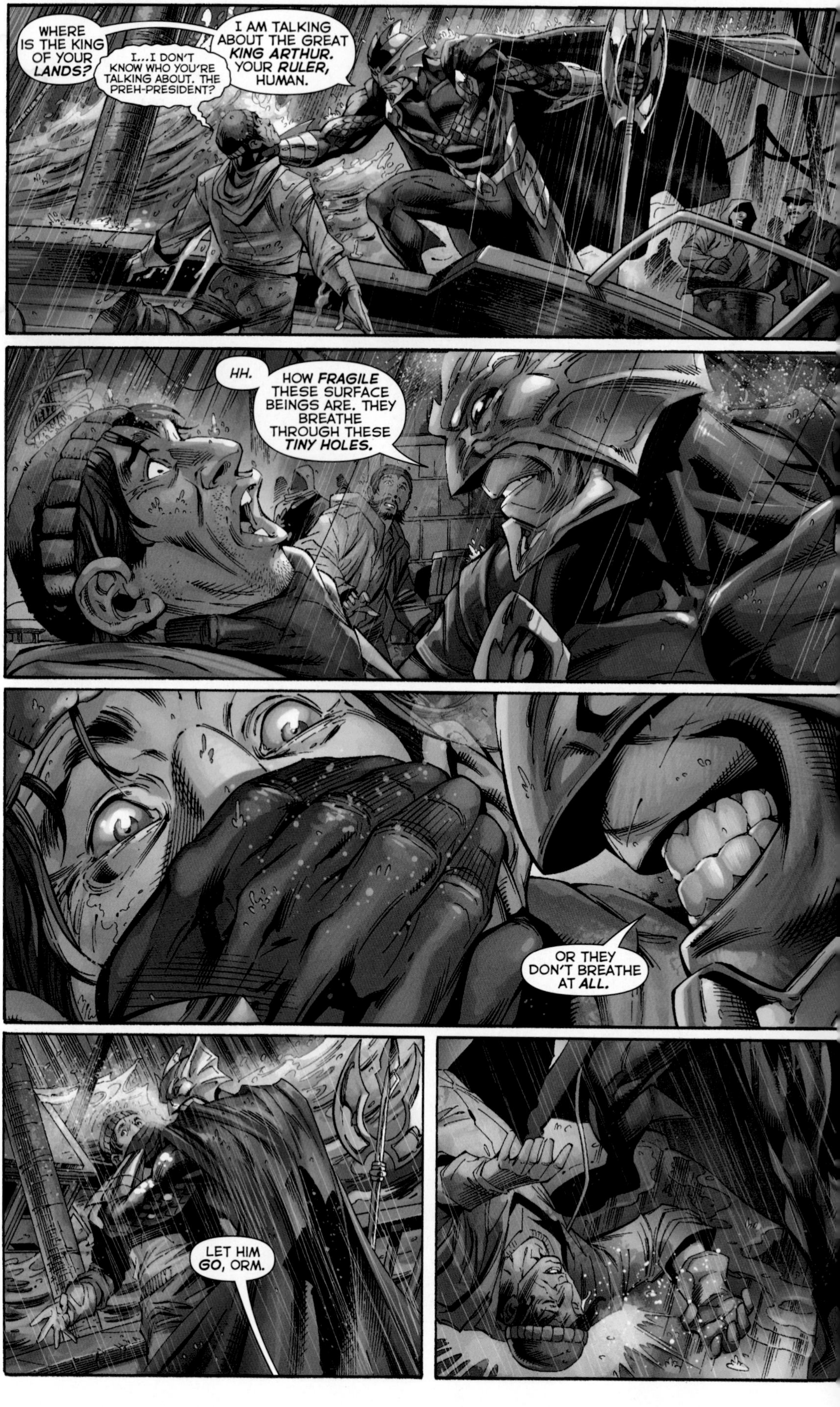
WHERE IS THE KING OF YOUR LANDS?
I...I DON'T KNOW WHO YOU'RE TALKING ABOUT. THE PREH-PRESIDENT?
I AM TALKING ABOUT THE GREAT KING ARTHUR. YOUR RULER, HUMAN.
HH.
HOW FRAGILE THESE SURFACE BEINGS ARE. THEY BREATHE THROUGH THESE TINY HOLES.
OR THEY DON'T BREATHE AT ALL.
LET HIM GO, ORM.

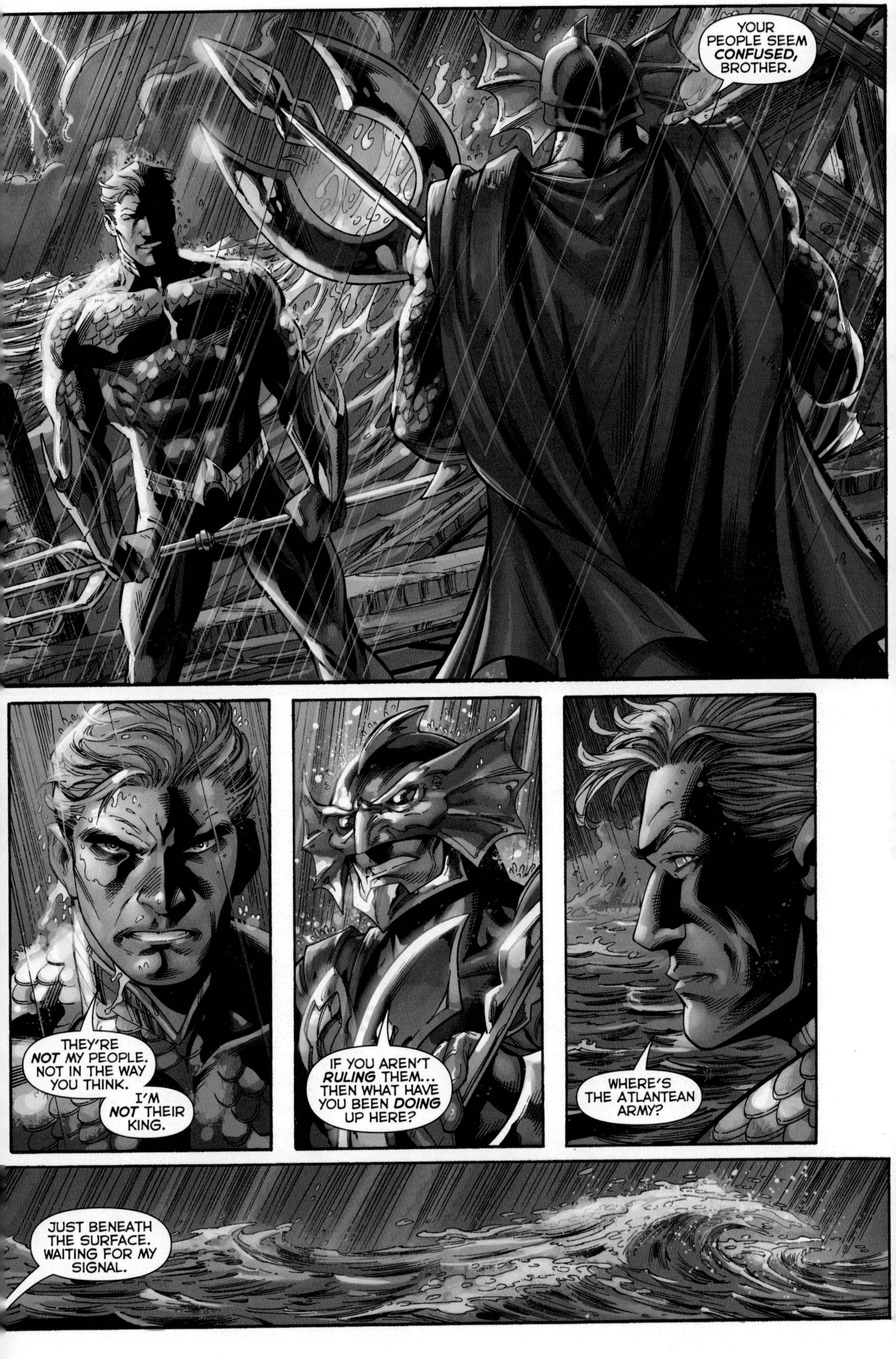
YOUR PEOPLE SEEM *CONFUSED,* BROTHER.
THEY'RE *NOT* MY PEOPLE. NOT IN THE WAY YOU THINK.
I'M *NOT* THEIR KING.
IF YOU AREN'T *RULING* THEM... THEN WHAT HAVE YOU BEEN *DOING* UP HERE?
WHERE'S THE ATLANTEAN ARMY?
JUST BENEATH THE SURFACE. WAITING FOR MY SIGNAL.

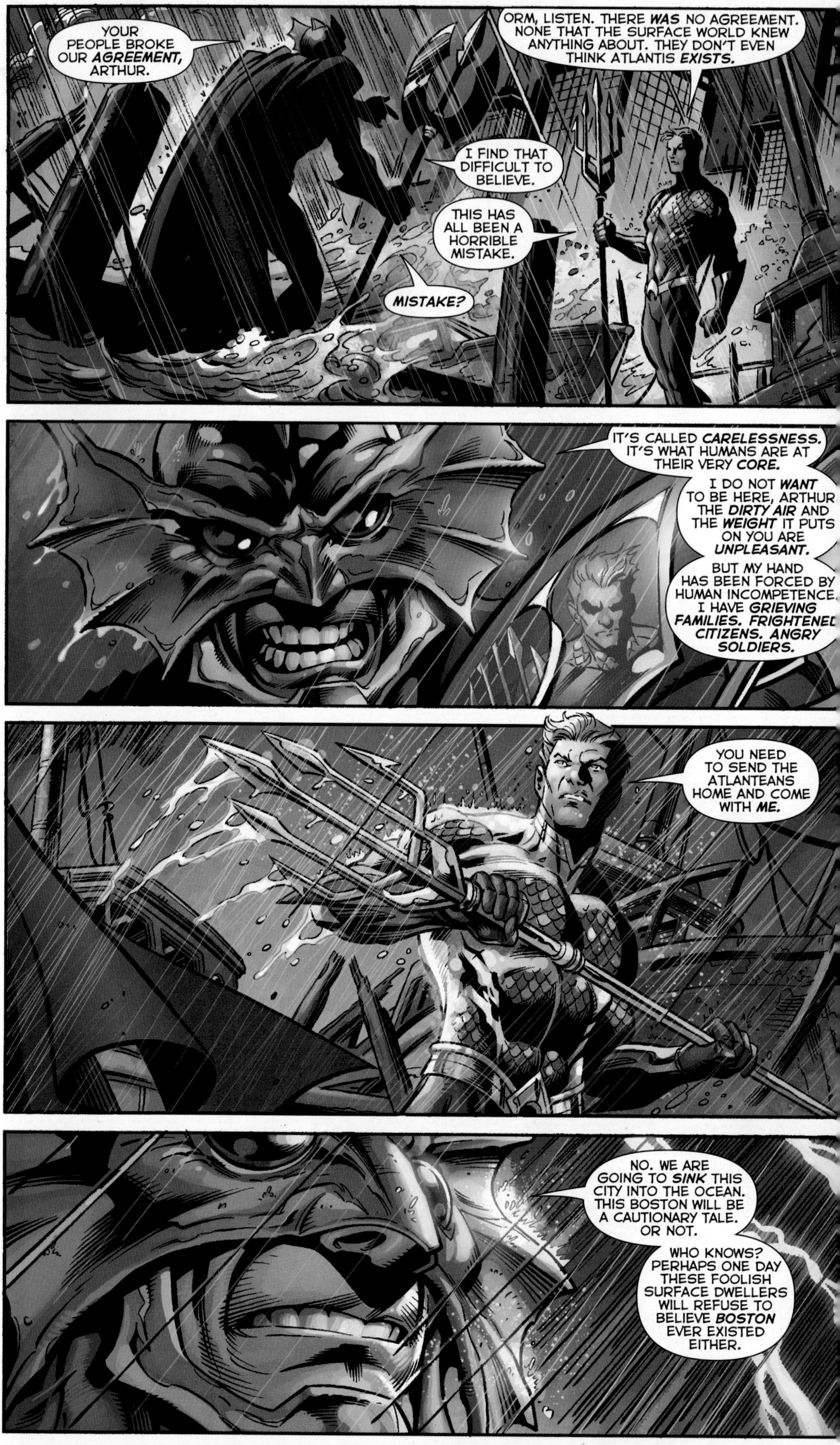
YOUR PEOPLE BROKE OUR AGREEMENT, ARTHUR.
ORM, LISTEN. THERE WAS NO AGREEMENT. NONE THAT THE SURFACE WORLD KNEW ANYTHING ABOUT. THEY DON'T EVEN THINK ATLANTIS EXISTS.
I FIND THAT DIFFICULT TO BELIEVE.
THIS HAS ALL BEEN A HORRIBLE MISTAKE.
MISTAKE?
IT'S CALLED CARELESSNESS. IT'S WHAT HUMANS ARE AT THEIR VERY CORE.
I DO NOT WANT TO BE HERE, ARTHUR THE DIRTY AIR AND THE WEIGHT IT PUTS ON YOU ARE UNPLEASANT.
BUT MY HAND HAS BEEN FORCED BY HUMAN INCOMPETENCE. I HAVE GRIEVING FAMILIES. FRIGHTENED CITIZENS. ANGRY SOLDIERS.
YOU NEED TO SEND THE ATLANTEANS HOME AND COME WITH ME.
NO. WE ARE GOING TO SINK THIS CITY INTO THE OCEAN. THIS BOSTON WILL BE A CAUTIONARY TALE. OR NOT.
WHO KNOWS? PERHAPS ONE DAY THESE FOOLISH SURFACE DWELLERS WILL REFUSE TO BELIEVE BOSTON EVER EXISTED EITHER.

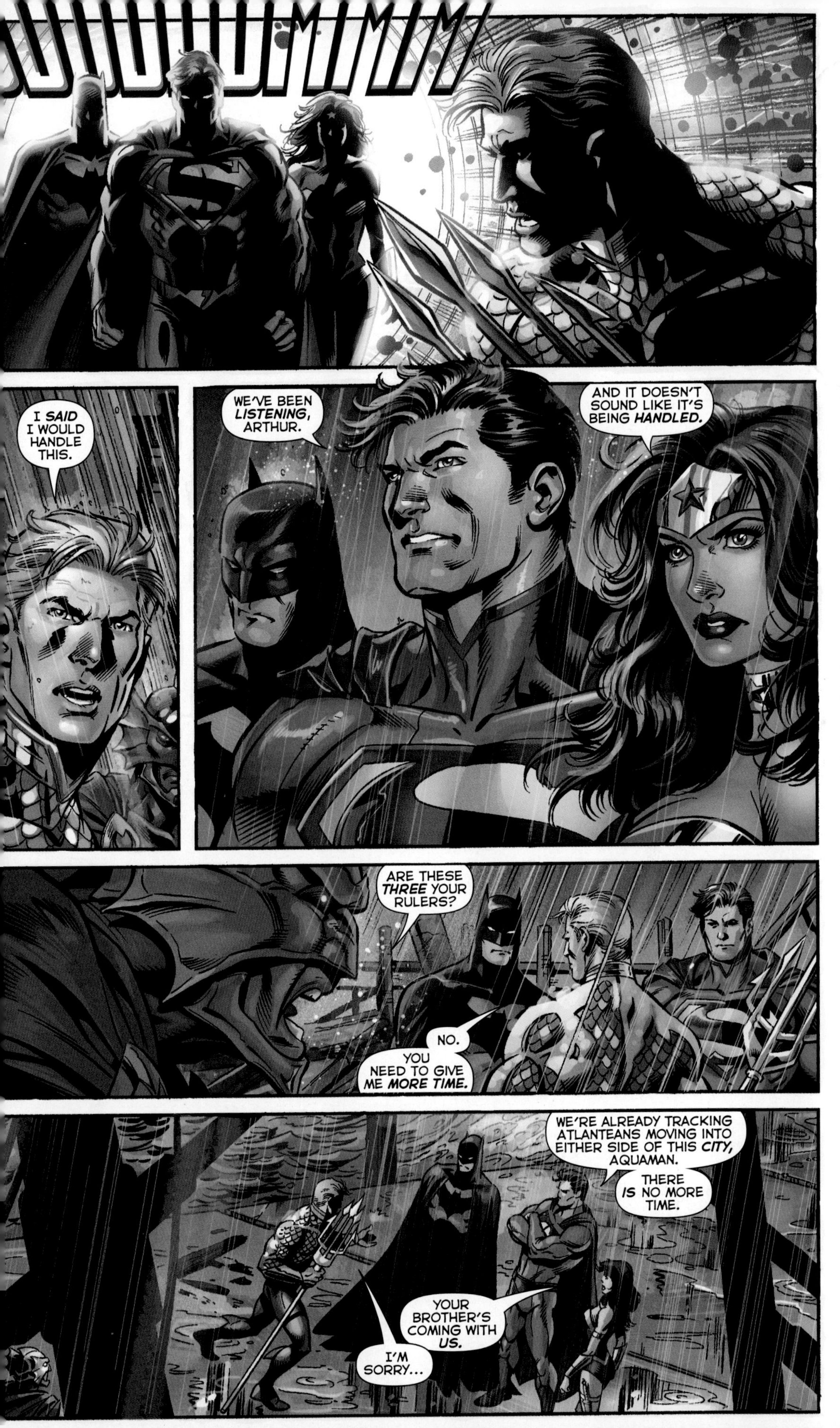
I SAID I WOULD HANDLE THIS.
WE'VE BEEN LISTENING, ARTHUR.
AND IT DOESN'T SOUND LIKE IT'S BEING HANDLED.
ARE THESE THREE YOUR RULERS?
NO.
YOU NEED TO GIVE ME MORE TIME.
WE'RE ALREADY TRACKING ATLANTEANS MOVING INTO EITHER SIDE OF THIS CITY, AQUAMAN.
THERE IS NO MORE TIME.
YOUR BROTHER'S COMING WITH US.
I'M SORRY...

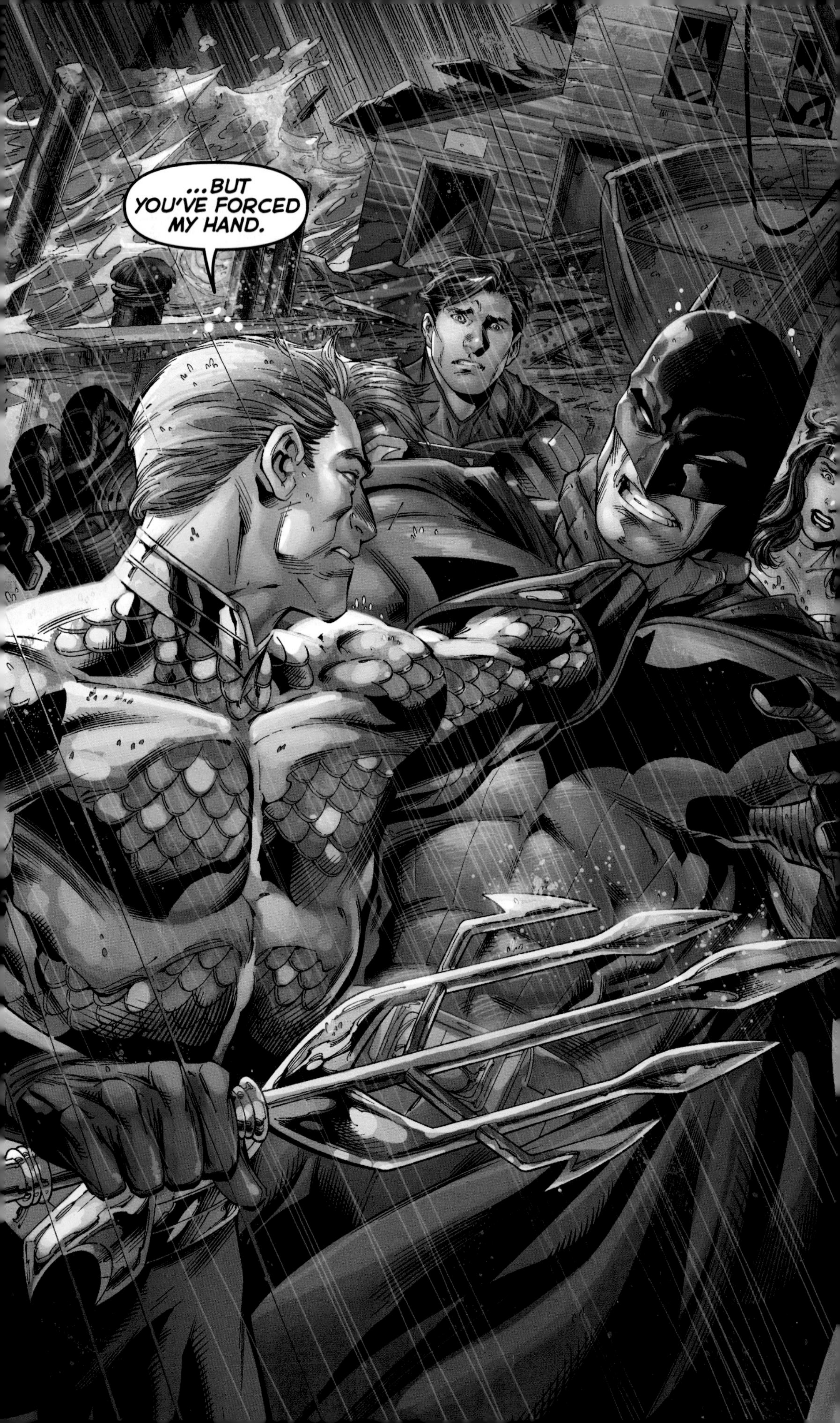
...BUT YOU'VE FORCED MY HAND.

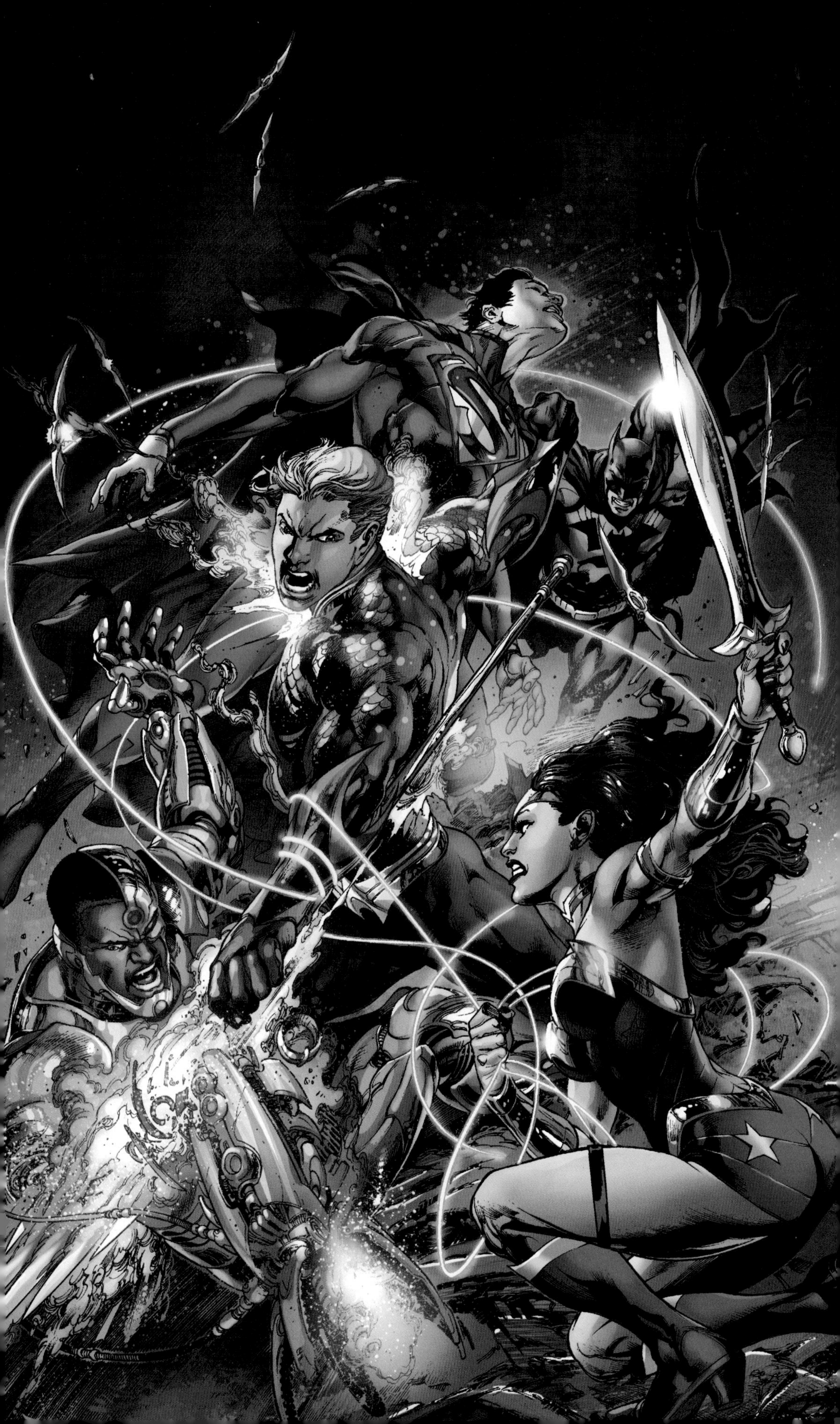

GEOFF JOHNS writer **IVAN REIS** penciller **JOE PRADO & IVAN REIS** inkers cover by **IVAN REIS, JOE PRADO & ROD REIS**

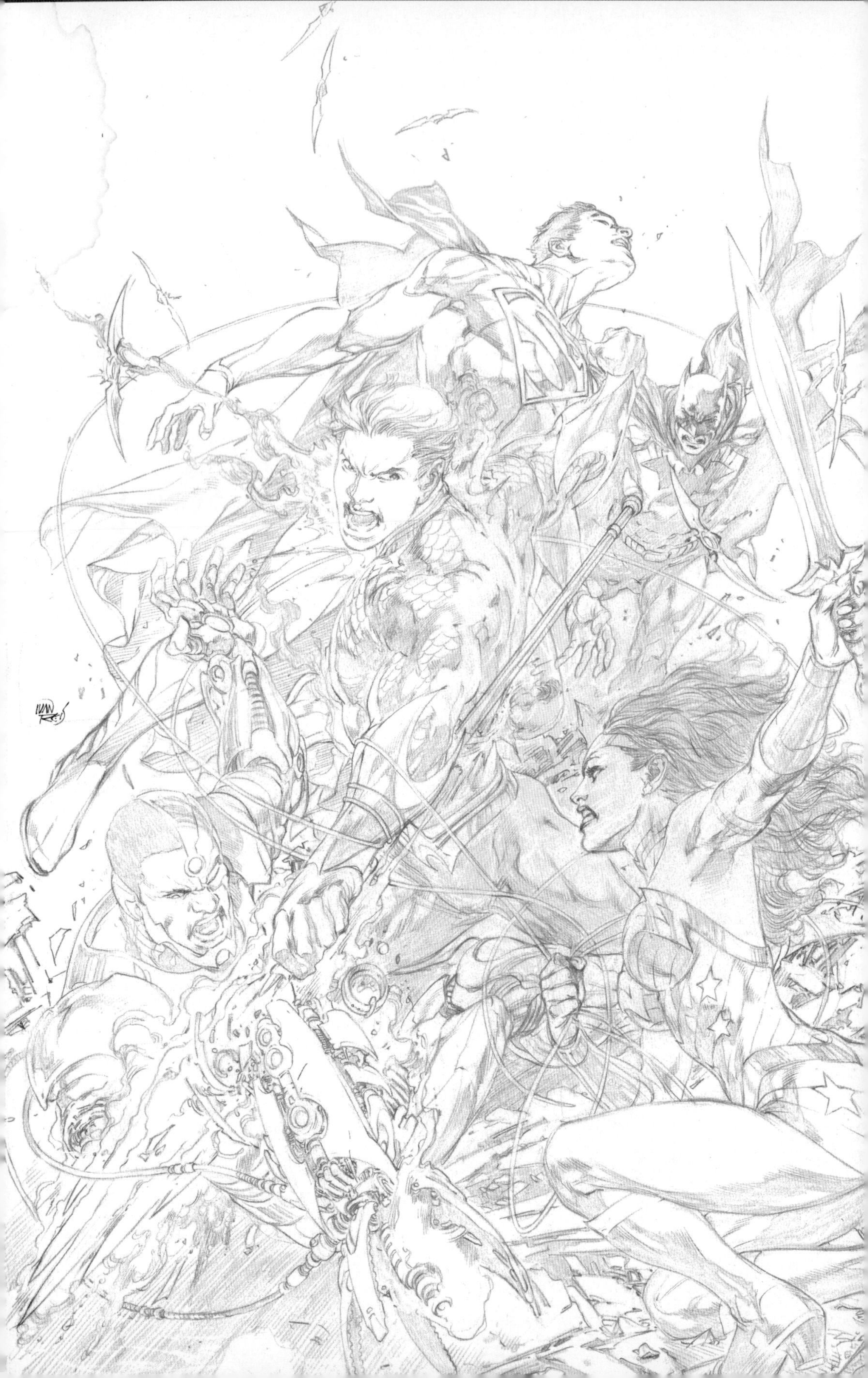

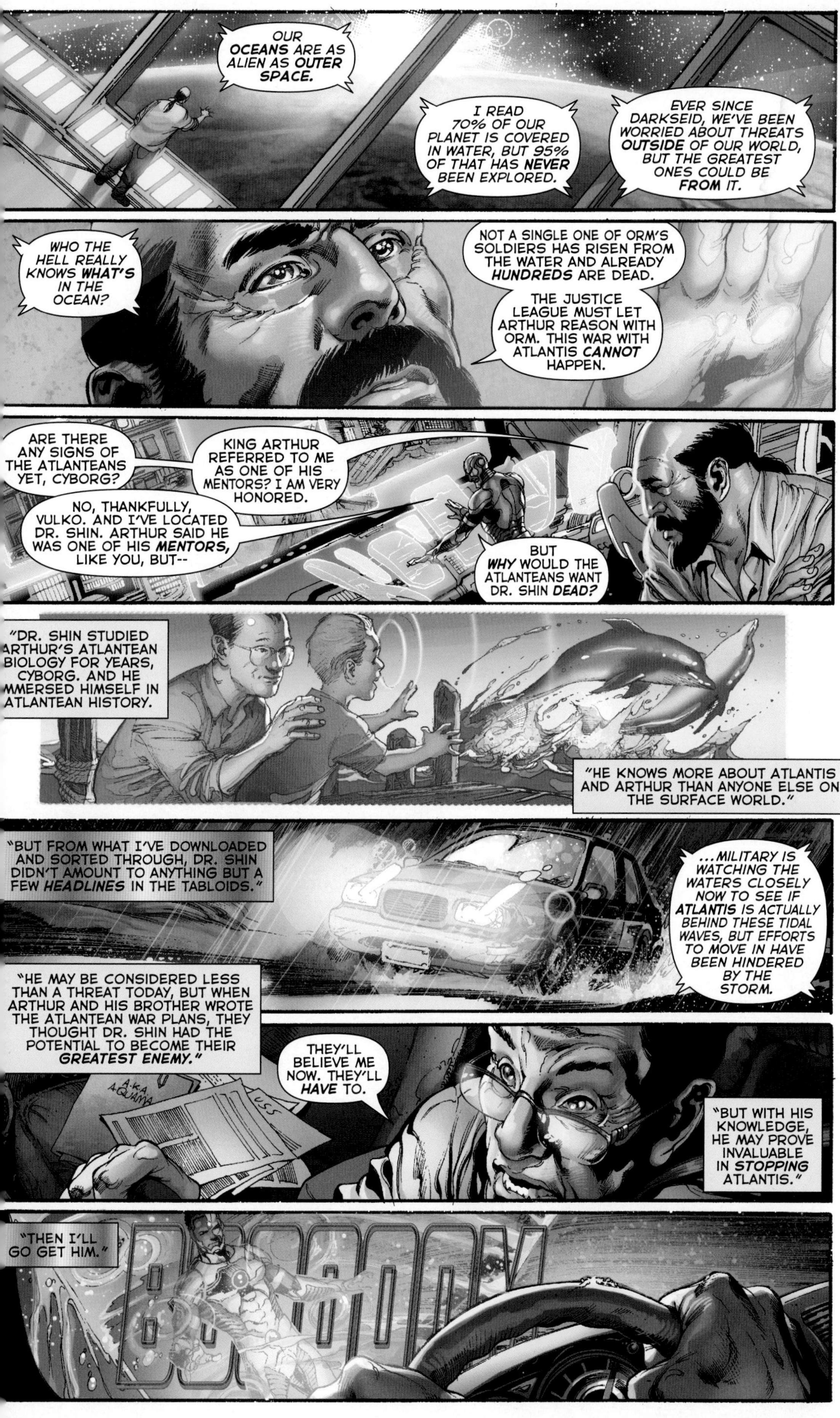

OUR OCEANS ARE AS ALIEN AS OUTER SPACE.
I READ 70% OF OUR PLANET IS COVERED IN WATER, BUT 95% OF THAT HAS NEVER BEEN EXPLORED.
EVER SINCE DARKSEID, WE'VE BEEN WORRIED ABOUT THREATS OUTSIDE OF OUR WORLD, BUT THE GREATEST ONES COULD BE FROM IT.
WHO THE HELL REALLY KNOWS WHAT'S IN THE OCEAN?
NOT A SINGLE ONE OF ORM'S SOLDIERS HAS RISEN FROM THE WATER AND ALREADY HUNDREDS ARE DEAD.
THE JUSTICE LEAGUE MUST LET ARTHUR REASON WITH ORM. THIS WAR WITH ATLANTIS CANNOT HAPPEN.
ARE THERE ANY SIGNS OF THE ATLANTEANS YET, CYBORG?
NO, THANKFULLY, VULKO. AND I'VE LOCATED DR. SHIN. ARTHUR SAID HE WAS ONE OF HIS MENTORS, LIKE YOU, BUT--
KING ARTHUR REFERRED TO ME AS ONE OF HIS MENTORS? I AM VERY HONORED.
BUT WHY WOULD THE ATLANTEANS WANT DR. SHIN DEAD?
"DR. SHIN STUDIED ARTHUR'S ATLANTEAN BIOLOGY FOR YEARS, CYBORG. AND HE IMMERSED HIMSELF IN ATLANTEAN HISTORY.
"HE KNOWS MORE ABOUT ATLANTIS AND ARTHUR THAN ANYONE ELSE ON THE SURFACE WORLD."
"BUT FROM WHAT I'VE DOWNLOADED AND SORTED THROUGH, DR. SHIN DIDN'T AMOUNT TO ANYTHING BUT A FEW HEADLINES IN THE TABLOIDS."
...MILITARY IS WATCHING THE WATERS CLOSELY NOW TO SEE IF ATLANTIS IS ACTUALLY BEHIND THESE TIDAL WAVES, BUT EFFORTS TO MOVE IN HAVE BEEN HINDERED BY THE STORM.
"HE MAY BE CONSIDERED LESS THAN A THREAT TODAY, BUT WHEN ARTHUR AND HIS BROTHER WROTE THE ATLANTEAN WAR PLANS, THEY THOUGHT DR. SHIN HAD THE POTENTIAL TO BECOME THEIR GREATEST ENEMY."
THEY'LL BELIEVE ME NOW. THEY'LL HAVE TO.
A.K.A. AQUAMA
"BUT WITH HIS KNOWLEDGE, HE MAY PROVE INVALUABLE IN STOPPING ATLANTIS."
"THEN I'LL GO GET HIM."
BOOOOOM

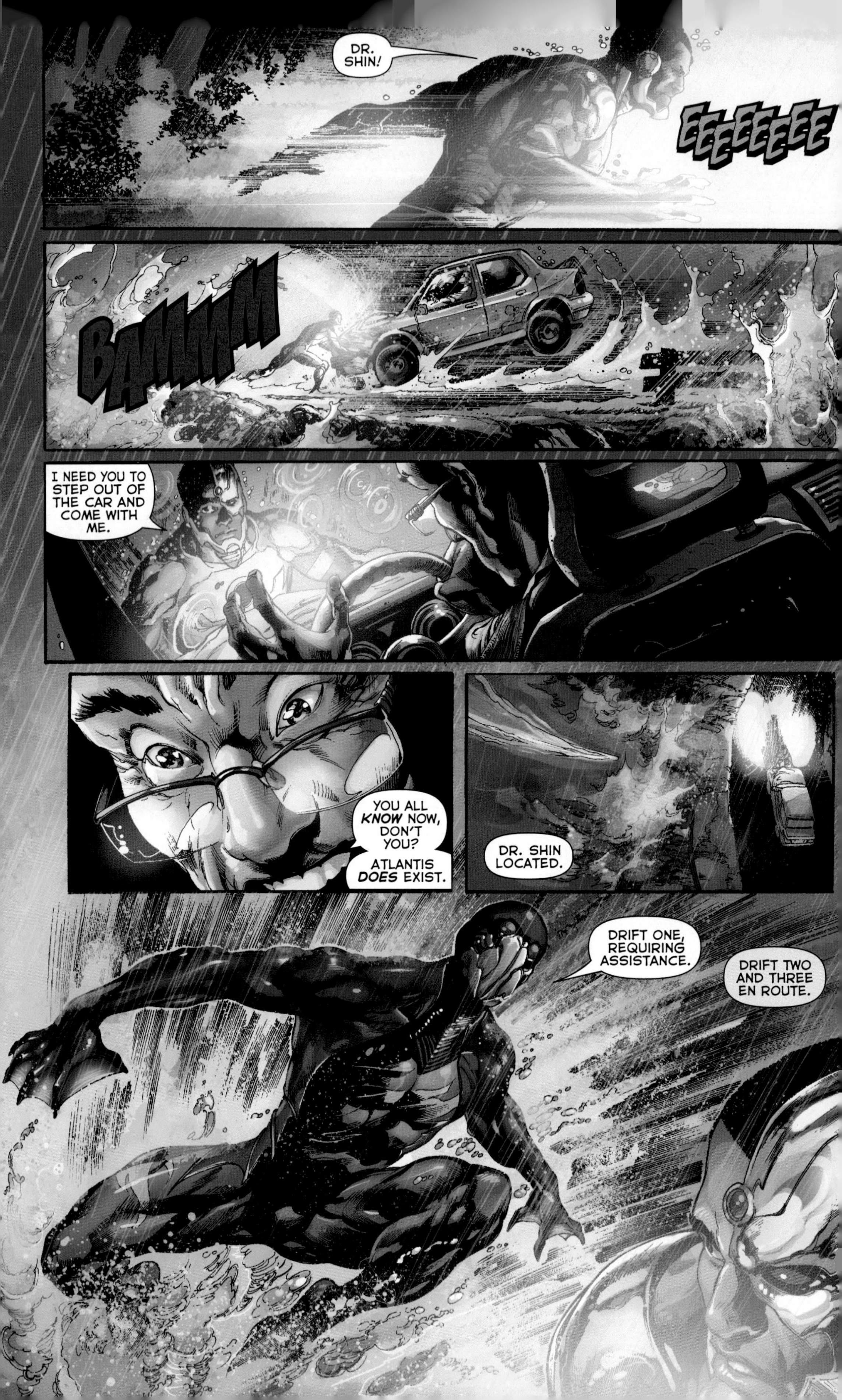
DR. SHIN!
EEEEEEEE
BAMMMM
I NEED YOU TO STEP OUT OF THE CAR AND COME WITH ME.
YOU ALL KNOW NOW, DON'T YOU?
ATLANTIS DOES EXIST.
DR. SHIN LOCATED.
DRIFT ONE, REQUIRING ASSISTANCE.
DRIFT TWO AND THREE EN ROUTE.

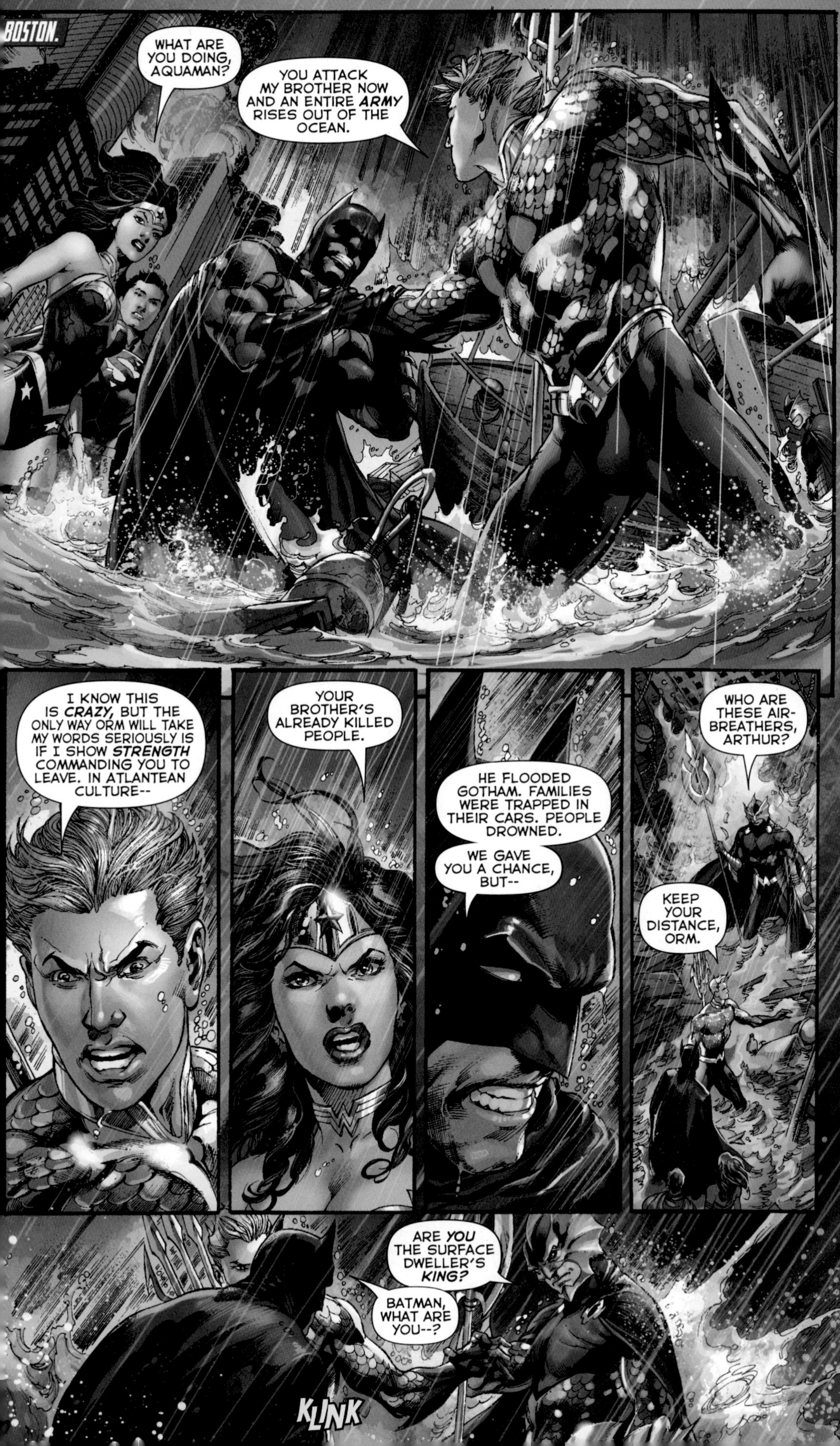
BOSTON.
WHAT ARE YOU DOING, AQUAMAN?
YOU ATTACK MY BROTHER NOW AND AN ENTIRE ARMY RISES OUT OF THE OCEAN.
I KNOW THIS IS CRAZY, BUT THE ONLY WAY ORM WILL TAKE MY WORDS SERIOUSLY IS IF I SHOW STRENGTH COMMANDING YOU TO LEAVE. IN ATLANTEAN CULTURE--
YOUR BROTHER'S ALREADY KILLED PEOPLE.
HE FLOODED GOTHAM. FAMILIES WERE TRAPPED IN THEIR CARS. PEOPLE DROWNED.
WE GAVE YOU A CHANCE, BUT--
WHO ARE THESE AIR-BREATHERS, ARTHUR?
KEEP YOUR DISTANCE, ORM.
ARE YOU THE SURFACE DWELLER'S KING?
BATMAN, WHAT ARE YOU--?
KLINK

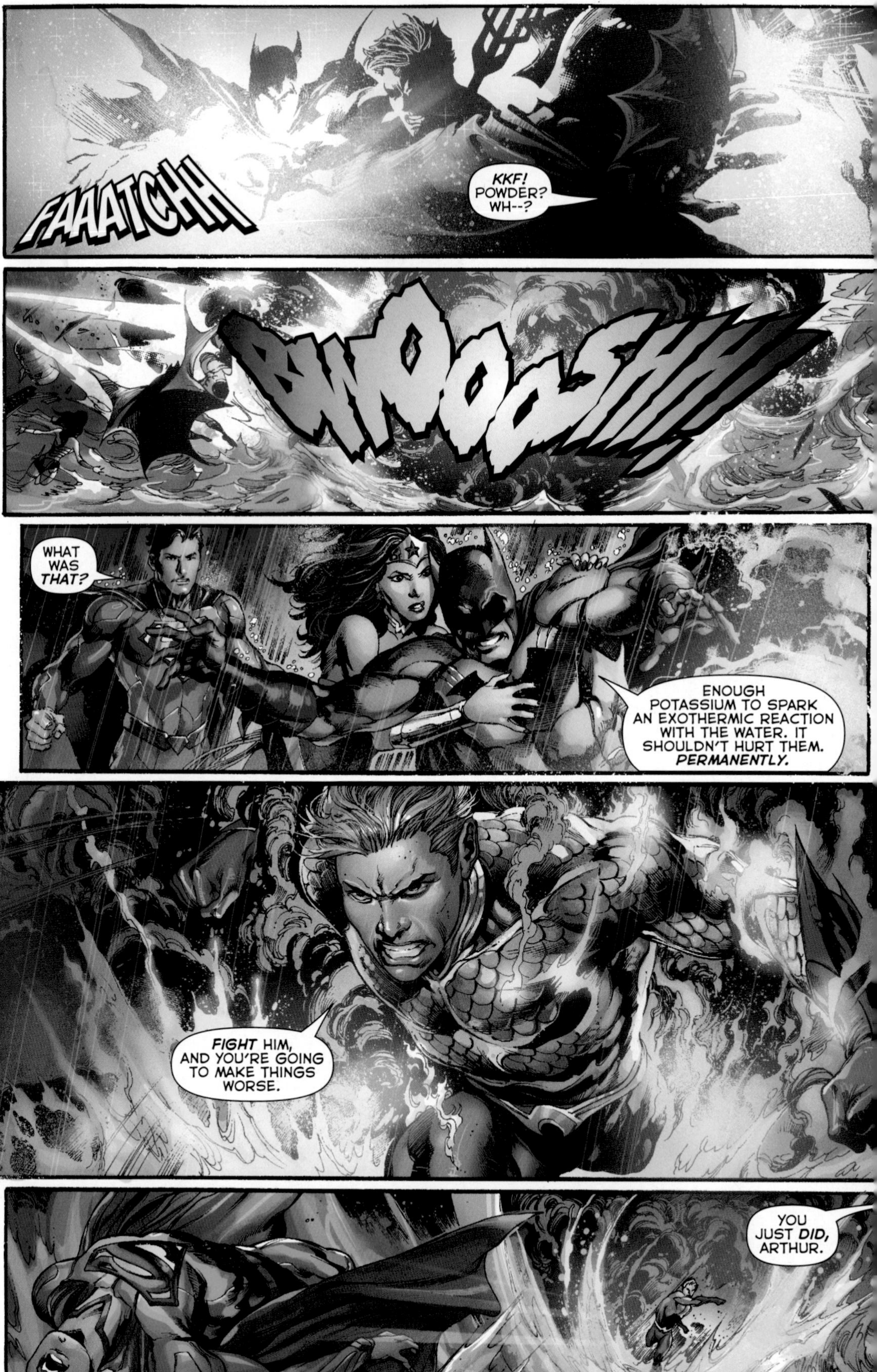

FAAATCHH
KKF! POWDER? WH--?
BWOOSHH
WHAT WAS THAT?
ENOUGH POTASSIUM TO SPARK AN EXOTHERMIC REACTION WITH THE WATER. IT SHOULDN'T HURT THEM. PERMANENTLY.
FIGHT HIM, AND YOU'RE GOING TO MAKE THINGS WORSE.
YOU JUST DID, ARTHUR.

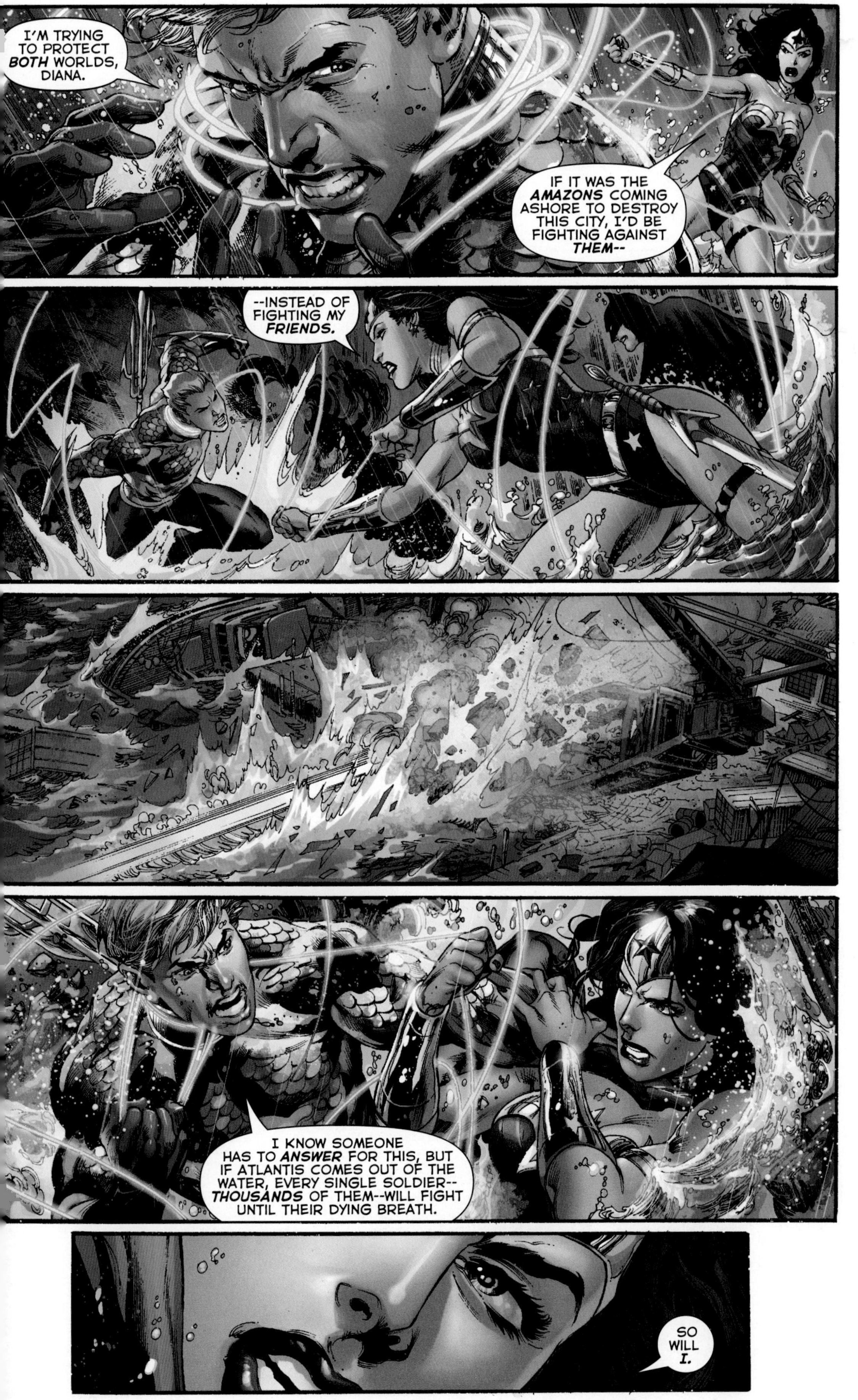

I'M TRYING TO PROTECT *BOTH* WORLDS, DIANA.
IF IT WAS THE *AMAZONS* COMING ASHORE TO DESTROY THIS CITY, I'D BE FIGHTING AGAINST *THEM*--
--INSTEAD OF FIGHTING MY *FRIENDS.*
I KNOW SOMEONE HAS TO *ANSWER* FOR THIS, BUT IF ATLANTIS COMES OUT OF THE WATER, EVERY SINGLE SOLDIER-- *THOUSANDS* OF THEM--WILL FIGHT UNTIL THEIR DYING BREATH.
SO WILL *I.*

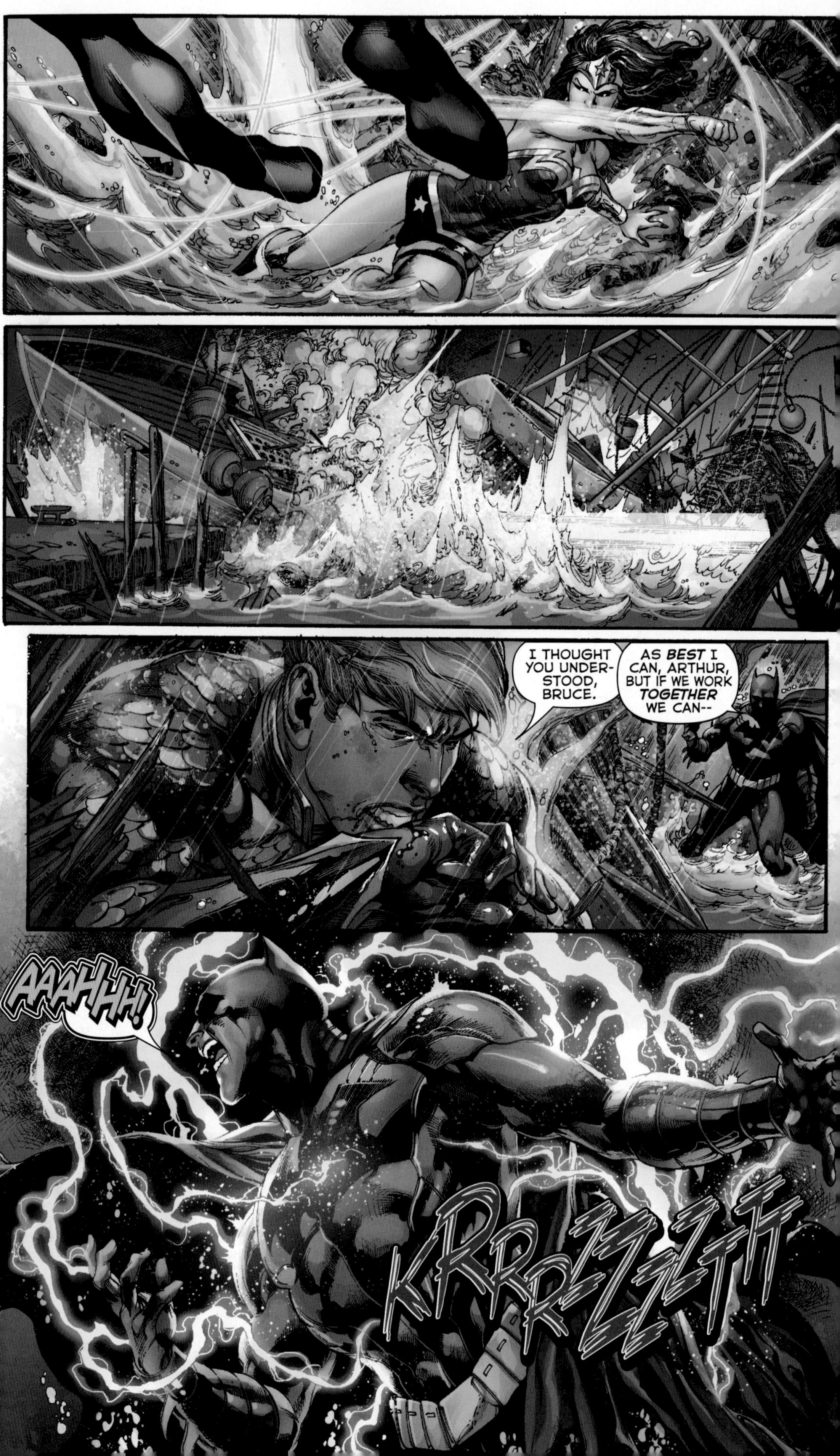

I THOUGHT YOU UNDER-STOOD, BRUCE.
AS *BEST* I CAN, ARTHUR, BUT IF WE WORK *TOGETHER* WE CAN--
AAAHHH!
KRRRZZZZTT

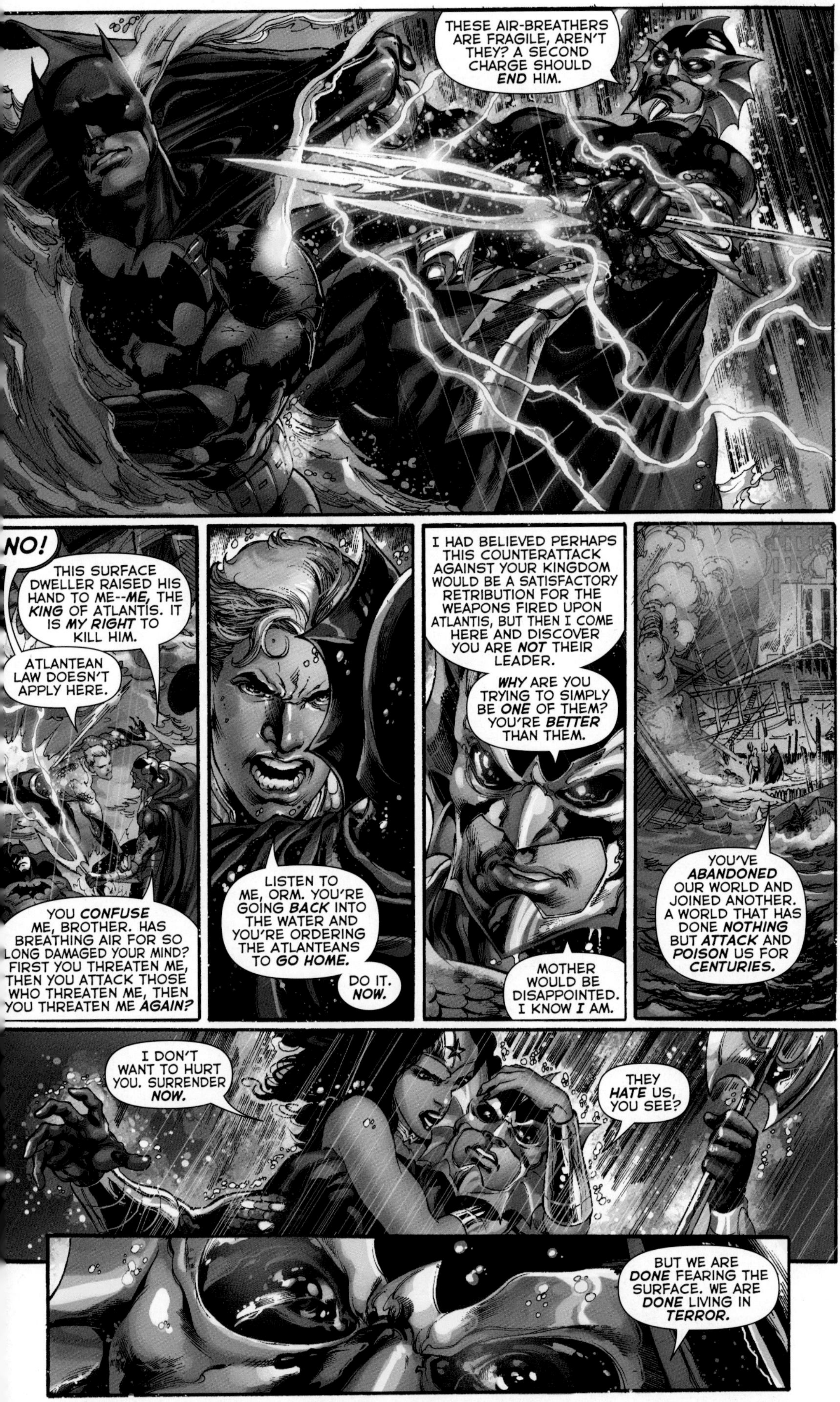

THESE AIR-BREATHERS ARE FRAGILE, AREN'T THEY? A SECOND CHARGE SHOULD END HIM.
NO!
THIS SURFACE DWELLER RAISED HIS HAND TO ME--ME, THE KING OF ATLANTIS. IT IS MY RIGHT TO KILL HIM.
ATLANTEAN LAW DOESN'T APPLY HERE.
YOU CONFUSE ME, BROTHER. HAS BREATHING AIR FOR SO LONG DAMAGED YOUR MIND? FIRST YOU THREATEN ME, THEN YOU ATTACK THOSE WHO THREATEN ME, THEN YOU THREATEN ME AGAIN?
LISTEN TO ME, ORM. YOU'RE GOING BACK INTO THE WATER AND YOU'RE ORDERING THE ATLANTEANS TO GO HOME.
DO IT. NOW.
I HAD BELIEVED PERHAPS THIS COUNTERATTACK AGAINST YOUR KINGDOM WOULD BE A SATISFACTORY RETRIBUTION FOR THE WEAPONS FIRED UPON ATLANTIS, BUT THEN I COME HERE AND DISCOVER YOU ARE NOT THEIR LEADER.
WHY ARE YOU TRYING TO SIMPLY BE ONE OF THEM? YOU'RE BETTER THAN THEM.
MOTHER WOULD BE DISAPPOINTED. I KNOW I AM.
YOU'VE ABANDONED OUR WORLD AND JOINED ANOTHER. A WORLD THAT HAS DONE NOTHING BUT ATTACK AND POISON US FOR CENTURIES.
I DON'T WANT TO HURT YOU. SURRENDER NOW.
THEY HATE US, YOU SEE?
BUT WE ARE DONE FEARING THE SURFACE. WE ARE DONE LIVING IN TERROR.

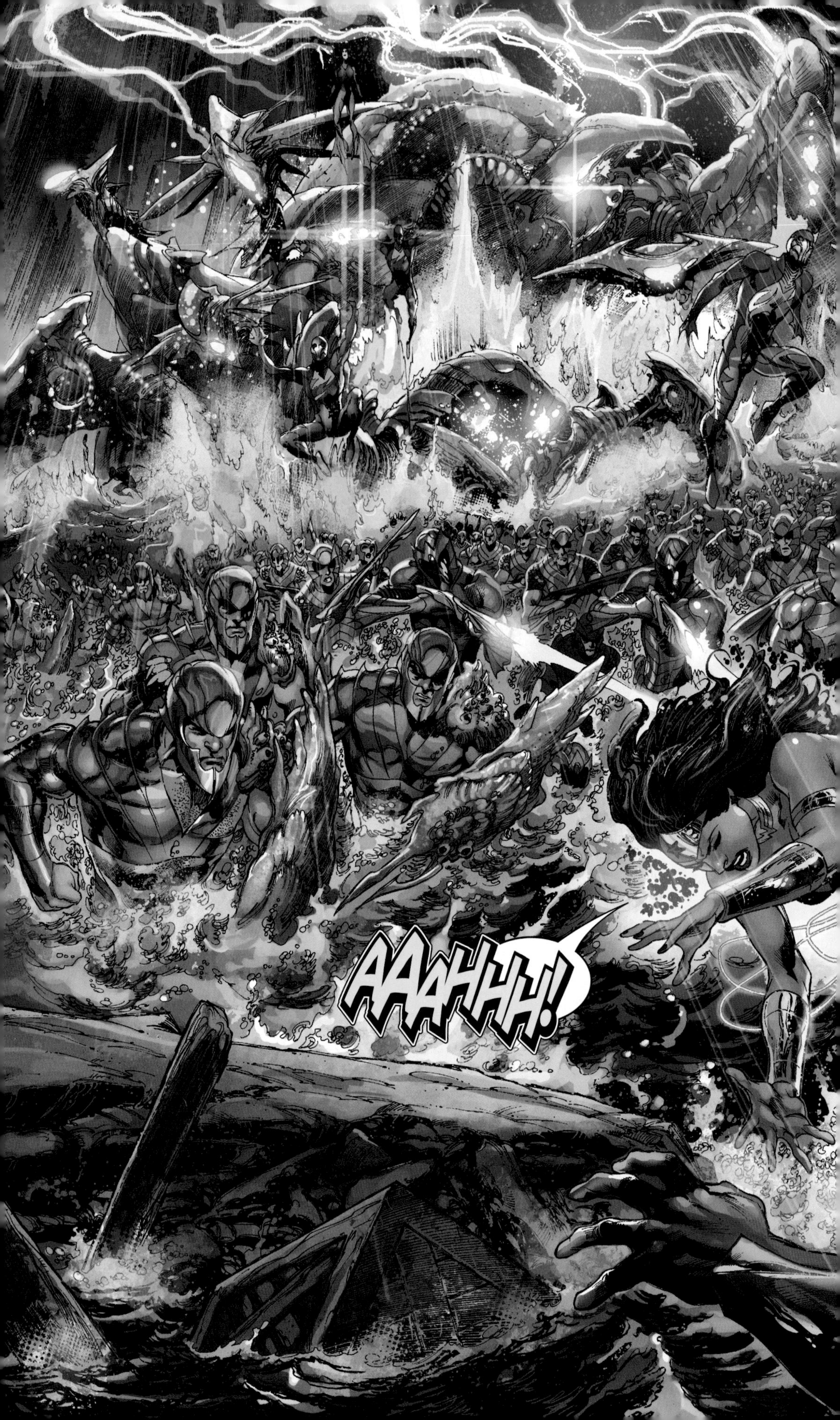
AAAHHH!

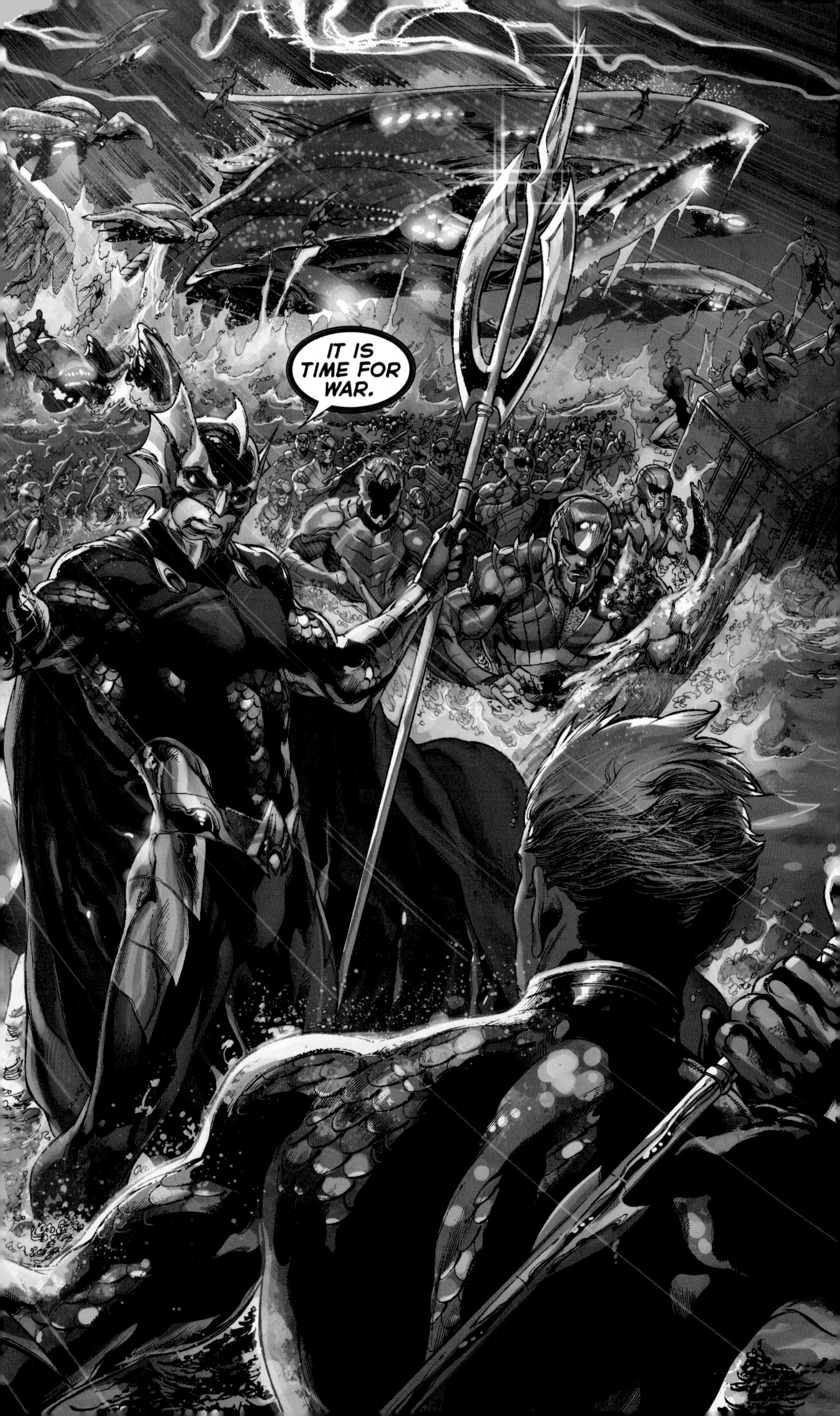
IT IS TIME FOR WAR.

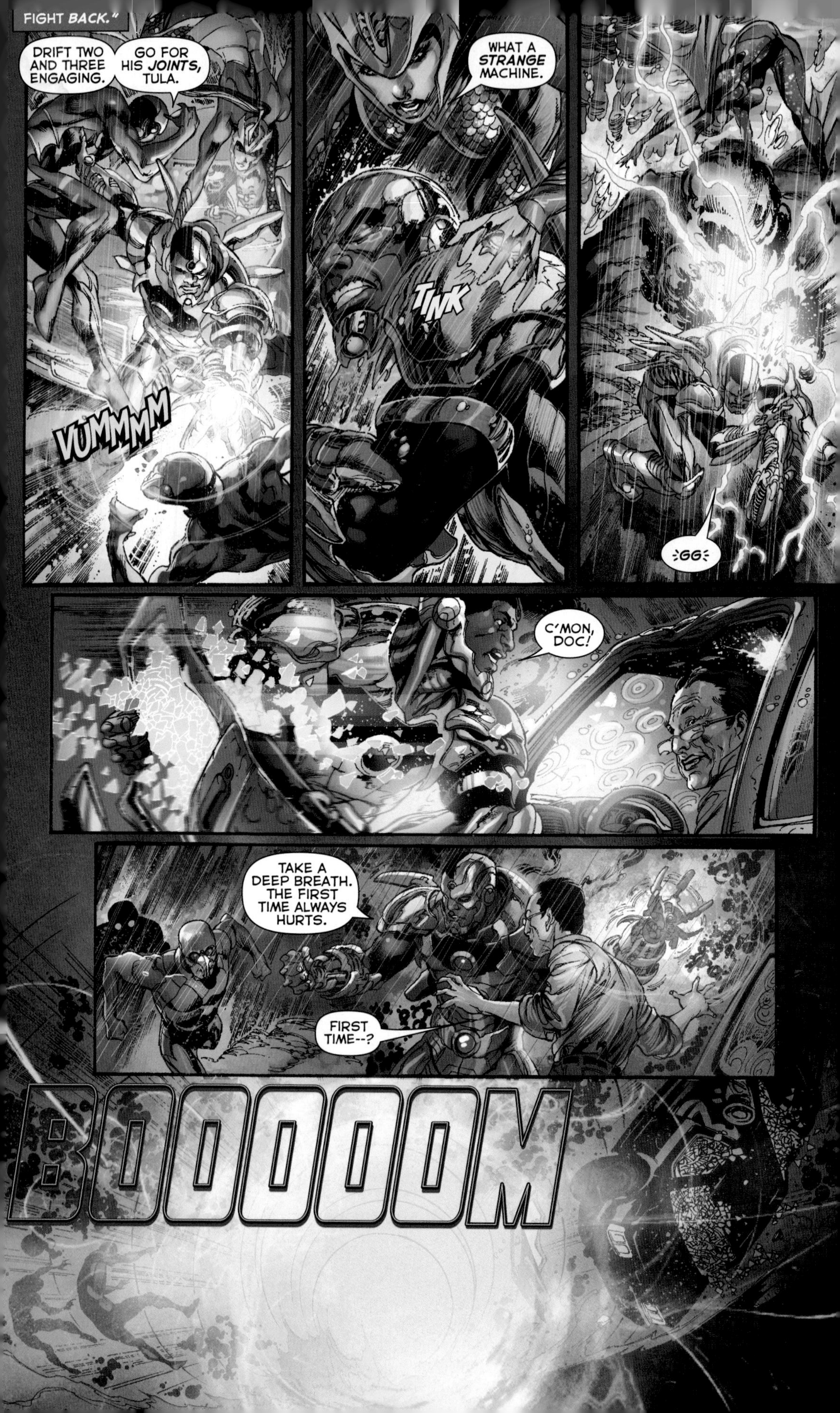
FIGHT BACK."
DRIFT TWO AND THREE ENGAGING.
GO FOR HIS JOINTS, TULA.
VUMMMM
WHAT A STRANGE MACHINE.
TINK
GG
C'MON, DOC!
TAKE A DEEP BREATH. THE FIRST TIME ALWAYS HURTS.
FIRST TIME--?
BOOOOOM

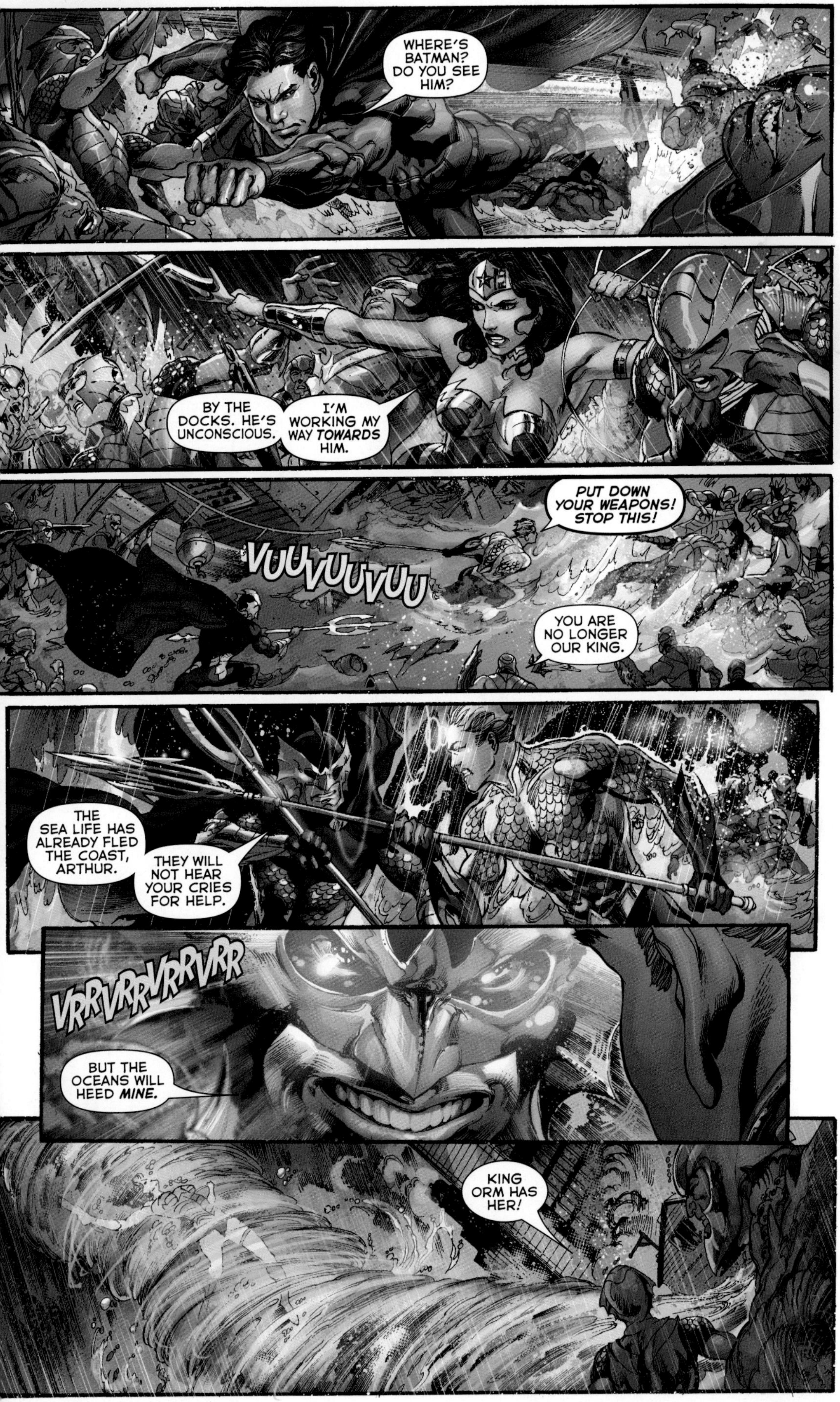
WHERE'S BATMAN? DO YOU SEE HIM?
BY THE DOCKS. HE'S UNCONSCIOUS.
I'M WORKING MY WAY TOWARDS HIM.
PUT DOWN YOUR WEAPONS! STOP THIS!
VUUVUUVUU
YOU ARE NO LONGER OUR KING.
THE SEA LIFE HAS ALREADY FLED THE COAST, ARTHUR.
THEY WILL NOT HEAR YOUR CRIES FOR HELP.
VRRVRRVRRVRR
BUT THE OCEANS WILL HEED MINE.
KING ORM HAS HER!

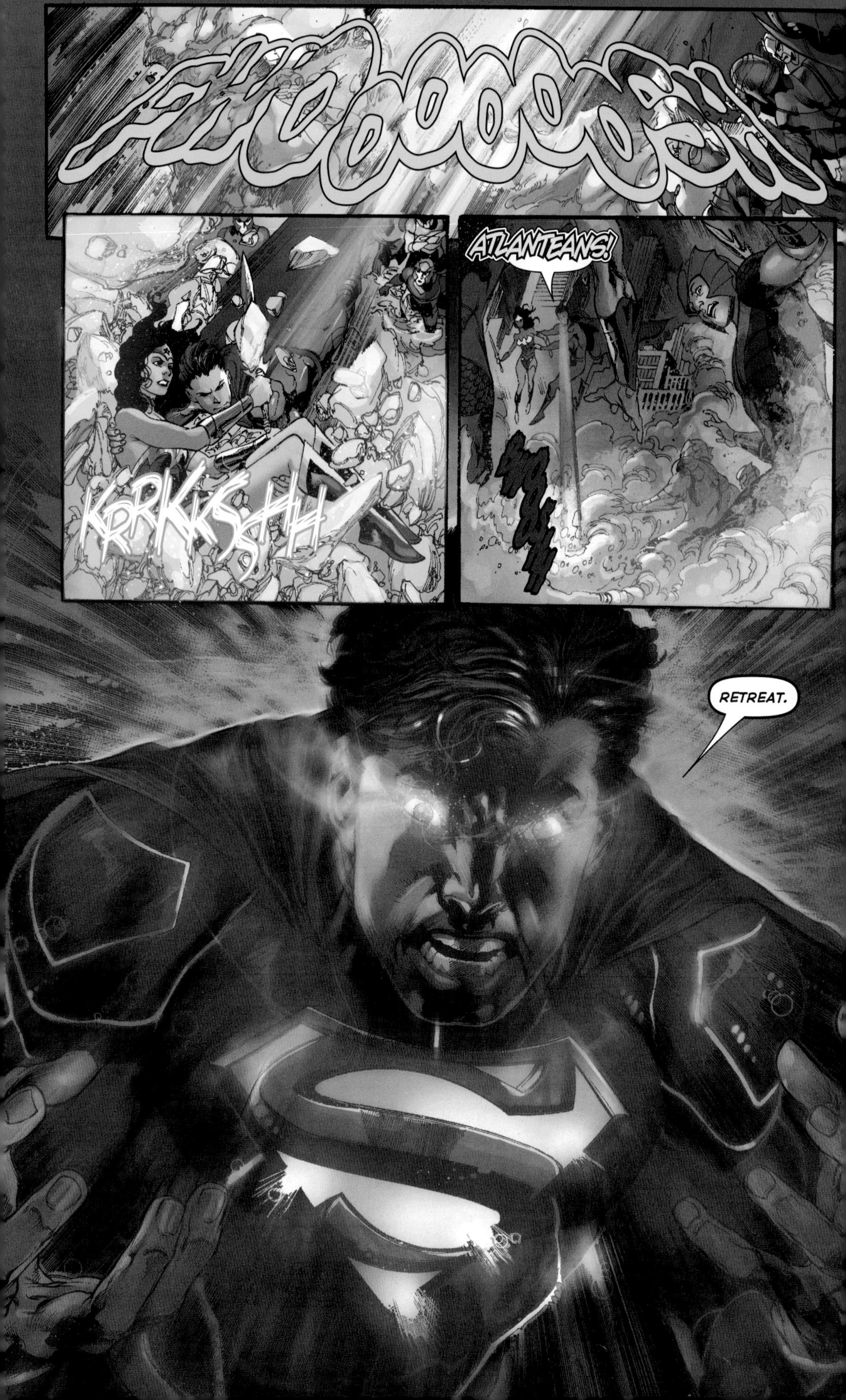
FZHOOOOOOOSH
KRRKKSSHH
ATLANTEANS!
RETREAT.

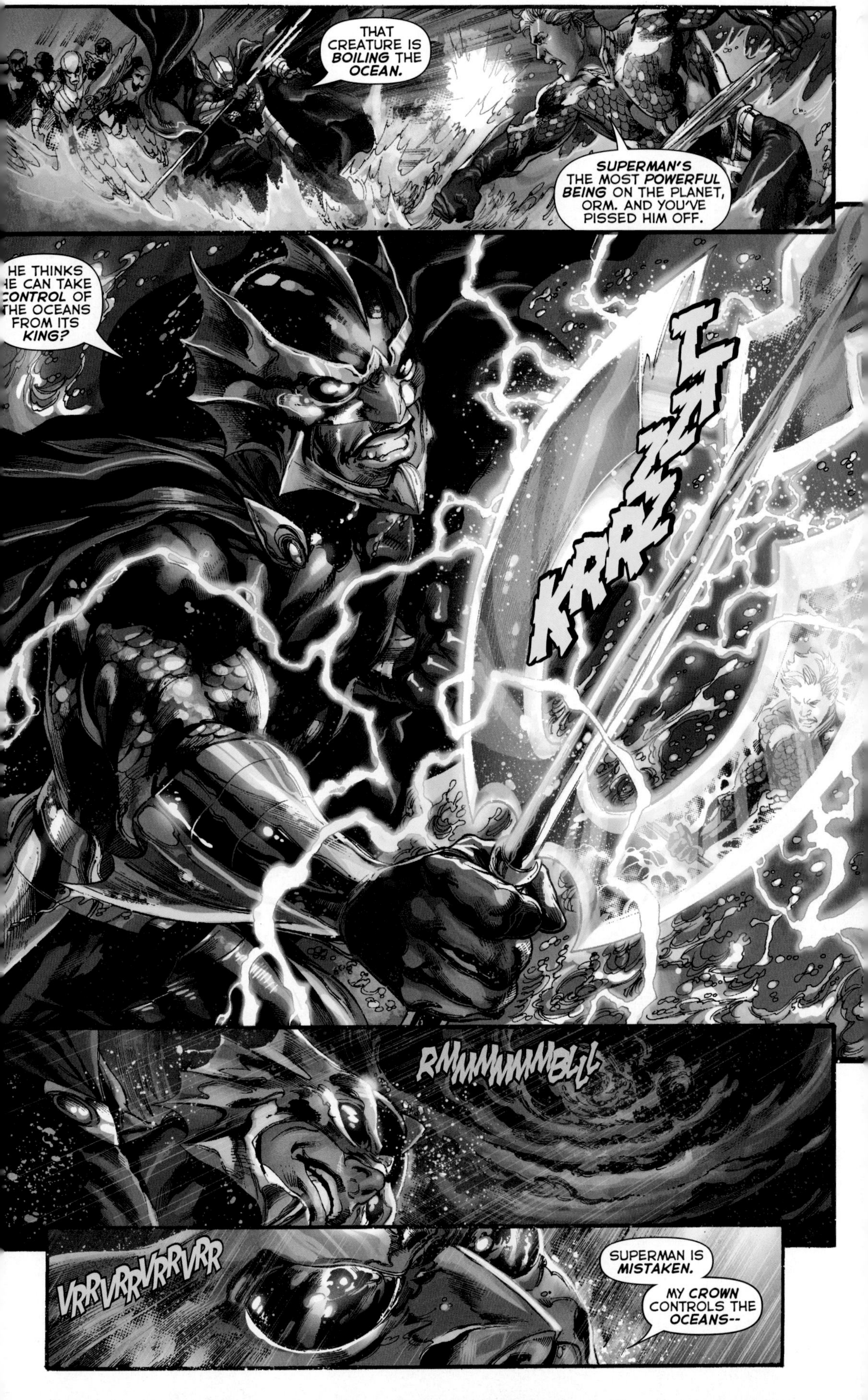

THAT CREATURE IS BOILING THE OCEAN.
SUPERMAN'S THE MOST POWERFUL BEING ON THE PLANET, ORM. AND YOU'VE PISSED HIM OFF.
HE THINKS HE CAN TAKE CONTROL OF THE OCEANS FROM ITS KING?
KRRZZZT
RMMMMMMBLLL
VRRVRRVRRVRR
SUPERMAN IS MISTAKEN.
MY CROWN CONTROLS THE OCEANS--

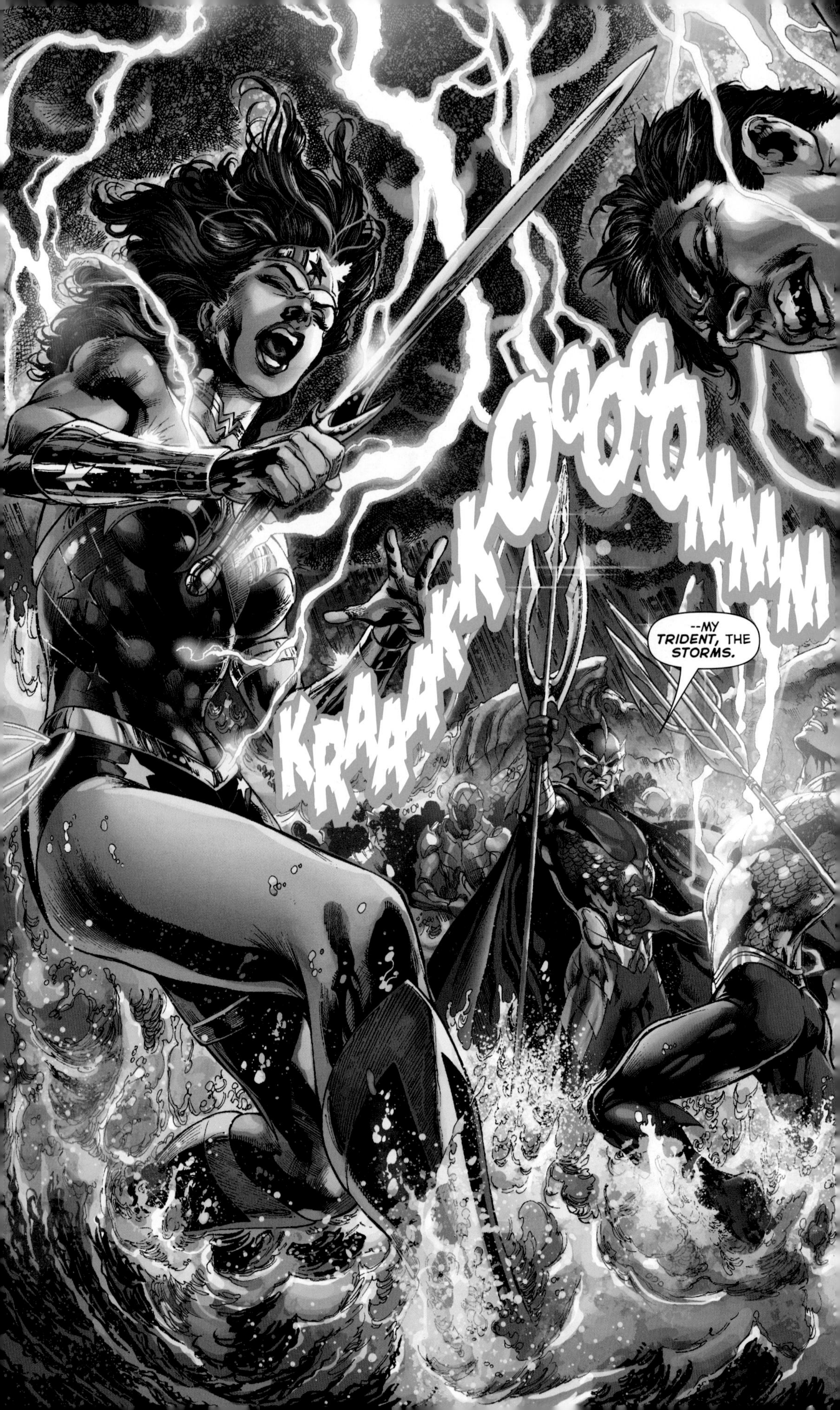
KRAAAKKOOOOOMMMM
--MY TRIDENT, THE STORMS.

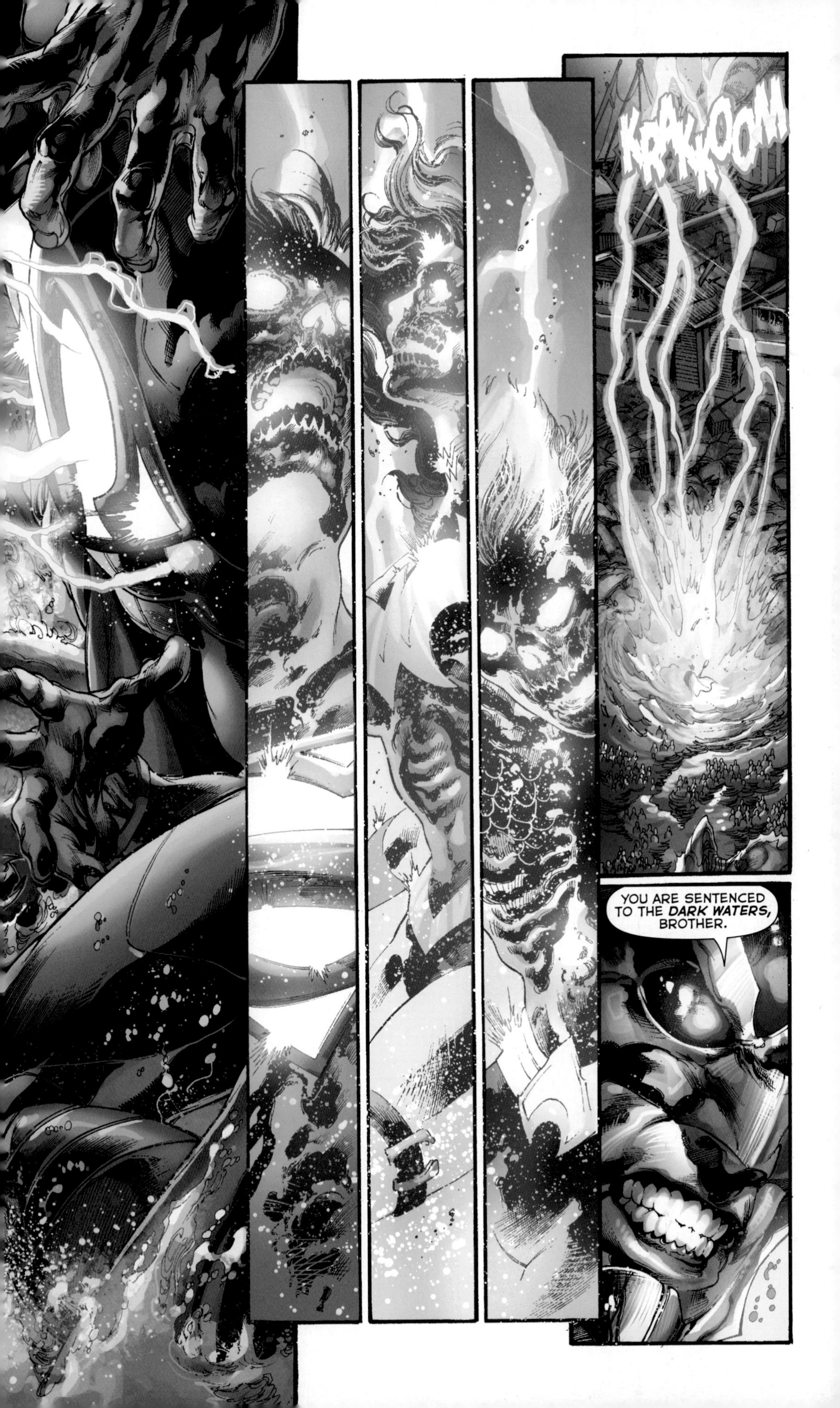
KRAKOOM
YOU ARE SENTENCED TO THE DARK WATERS, BROTHER.

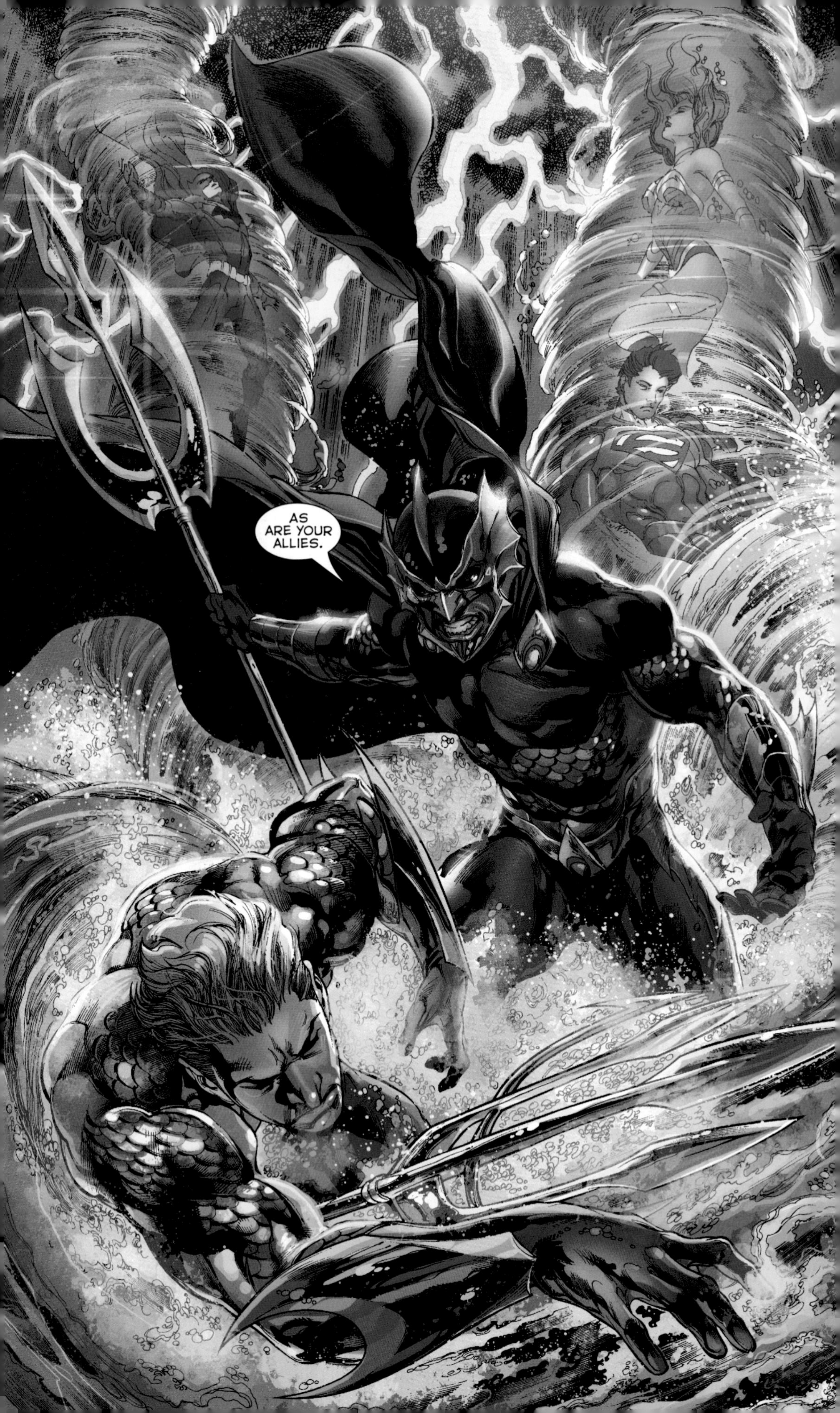
AS ARE YOUR ALLIES.

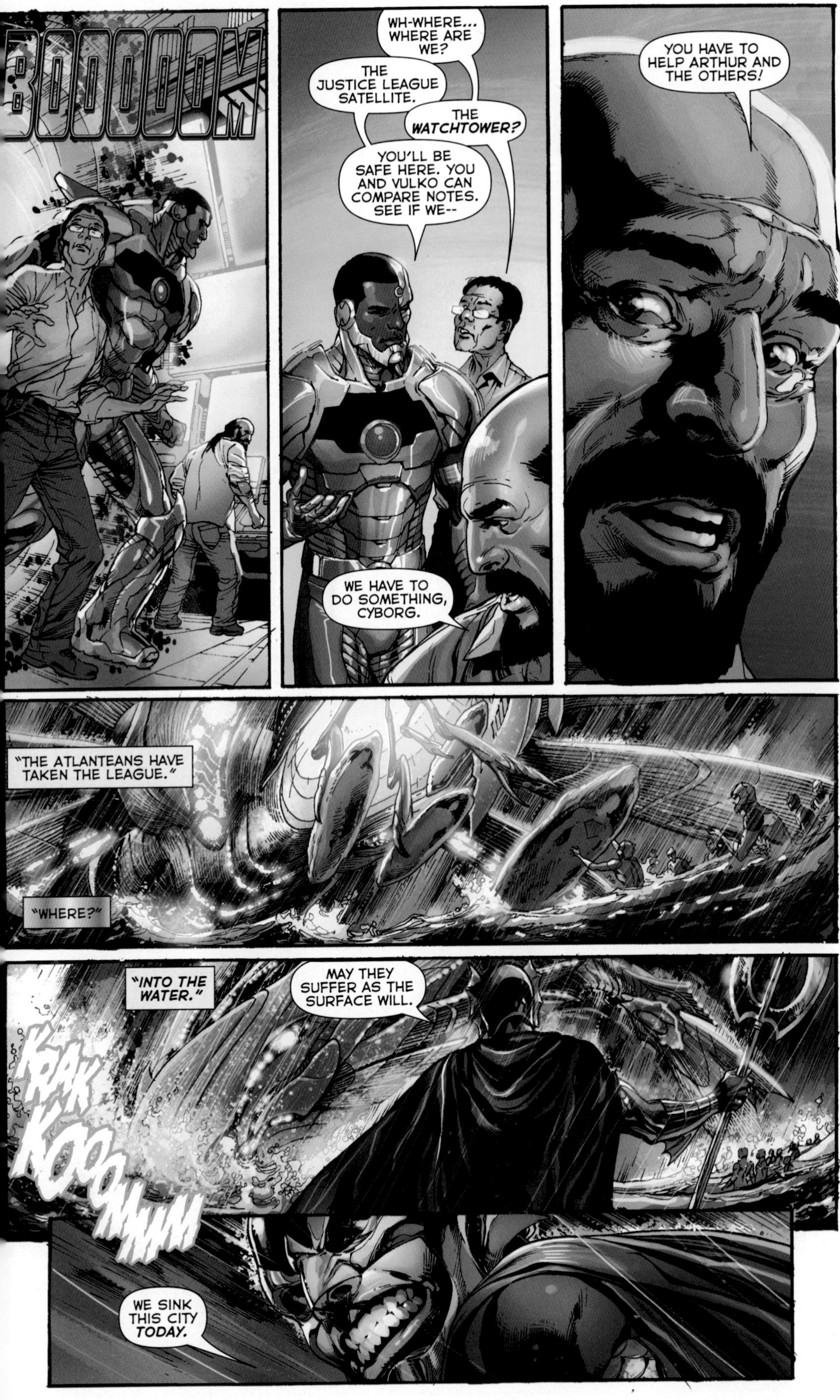
BOOOOOOM
WH-WHERE... WHERE ARE WE?
THE JUSTICE LEAGUE SATELLITE.
THE WATCHTOWER?
YOU'LL BE SAFE HERE. YOU AND VULKO CAN COMPARE NOTES. SEE IF WE--
WE HAVE TO DO SOMETHING, CYBORG.
YOU HAVE TO HELP ARTHUR AND THE OTHERS!
"THE ATLANTEANS HAVE TAKEN THE LEAGUE."
"WHERE?"
"INTO THE WATER."
MAY THEY SUFFER AS THE SURFACE WILL.
KRAK KOOOMMM
WE SINK THIS CITY TODAY.

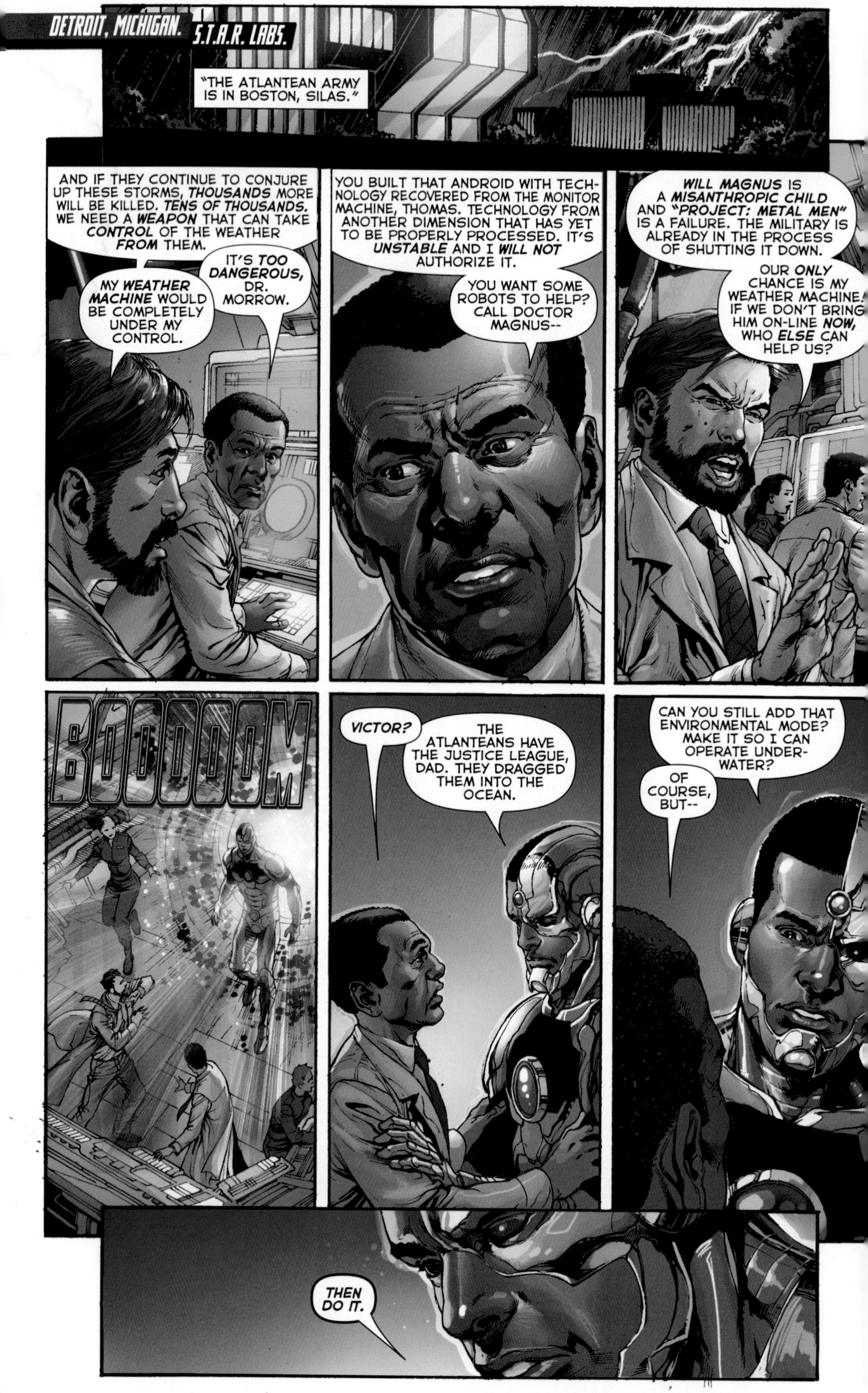
DETROIT, MICHIGAN.
S.T.A.R. LABS.
"THE ATLANTEAN ARMY IS IN BOSTON, SILAS."
AND IF THEY CONTINUE TO CONJURE UP THESE STORMS, THOUSANDS MORE WILL BE KILLED. TENS OF THOUSANDS. WE NEED A WEAPON THAT CAN TAKE CONTROL OF THE WEATHER FROM THEM.
MY WEATHER MACHINE WOULD BE COMPLETELY UNDER MY CONTROL.
IT'S TOO DANGEROUS, DR. MORROW.
YOU BUILT THAT ANDROID WITH TECHNOLOGY RECOVERED FROM THE MONITOR MACHINE, THOMAS. TECHNOLOGY FROM ANOTHER DIMENSION THAT HAS YET TO BE PROPERLY PROCESSED. IT'S UNSTABLE AND I WILL NOT AUTHORIZE IT.
YOU WANT SOME ROBOTS TO HELP? CALL DOCTOR MAGNUS--
WILL MAGNUS IS A MISANTHROPIC CHILD AND "PROJECT: METAL MEN" IS A FAILURE. THE MILITARY IS ALREADY IN THE PROCESS OF SHUTTING IT DOWN.
OUR ONLY CHANCE IS MY WEATHER MACHINE. IF WE DON'T BRING HIM ON-LINE NOW, WHO ELSE CAN HELP US?
BOOOOOM
VICTOR?
THE ATLANTEANS HAVE THE JUSTICE LEAGUE, DAD. THEY DRAGGED THEM INTO THE OCEAN.
CAN YOU STILL ADD THAT ENVIRONMENTAL MODE? MAKE IT SO I CAN OPERATE UNDER-WATER?
OF COURSE, BUT--
THEN DO IT.

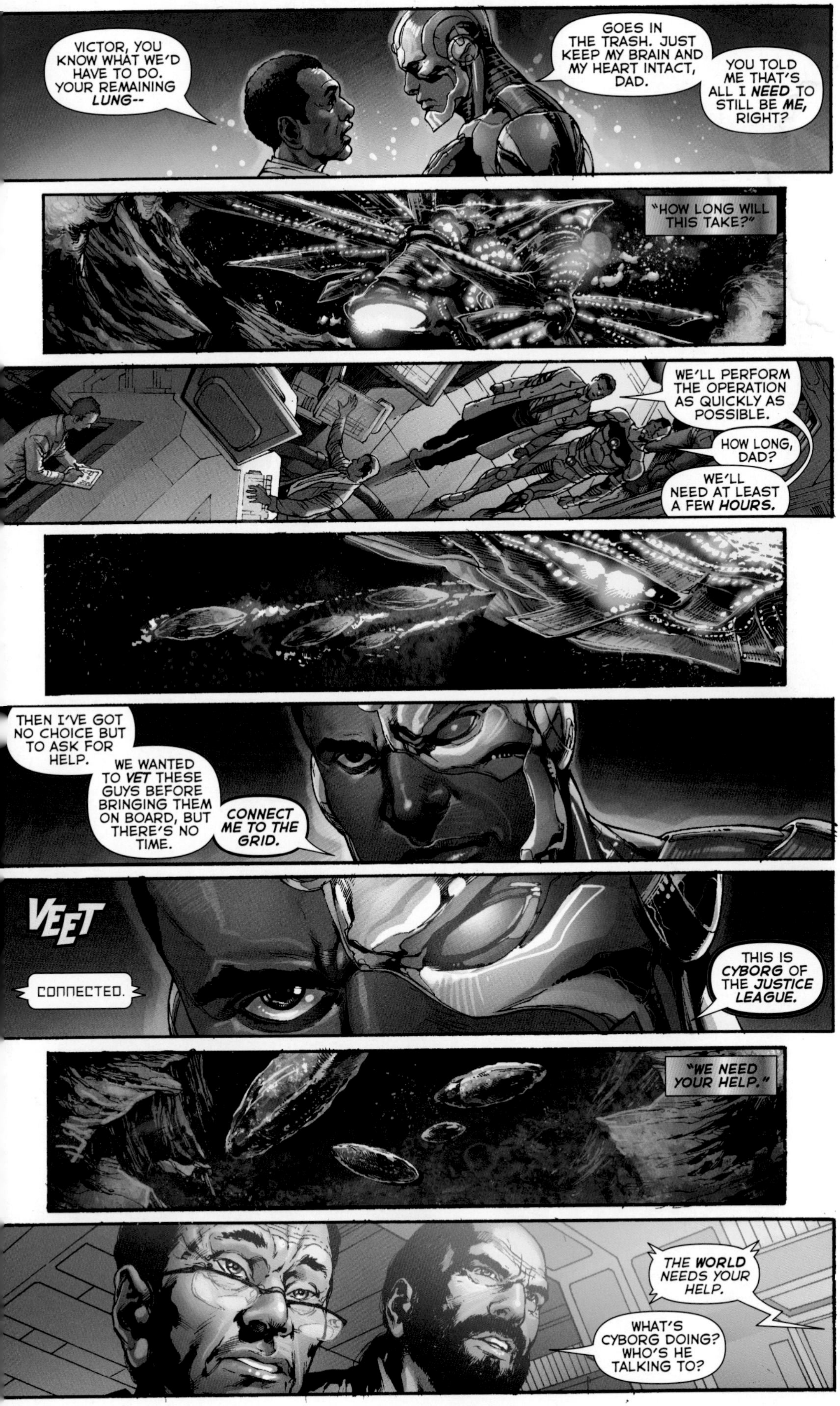
VICTOR, YOU KNOW WHAT WE'D HAVE TO DO. YOUR REMAINING LUNG--
GOES IN THE TRASH. JUST KEEP MY BRAIN AND MY HEART INTACT, DAD.
YOU TOLD ME THAT'S ALL I NEED TO STILL BE ME, RIGHT?
"HOW LONG WILL THIS TAKE?"
WE'LL PERFORM THE OPERATION AS QUICKLY AS POSSIBLE.
HOW LONG, DAD?
WE'LL NEED AT LEAST A FEW HOURS.
THEN I'VE GOT NO CHOICE BUT TO ASK FOR HELP.
WE WANTED TO VET THESE GUYS BEFORE BRINGING THEM ON BOARD, BUT THERE'S NO TIME.
CONNECT ME TO THE GRID.
VEET
CONNECTED.
THIS IS CYBORG OF THE JUSTICE LEAGUE.
"WE NEED YOUR HELP."
THE WORLD NEEDS YOUR HELP.
WHAT'S CYBORG DOING? WHO'S HE TALKING TO?

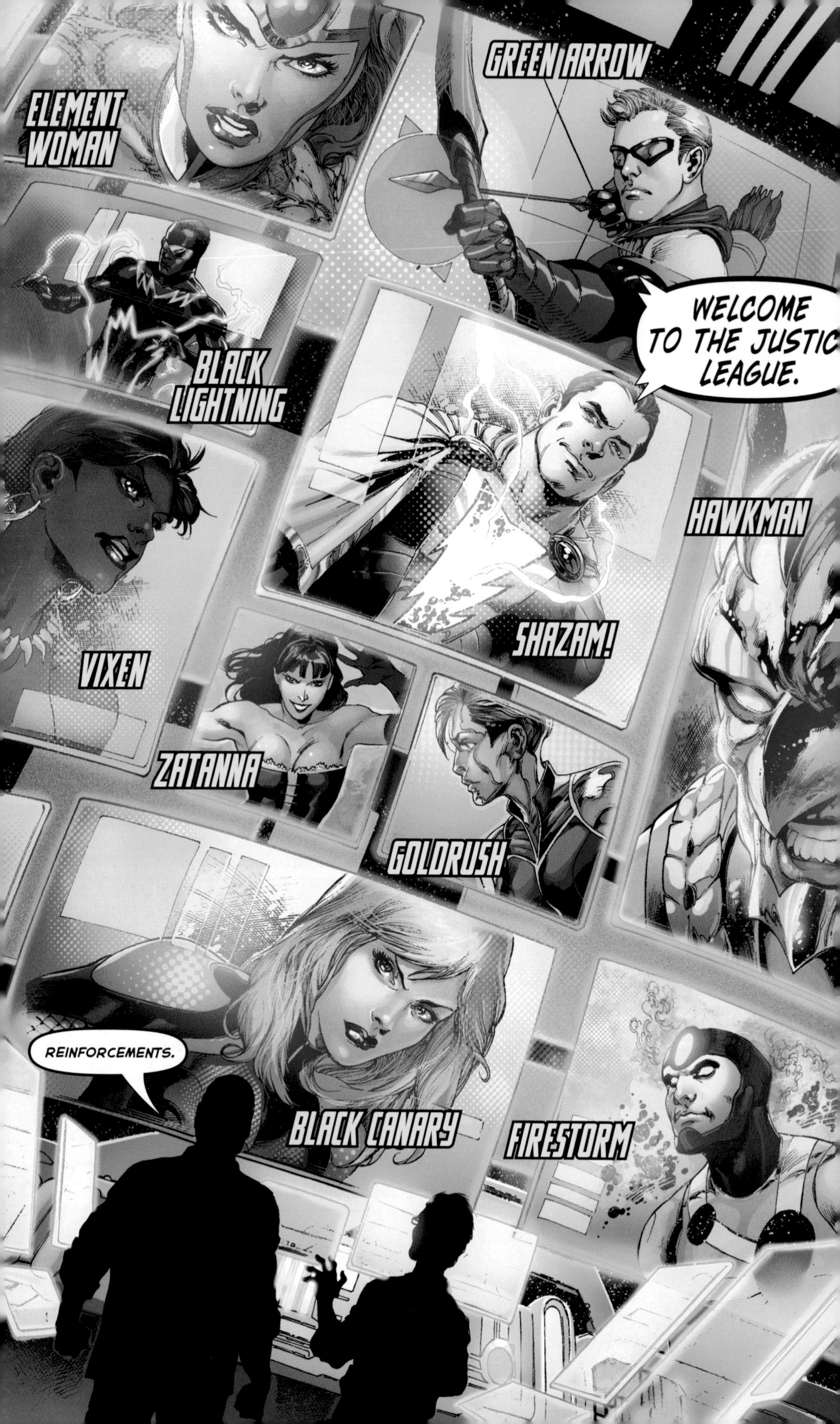
ELEMENT WOMAN
GREEN ARROW
BLACK LIGHTNING
WELCOME TO THE JUSTIC LEAGUE.
HAWKMAN
VIXEN
SHAZAM!
ZATANNA
GOLDRUSH
REINFORCEMENTS.
BLACK CANARY
FIRESTORM

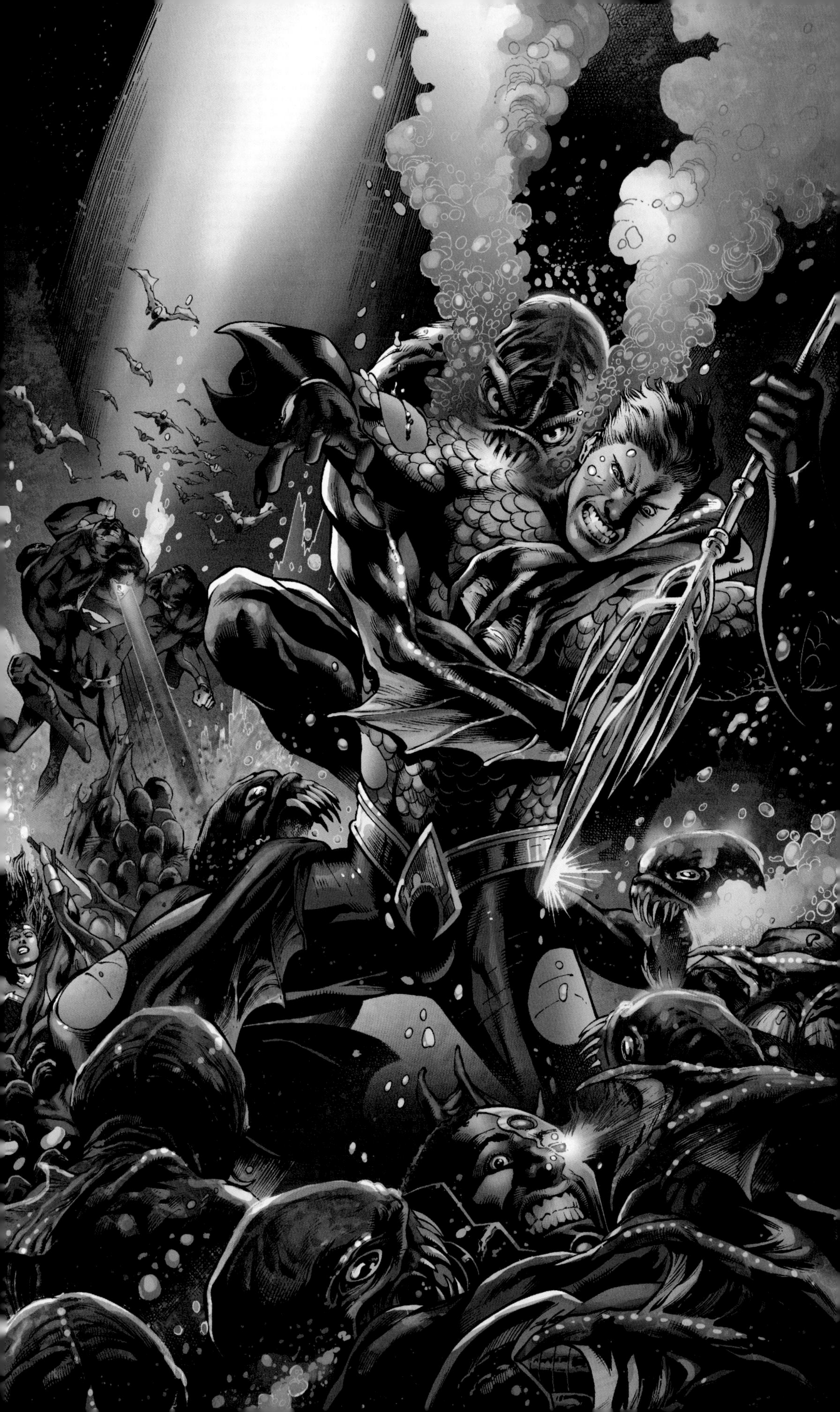

GEOFF JOHNS writer PAUL PELLETIER penciller SEAN PARSONS inker cover by PAUL PELLETIER, ART THIBERT & ROD REIS

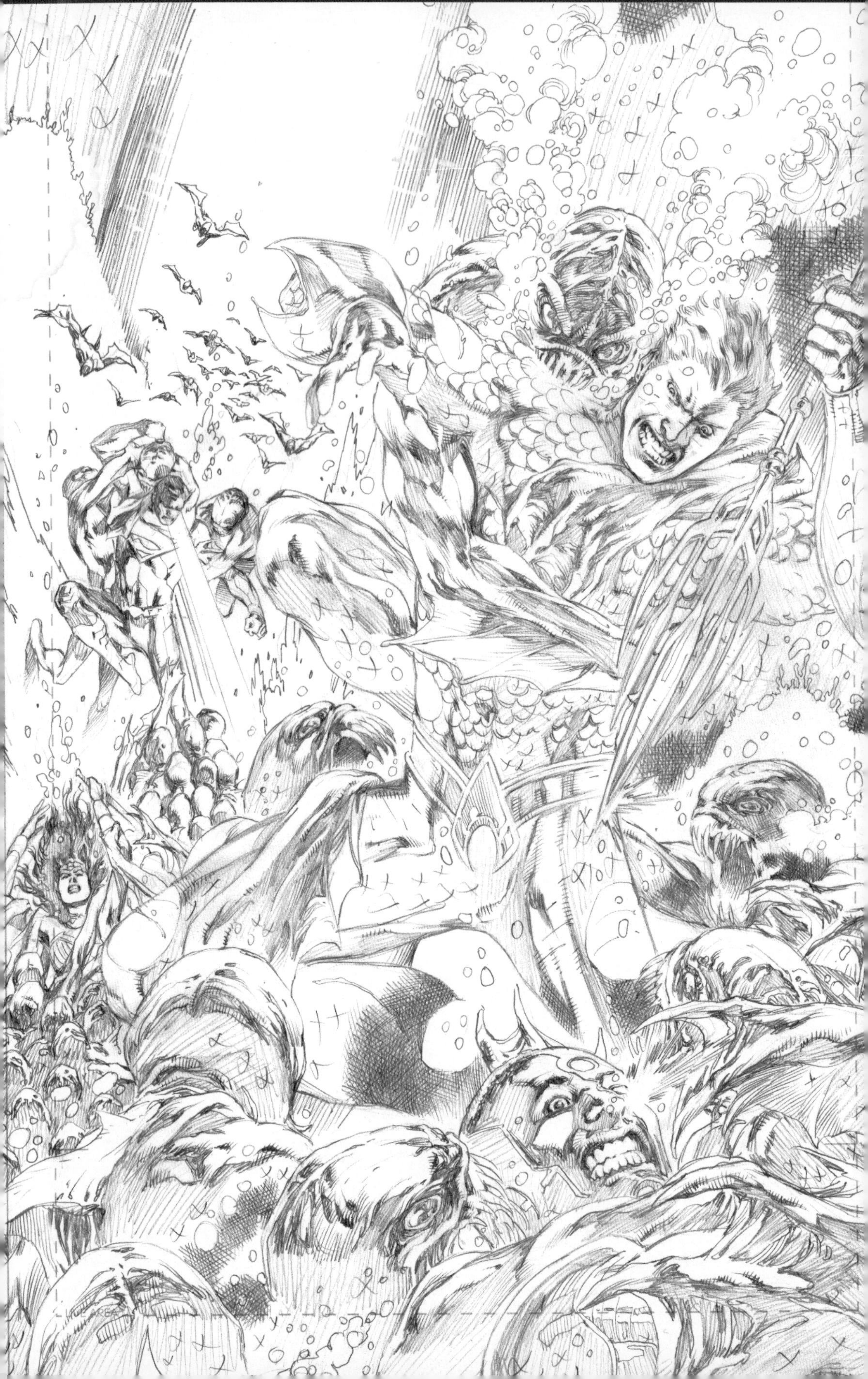

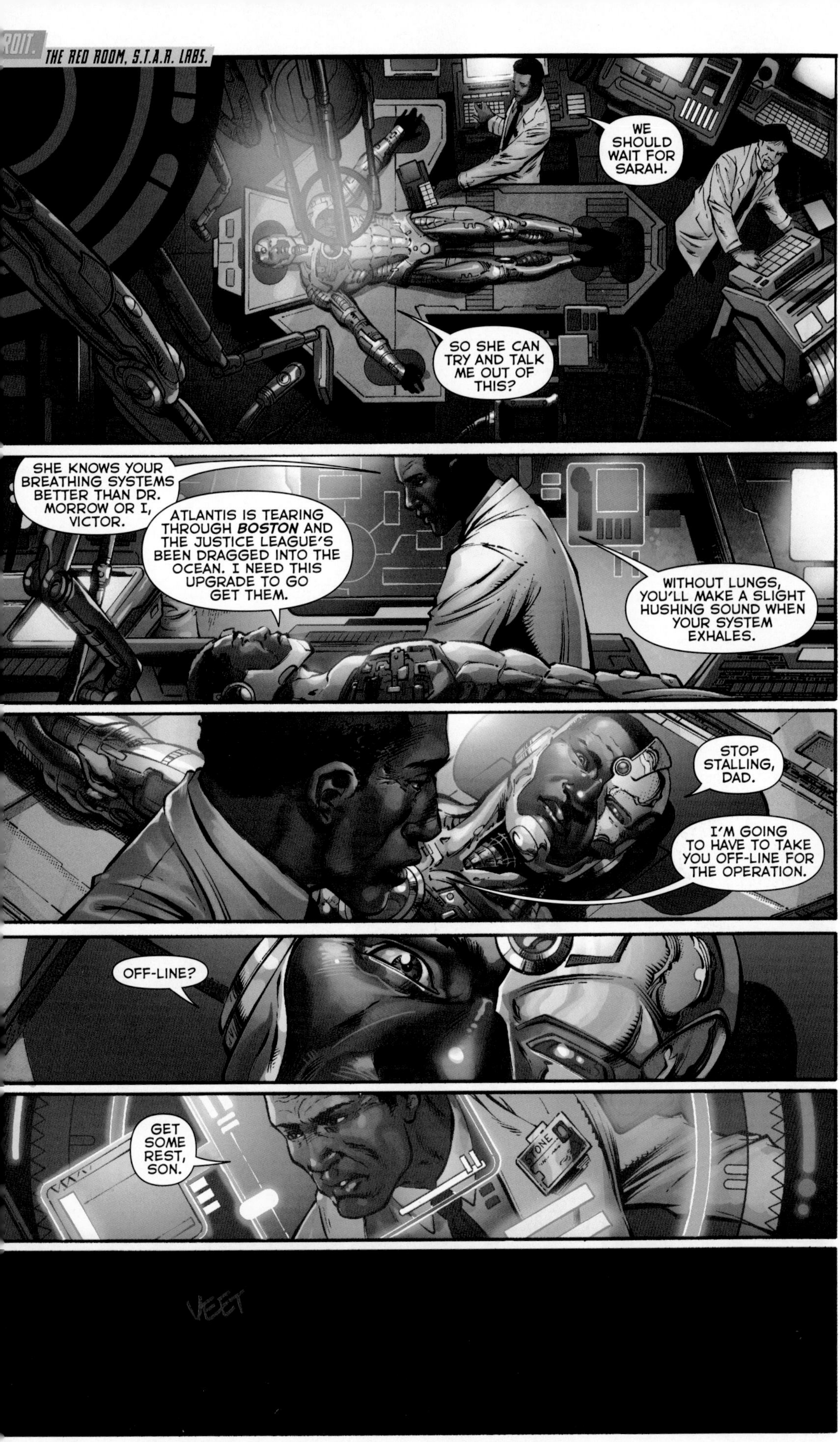

ROIT.
THE RED ROOM, S.T.A.R. LABS.
WE SHOULD WAIT FOR SARAH.
SO SHE CAN TRY AND TALK ME OUT OF THIS?
SHE KNOWS YOUR BREATHING SYSTEMS BETTER THAN DR. MORROW OR I, VICTOR.
ATLANTIS IS TEARING THROUGH BOSTON AND THE JUSTICE LEAGUE'S BEEN DRAGGED INTO THE OCEAN. I NEED THIS UPGRADE TO GO GET THEM.
WITHOUT LUNGS, YOU'LL MAKE A SLIGHT HUSHING SOUND WHEN YOUR SYSTEM EXHALES.
STOP STALLING, DAD.
I'M GOING TO HAVE TO TAKE YOU OFF-LINE FOR THE OPERATION.
OFF-LINE?
GET SOME REST, SON.
STONE
VEET

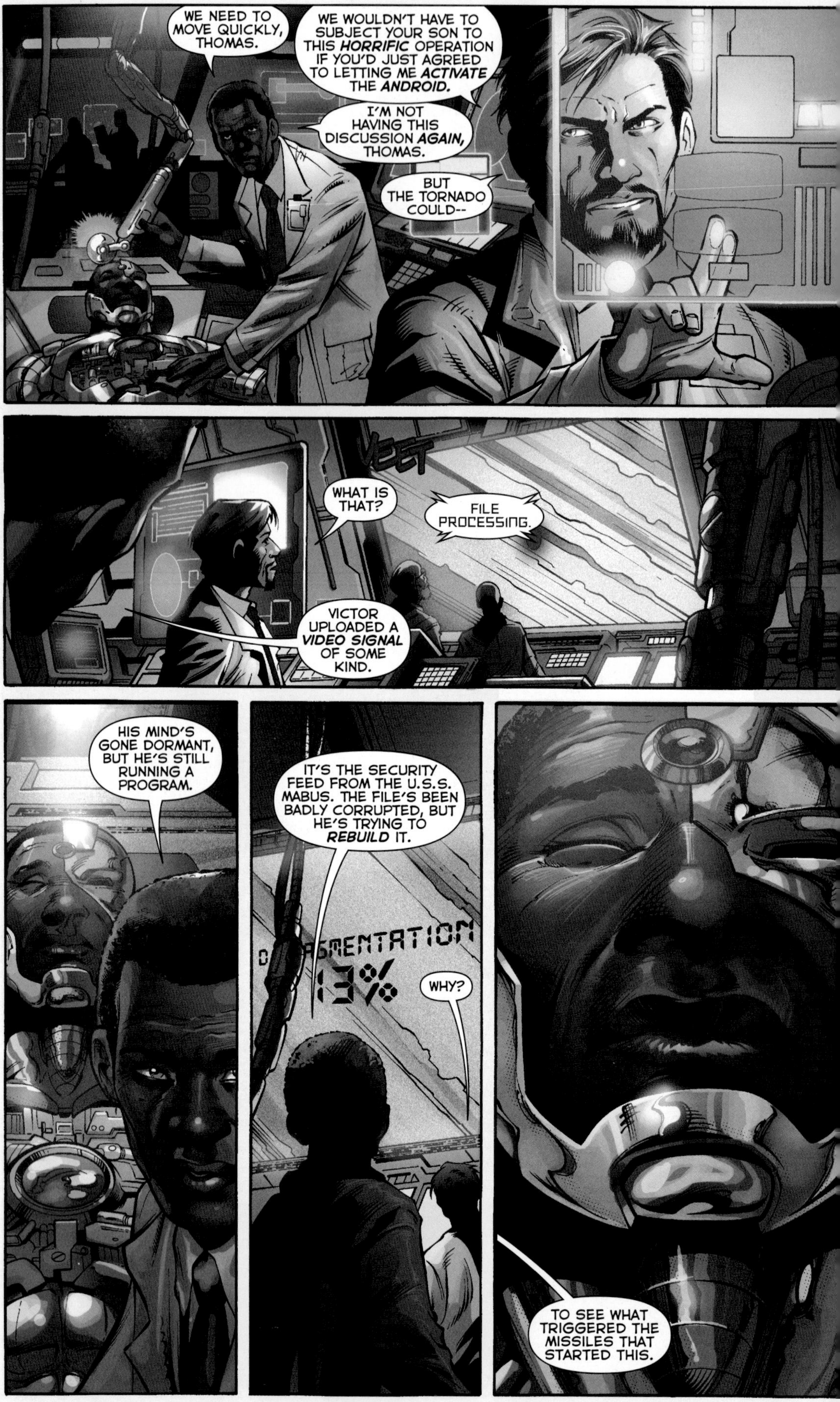
WE NEED TO MOVE QUICKLY, THOMAS.
WE WOULDN'T HAVE TO SUBJECT YOUR SON TO THIS HORRIFIC OPERATION IF YOU'D JUST AGREED TO LETTING ME ACTIVATE THE ANDROID.
I'M NOT HAVING THIS DISCUSSION AGAIN, THOMAS.
BUT THE TORNADO COULD--
WHAT IS THAT?
FILE PROCESSING.
VICTOR UPLOADED A VIDEO SIGNAL OF SOME KIND.
HIS MIND'S GONE DORMANT, BUT HE'S STILL RUNNING A PROGRAM.
IT'S THE SECURITY FEED FROM THE U.S.S. MABUS. THE FILE'S BEEN BADLY CORRUPTED, BUT HE'S TRYING TO REBUILD IT.
13%
WHY?
TO SEE WHAT TRIGGERED THE MISSILES THAT STARTED THIS.

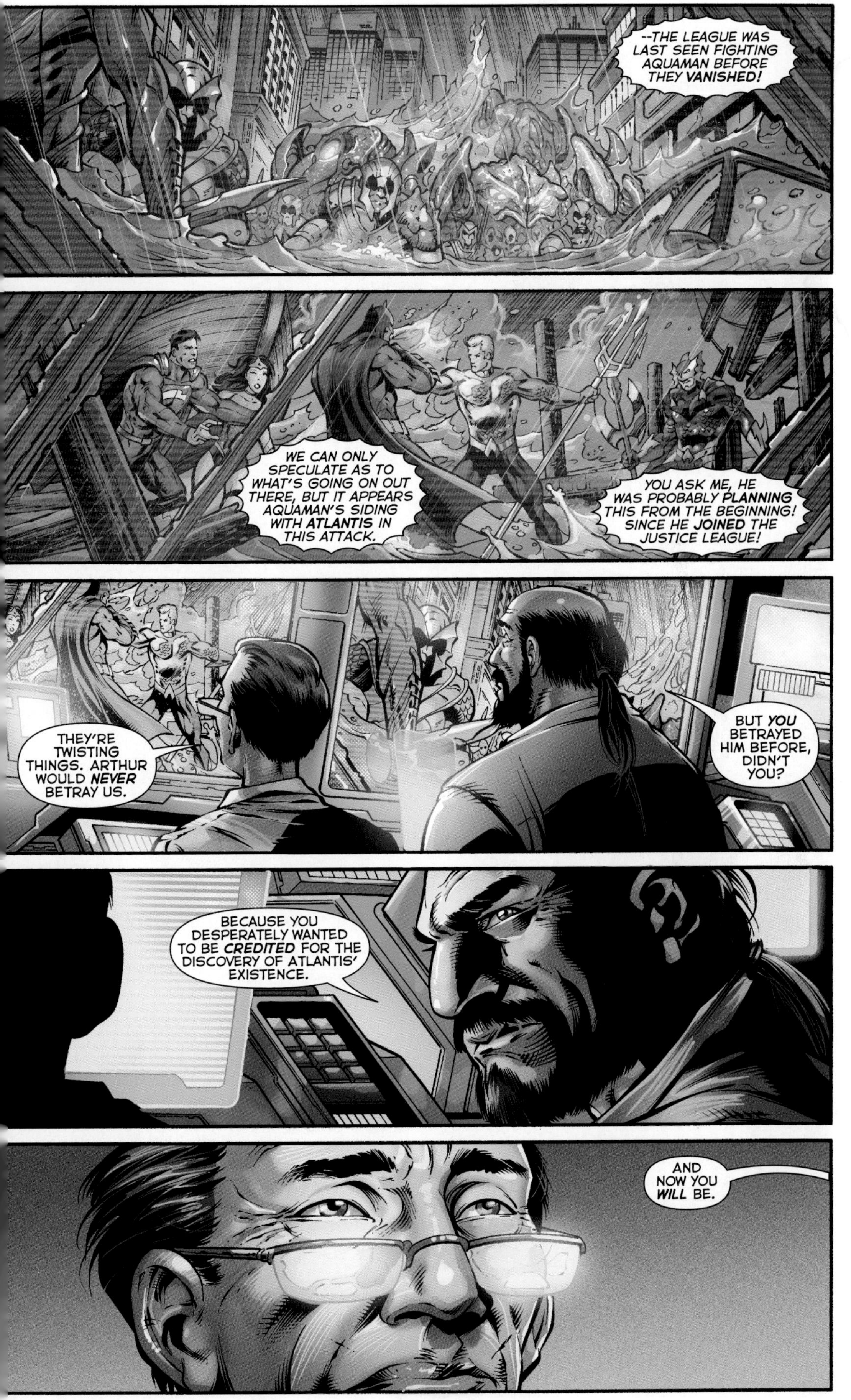
--THE LEAGUE WAS LAST SEEN FIGHTING AQUAMAN BEFORE THEY VANISHED!
WE CAN ONLY SPECULATE AS TO WHAT'S GOING ON OUT THERE, BUT IT APPEARS AQUAMAN'S SIDING WITH ATLANTIS IN THIS ATTACK.
YOU ASK ME, HE WAS PROBABLY PLANNING THIS FROM THE BEGINNING! SINCE HE JOINED THE JUSTICE LEAGUE!
THEY'RE TWISTING THINGS. ARTHUR WOULD NEVER BETRAY US.
BUT YOU BETRAYED HIM BEFORE, DIDN'T YOU?
BECAUSE YOU DESPERATELY WANTED TO BE CREDITED FOR THE DISCOVERY OF ATLANTIS' EXISTENCE.
AND NOW YOU WILL BE.

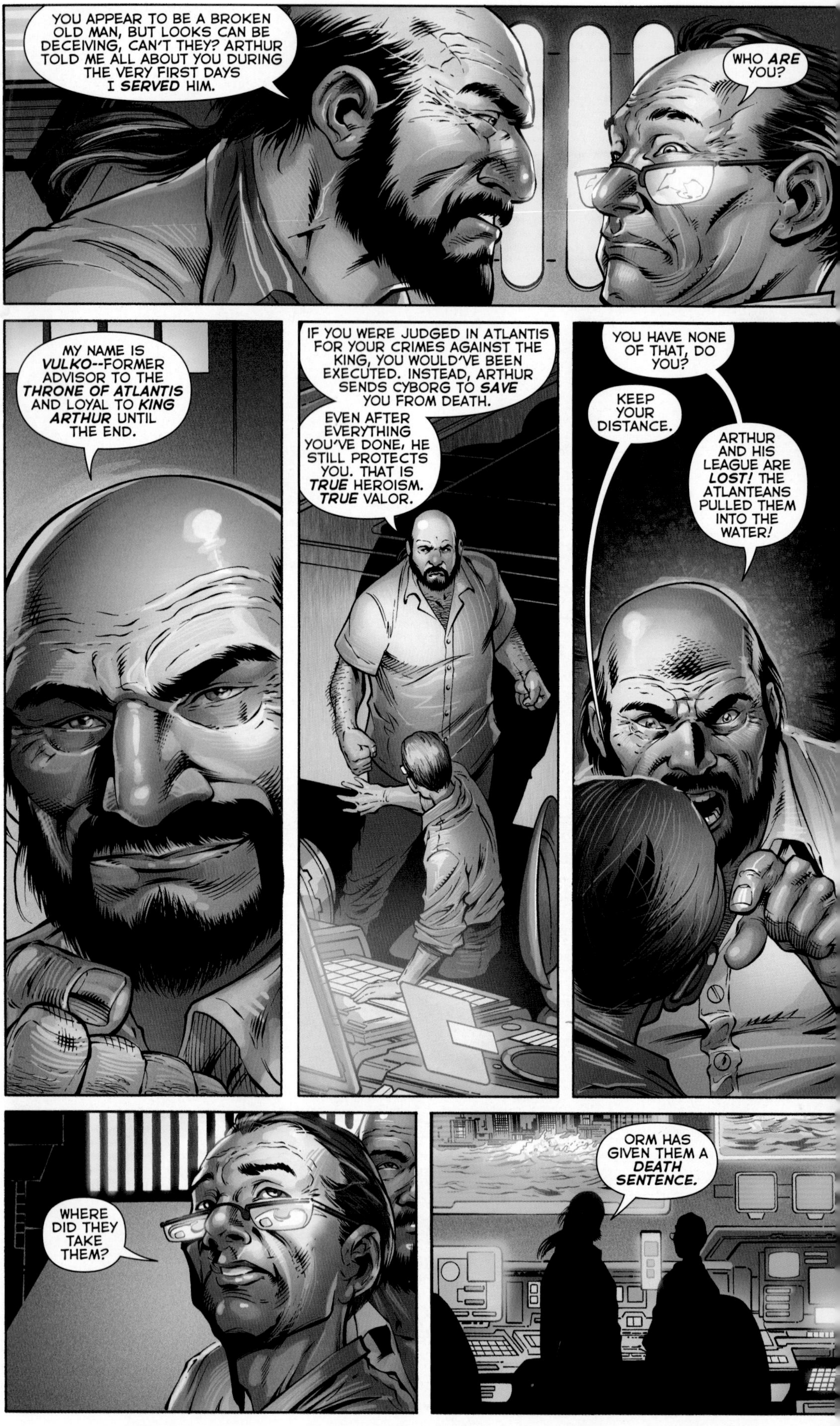
YOU APPEAR TO BE A BROKEN OLD MAN, BUT LOOKS CAN BE DECEIVING, CAN'T THEY? ARTHUR TOLD ME ALL ABOUT YOU DURING THE VERY FIRST DAYS I *SERVED* HIM.
WHO *ARE* YOU?
MY NAME IS *VULKO*--FORMER ADVISOR TO THE *THRONE OF ATLANTIS* AND LOYAL TO *KING ARTHUR* UNTIL THE END.
IF YOU WERE JUDGED IN ATLANTIS FOR YOUR CRIMES AGAINST THE KING, YOU WOULD'VE BEEN EXECUTED. INSTEAD, ARTHUR SENDS CYBORG TO *SAVE* YOU FROM DEATH.
EVEN AFTER EVERYTHING YOU'VE DONE, HE STILL PROTECTS YOU. THAT IS *TRUE* HEROISM. *TRUE* VALOR.
YOU HAVE NONE OF THAT, DO YOU?
KEEP YOUR DISTANCE.
ARTHUR AND HIS LEAGUE ARE *LOST!* THE ATLANTEANS PULLED THEM INTO THE WATER!
WHERE DID THEY TAKE THEM?
ORM HAS GIVEN THEM A *DEATH SENTENCE.*

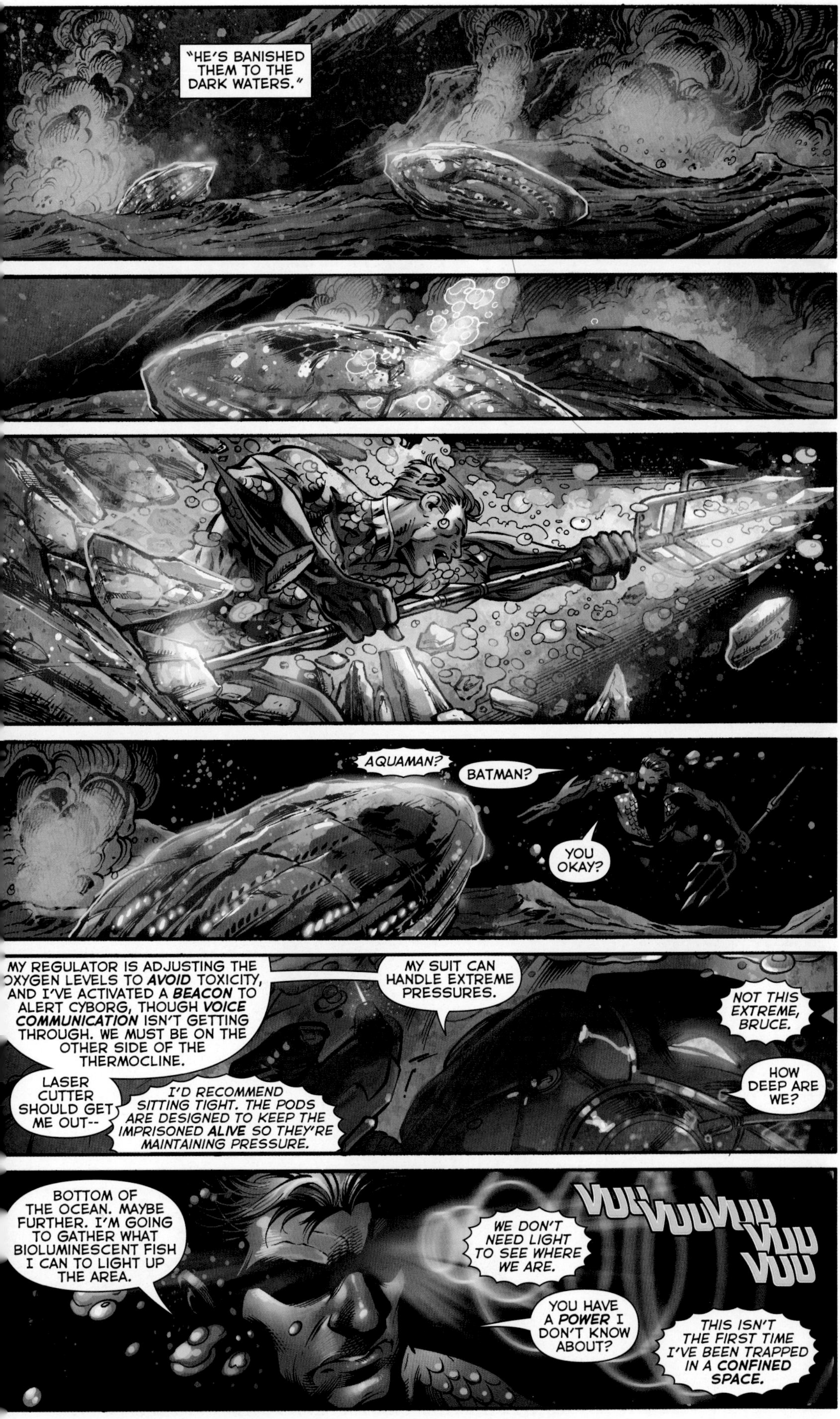
"HE'S BANISHED THEM TO THE DARK WATERS."
AQUAMAN?
BATMAN?
YOU OKAY?
MY REGULATOR IS ADJUSTING THE OXYGEN LEVELS TO AVOID TOXICITY, AND I'VE ACTIVATED A BEACON TO ALERT CYBORG, THOUGH VOICE COMMUNICATION ISN'T GETTING THROUGH. WE MUST BE ON THE OTHER SIDE OF THE THERMOCLINE.
MY SUIT CAN HANDLE EXTREME PRESSURES.
NOT THIS EXTREME, BRUCE.
LASER CUTTER SHOULD GET ME OUT--
I'D RECOMMEND SITTING TIGHT. THE PODS ARE DESIGNED TO KEEP THE IMPRISONED ALIVE SO THEY'RE MAINTAINING PRESSURE.
HOW DEEP ARE WE?
BOTTOM OF THE OCEAN. MAYBE FURTHER. I'M GOING TO GATHER WHAT BIOLUMINESCENT FISH I CAN TO LIGHT UP THE AREA.
VUU VUUVUU VUU VUU
WE DON'T NEED LIGHT TO SEE WHERE WE ARE.
YOU HAVE A POWER I DON'T KNOW ABOUT?
THIS ISN'T THE FIRST TIME I'VE BEEN TRAPPED IN A CONFINED SPACE.

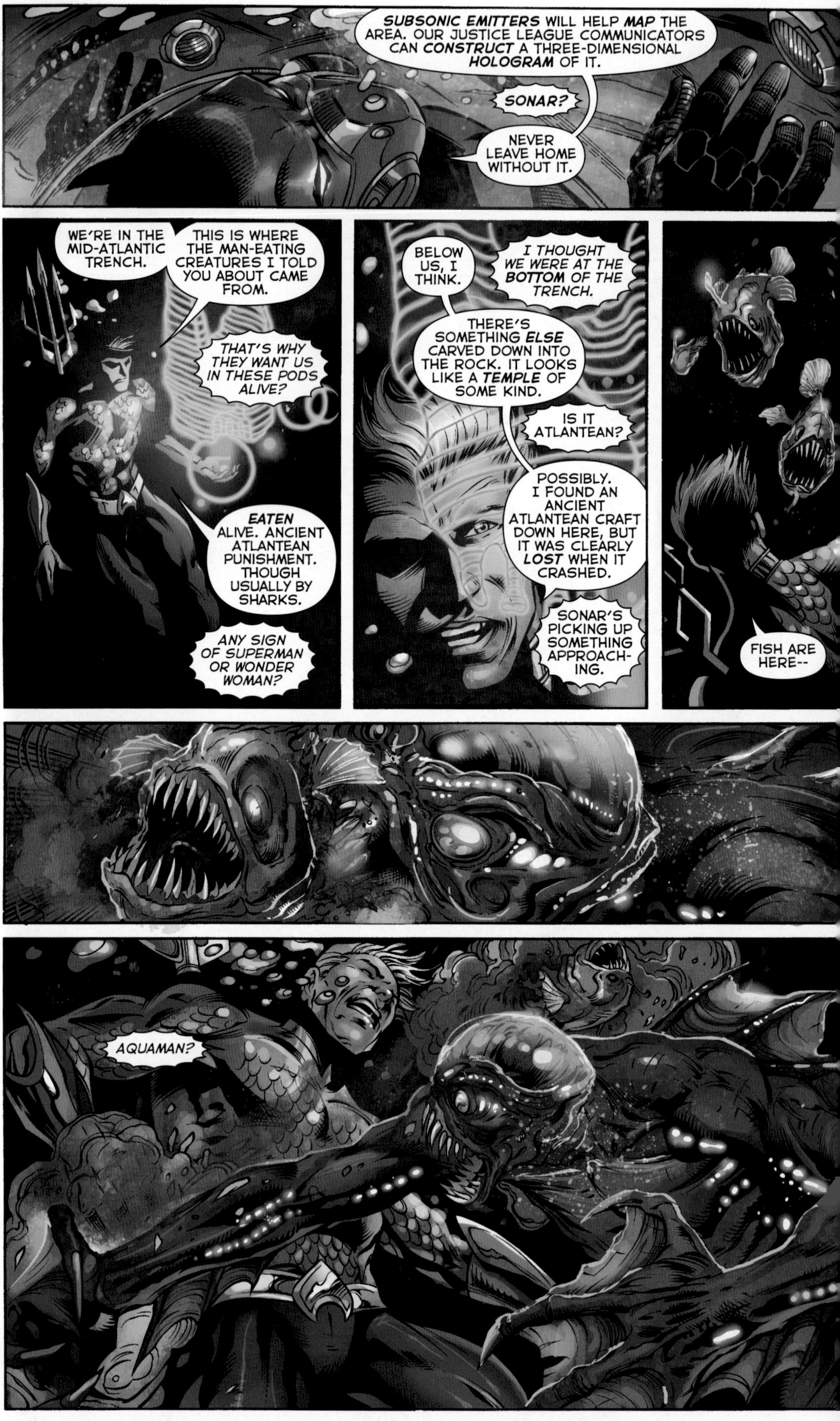
SUBSONIC EMITTERS WILL HELP MAP THE AREA. OUR JUSTICE LEAGUE COMMUNICATORS CAN CONSTRUCT A THREE-DIMENSIONAL HOLOGRAM OF IT.
SONAR?
NEVER LEAVE HOME WITHOUT IT.
WE'RE IN THE MID-ATLANTIC TRENCH.
THIS IS WHERE THE MAN-EATING CREATURES I TOLD YOU ABOUT CAME FROM.
THAT'S WHY THEY WANT US IN THESE PODS ALIVE?
EATEN ALIVE. ANCIENT ATLANTEAN PUNISHMENT. THOUGH USUALLY BY SHARKS.
ANY SIGN OF SUPERMAN OR WONDER WOMAN?
BELOW US, I THINK.
I THOUGHT WE WERE AT THE BOTTOM OF THE TRENCH.
THERE'S SOMETHING ELSE CARVED DOWN INTO THE ROCK. IT LOOKS LIKE A TEMPLE OF SOME KIND.
IS IT ATLANTEAN?
POSSIBLY. I FOUND AN ANCIENT ATLANTEAN CRAFT DOWN HERE, BUT IT WAS CLEARLY LOST WHEN IT CRASHED.
SONAR'S PICKING UP SOMETHING APPROACH-ING.
FISH ARE HERE--
AQUAMAN?

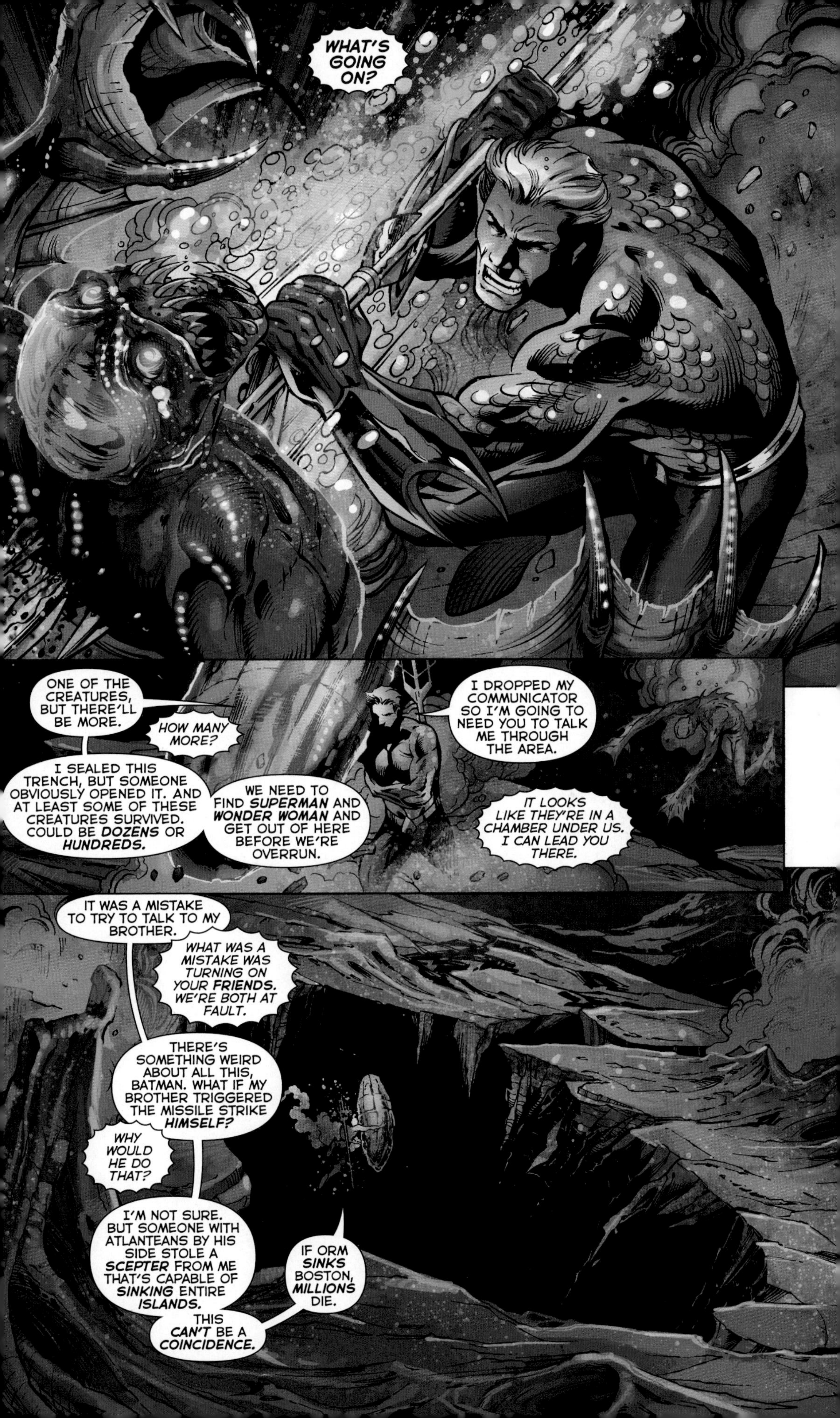
WHAT'S GOING ON?
ONE OF THE CREATURES, BUT THERE'LL BE MORE.
HOW MANY MORE?
I SEALED THIS TRENCH, BUT SOMEONE OBVIOUSLY OPENED IT. AND AT LEAST SOME OF THESE CREATURES SURVIVED. COULD BE DOZENS OR HUNDREDS.
WE NEED TO FIND SUPERMAN AND WONDER WOMAN AND GET OUT OF HERE BEFORE WE'RE OVERRUN.
I DROPPED MY COMMUNICATOR SO I'M GOING TO NEED YOU TO TALK ME THROUGH THE AREA.
IT LOOKS LIKE THEY'RE IN A CHAMBER UNDER US. I CAN LEAD YOU THERE.
IT WAS A MISTAKE TO TRY TO TALK TO MY BROTHER.
WHAT WAS A MISTAKE WAS TURNING ON YOUR FRIENDS. WE'RE BOTH AT FAULT.
THERE'S SOMETHING WEIRD ABOUT ALL THIS, BATMAN. WHAT IF MY BROTHER TRIGGERED THE MISSILE STRIKE HIMSELF?
WHY WOULD HE DO THAT?
I'M NOT SURE. BUT SOMEONE WITH ATLANTEANS BY HIS SIDE STOLE A SCEPTER FROM ME THAT'S CAPABLE OF SINKING ENTIRE ISLANDS.
IF ORM SINKS BOSTON, MILLIONS DIE.
THIS CAN'T BE A COINCIDENCE.

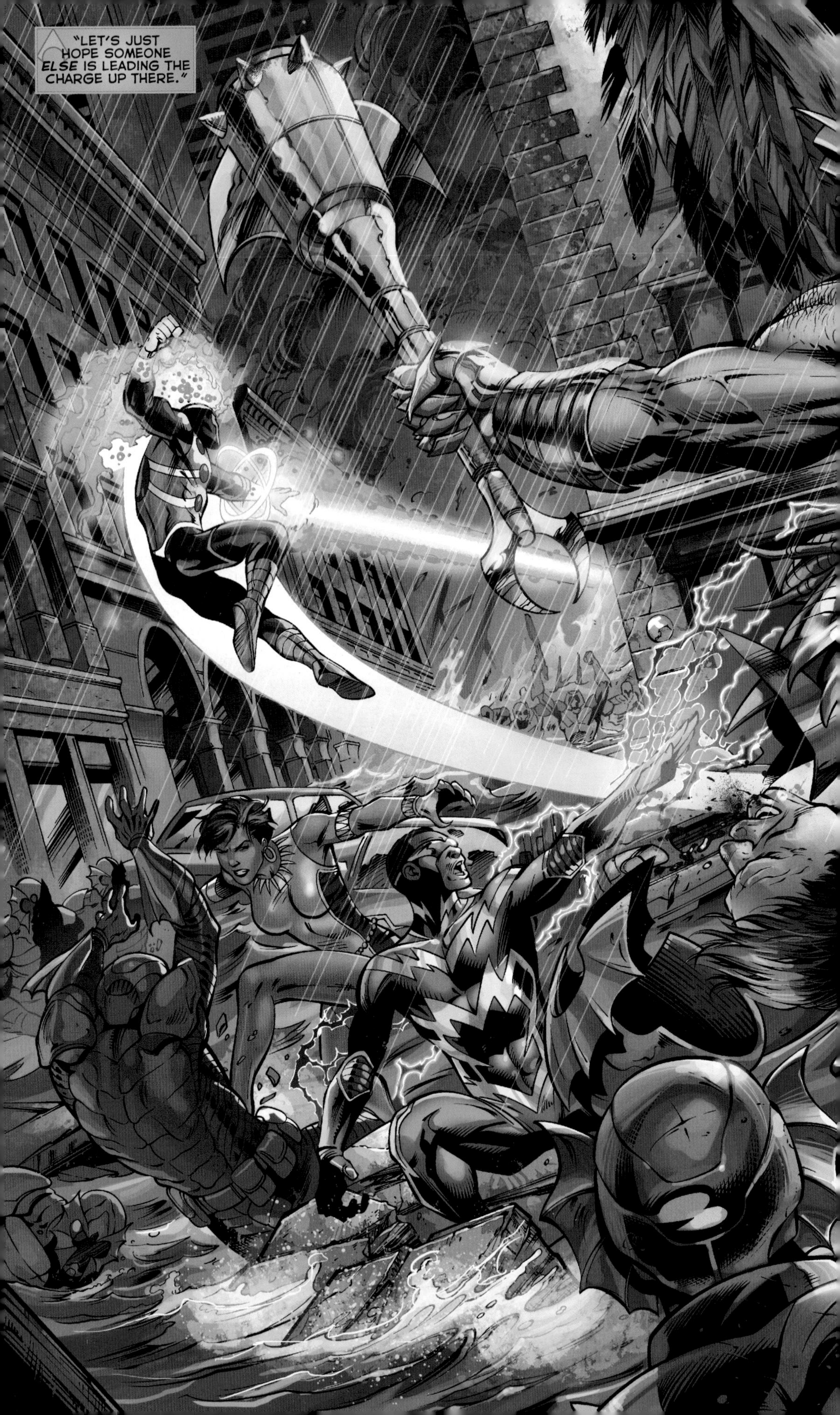
"LET'S JUST HOPE SOMEONE *ELSE* IS LEADING THE CHARGE UP THERE."

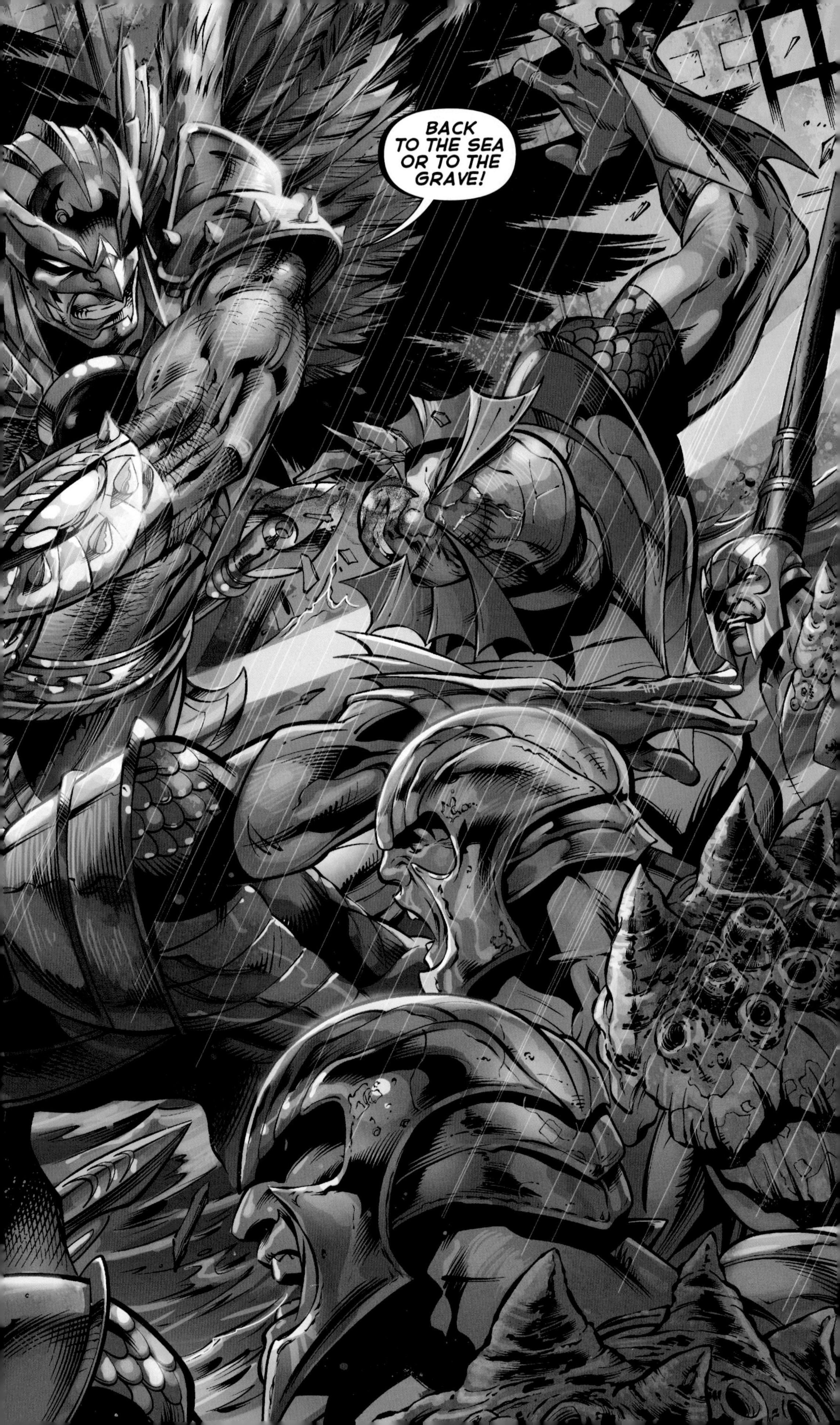
BACK TO THE SEA OR TO THE GRAVE!

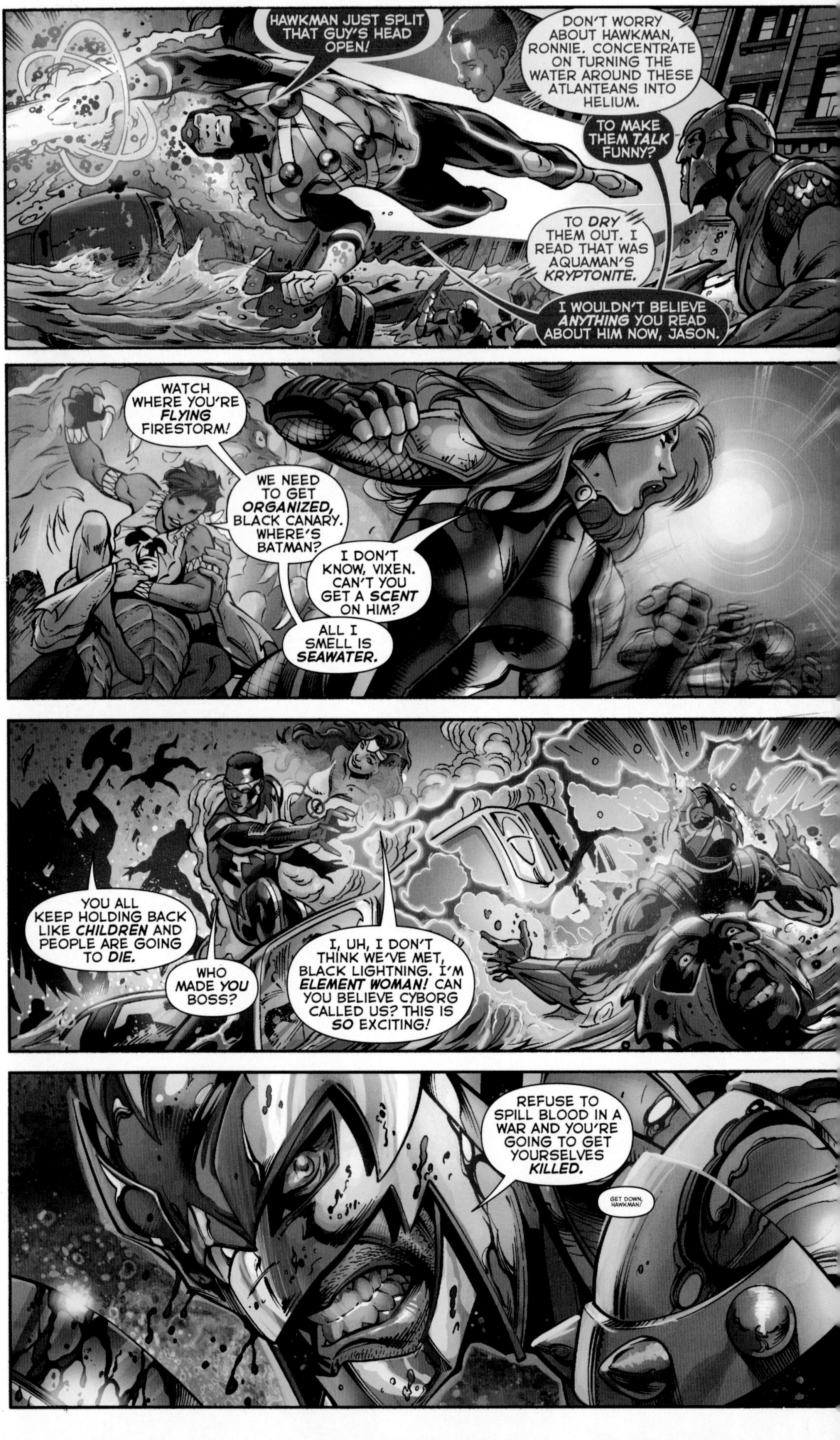
HAWKMAN JUST SPLIT THAT GUY'S HEAD OPEN!
DON'T WORRY ABOUT HAWKMAN, RONNIE. CONCENTRATE ON TURNING THE WATER AROUND THESE ATLANTEANS INTO HELIUM.
TO MAKE THEM TALK FUNNY?
TO DRY THEM OUT. I READ THAT WAS AQUAMAN'S KRYPTONITE.
I WOULDN'T BELIEVE ANYTHING YOU READ ABOUT HIM NOW, JASON.
WATCH WHERE YOU'RE FLYING FIRESTORM!
WE NEED TO GET ORGANIZED, BLACK CANARY. WHERE'S BATMAN?
I DON'T KNOW, VIXEN. CAN'T YOU GET A SCENT ON HIM?
ALL I SMELL IS SEAWATER.
YOU ALL KEEP HOLDING BACK LIKE CHILDREN AND PEOPLE ARE GOING TO DIE.
WHO MADE YOU BOSS?
I, UH, I DON'T THINK WE'VE MET, BLACK LIGHTNING. I'M ELEMENT WOMAN! CAN YOU BELIEVE CYBORG CALLED US? THIS IS SO EXCITING!
REFUSE TO SPILL BLOOD IN A WAR AND YOU'RE GOING TO GET YOURSELVES KILLED.
GET DOWN, HAWKMAN!

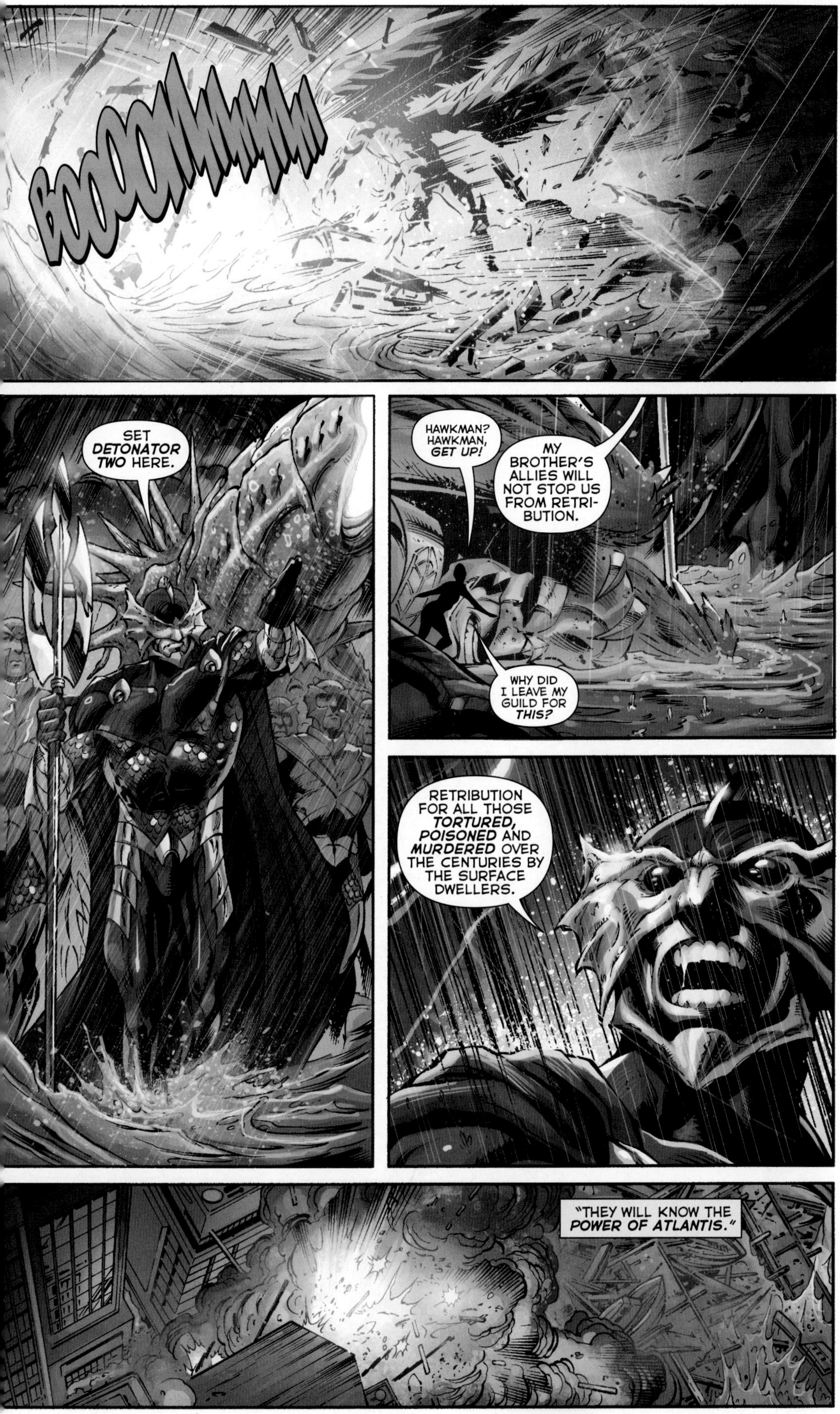
BOOOOMMMMM
SET DETONATOR TWO HERE.
HAWKMAN? HAWKMAN, GET UP!
MY BROTHER'S ALLIES WILL NOT STOP US FROM RETRIBUTION.
WHY DID I LEAVE MY GUILD FOR THIS?
RETRIBUTION FOR ALL THOSE TORTURED, POISONED AND MURDERED OVER THE CENTURIES BY THE SURFACE DWELLERS.
"THEY WILL KNOW THE POWER OF ATLANTIS."

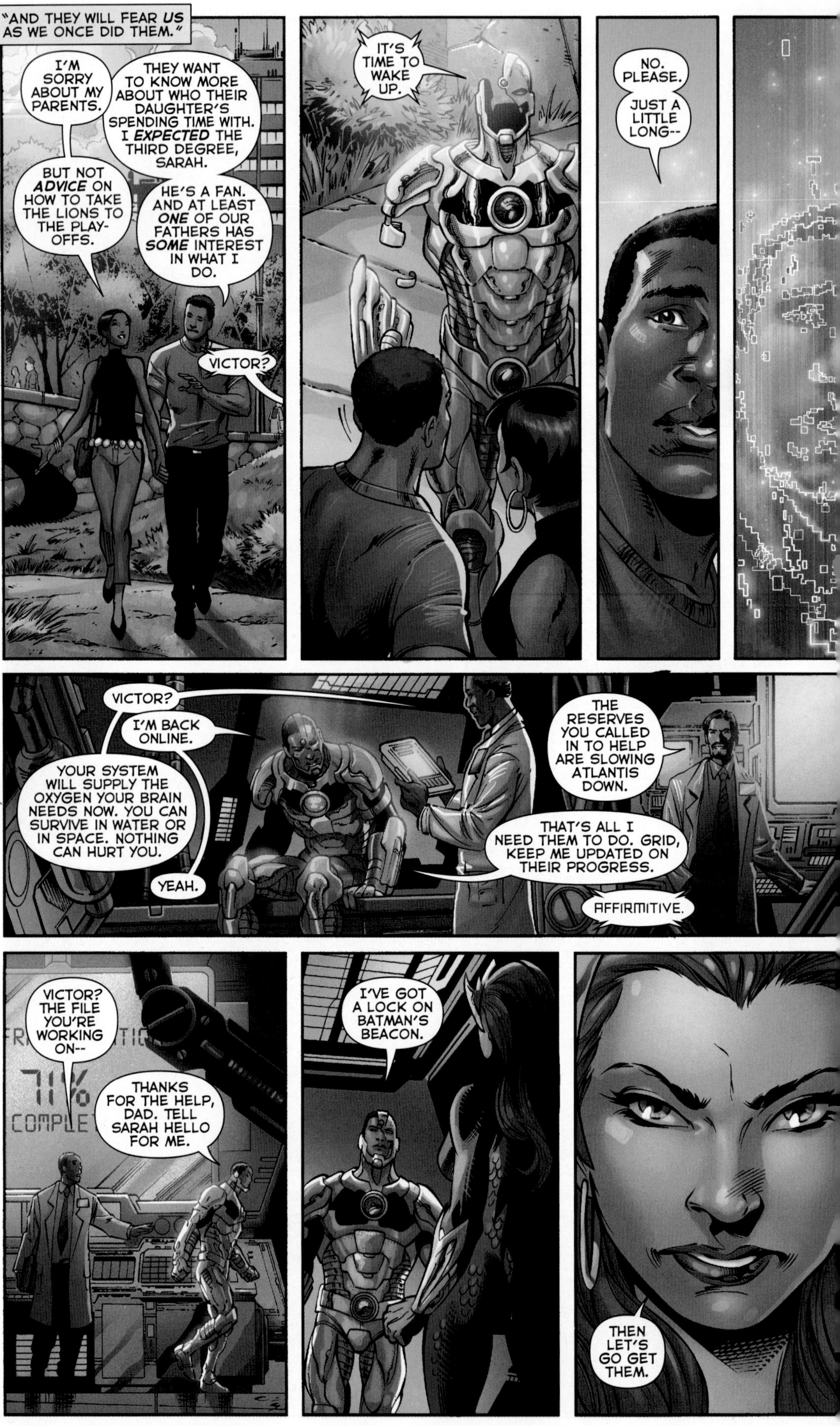
"AND THEY WILL FEAR US AS WE ONCE DID THEM."
I'M SORRY ABOUT MY PARENTS.
THEY WANT TO KNOW MORE ABOUT WHO THEIR DAUGHTER'S SPENDING TIME WITH. I EXPECTED THE THIRD DEGREE, SARAH.
BUT NOT ADVICE ON HOW TO TAKE THE LIONS TO THE PLAY-OFFS.
HE'S A FAN. AND AT LEAST ONE OF OUR FATHERS HAS SOME INTEREST IN WHAT I DO.
VICTOR?
IT'S TIME TO WAKE UP.
NO. PLEASE.
JUST A LITTLE LONG--
VICTOR?
I'M BACK ONLINE.
YOUR SYSTEM WILL SUPPLY THE OXYGEN YOUR BRAIN NEEDS NOW. YOU CAN SURVIVE IN WATER OR IN SPACE. NOTHING CAN HURT YOU.
YEAH.
THE RESERVES YOU CALLED IN TO HELP ARE SLOWING ATLANTIS DOWN.
THAT'S ALL I NEED THEM TO DO. GRID, KEEP ME UPDATED ON THEIR PROGRESS.
AFFIRMITIVE.
VICTOR? THE FILE YOU'RE WORKING ON--
71%
THANKS FOR THE HELP, DAD. TELL SARAH HELLO FOR ME.
I'VE GOT A LOCK ON BATMAN'S BEACON.
THEN LET'S GO GET THEM.

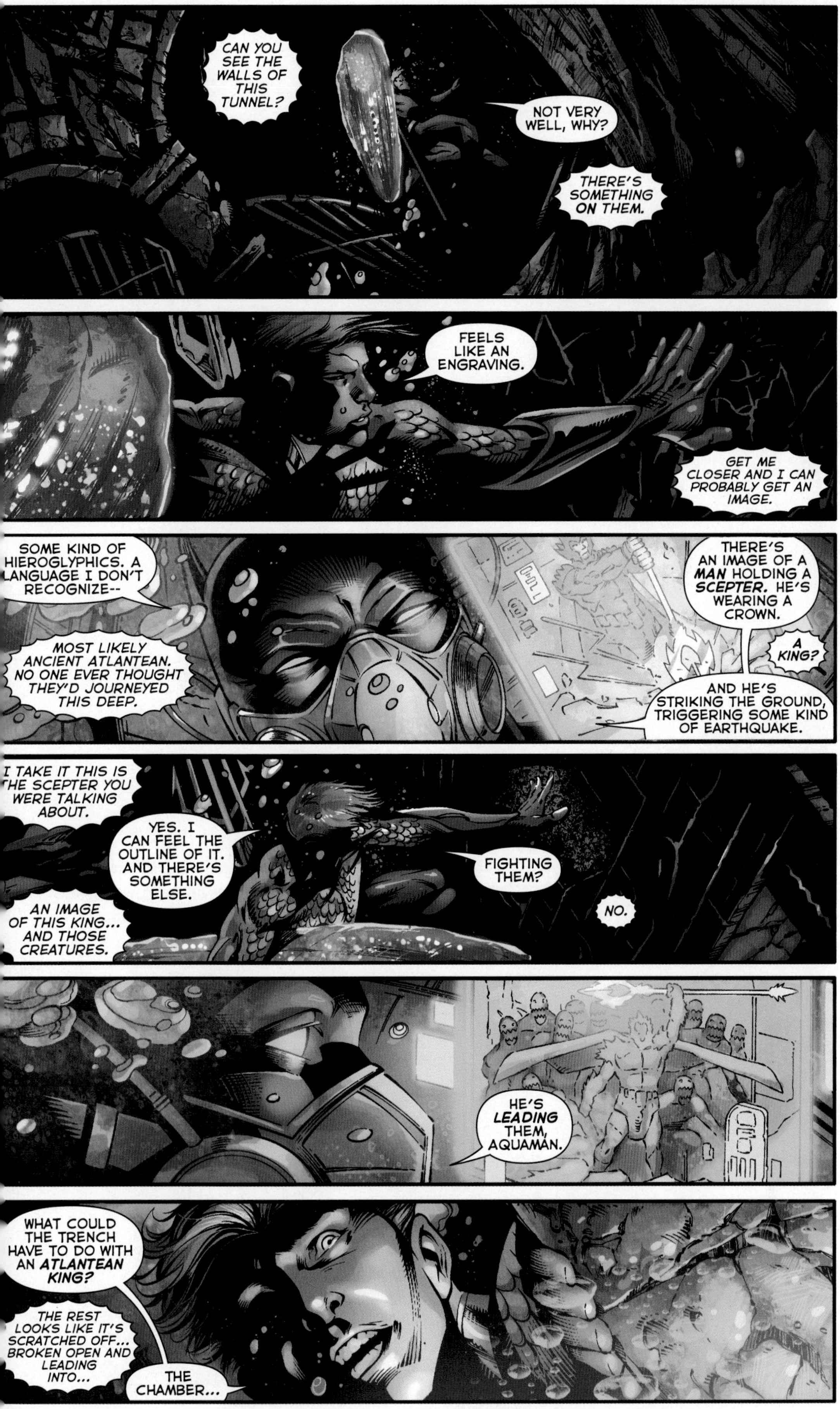
CAN YOU SEE THE WALLS OF THIS TUNNEL?
NOT VERY WELL, WHY?
THERE'S SOMETHING ON THEM.
FEELS LIKE AN ENGRAVING.
GET ME CLOSER AND I CAN PROBABLY GET AN IMAGE.
SOME KIND OF HIEROGLYPHICS. A LANGUAGE I DON'T RECOGNIZE--
MOST LIKELY ANCIENT ATLANTEAN. NO ONE EVER THOUGHT THEY'D JOURNEYED THIS DEEP.
THERE'S AN IMAGE OF A MAN HOLDING A SCEPTER. HE'S WEARING A CROWN.
A KING?
AND HE'S STRIKING THE GROUND, TRIGGERING SOME KIND OF EARTHQUAKE.
I TAKE IT THIS IS THE SCEPTER YOU WERE TALKING ABOUT.
YES. I CAN FEEL THE OUTLINE OF IT. AND THERE'S SOMETHING ELSE.
AN IMAGE OF THIS KING... AND THOSE CREATURES.
FIGHTING THEM?
NO.
HE'S LEADING THEM, AQUAMAN.
WHAT COULD THE TRENCH HAVE TO DO WITH AN ATLANTEAN KING?
THE REST LOOKS LIKE IT'S SCRATCHED OFF... BROKEN OPEN AND LEADING INTO...
THE CHAMBER...

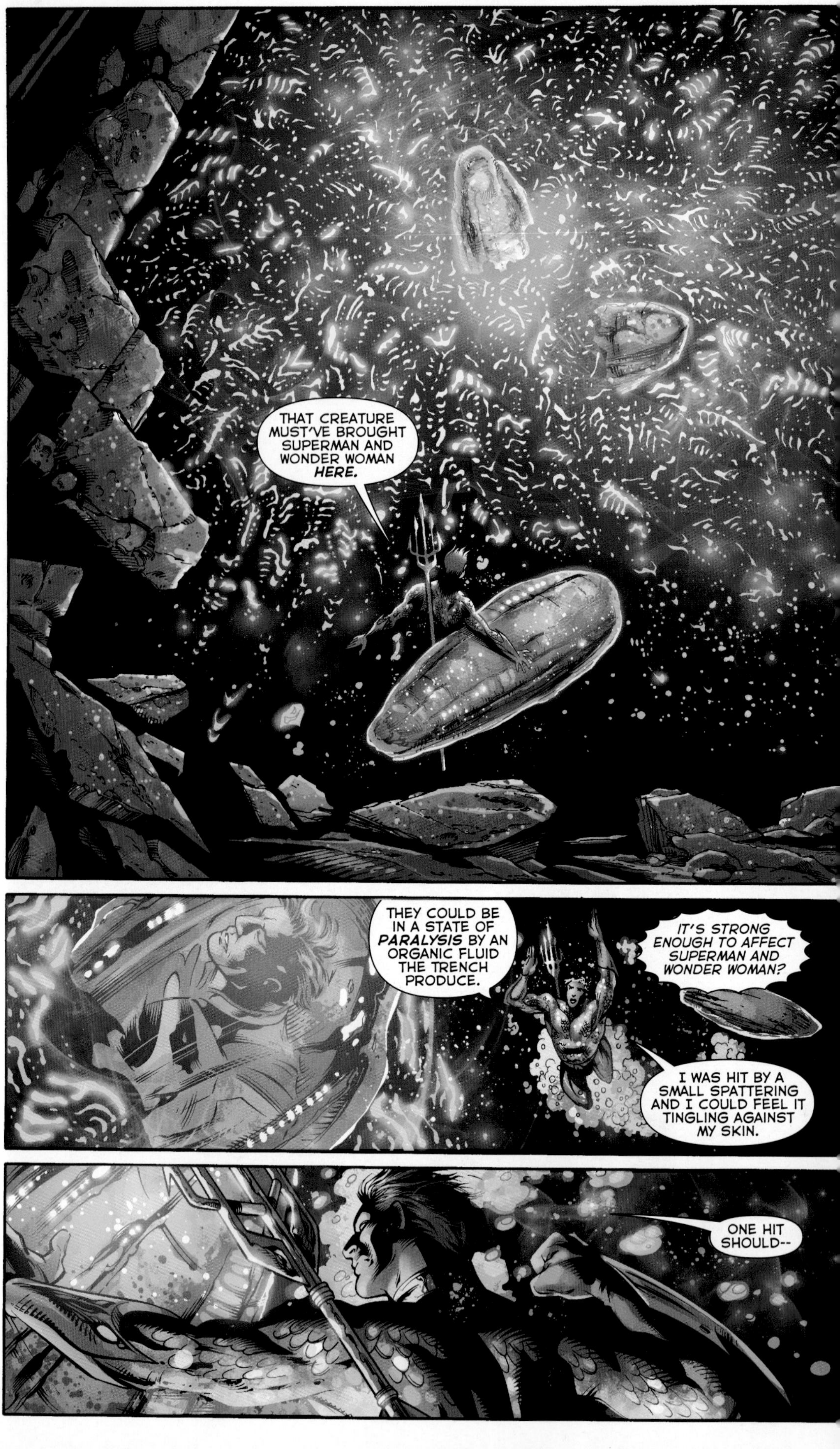
THAT CREATURE MUST'VE BROUGHT SUPERMAN AND WONDER WOMAN *HERE.*
THEY COULD BE IN A STATE OF *PARALYSIS* BY AN ORGANIC FLUID THE TRENCH PRODUCE.
IT'S STRONG ENOUGH TO AFFECT SUPERMAN AND WONDER WOMAN?
I WAS HIT BY A SMALL SPATTERING AND I COULD FEEL IT TINGLING AGAINST MY SKIN.
ONE HIT SHOULD--

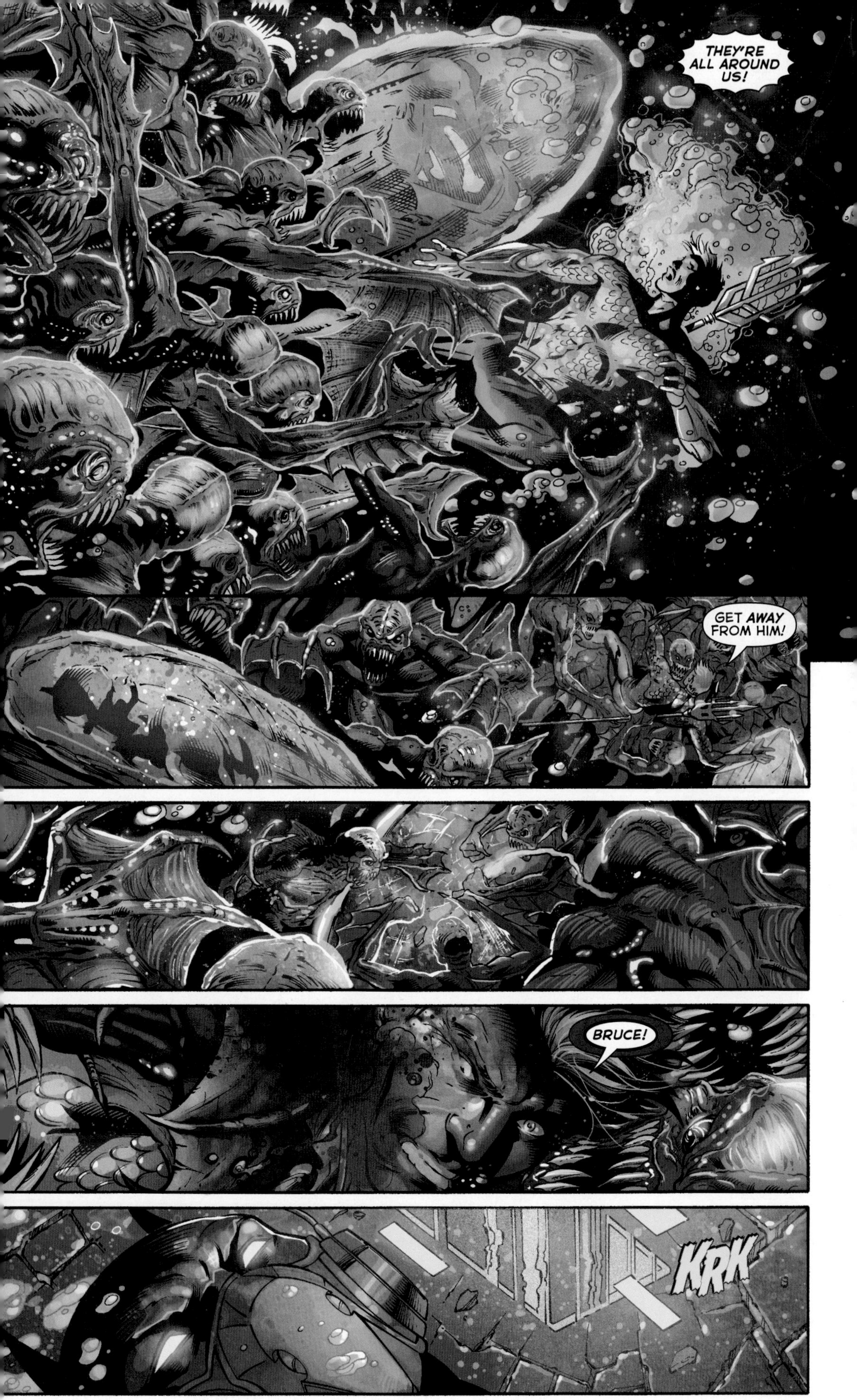
THEY'RE ALL AROUND US!
GET AWAY FROM HIM!
BRUCE!
KRK

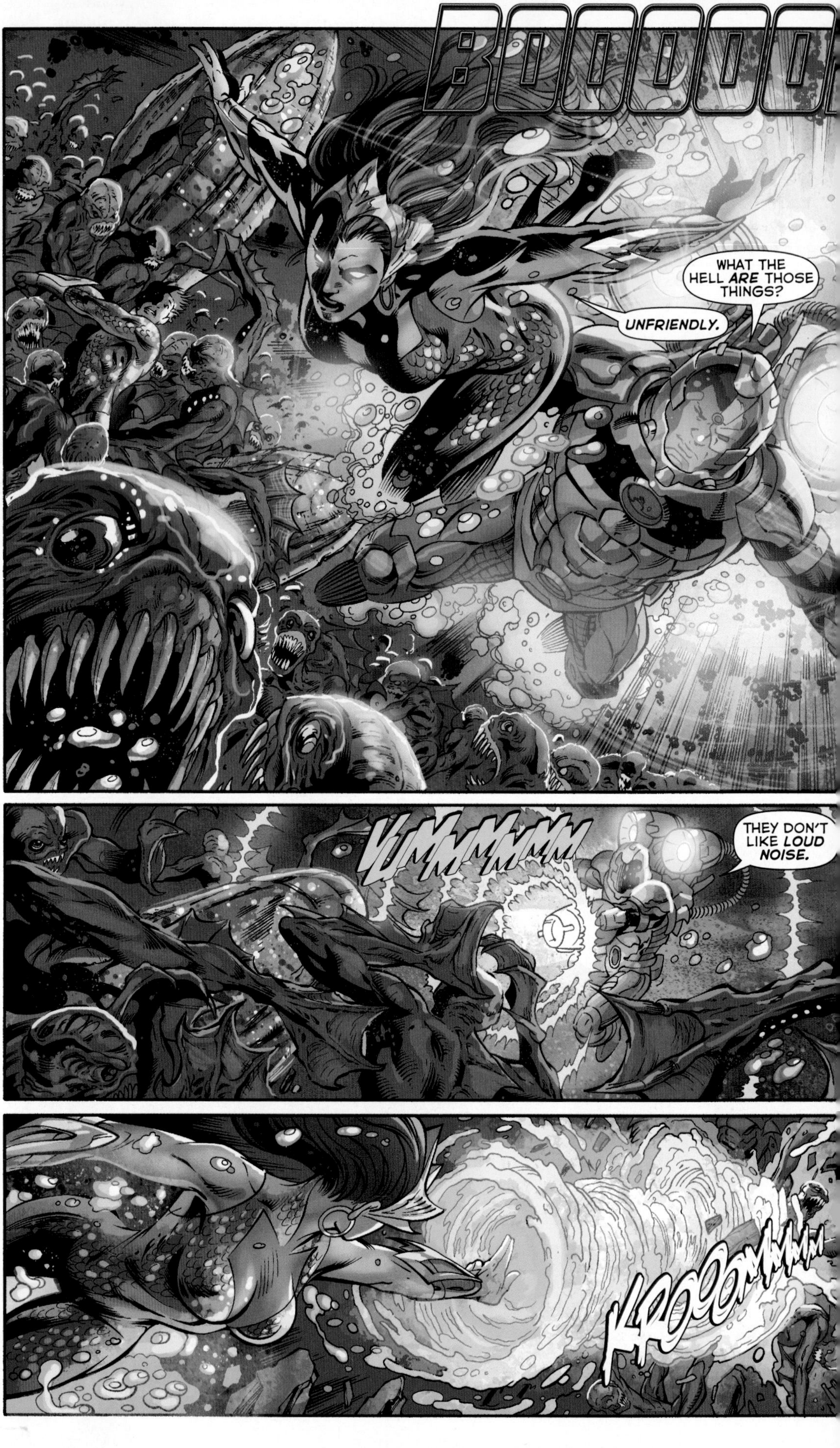
BOOOOOO
WHAT THE HELL ARE THOSE THINGS?
UNFRIENDLY.
VUMMMMMM
THEY DON'T LIKE LOUD NOISE.
KROOOOMMMM

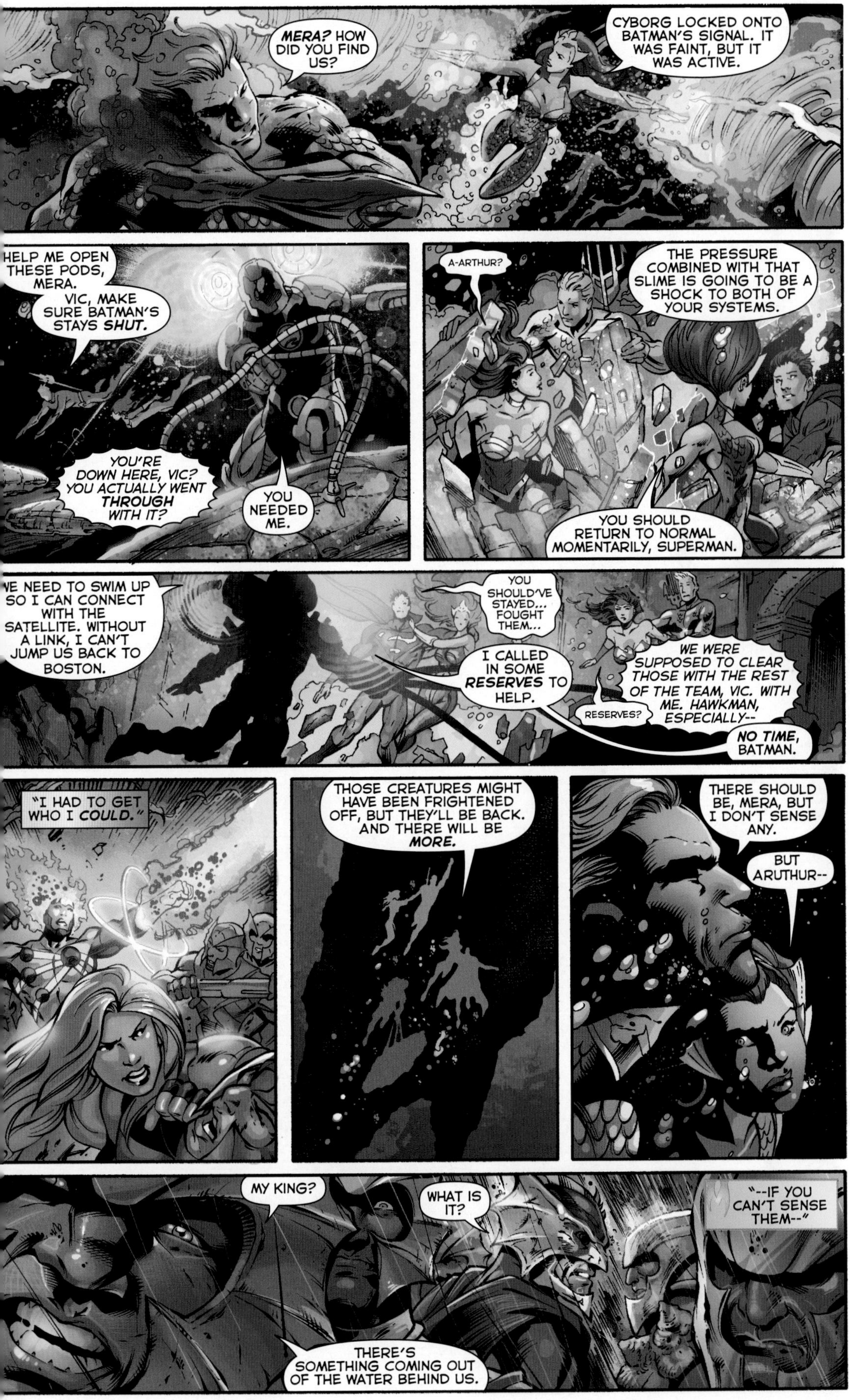
MERA? HOW DID YOU FIND US?
CYBORG LOCKED ONTO BATMAN'S SIGNAL. IT WAS FAINT, BUT IT WAS ACTIVE.
HELP ME OPEN THESE PODS, MERA.
VIC, MAKE SURE BATMAN'S STAYS SHUT.
YOU'RE DOWN HERE, VIC? YOU ACTUALLY WENT THROUGH WITH IT?
YOU NEEDED ME.
A-ARTHUR?
THE PRESSURE COMBINED WITH THAT SLIME IS GOING TO BE A SHOCK TO BOTH OF YOUR SYSTEMS.
YOU SHOULD RETURN TO NORMAL MOMENTARILY, SUPERMAN.
WE NEED TO SWIM UP SO I CAN CONNECT WITH THE SATELLITE. WITHOUT A LINK, I CAN'T JUMP US BACK TO BOSTON.
YOU SHOULD'VE STAYED... FOUGHT THEM...
I CALLED IN SOME RESERVES TO HELP.
RESERVES?
WE WERE SUPPOSED TO CLEAR THOSE WITH THE REST OF THE TEAM, VIC. WITH ME. HAWKMAN, ESPECIALLY--
NO TIME, BATMAN.
"I HAD TO GET WHO I COULD."
THOSE CREATURES MIGHT HAVE BEEN FRIGHTENED OFF, BUT THEY'LL BE BACK. AND THERE WILL BE MORE.
THERE SHOULD BE, MERA, BUT I DON'T SENSE ANY.
BUT ARUTHUR--
MY KING?
WHAT IS IT?
"--IF YOU CAN'T SENSE THEM--"
THERE'S SOMETHING COMING OUT OF THE WATER BEHIND US.

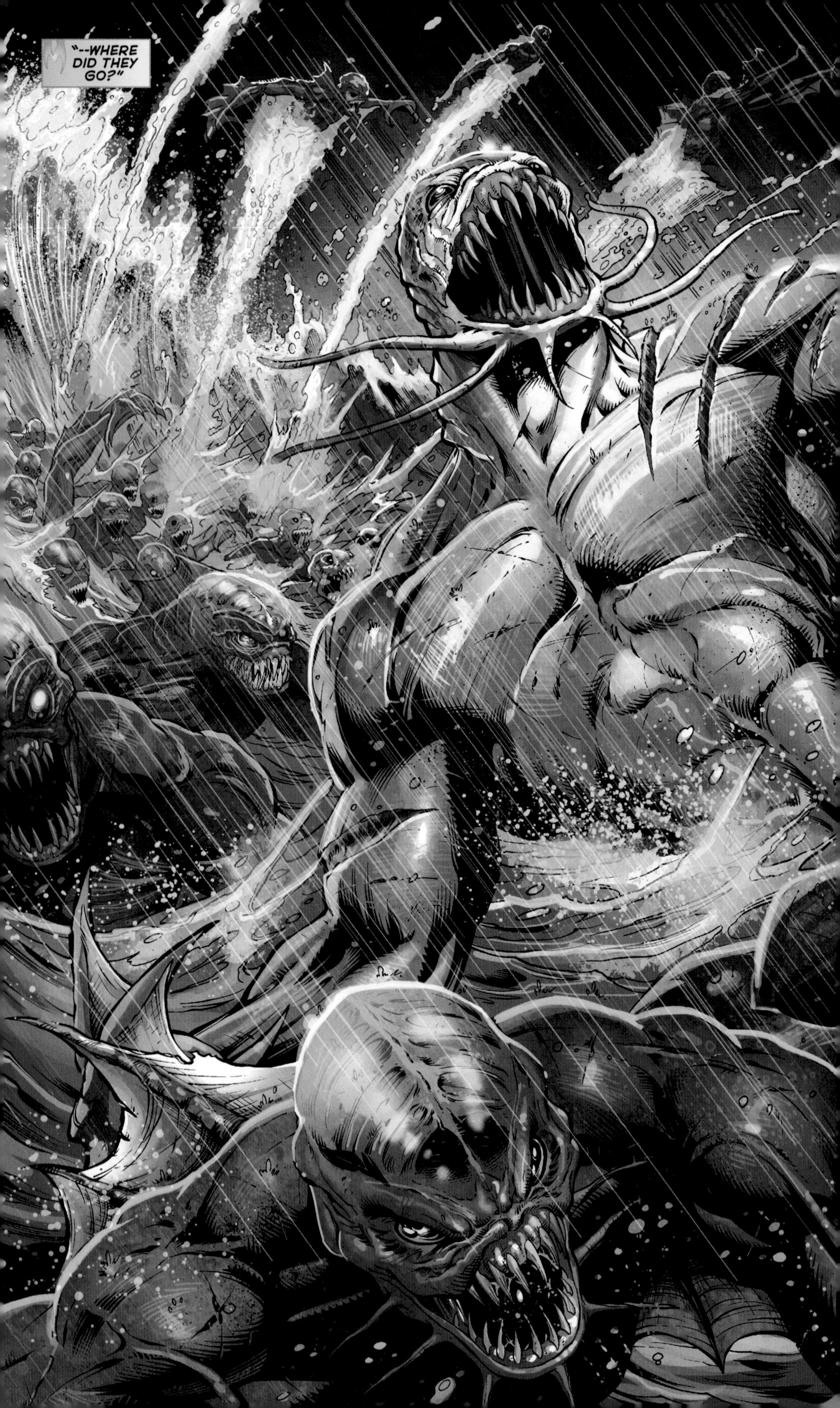
"--WHERE DID THEY GO?"

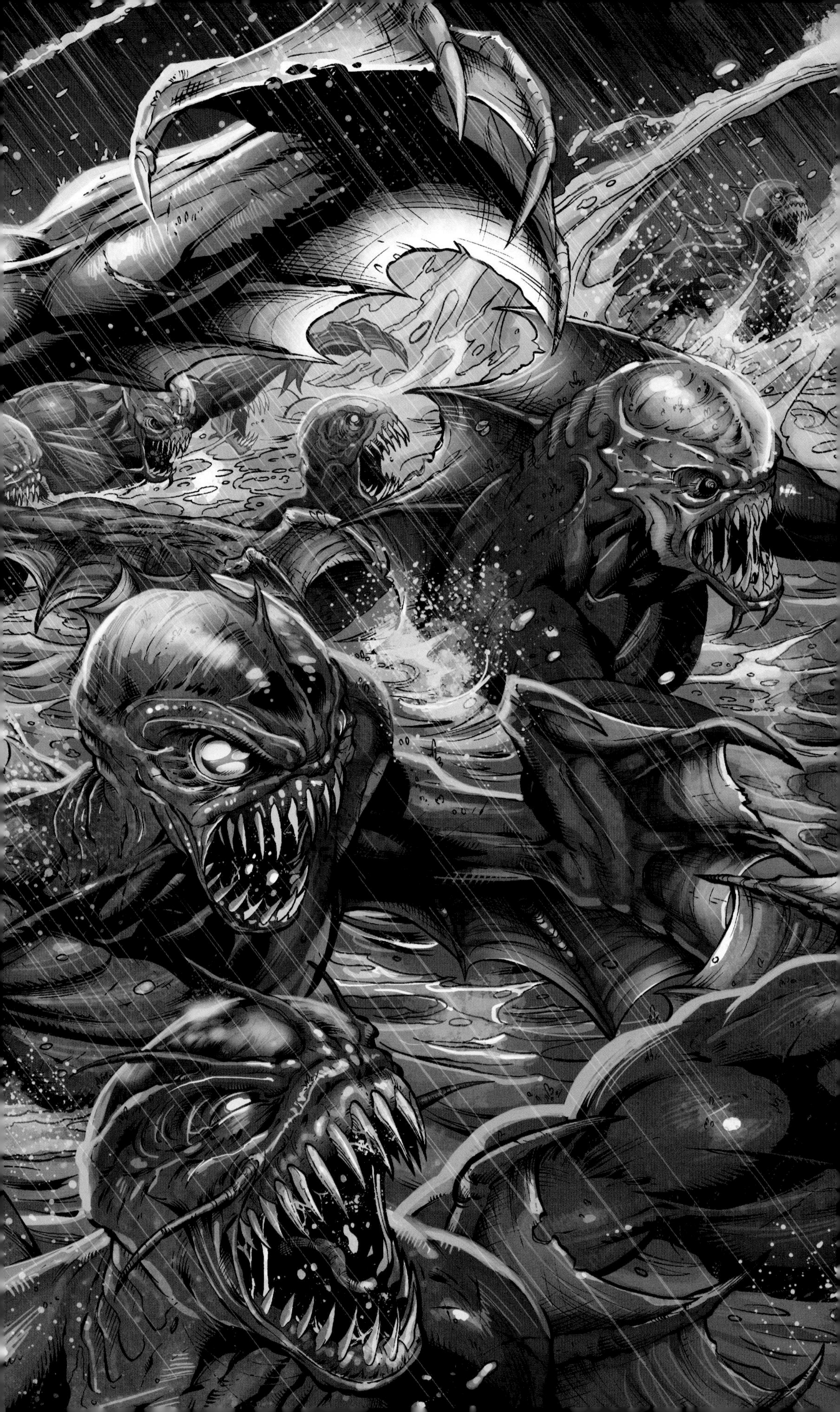

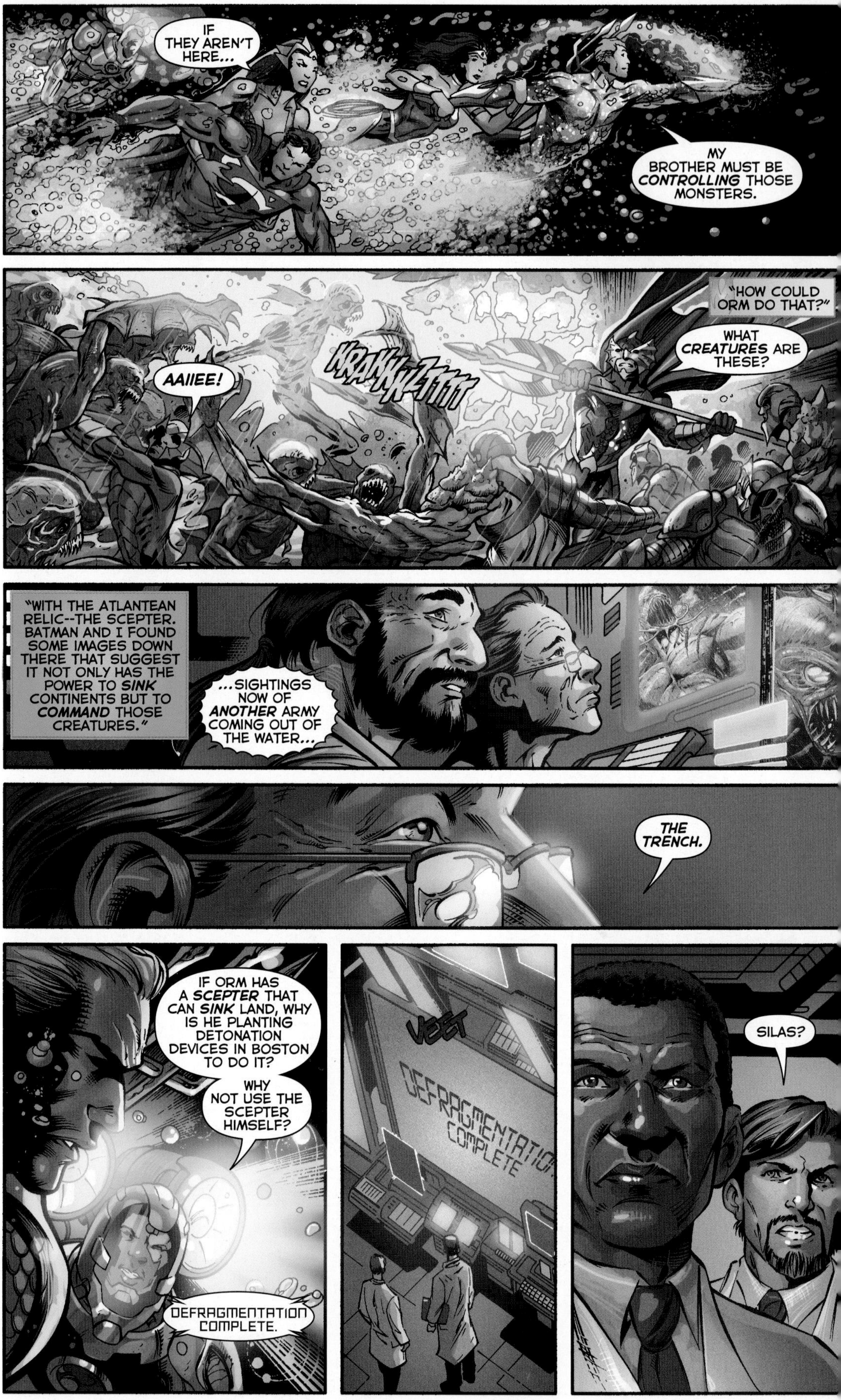
IF THEY AREN'T HERE...
MY BROTHER MUST BE *CONTROLLING* THOSE MONSTERS.
"HOW COULD ORM DO THAT?"
WHAT *CREATURES* ARE THESE?
KRAKKKZZTTTTT
AAIIEE!
"WITH THE ATLANTEAN RELIC--THE SCEPTER. BATMAN AND I FOUND SOME IMAGES DOWN THERE THAT SUGGEST IT NOT ONLY HAS THE POWER TO *SINK* CONTINENTS BUT TO *COMMAND* THOSE CREATURES."
...SIGHTINGS NOW OF *ANOTHER* ARMY COMING OUT OF THE WATER...
THE TRENCH.
IF ORM HAS A *SCEPTER* THAT CAN *SINK* LAND, WHY IS HE PLANTING DETONATION DEVICES IN BOSTON TO DO IT?
WHY NOT USE THE SCEPTER HIMSELF?
DEFRAGMENTATION COMPLETE.
DEFRAGMENTATIO COMPLETE
SILAS?

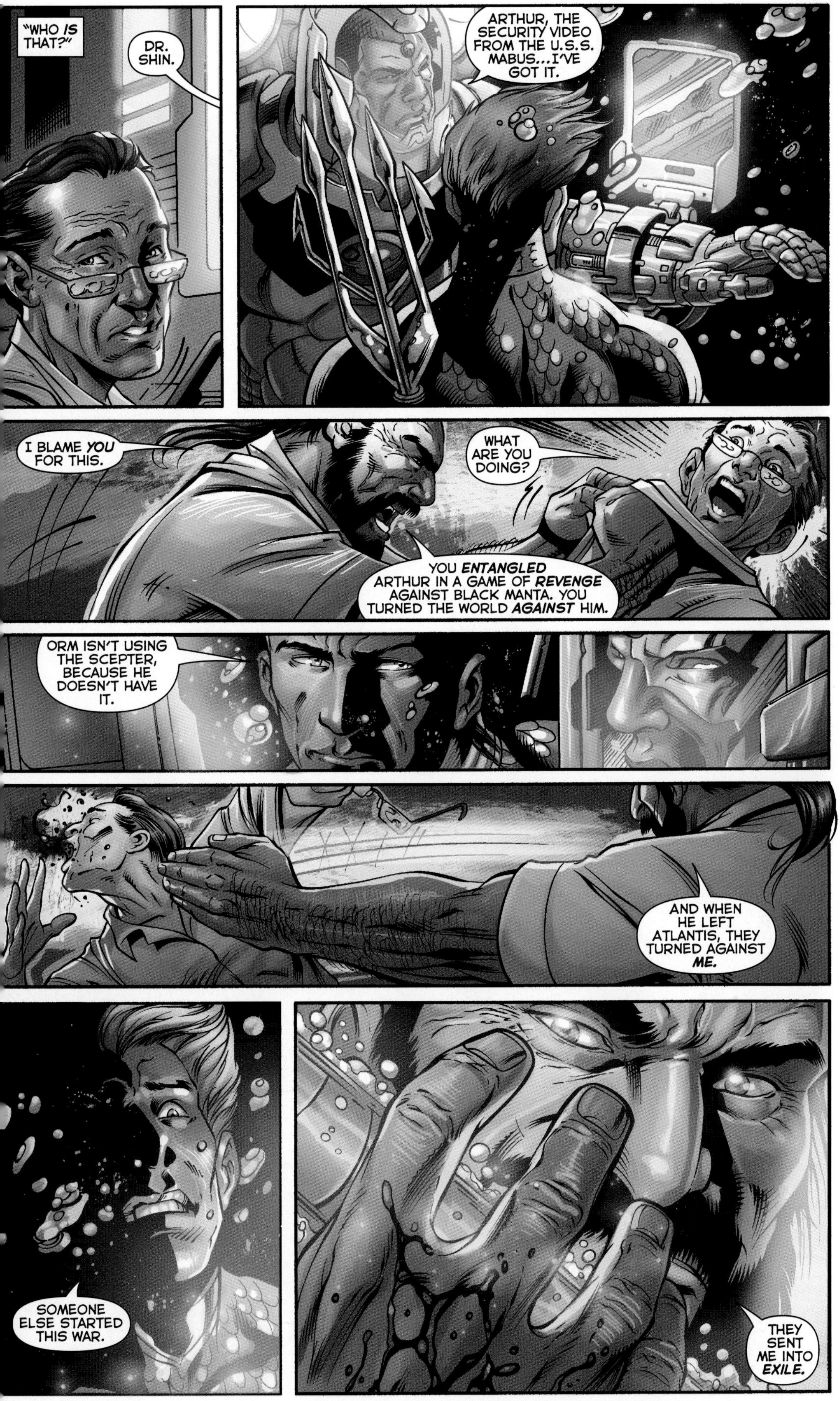
"WHO IS THAT?"
DR. SHIN.
ARTHUR, THE SECURITY VIDEO FROM THE U.S.S. MABUS...I'VE GOT IT.
I BLAME YOU FOR THIS.
WHAT ARE YOU DOING?
YOU ENTANGLED ARTHUR IN A GAME OF REVENGE AGAINST BLACK MANTA. YOU TURNED THE WORLD AGAINST HIM.
ORM ISN'T USING THE SCEPTER, BECAUSE HE DOESN'T HAVE IT.
AND WHEN HE LEFT ATLANTIS, THEY TURNED AGAINST ME.
SOMEONE ELSE STARTED THIS WAR.
THEY SENT ME INTO EXILE.

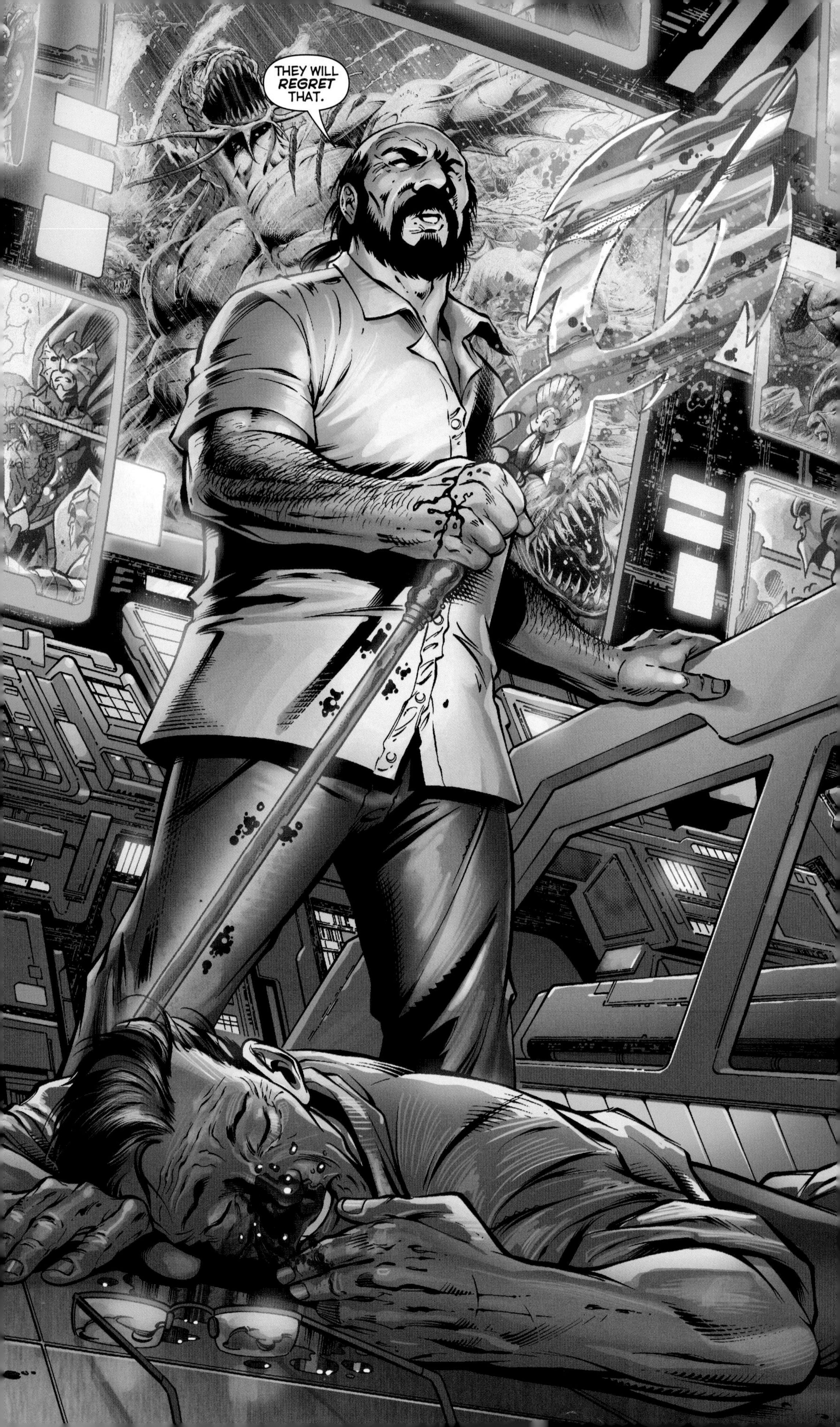
THEY WILL REGRET THAT.

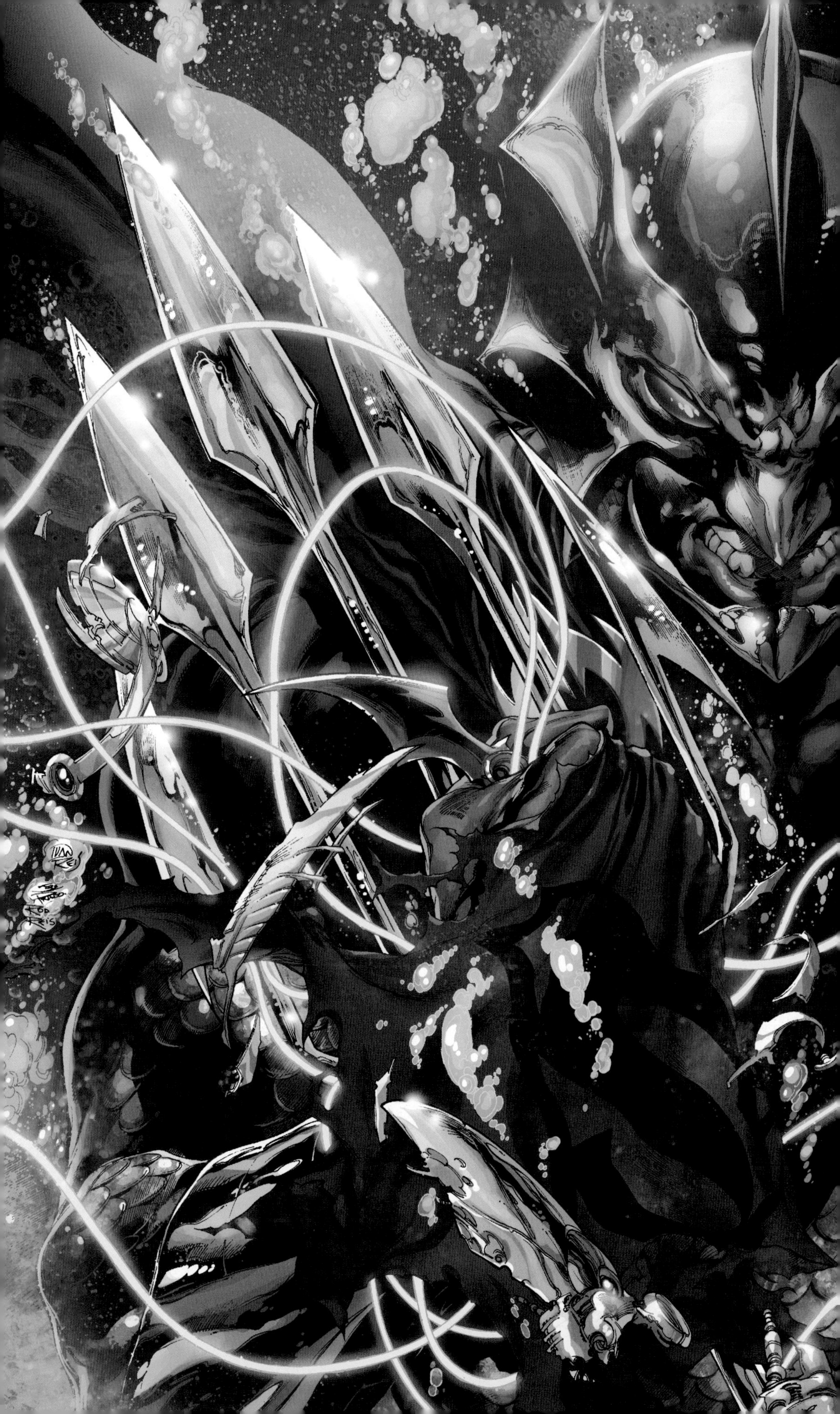

EPILOGUE

GEOFF JOHNS & JEFF LEMIRE writers BRAD WALKER penciller DREW HENNESSY inker

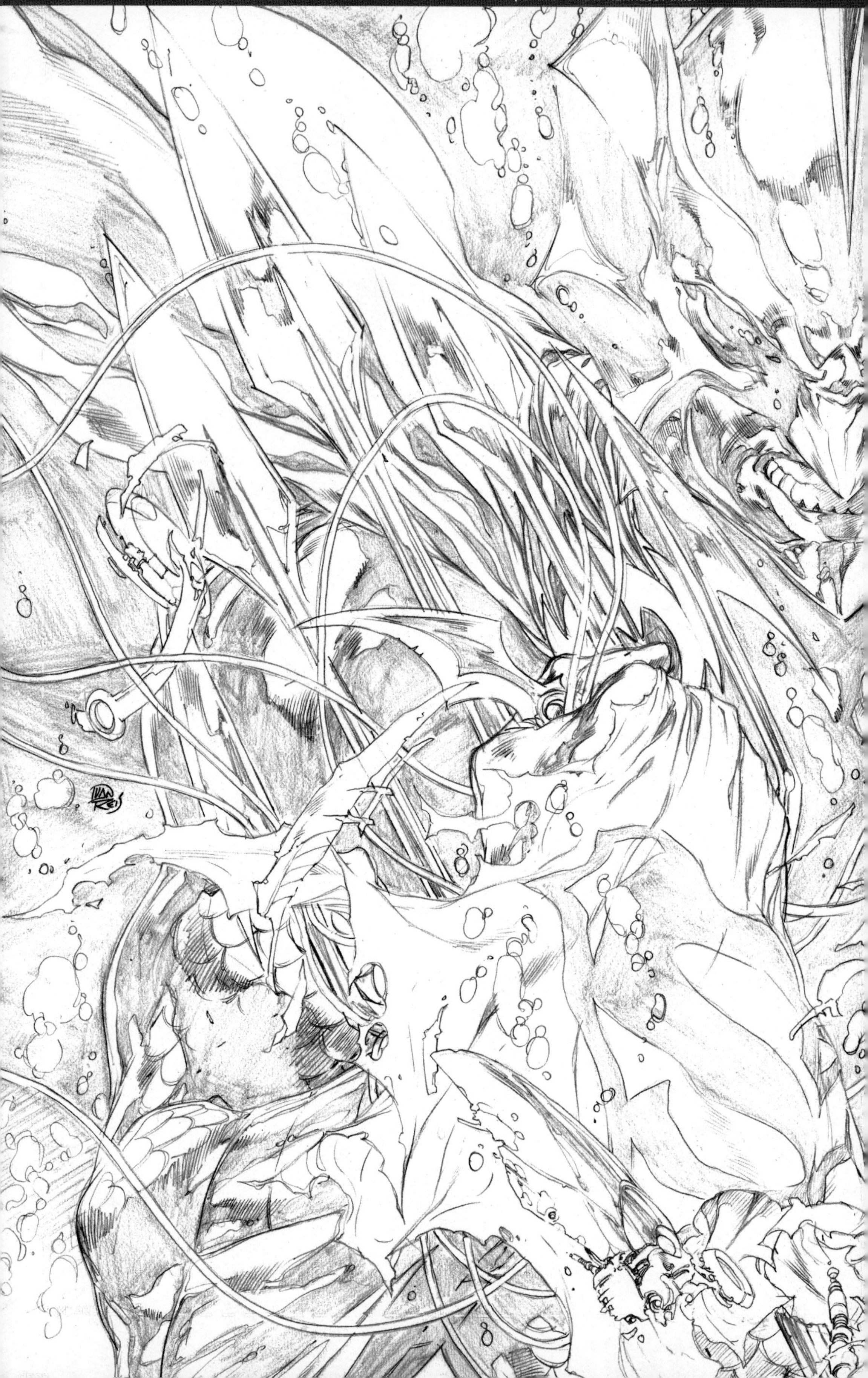

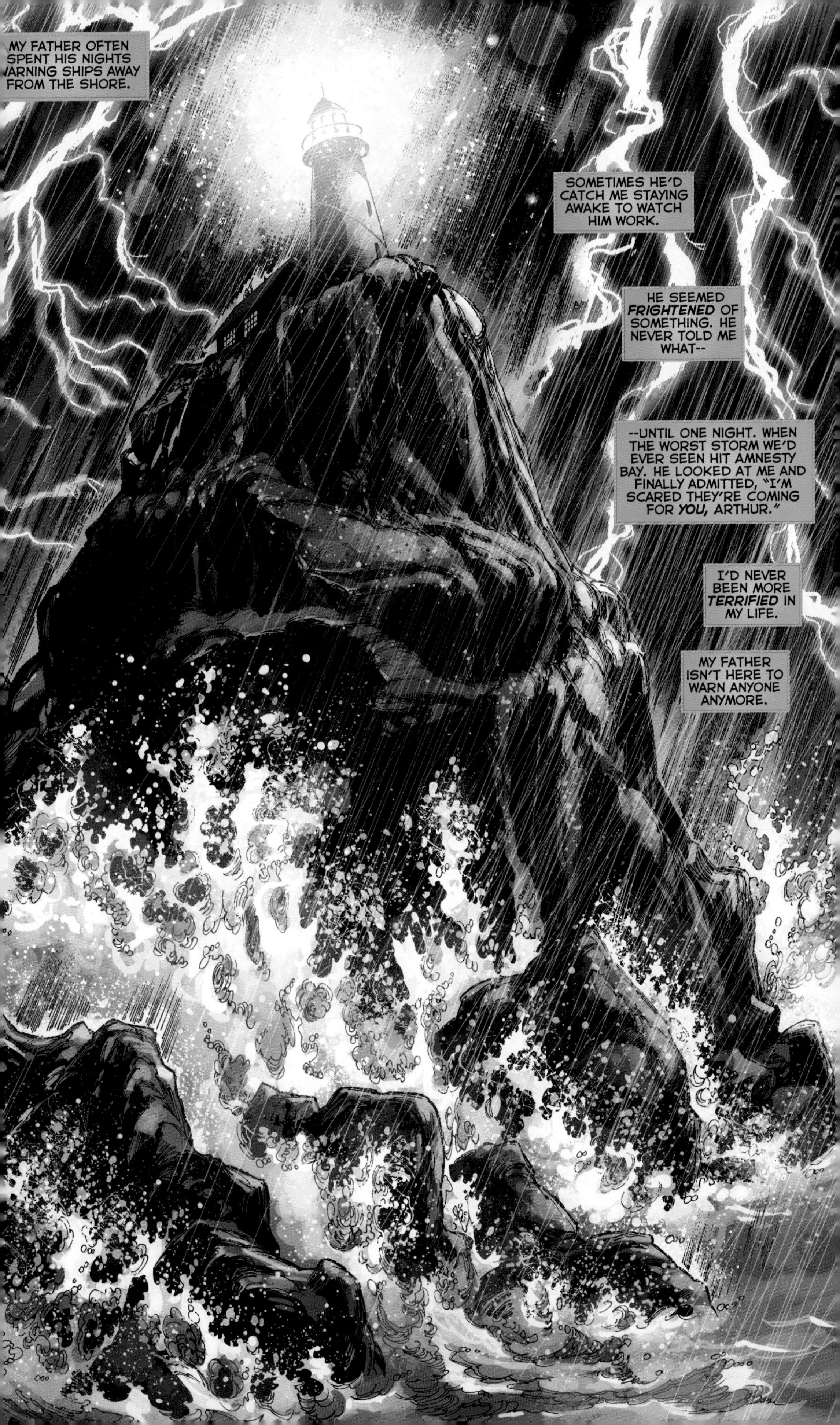
MY FATHER OFTEN SPENT HIS NIGHTS WARNING SHIPS AWAY FROM THE SHORE.
SOMETIMES HE'D CATCH ME STAYING AWAKE TO WATCH HIM WORK.
HE SEEMED *FRIGHTENED* OF SOMETHING. HE NEVER TOLD ME WHAT--
--UNTIL ONE NIGHT. WHEN THE WORST STORM WE'D EVER SEEN HIT AMNESTY BAY. HE LOOKED AT ME AND FINALLY ADMITTED, "I'M SCARED THEY'RE COMING FOR *YOU,* ARTHUR."
I'D NEVER BEEN MORE *TERRIFIED* IN MY LIFE.
MY FATHER ISN'T HERE TO WARN ANYONE ANYMORE.

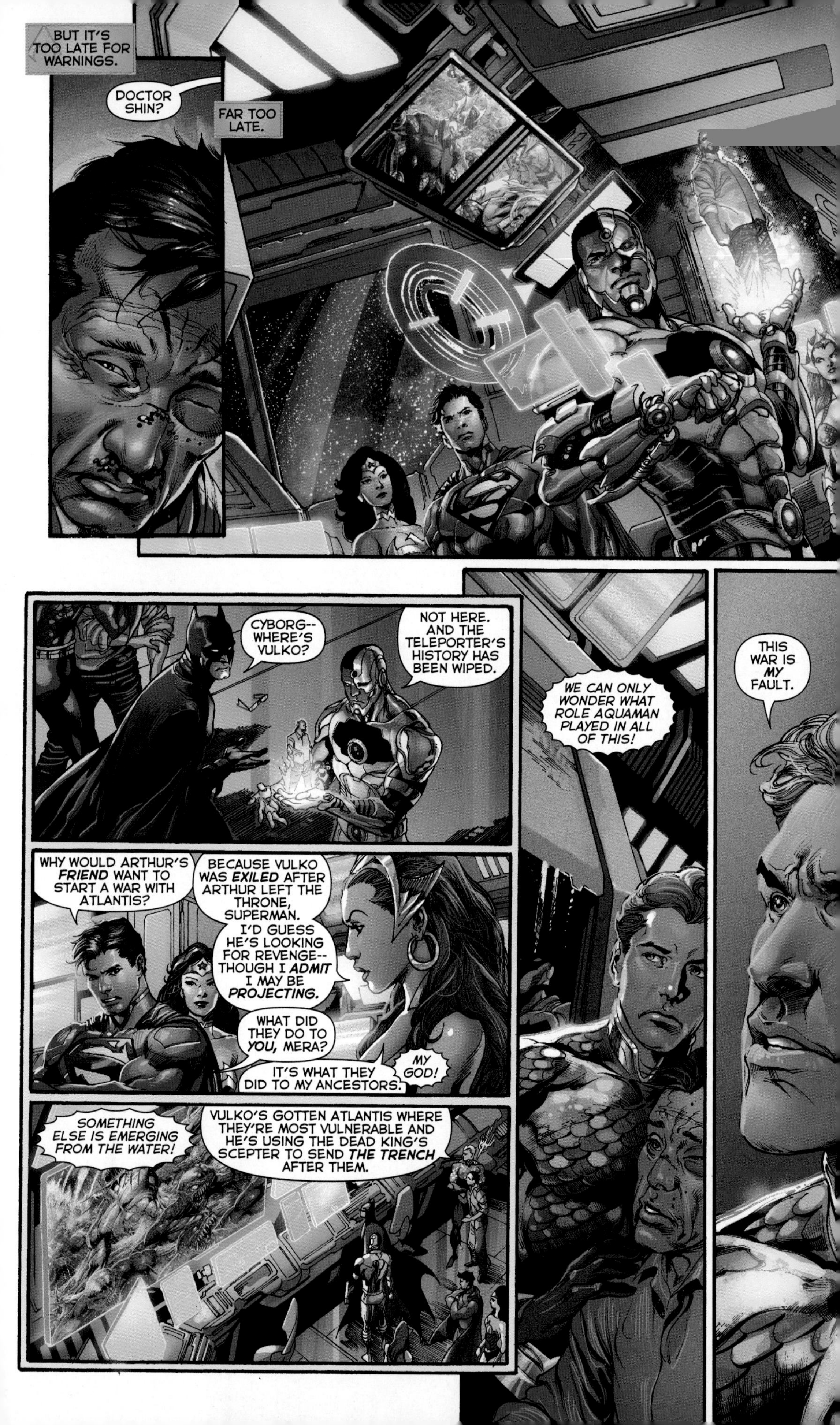
BUT IT'S TOO LATE FOR WARNINGS.
DOCTOR SHIN?
FAR TOO LATE.
CYBORG-- WHERE'S VULKO?
NOT HERE. AND THE TELEPORTER'S HISTORY HAS BEEN WIPED.
WE CAN ONLY WONDER WHAT ROLE AQUAMAN PLAYED IN ALL OF THIS!
THIS WAR IS MY FAULT.
WHY WOULD ARTHUR'S FRIEND WANT TO START A WAR WITH ATLANTIS?
BECAUSE VULKO WAS EXILED AFTER ARTHUR LEFT THE THRONE, SUPERMAN.
I'D GUESS HE'S LOOKING FOR REVENGE-- THOUGH I ADMIT I MAY BE PROJECTING.
WHAT DID THEY DO TO YOU, MERA?
IT'S WHAT THEY DID TO MY ANCESTORS.
MY GOD!
SOMETHING ELSE IS EMERGING FROM THE WATER!
VULKO'S GOTTEN ATLANTIS WHERE THEY'RE MOST VULNERABLE AND HE'S USING THE DEAD KING'S SCEPTER TO SEND THE TRENCH AFTER THEM.

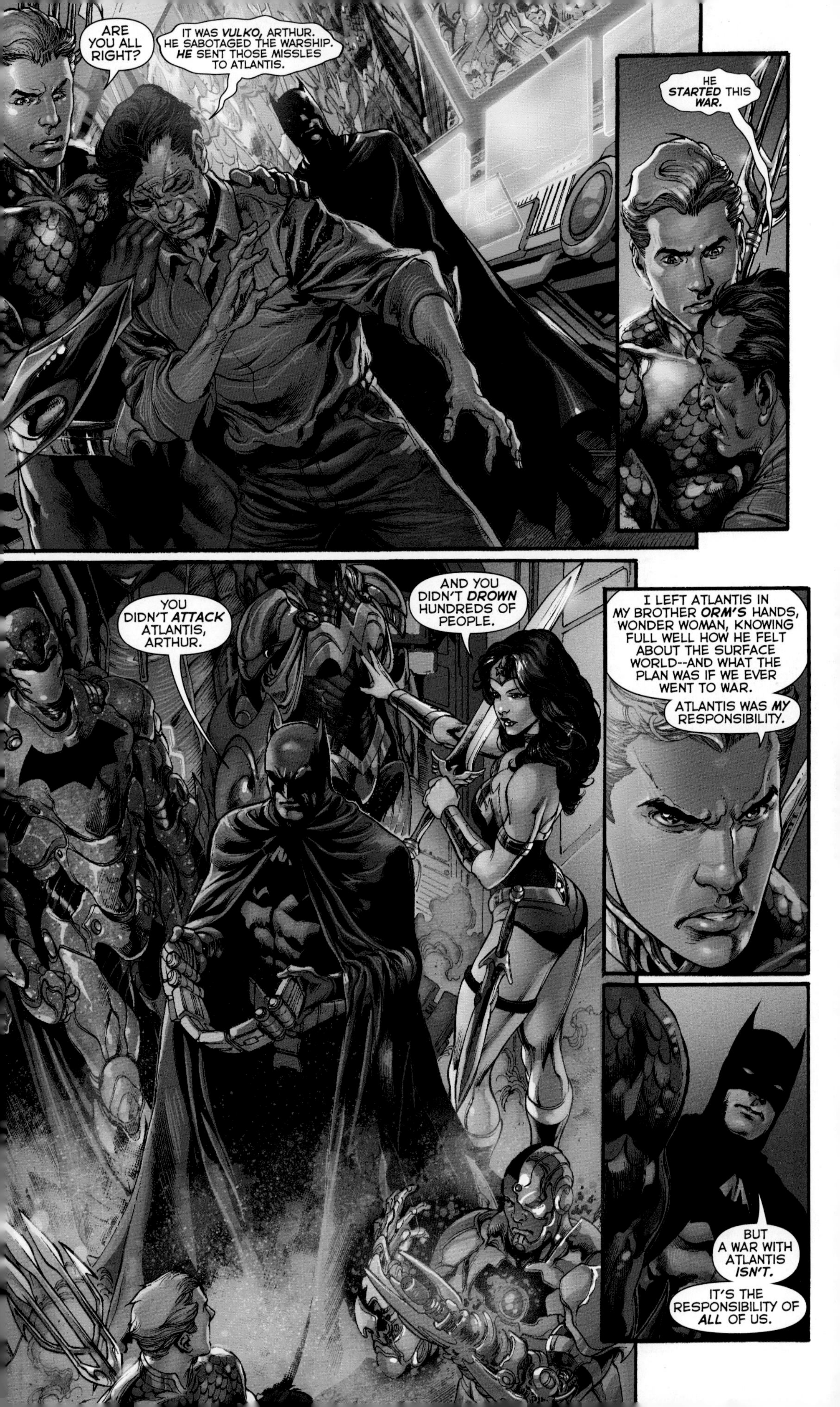
ARE YOU ALL RIGHT?
IT WAS VULKO, ARTHUR. HE SABOTAGED THE WARSHIP. HE SENT THOSE MISSLES TO ATLANTIS.
HE STARTED THIS WAR.
YOU DIDN'T ATTACK ATLANTIS, ARTHUR.
AND YOU DIDN'T DROWN HUNDREDS OF PEOPLE.
I LEFT ATLANTIS IN MY BROTHER ORM'S HANDS, WONDER WOMAN, KNOWING FULL WELL HOW HE FELT ABOUT THE SURFACE WORLD--AND WHAT THE PLAN WAS IF WE EVER WENT TO WAR.
ATLANTIS WAS MY RESPONSIBILITY.
BUT A WAR WITH ATLANTIS ISN'T.
IT'S THE RESPONSIBILITY OF ALL OF US.

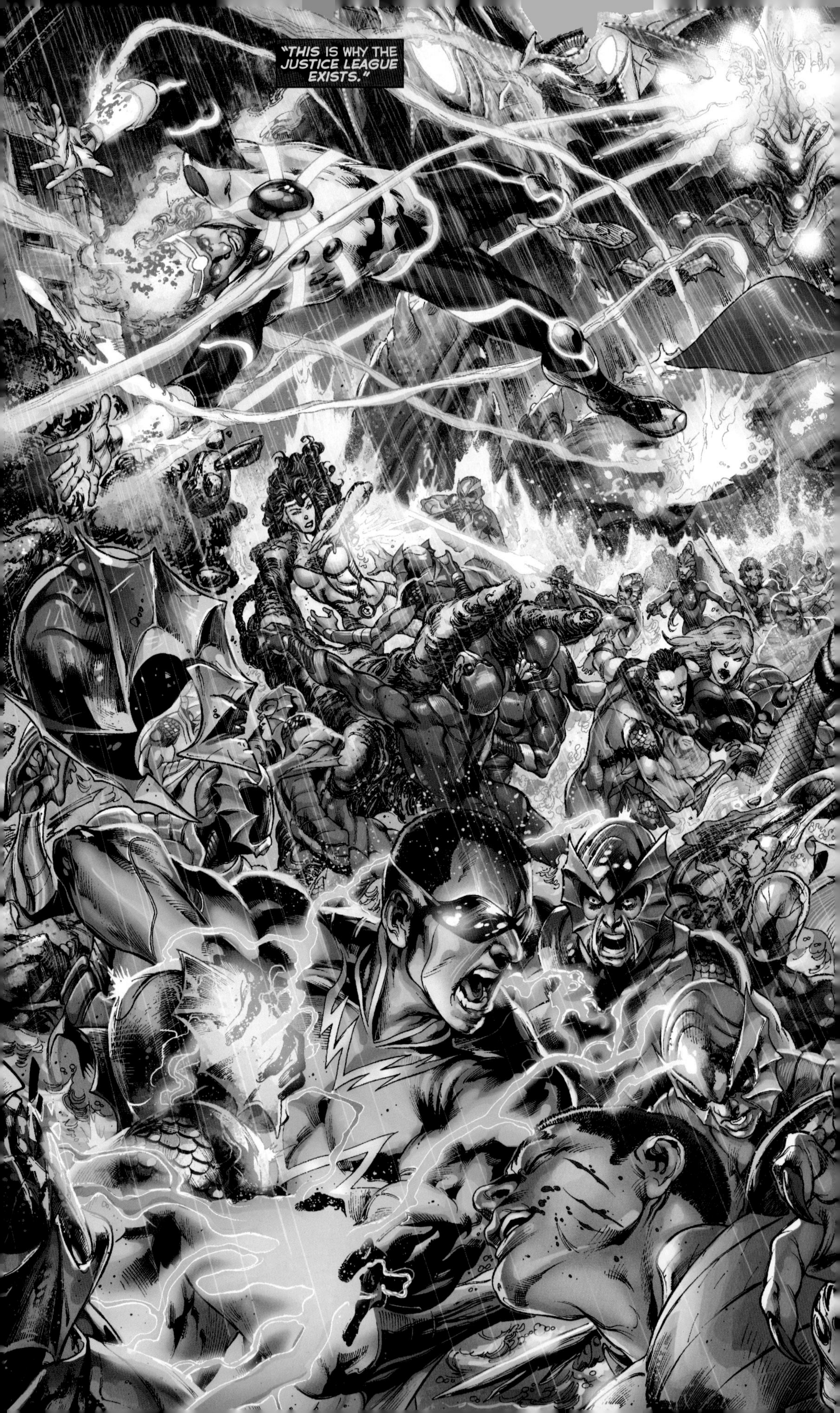
"THIS IS WHY THE JUSTICE LEAGUE EXISTS."

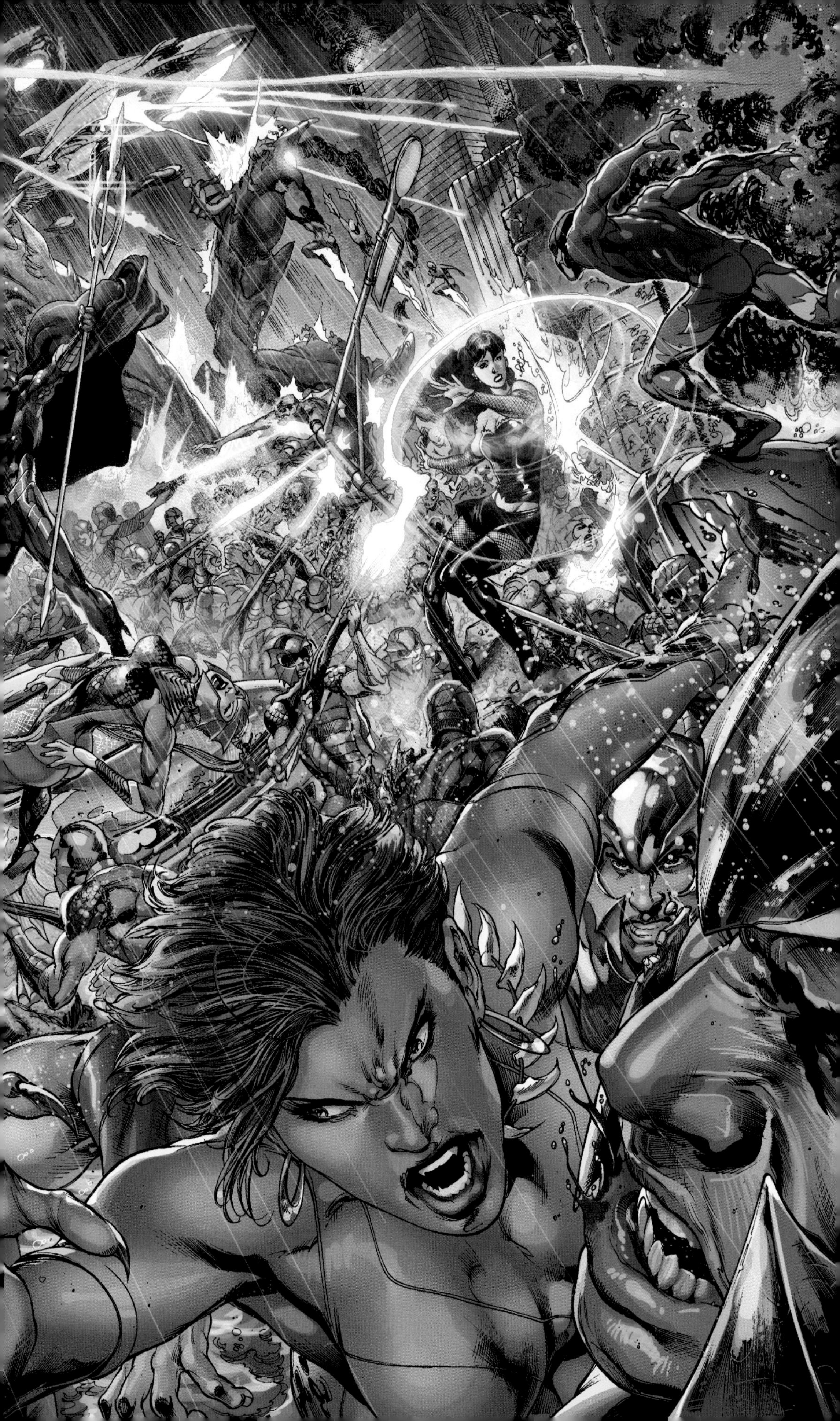

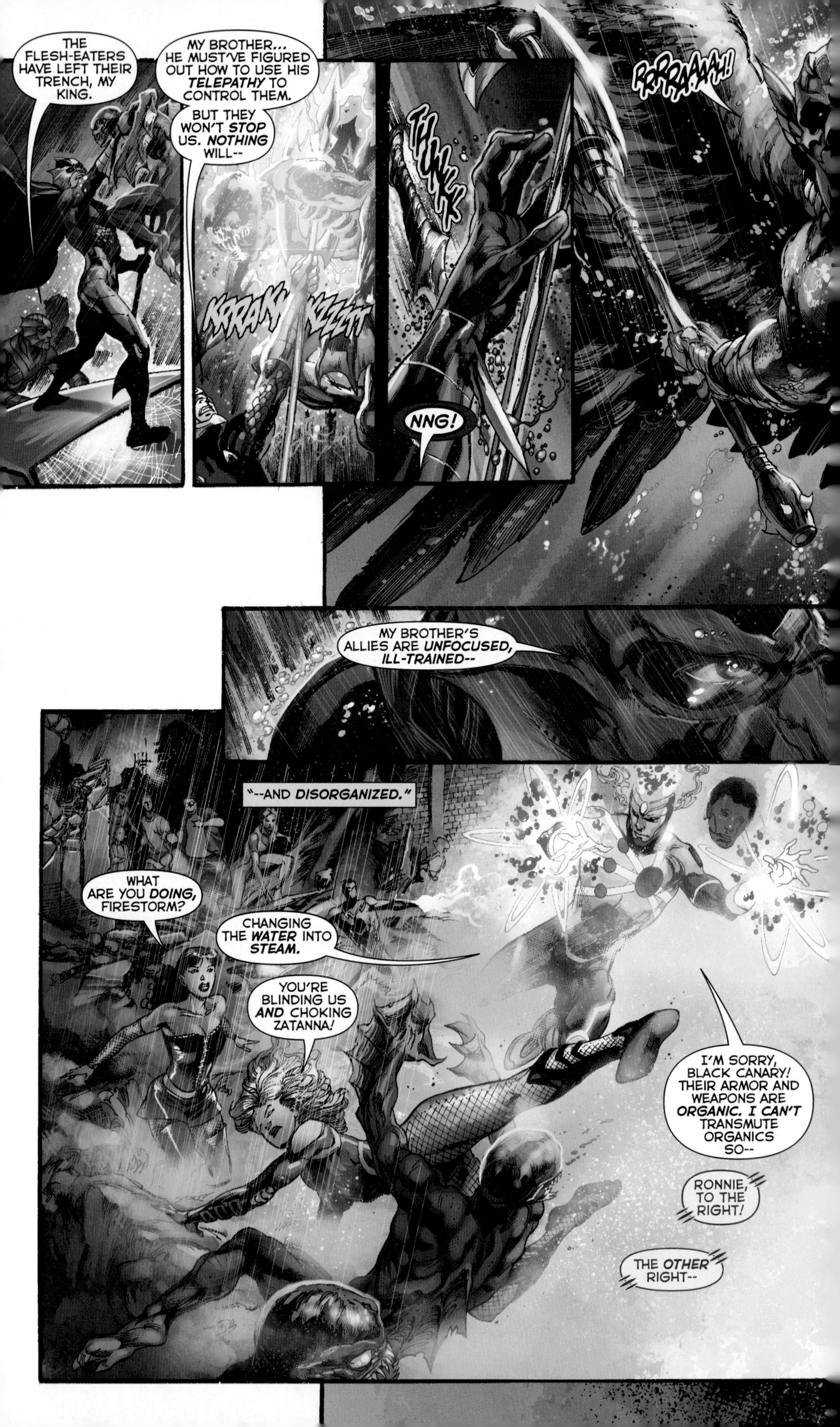
THE FLESH-EATERS HAVE LEFT THEIR TRENCH, MY KING.
MY BROTHER... HE MUST'VE FIGURED OUT HOW TO USE HIS *TELEPATHY* TO CONTROL THEM.
BUT THEY WON'T *STOP* US. *NOTHING* WILL--
KRRAK
KZZZTT
THUNKK
NNG!
RRRRAAAH!
MY BROTHER'S ALLIES ARE *UNFOCUSED, ILL-TRAINED*--
"--AND *DISORGANIZED.*"
WHAT ARE YOU *DOING,* FIRESTORM?
CHANGING THE *WATER* INTO *STEAM.*
YOU'RE BLINDING US *AND* CHOKING ZATANNA!
I'M SORRY, BLACK CANARY! THEIR ARMOR AND WEAPONS ARE *ORGANIC. I CAN'T* TRANSMUTE ORGANICS SO--
RONNIE, TO THE *RIGHT!*
THE *OTHER* RIGHT--

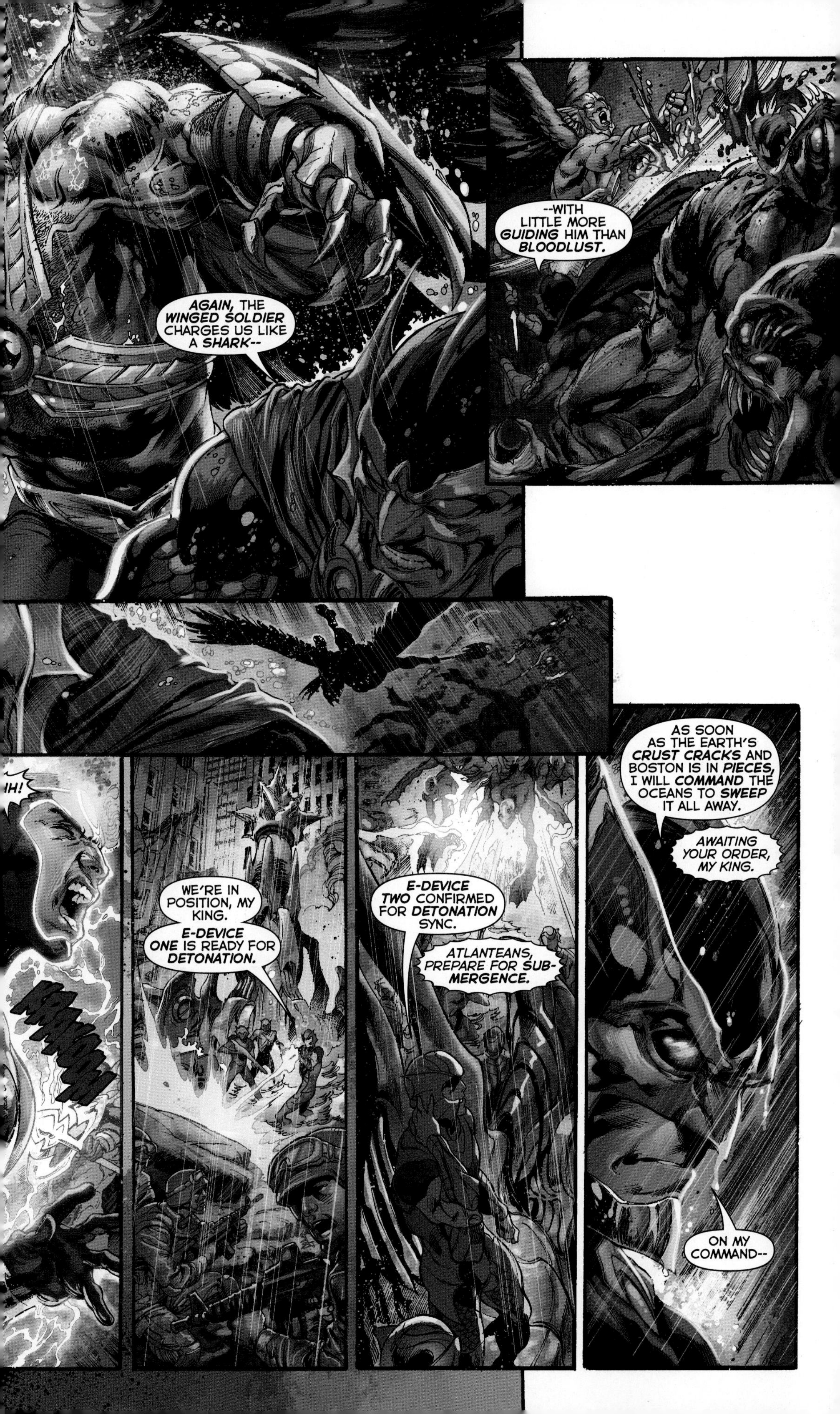
AGAIN, THE WINGED SOLDIER CHARGES US LIKE A SHARK--
--WITH LITTLE MORE GUIDING HIM THAN BLOODLUST.
WE'RE IN POSITION, MY KING.
E-DEVICE ONE IS READY FOR DETONATION.
E-DEVICE TWO CONFIRMED FOR DETONATION SYNC.
ATLANTEANS, PREPARE FOR SUB-MERGENCE.
AS SOON AS THE EARTH'S CRUST CRACKS AND BOSTON IS IN PIECES, I WILL COMMAND THE OCEANS TO SWEEP IT ALL AWAY.
AWAITING YOUR ORDER, MY KING.
ON MY COMMAND--

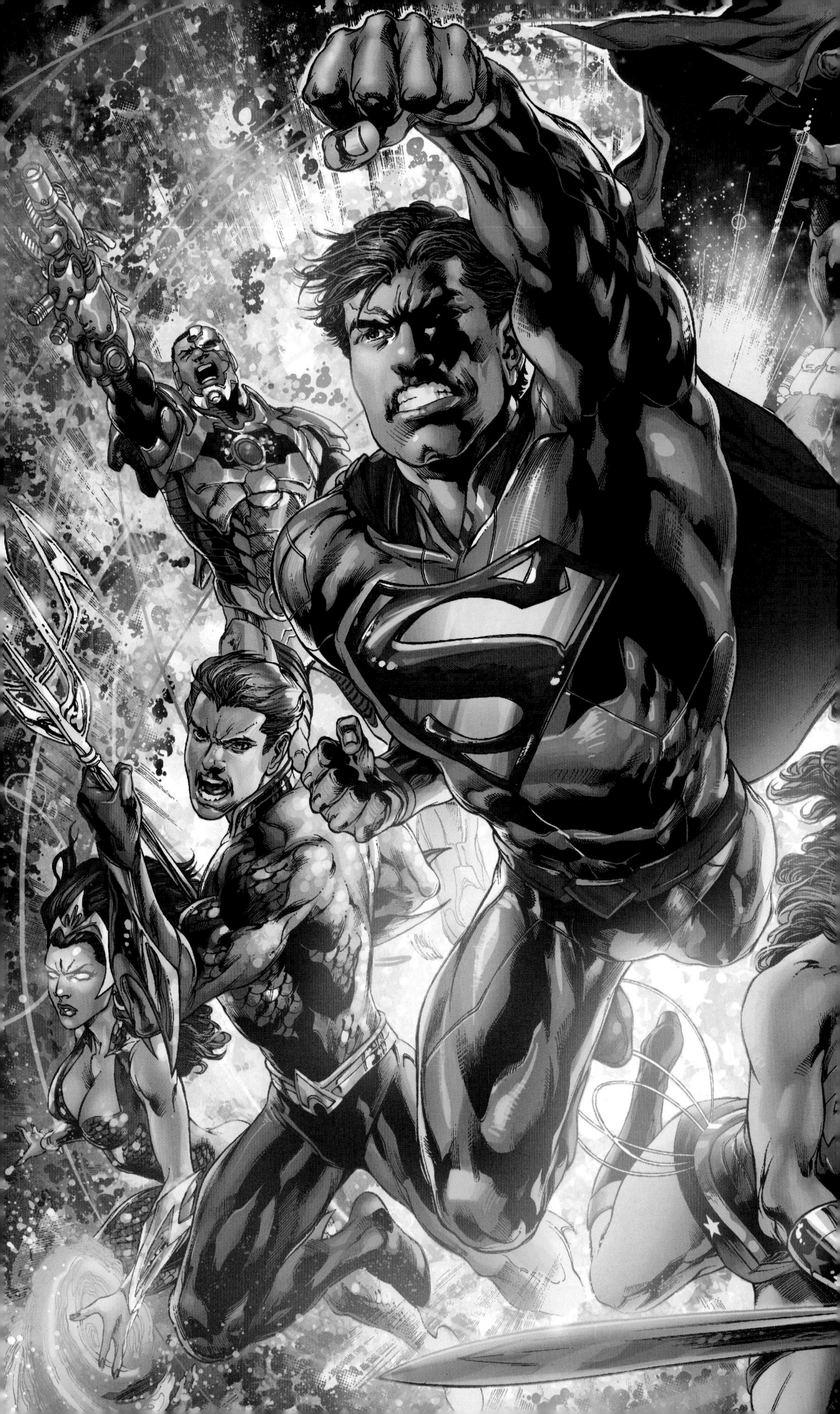

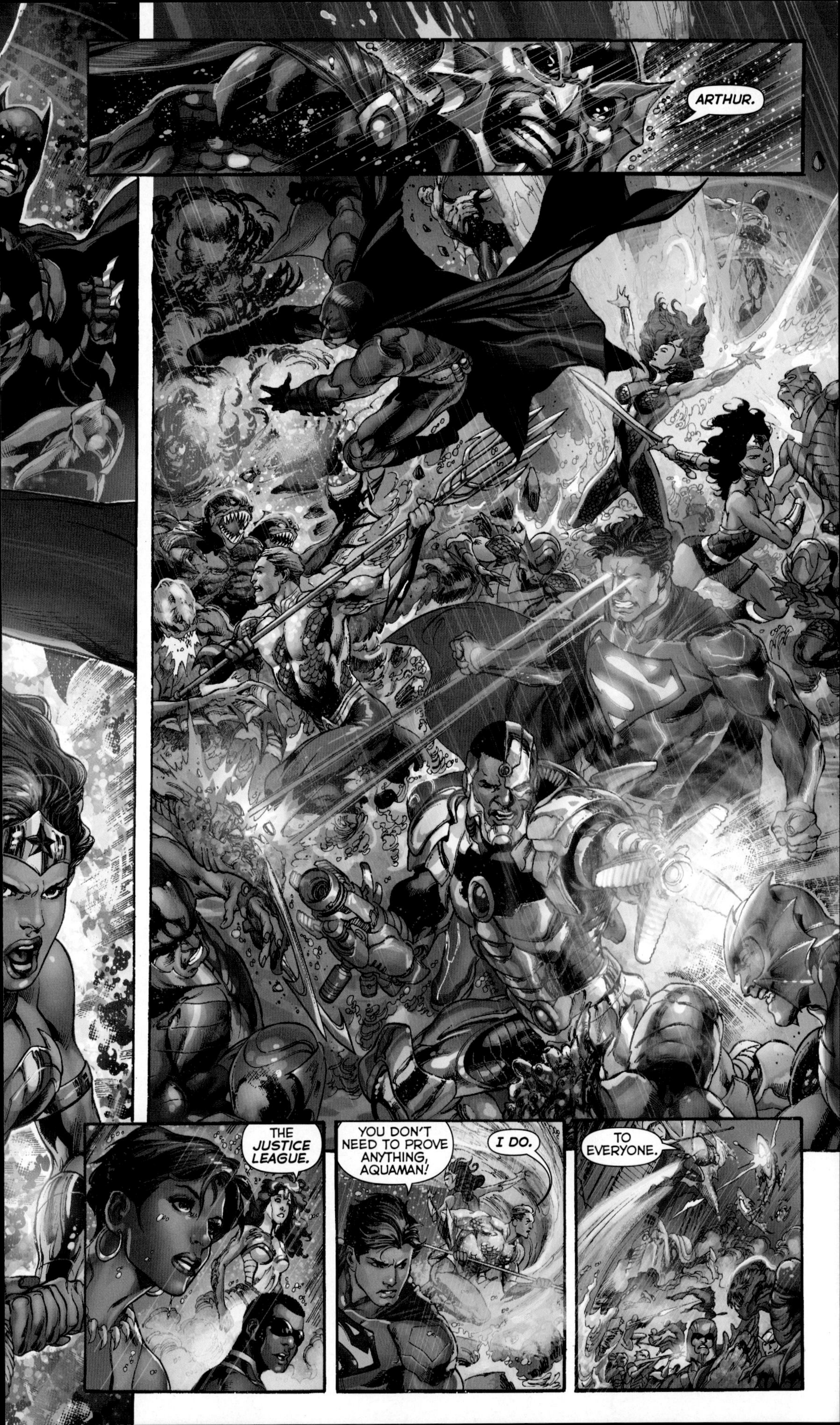
ARTHUR.
THE JUSTICE LEAGUE.
YOU DON'T NEED TO PROVE ANYTHING, AQUAMAN!
I DO.
TO EVERYONE.

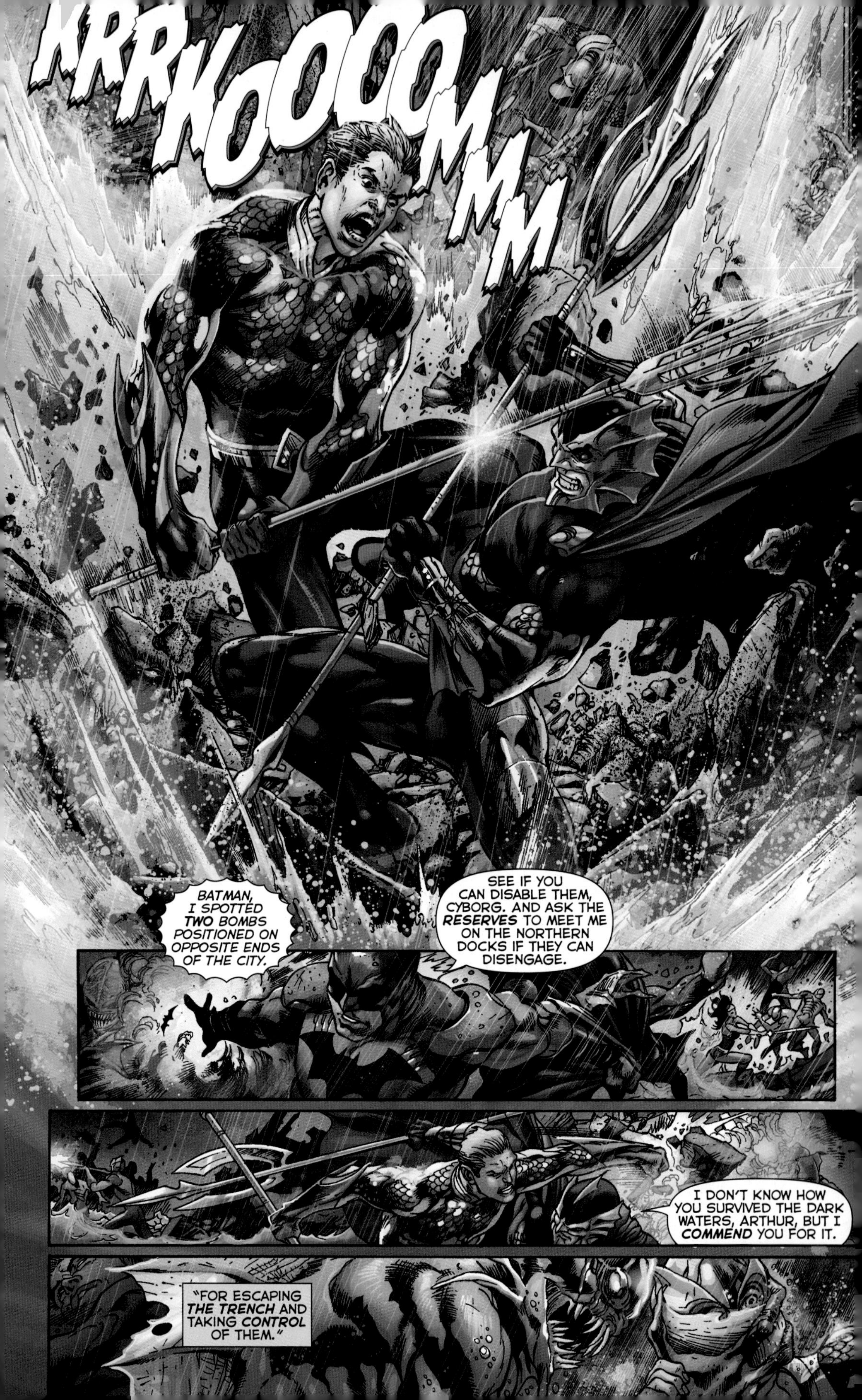

KRRKOOOOMMM
BATMAN, I SPOTTED TWO BOMBS POSITIONED ON OPPOSITE ENDS OF THE CITY.
SEE IF YOU CAN DISABLE THEM, CYBORG. AND ASK THE RESERVES TO MEET ME ON THE NORTHERN DOCKS IF THEY CAN DISENGAGE.
I DON'T KNOW HOW YOU SURVIVED THE DARK WATERS, ARTHUR, BUT I COMMEND YOU FOR IT.
"FOR ESCAPING THE TRENCH AND TAKING CONTROL OF THEM."

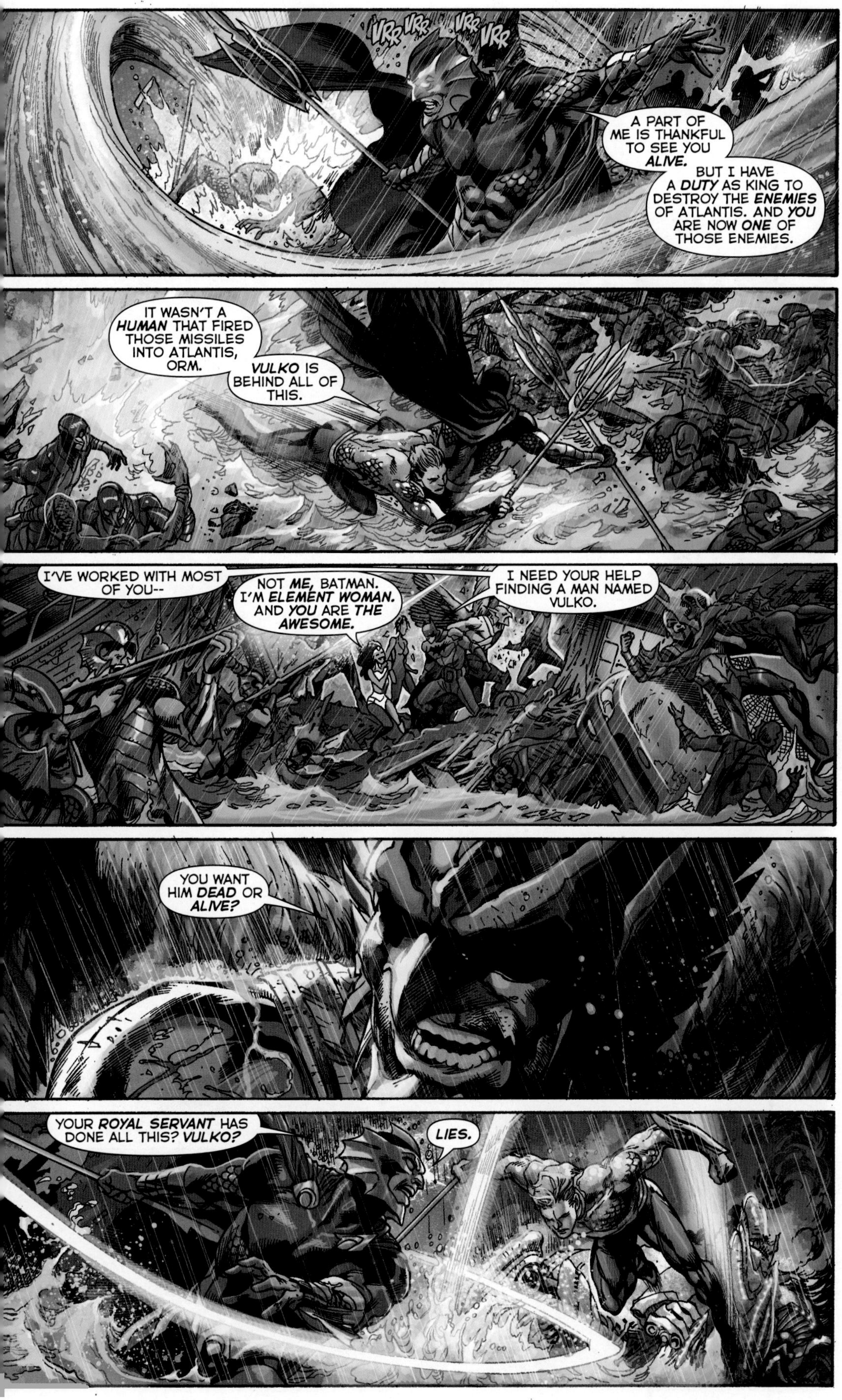
VRR VRR VRR VRR
A PART OF ME IS THANKFUL TO SEE YOU ALIVE.
BUT I HAVE A DUTY AS KING TO DESTROY THE ENEMIES OF ATLANTIS. AND YOU ARE NOW ONE OF THOSE ENEMIES.
IT WASN'T A HUMAN THAT FIRED THOSE MISSILES INTO ATLANTIS, ORM.
VULKO IS BEHIND ALL OF THIS.
I'VE WORKED WITH MOST OF YOU--
NOT ME, BATMAN. I'M ELEMENT WOMAN. AND YOU ARE THE AWESOME.
I NEED YOUR HELP FINDING A MAN NAMED VULKO.
YOU WANT HIM DEAD OR ALIVE?
YOUR ROYAL SERVANT HAS DONE ALL THIS? VULKO?
LIES.

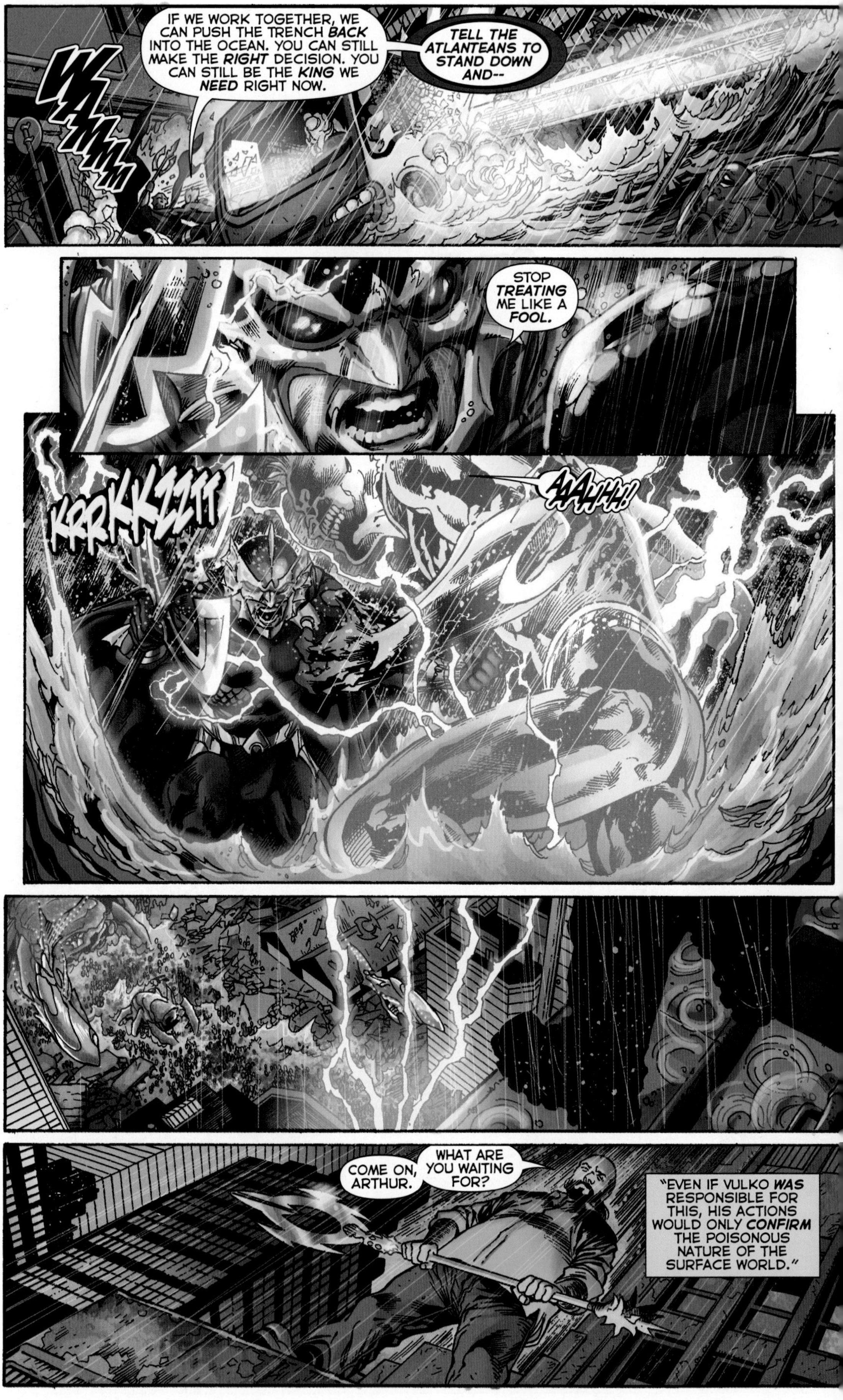

IF WE WORK TOGETHER, WE CAN PUSH THE TRENCH BACK INTO THE OCEAN. YOU CAN STILL MAKE THE RIGHT DECISION. YOU CAN STILL BE THE KING WE NEED RIGHT NOW.
TELL THE ATLANTEANS TO STAND DOWN AND--
STOP TREATING ME LIKE A FOOL.
KRRKKZZTT
AAAHHH!
COME ON, ARTHUR.
WHAT ARE YOU WAITING FOR?
"EVEN IF VULKO WAS RESPONSIBLE FOR THIS, HIS ACTIONS WOULD ONLY CONFIRM THE POISONOUS NATURE OF THE SURFACE WORLD."

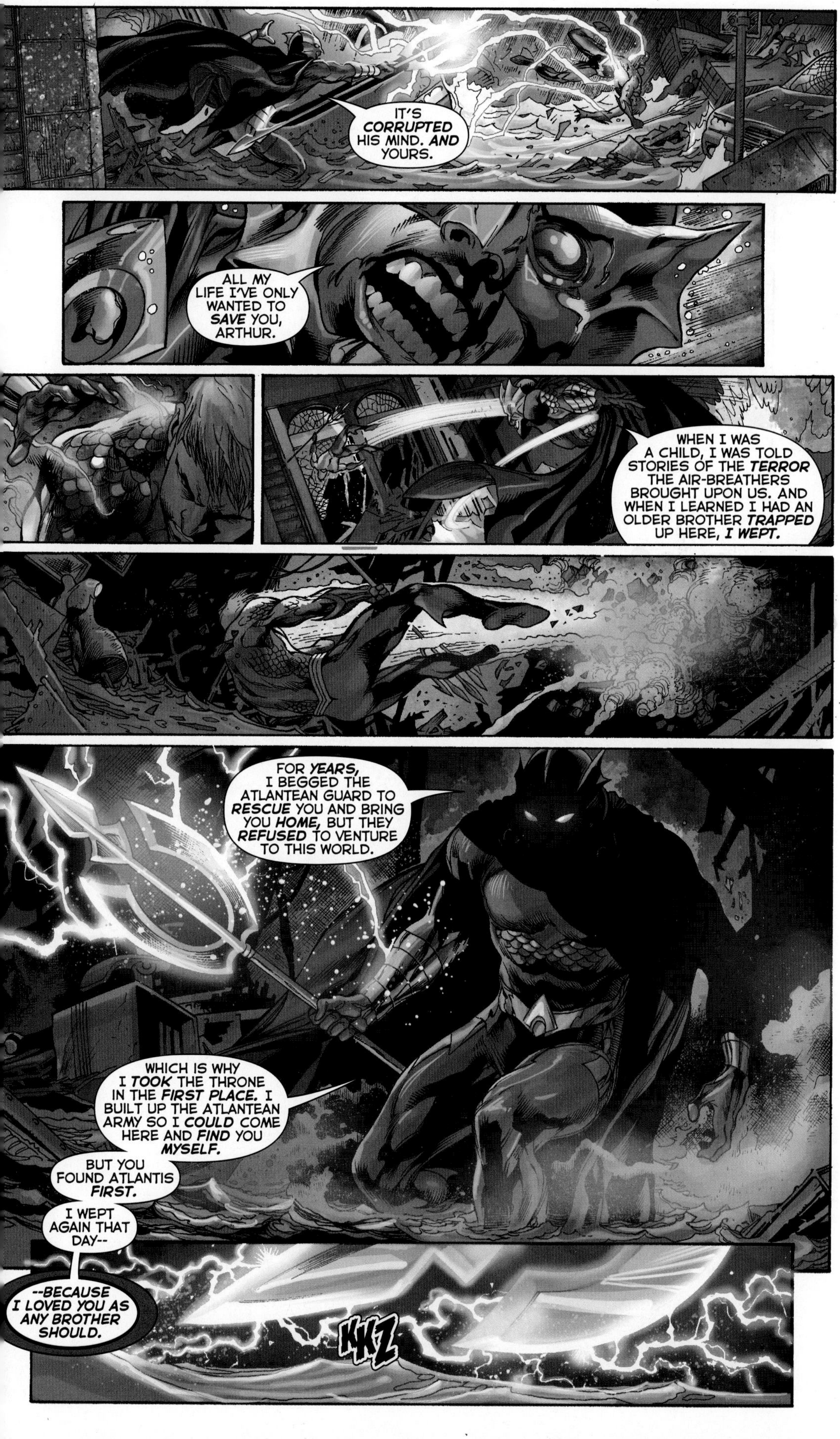
IT'S CORRUPTED HIS MIND. AND YOURS.
ALL MY LIFE I'VE ONLY WANTED TO SAVE YOU, ARTHUR.
WHEN I WAS A CHILD, I WAS TOLD STORIES OF THE TERROR THE AIR-BREATHERS BROUGHT UPON US. AND WHEN I LEARNED I HAD AN OLDER BROTHER TRAPPED UP HERE, I WEPT.
FOR YEARS, I BEGGED THE ATLANTEAN GUARD TO RESCUE YOU AND BRING YOU HOME, BUT THEY REFUSED TO VENTURE TO THIS WORLD.
WHICH IS WHY I TOOK THE THRONE IN THE FIRST PLACE. I BUILT UP THE ATLANTEAN ARMY SO I COULD COME HERE AND FIND YOU MYSELF.
BUT YOU FOUND ATLANTIS FIRST.
I WEPT AGAIN THAT DAY--
--BECAUSE I LOVED YOU AS ANY BROTHER SHOULD.
KKZ

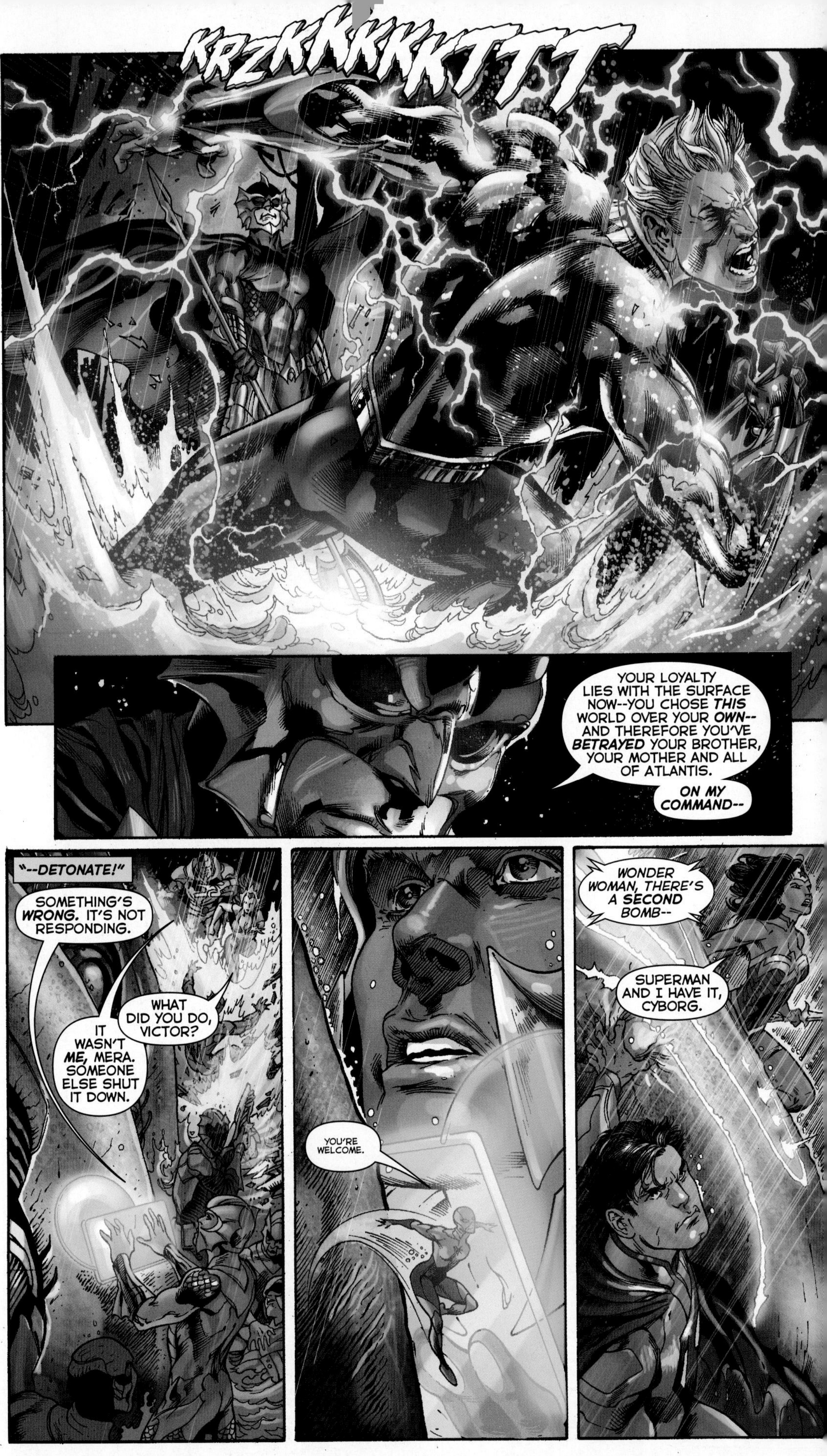
KRZKKKKKKTTTT
YOUR LOYALTY LIES WITH THE SURFACE NOW--YOU CHOSE THIS WORLD OVER YOUR OWN-- AND THEREFORE YOU'VE BETRAYED YOUR BROTHER, YOUR MOTHER AND ALL OF ATLANTIS.
ON MY COMMAND--
"--DETONATE!"
SOMETHING'S WRONG. IT'S NOT RESPONDING.
WHAT DID YOU DO, VICTOR?
IT WASN'T ME, MERA. SOMEONE ELSE SHUT IT DOWN.
YOU'RE WELCOME.
WONDER WOMAN, THERE'S A SECOND BOMB--
SUPERMAN AND I HAVE IT, CYBORG.

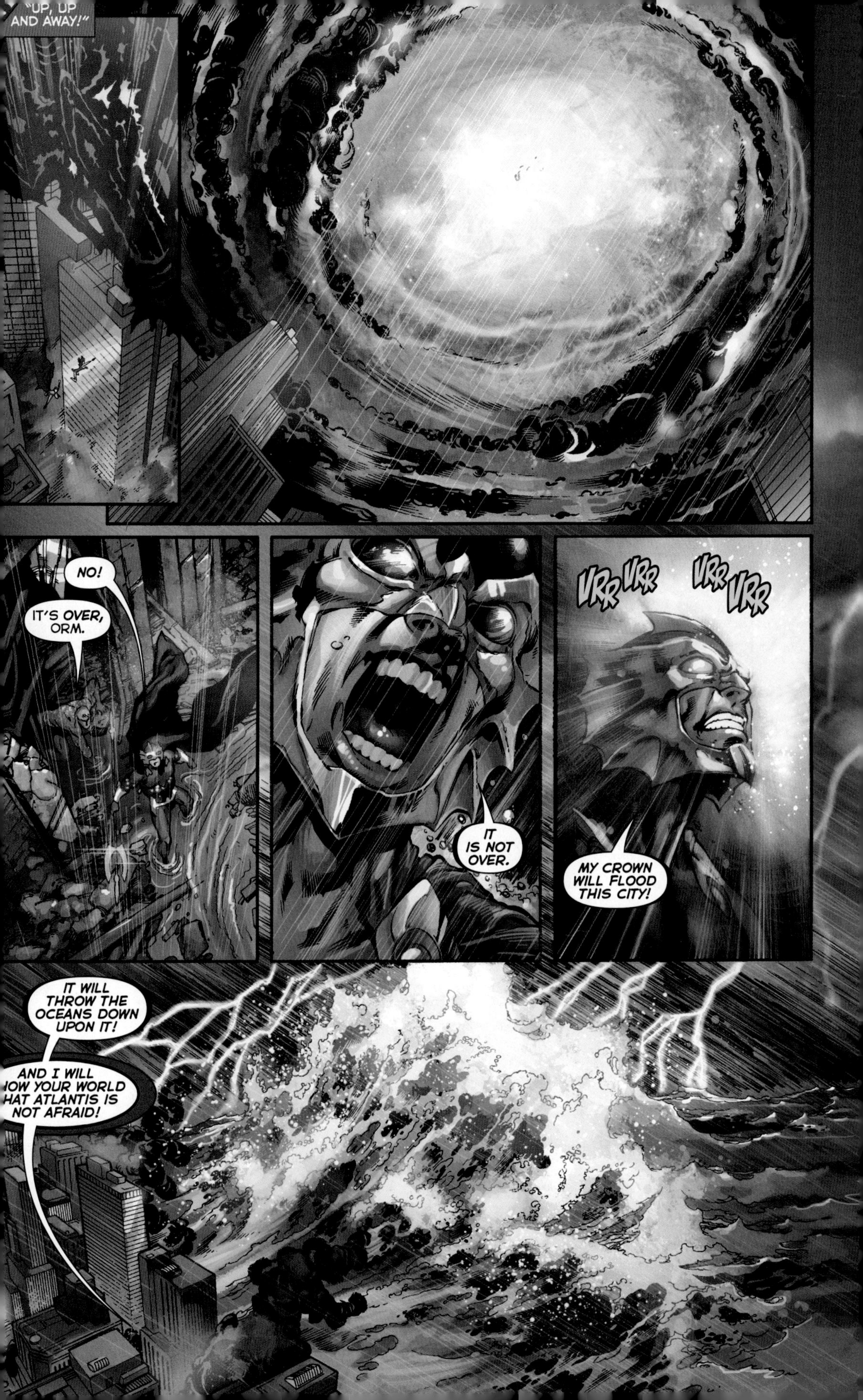
"UP, UP AND AWAY!"
NO!
IT'S OVER, ORM.
IT IS NOT OVER.
VRR VRR VRR VRR
MY CROWN WILL FLOOD THIS CITY!
IT WILL THROW THE OCEANS DOWN UPON IT!
AND I WILL HOW YOUR WORLD HAT ATLANTIS IS NOT AFRAID!

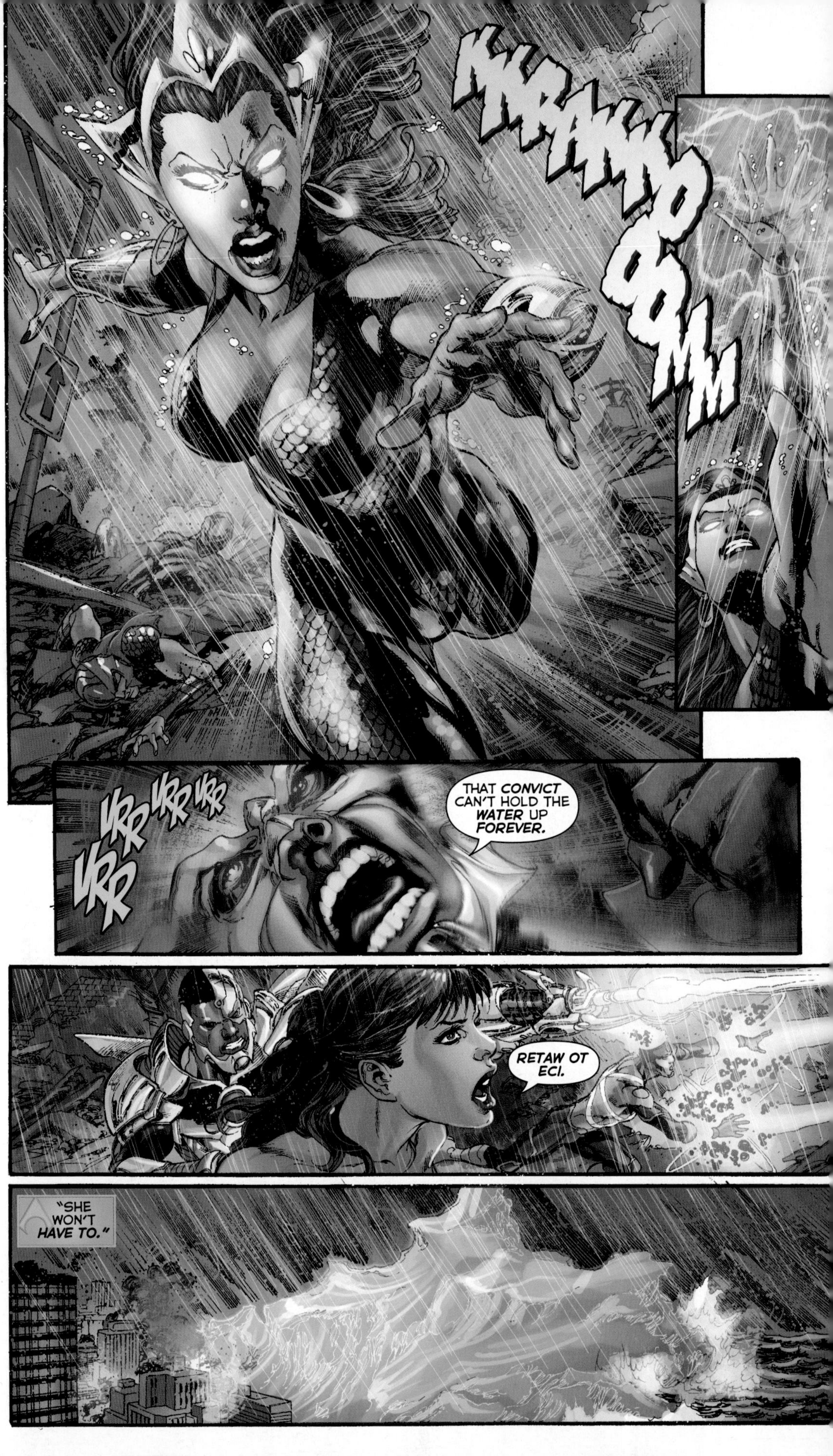
KKRAKKOOOMMM
URR URR URR URR
THAT CONVICT CAN'T HOLD THE WATER UP FOREVER.
RETAW OT ECI.
"SHE WON'T HAVE TO."

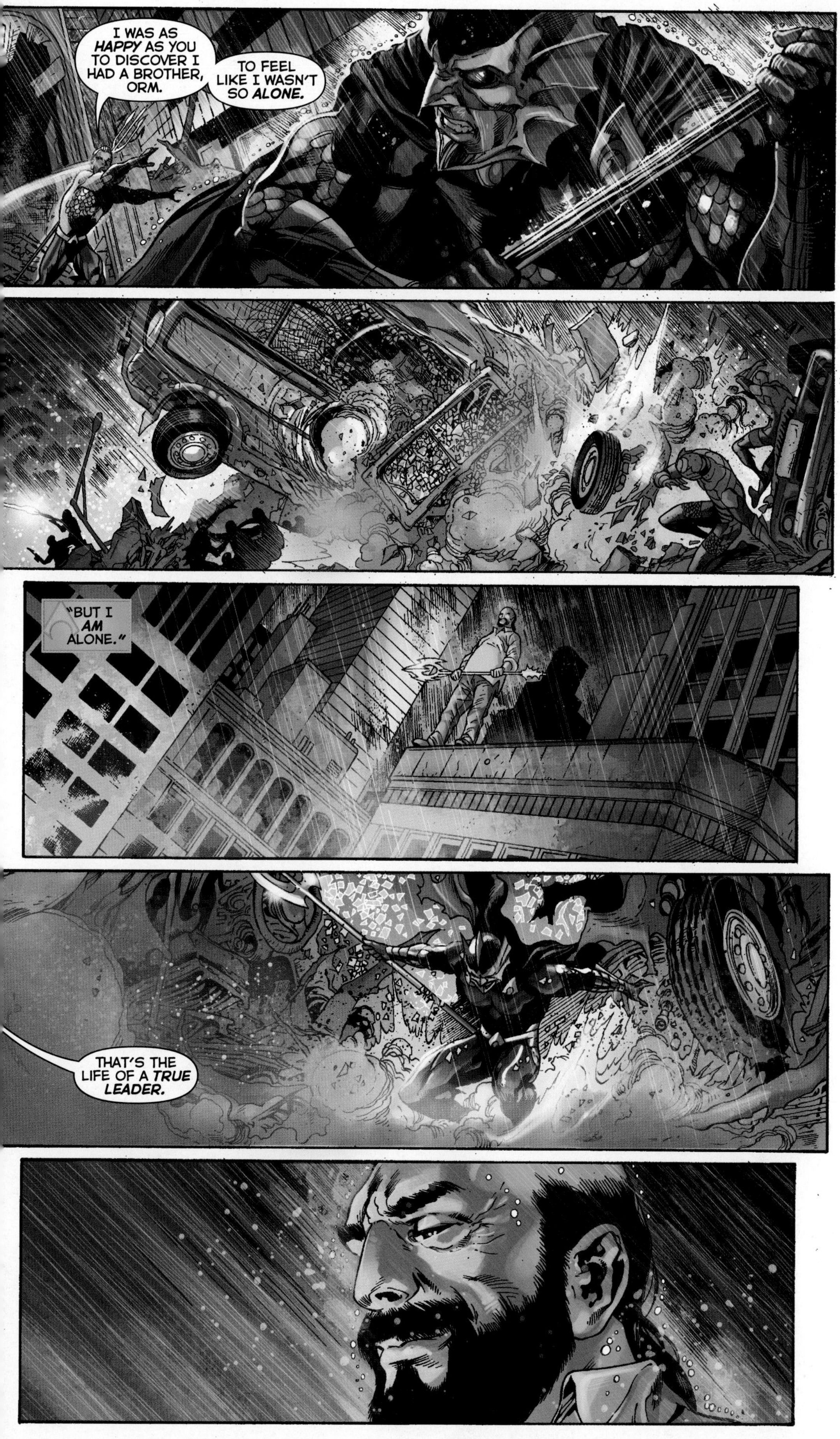
I WAS AS HAPPY AS YOU TO DISCOVER I HAD A BROTHER, ORM.
TO FEEL LIKE I WASN'T SO ALONE.
"BUT I AM ALONE."
THAT'S THE LIFE OF A TRUE LEADER.

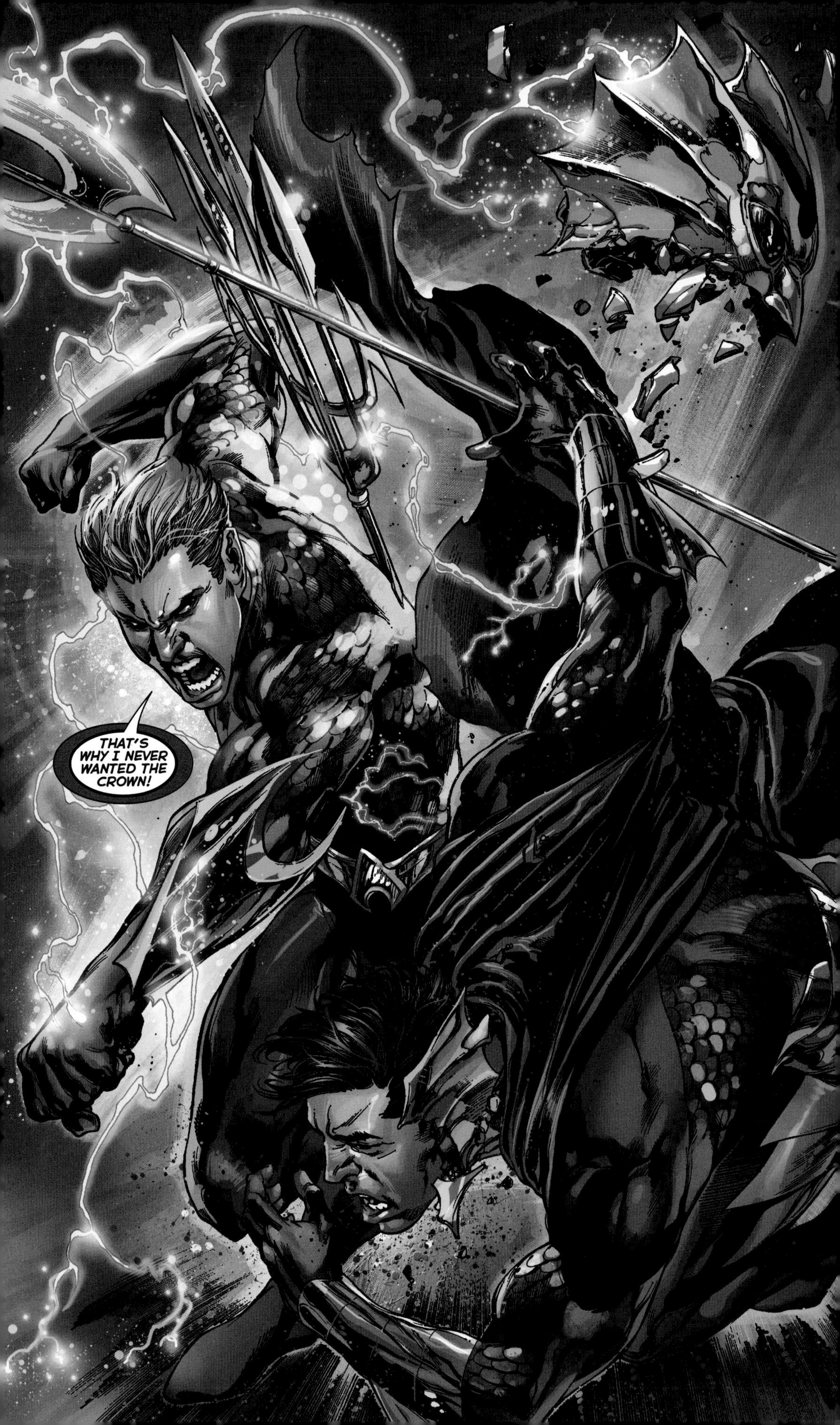
THAT'S WHY I NEVER WANTED THE CROWN!

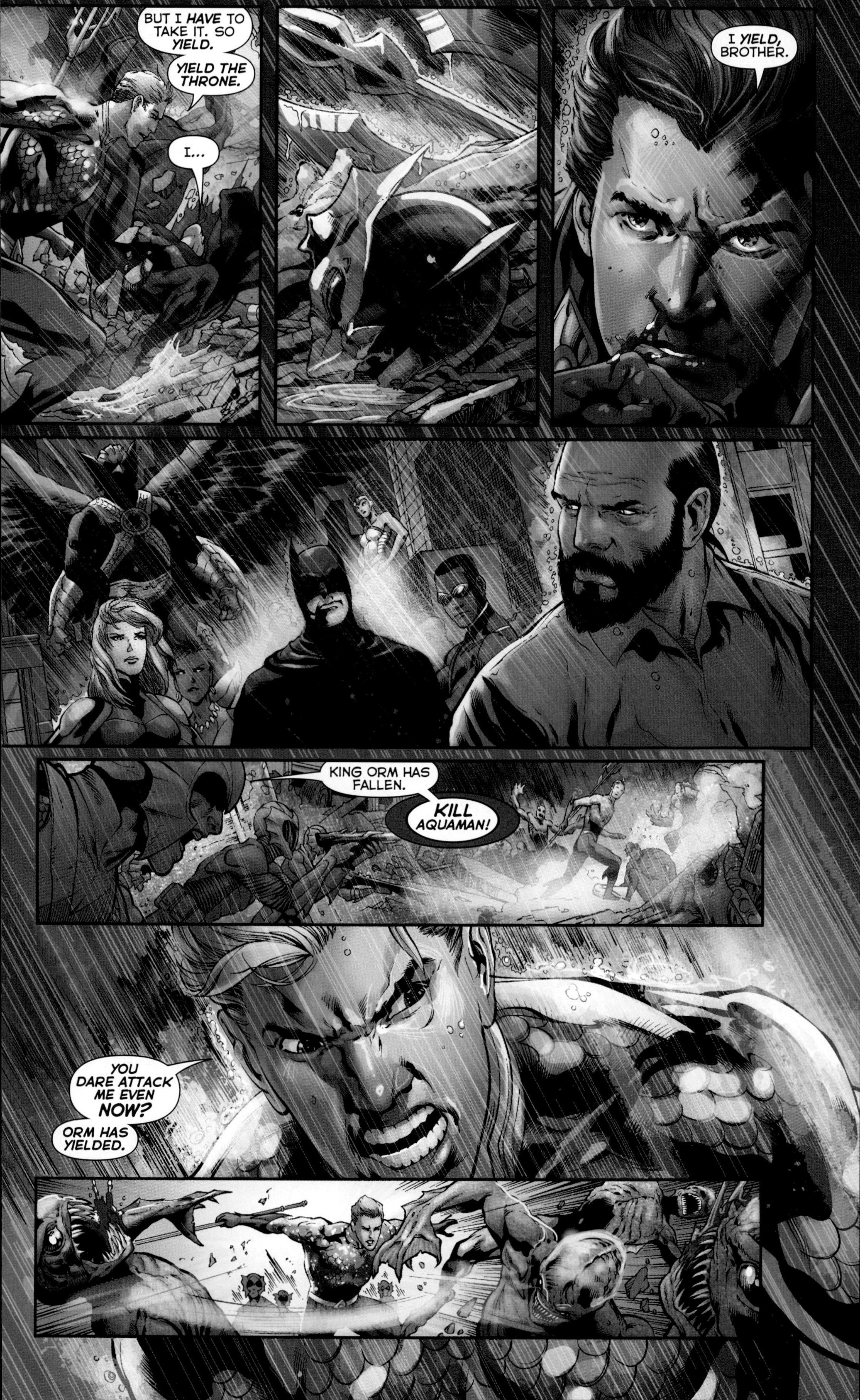
BUT I HAVE TO TAKE IT. SO YIELD.
YIELD THE THRONE.
I...
I YIELD, BROTHER.
KING ORM HAS FALLEN.
KILL AQUAMAN!
YOU DARE ATTACK ME EVEN NOW?
ORM HAS YIELDED.

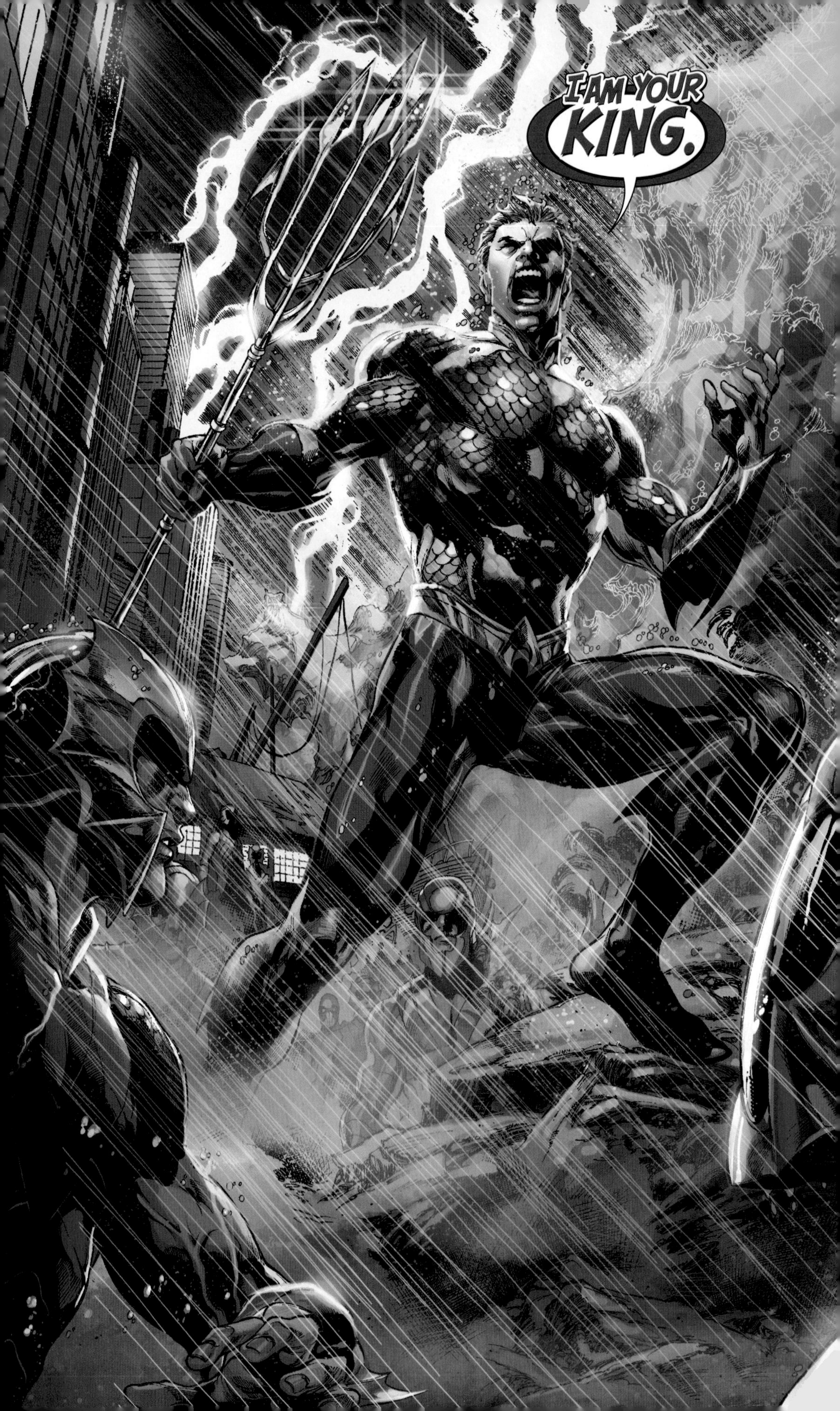
I-AM-YOUR KING.

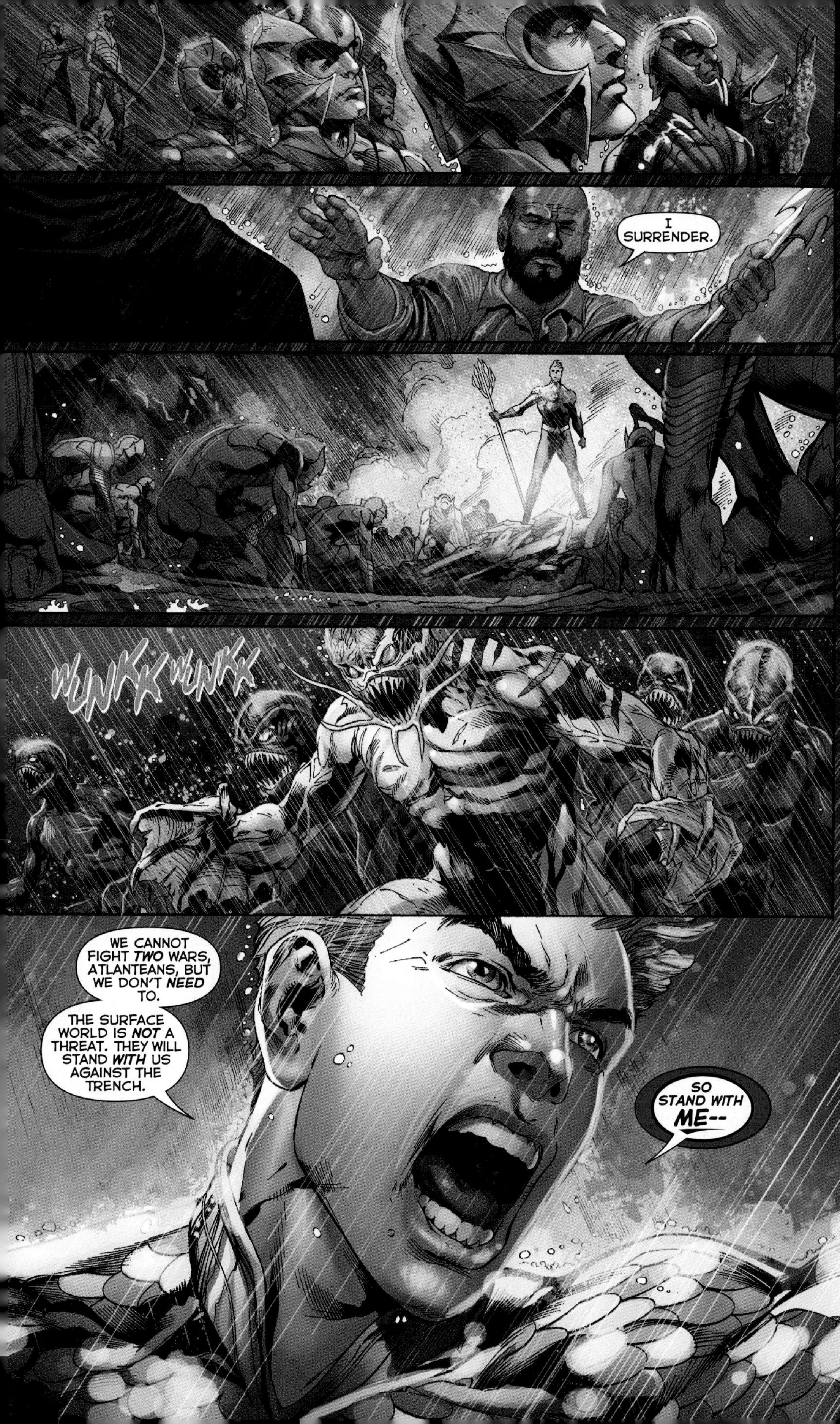

I SURRENDER.
WUNKK WUNKK
WE CANNOT FIGHT *TWO* WARS, ATLANTEANS, BUT WE DON'T *NEED* TO.
THE SURFACE WORLD IS *NOT* A THREAT. THEY WILL STAND *WITH* US AGAINST THE TRENCH.
SO STAND WITH *ME*--

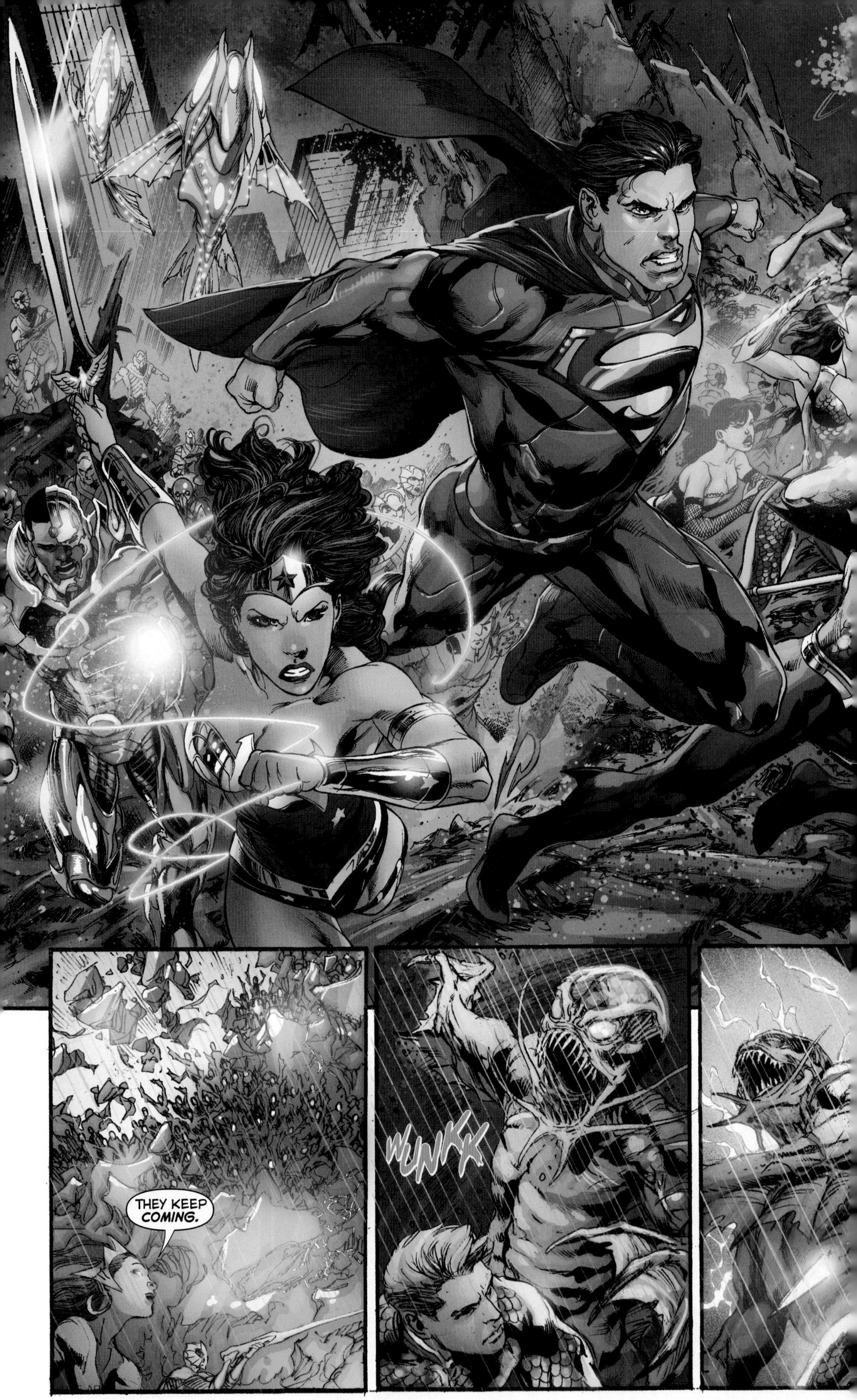
THEY KEEP COMING.
WUNKK

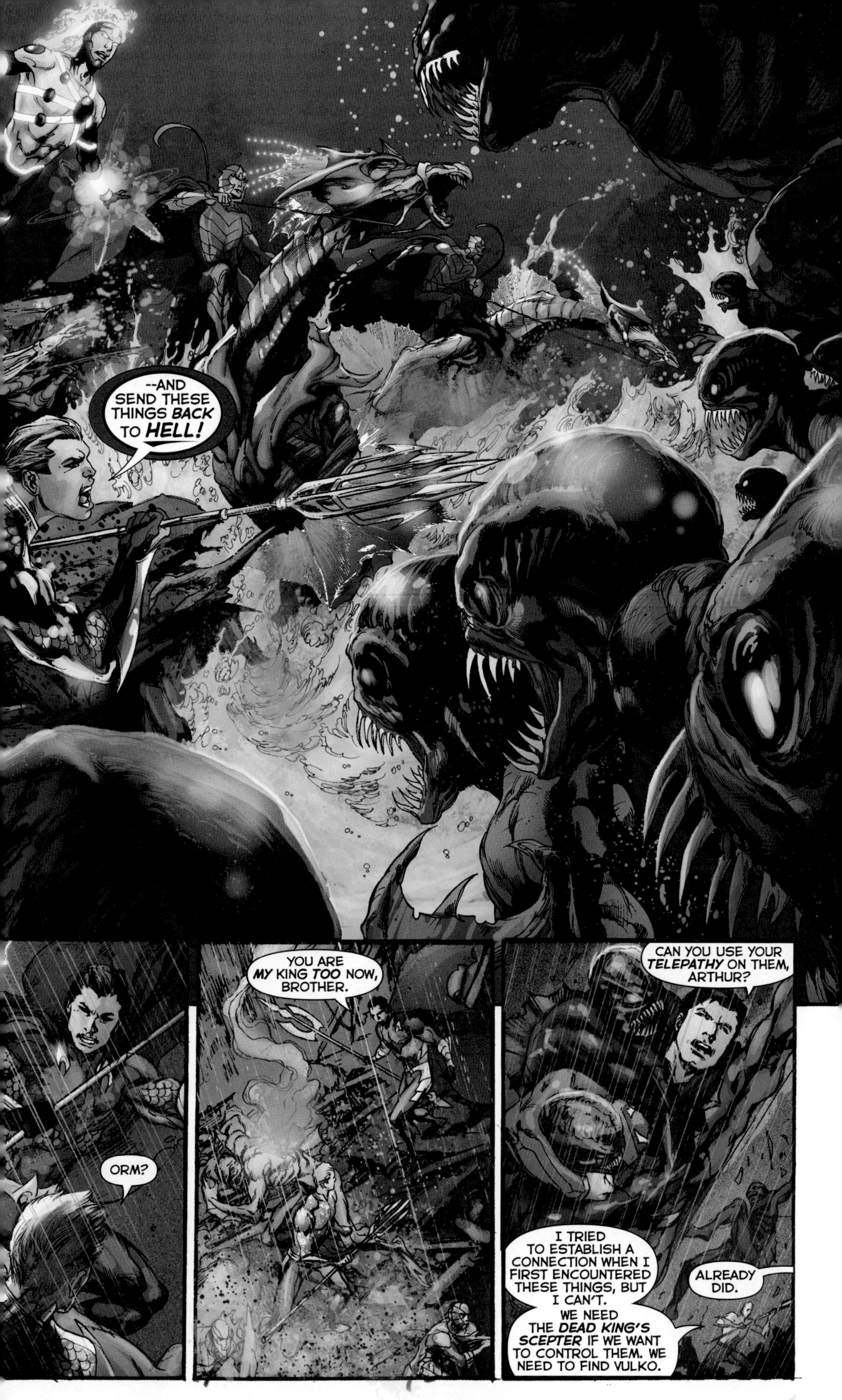
--AND SEND THESE THINGS *BACK* TO *HELL!*
ORM?
YOU ARE *MY* KING *TOO* NOW, BROTHER.
CAN YOU USE YOUR *TELEPATHY* ON THEM, ARTHUR?
I TRIED TO ESTABLISH A CONNECTION WHEN I FIRST ENCOUNTERED THESE THINGS, BUT I CAN'T.
WE NEED THE *DEAD KING'S SCEPTER* IF WE WANT TO CONTROL THEM. WE NEED TO FIND VULKO.
ALREADY DID.

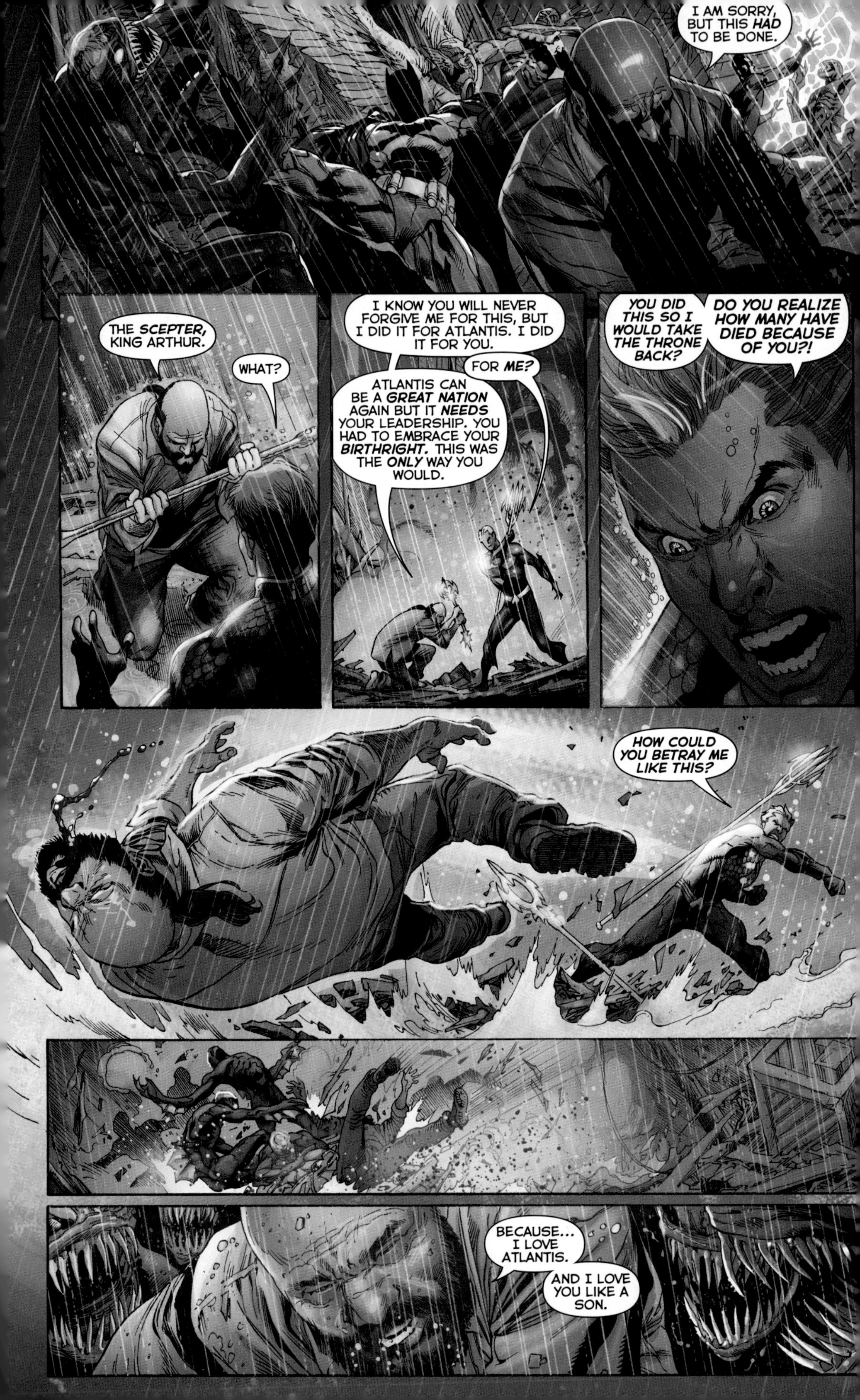
I AM SORRY, BUT THIS HAD TO BE DONE.
THE SCEPTER, KING ARTHUR.
WHAT?
I KNOW YOU WILL NEVER FORGIVE ME FOR THIS, BUT I DID IT FOR ATLANTIS. I DID IT FOR YOU.
FOR ME?
ATLANTIS CAN BE A GREAT NATION AGAIN BUT IT NEEDS YOUR LEADERSHIP. YOU HAD TO EMBRACE YOUR BIRTHRIGHT. THIS WAS THE ONLY WAY YOU WOULD.
YOU DID THIS SO I WOULD TAKE THE THRONE BACK?
DO YOU REALIZE HOW MANY HAVE DIED BECAUSE OF YOU?!
HOW COULD YOU BETRAY ME LIKE THIS?
BECAUSE... I LOVE ATLANTIS.
AND I LOVE YOU LIKE A SON.

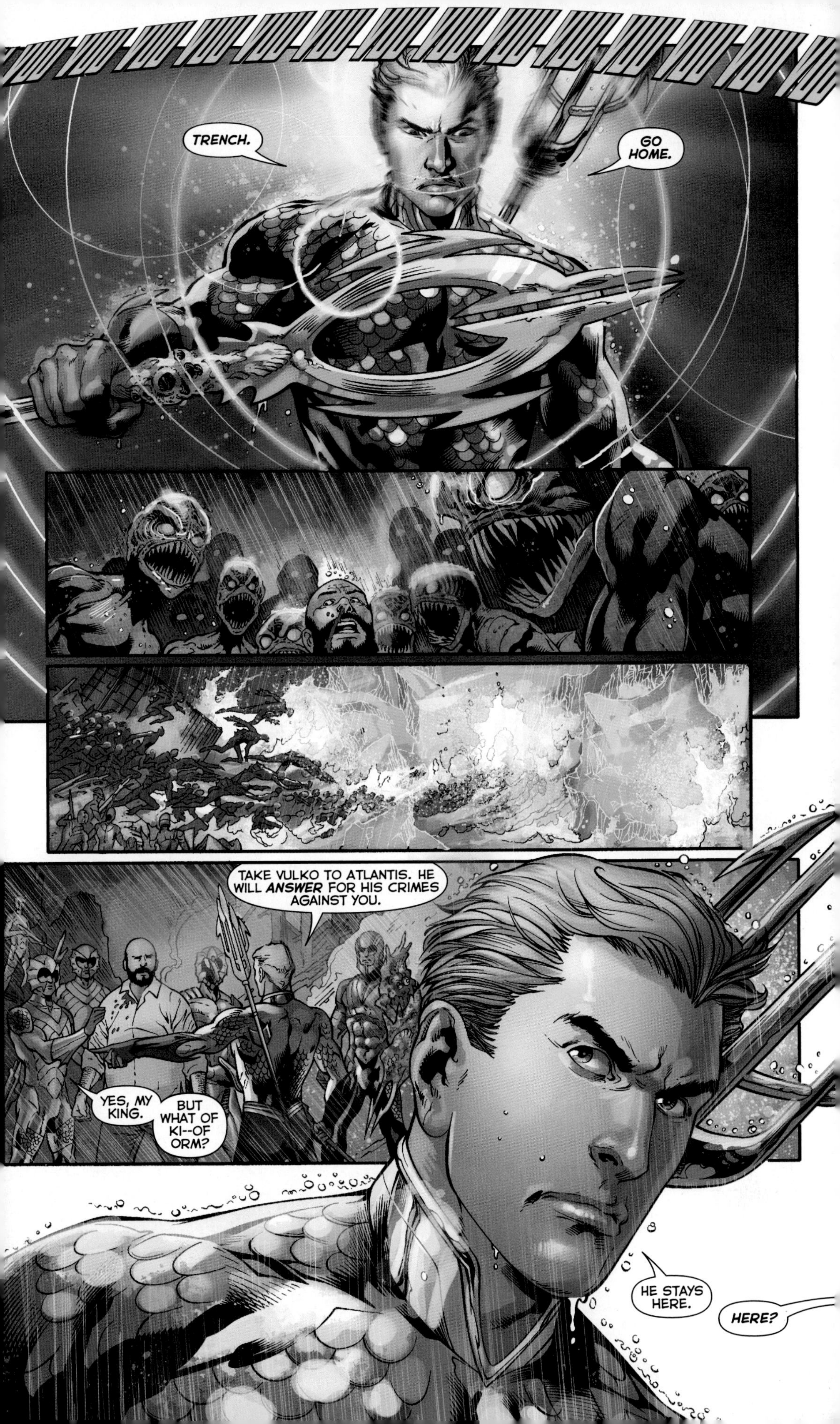
VOO-VOO-VOO-VOO-VOO-VOO-VOO-VOO-VOO-VOO-VOO-VOO-VOO-VOO-VOO-VOO-VOO
TRENCH.
GO HOME.
TAKE VULKO TO ATLANTIS. HE WILL ANSWER FOR HIS CRIMES AGAINST YOU.
YES, MY KING.
BUT WHAT OF KI--OF ORM?
HE STAYS HERE.
HERE?

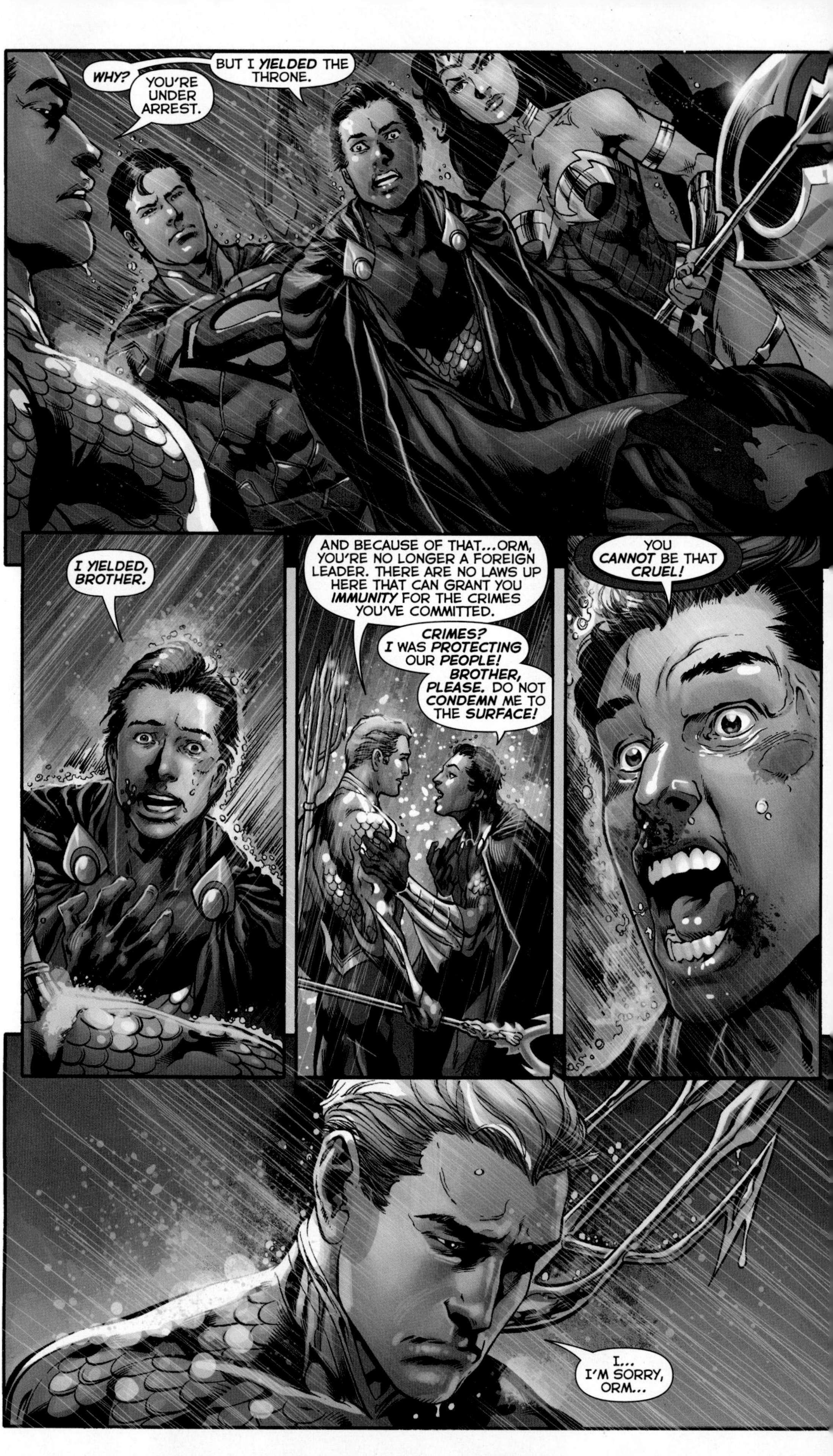
WHY?
YOU'RE UNDER ARREST.
BUT I YIELDED THE THRONE.
I YIELDED, BROTHER.
AND BECAUSE OF THAT...ORM, YOU'RE NO LONGER A FOREIGN LEADER. THERE ARE NO LAWS UP HERE THAT CAN GRANT YOU IMMUNITY FOR THE CRIMES YOU'VE COMMITTED.
CRIMES? I WAS PROTECTING OUR PEOPLE! BROTHER, PLEASE. DO NOT CONDEMN ME TO THE SURFACE!
YOU CANNOT BE THAT CRUEL!
I... I'M SORRY, ORM...

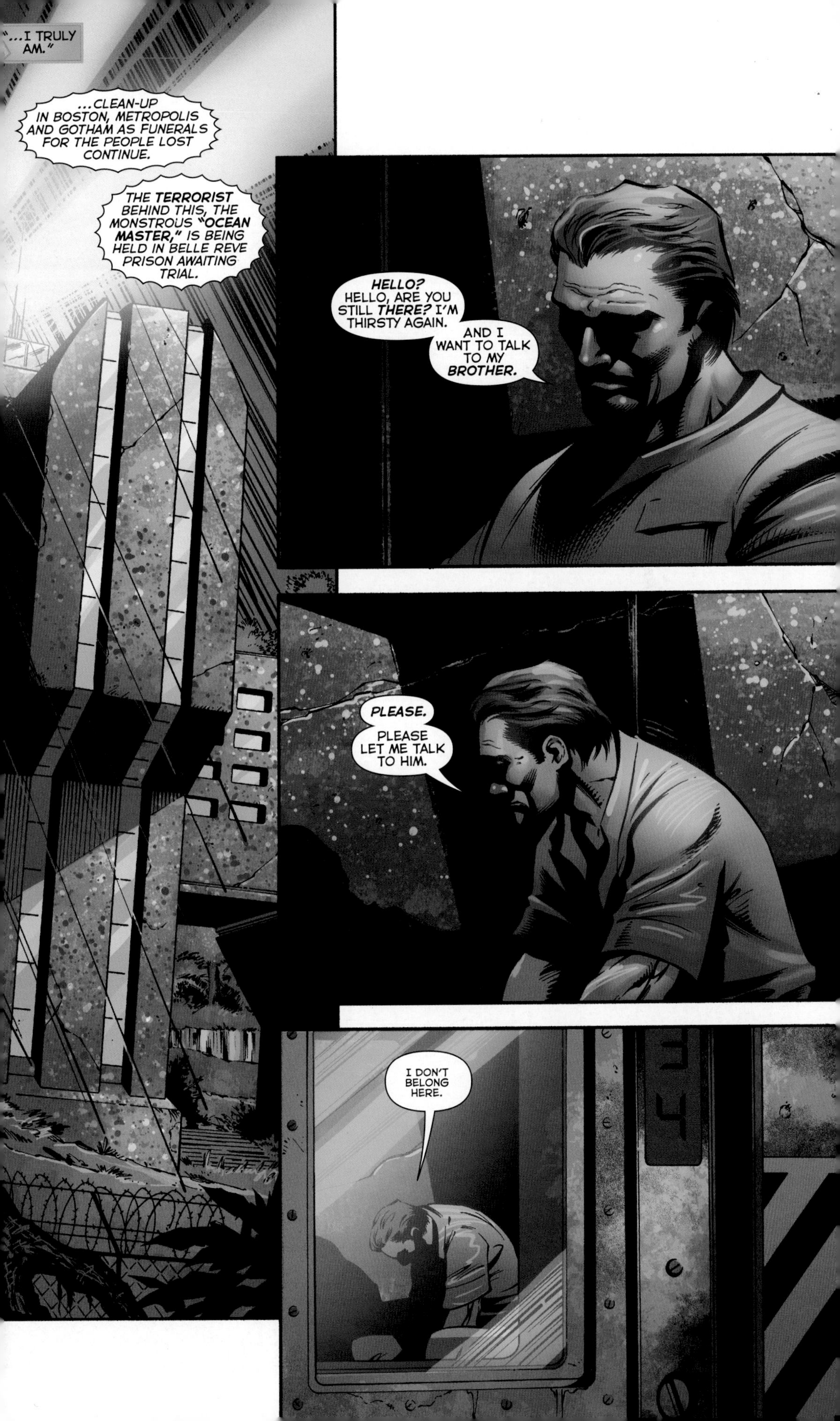
"...I TRULY AM."
...CLEAN-UP IN BOSTON, METROPOLIS AND GOTHAM AS FUNERALS FOR THE PEOPLE LOST CONTINUE.
THE TERRORIST BEHIND THIS, THE MONSTROUS "OCEAN MASTER," IS BEING HELD IN BELLE REVE PRISON AWAITING TRIAL.
HELLO? HELLO, ARE YOU STILL THERE? I'M THIRSTY AGAIN.
AND I WANT TO TALK TO MY BROTHER.
PLEASE.
PLEASE LET ME TALK TO HIM.
I DON'T BELONG HERE.

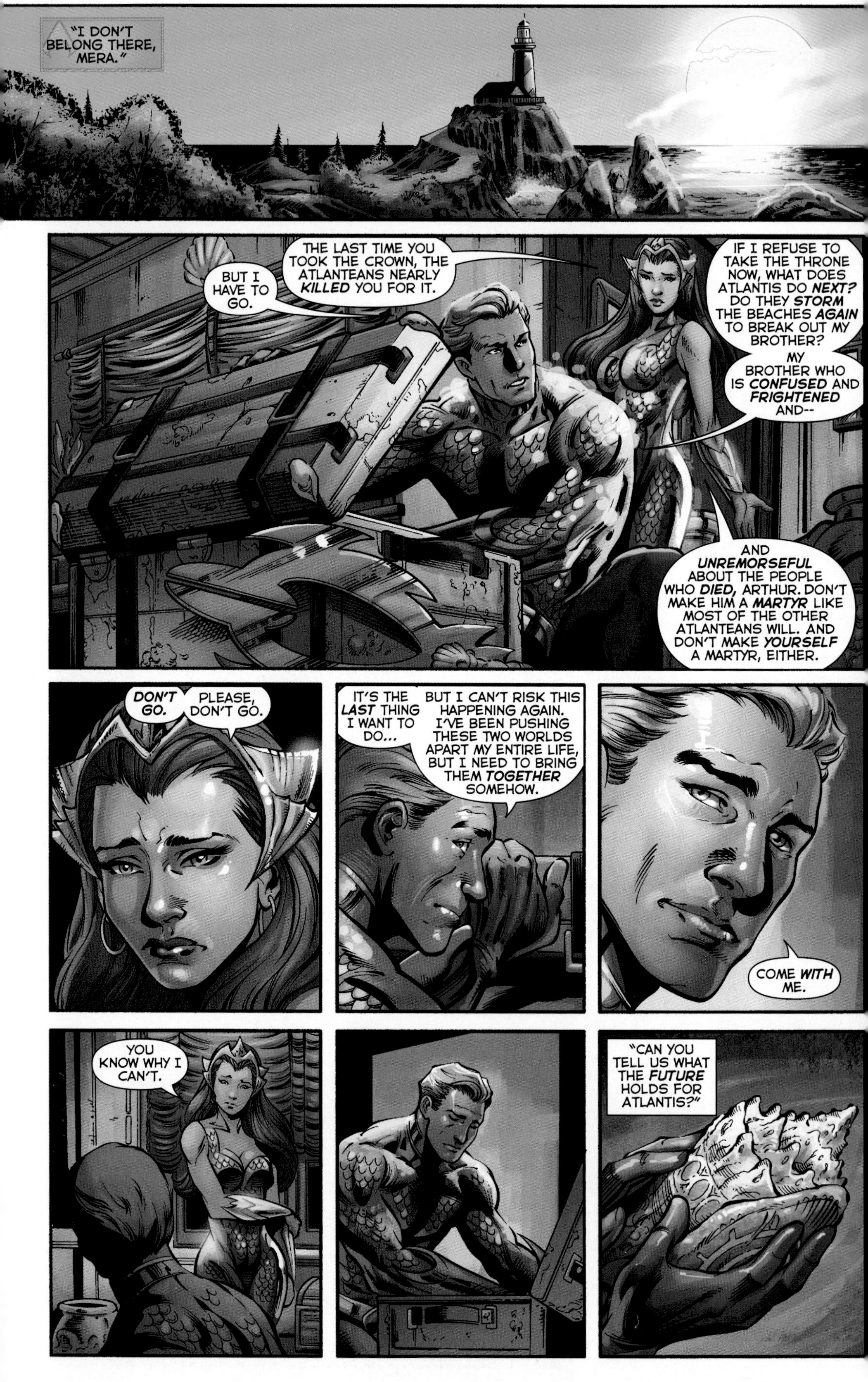
"I DON'T BELONG THERE, MERA."
BUT I HAVE TO GO.
THE LAST TIME YOU TOOK THE CROWN, THE ATLANTEANS NEARLY KILLED YOU FOR IT.
IF I REFUSE TO TAKE THE THRONE NOW, WHAT DOES ATLANTIS DO NEXT? DO THEY STORM THE BEACHES AGAIN TO BREAK OUT MY BROTHER?
MY BROTHER WHO IS CONFUSED AND FRIGHTENED AND--
AND UNREMORSEFUL ABOUT THE PEOPLE WHO DIED, ARTHUR. DON'T MAKE HIM A MARTYR LIKE MOST OF THE OTHER ATLANTEANS WILL. AND DON'T MAKE YOURSELF A MARTYR, EITHER.
DON'T GO.
PLEASE, DON'T GO.
IT'S THE LAST THING I WANT TO DO...
BUT I CAN'T RISK THIS HAPPENING AGAIN. I'VE BEEN PUSHING THESE TWO WORLDS APART MY ENTIRE LIFE, BUT I NEED TO BRING THEM TOGETHER SOMEHOW.
COME WITH ME.
YOU KNOW WHY I CAN'T.
"CAN YOU TELL US WHAT THE FUTURE HOLDS FOR ATLANTIS?"

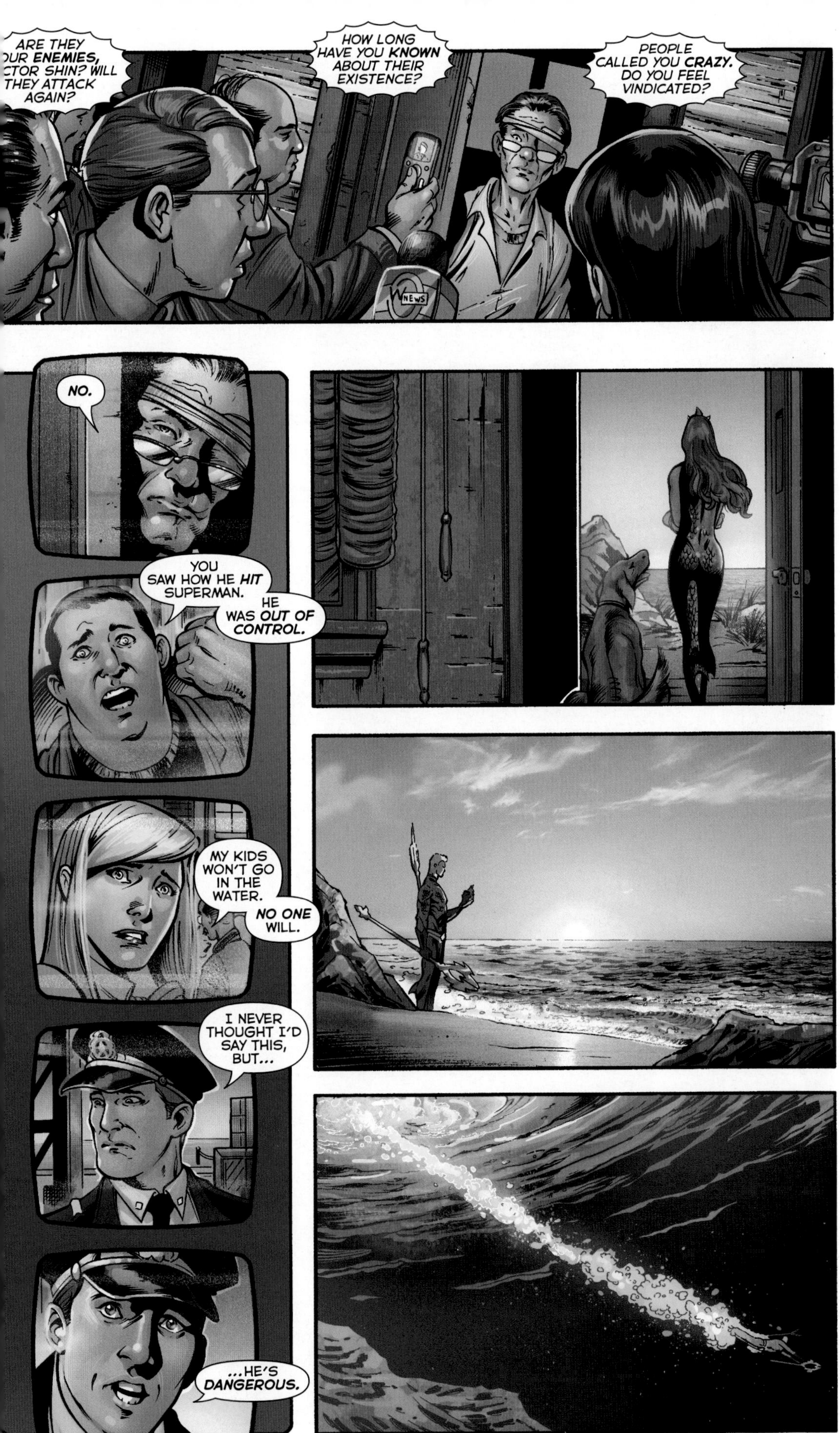
ARE THEY OUR ENEMIES, DOCTOR SHIN? WILL THEY ATTACK AGAIN?
HOW LONG HAVE YOU KNOWN ABOUT THEIR EXISTENCE?
PEOPLE CALLED YOU CRAZY. DO YOU FEEL VINDICATED?
NEWS
NO.
YOU SAW HOW HE HIT SUPERMAN. HE WAS OUT OF CONTROL.
MY KIDS WON'T GO IN THE WATER. NO ONE WILL.
I NEVER THOUGHT I'D SAY THIS, BUT...
...HE'S DANGEROUS.

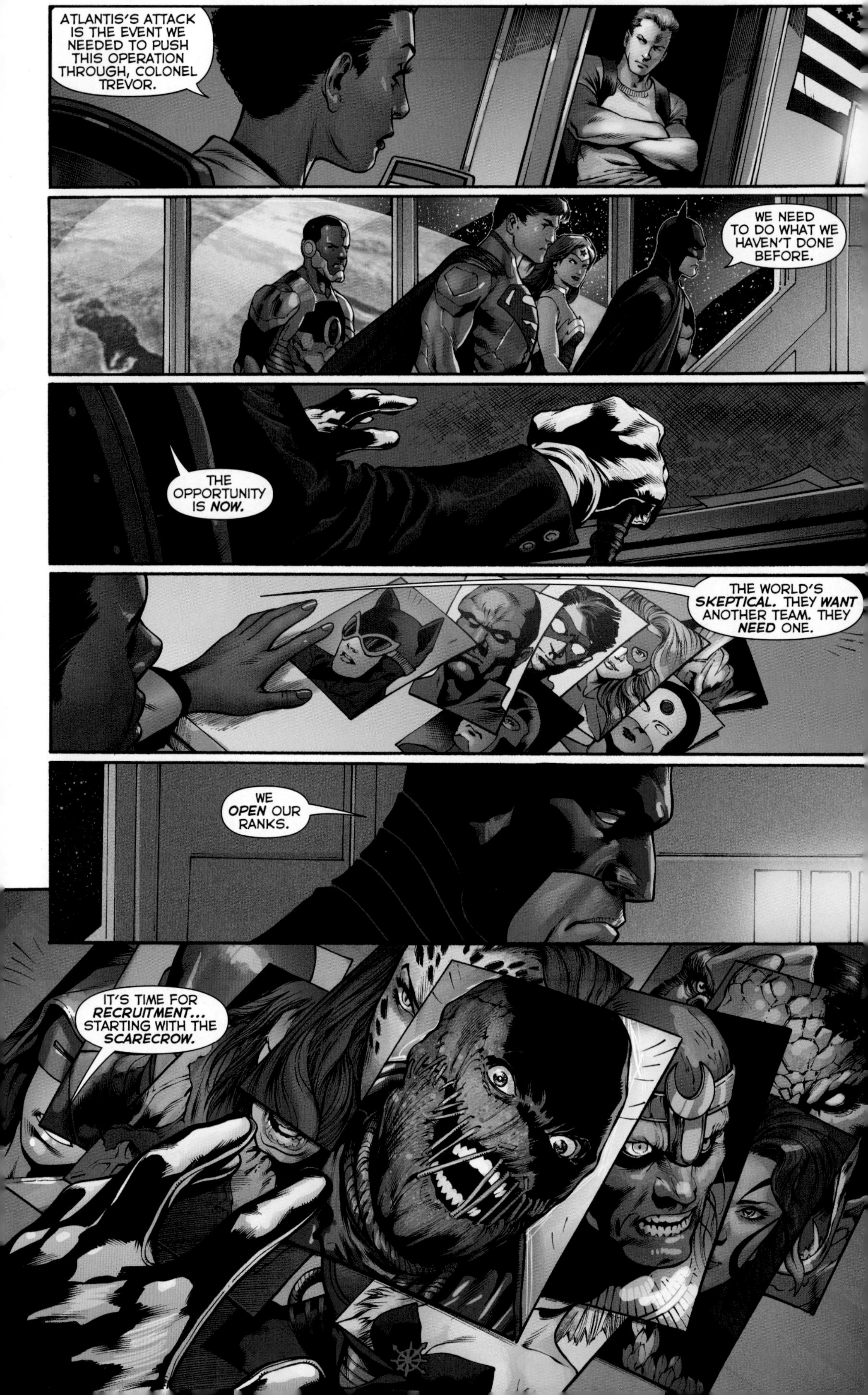
ATLANTIS'S ATTACK IS THE EVENT WE NEEDED TO PUSH THIS OPERATION THROUGH, COLONEL TREVOR.
WE NEED TO DO WHAT WE HAVEN'T DONE BEFORE.
THE OPPORTUNITY IS NOW.
THE WORLD'S SKEPTICAL. THEY WANT ANOTHER TEAM. THEY NEED ONE.
WE OPEN OUR RANKS.
IT'S TIME FOR RECRUITMENT... STARTING WITH THE SCARECROW.

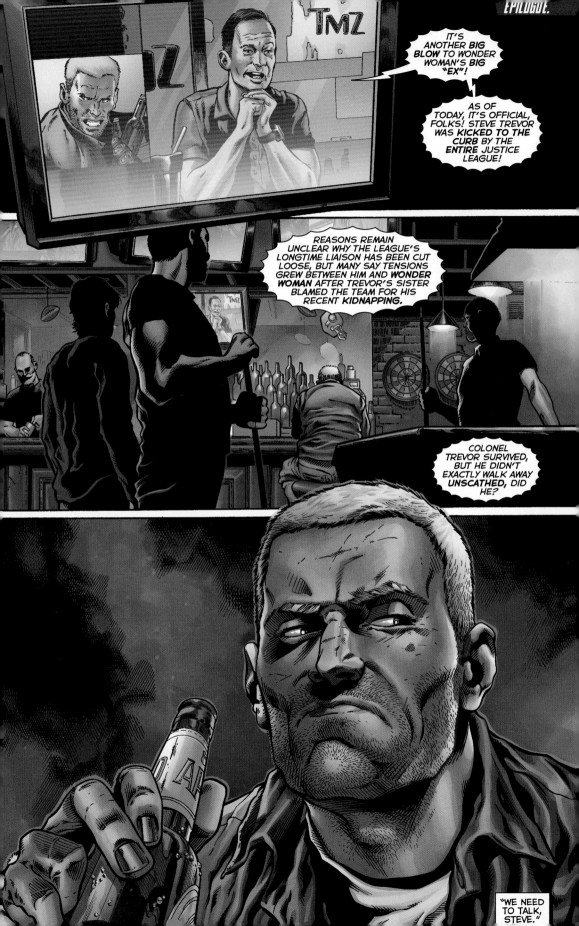

IT'S ANOTHER BIG BLOW TO WONDER WOMAN'S BIG "EX"!

AS OF TODAY, IT'S OFFICIAL, FOLKS! STEVE TREVOR WAS KICKED TO THE CURB BY THE ENTIRE JUSTICE LEAGUE!

REASONS REMAIN UNCLEAR WHY THE LEAGUE'S LONGTIME LIAISON HAS BEEN CUT LOOSE, BUT MANY SAY TENSIONS GREW BETWEEN HIM AND WONDER WOMAN AFTER TREVOR'S SISTER BLAMED THE TEAM FOR HIS RECENT KIDNAPPING.

COLONEL TREVOR SURVIVED, BUT HE DIDN'T EXACTLY WALK AWAY UNSCATHED, DID HE?

"WE NEED TO TALK, STEVE."

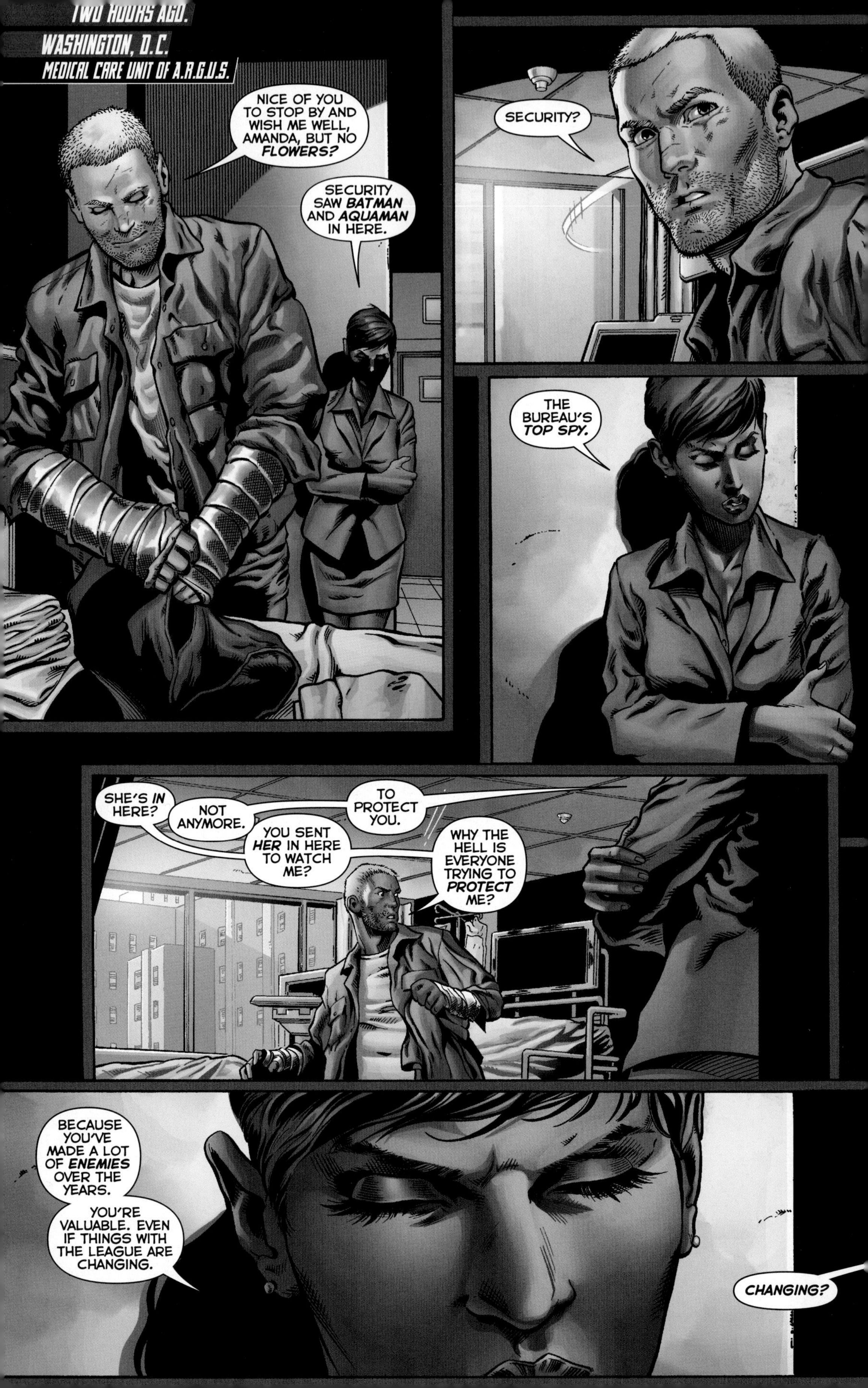
TWO HOURS AGO.
WASHINGTON, D.C.
MEDICAL CARE UNIT OF A.R.G.U.S.
NICE OF YOU TO STOP BY AND WISH ME WELL, AMANDA, BUT NO *FLOWERS?*
SECURITY SAW *BATMAN* AND *AQUAMAN* IN HERE.
SECURITY?
THE BUREAU'S *TOP SPY.*
SHE'S *IN* HERE?
NOT ANYMORE.
YOU SENT *HER* IN HERE TO WATCH ME?
TO PROTECT YOU.
WHY THE HELL IS EVERYONE TRYING TO *PROTECT* ME?
BECAUSE YOU'VE MADE A LOT OF *ENEMIES* OVER THE YEARS.
YOU'RE VALUABLE. EVEN IF THINGS WITH THE LEAGUE ARE CHANGING.
CHANGING?

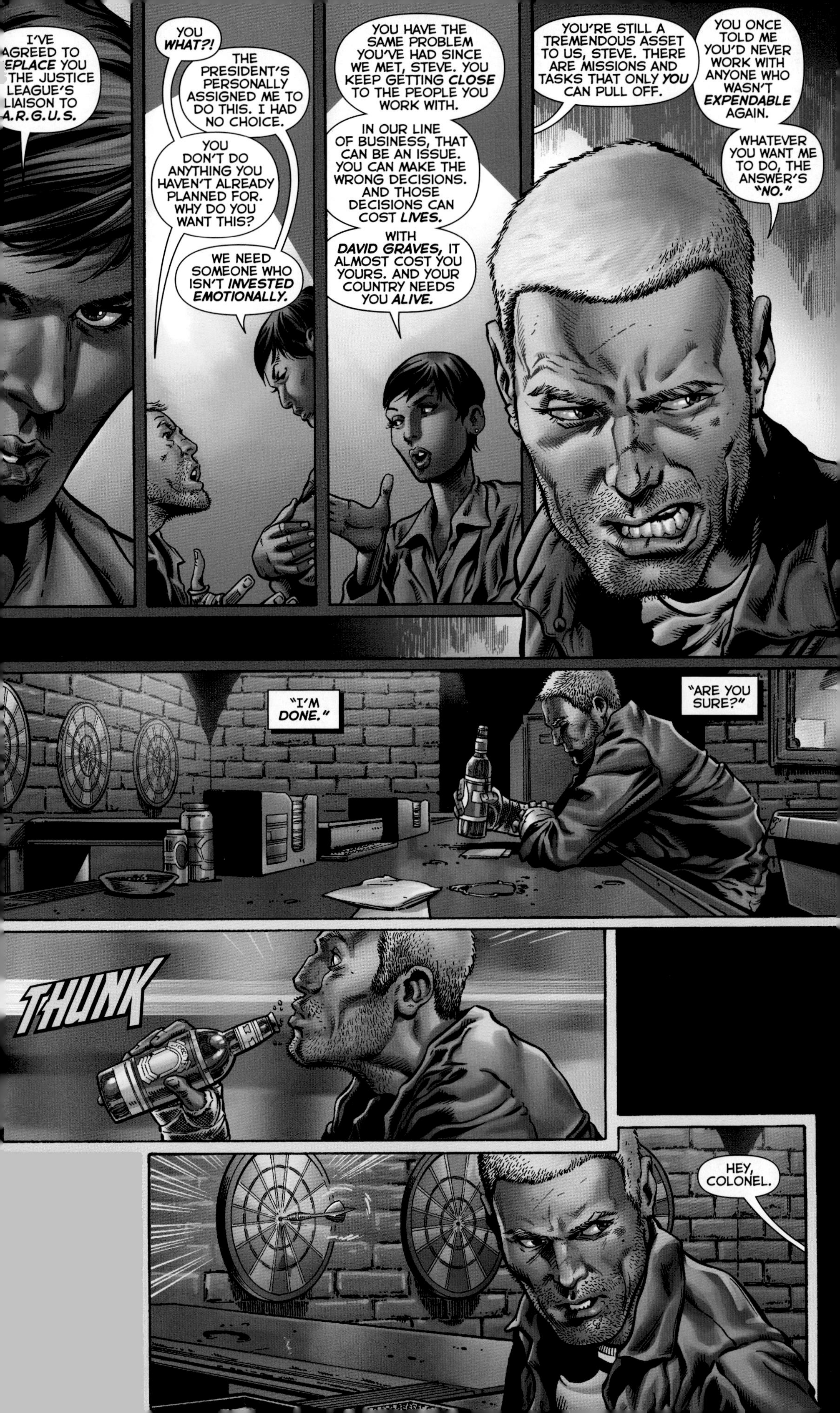

I'VE AGREED TO EPLACE YOU THE JUSTICE LEAGUE'S LIAISON TO A.R.G.U.S.
YOU WHAT?!
THE PRESIDENT'S PERSONALLY ASSIGNED ME TO DO THIS. I HAD NO CHOICE.
YOU DON'T DO ANYTHING YOU HAVEN'T ALREADY PLANNED FOR. WHY DO YOU WANT THIS?
WE NEED SOMEONE WHO ISN'T INVESTED EMOTIONALLY.
YOU HAVE THE SAME PROBLEM YOU'VE HAD SINCE WE MET, STEVE. YOU KEEP GETTING CLOSE TO THE PEOPLE YOU WORK WITH.
IN OUR LINE OF BUSINESS, THAT CAN BE AN ISSUE. YOU CAN MAKE THE WRONG DECISIONS. AND THOSE DECISIONS CAN COST LIVES.
WITH DAVID GRAVES, IT ALMOST COST YOU YOURS. AND YOUR COUNTRY NEEDS YOU ALIVE.
YOU'RE STILL A TREMENDOUS ASSET TO US, STEVE. THERE ARE MISSIONS AND TASKS THAT ONLY YOU CAN PULL OFF.
YOU ONCE TOLD ME YOU'D NEVER WORK WITH ANYONE WHO WASN'T EXPENDABLE AGAIN.
WHATEVER YOU WANT ME TO DO, THE ANSWER'S "NO."
"I'M DONE."
"ARE YOU SURE?"
THUNK
HEY, COLONEL.

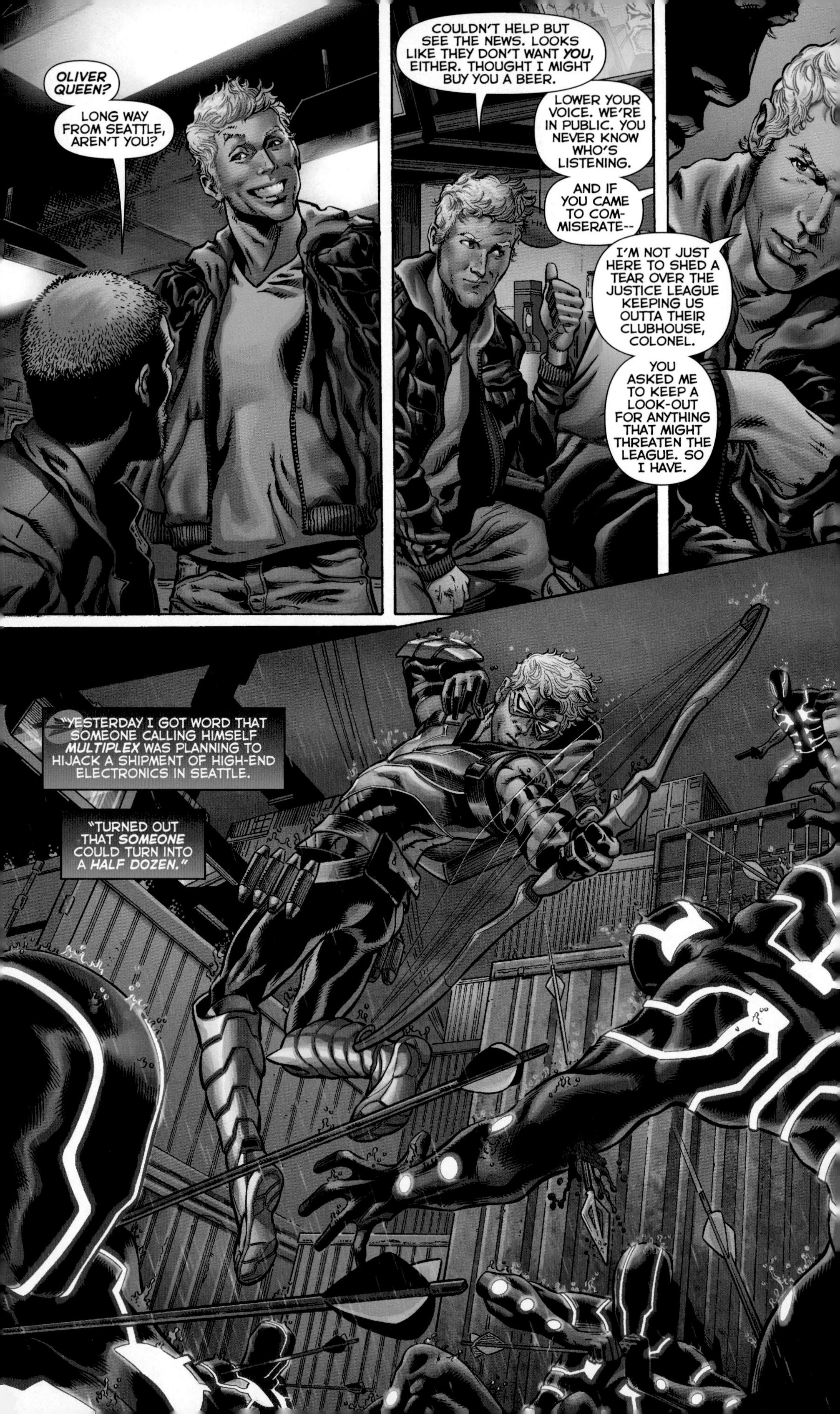

OLIVER QUEEN?
LONG WAY FROM SEATTLE, AREN'T YOU?
COULDN'T HELP BUT SEE THE NEWS. LOOKS LIKE THEY DON'T WANT YOU, EITHER. THOUGHT I MIGHT BUY YOU A BEER.
LOWER YOUR VOICE. WE'RE IN PUBLIC. YOU NEVER KNOW WHO'S LISTENING.
AND IF YOU CAME TO COM-MISERATE--
I'M NOT JUST HERE TO SHED A TEAR OVER THE JUSTICE LEAGUE KEEPING US OUTTA THEIR CLUBHOUSE, COLONEL.
YOU ASKED ME TO KEEP A LOOK-OUT FOR ANYTHING THAT MIGHT THREATEN THE LEAGUE. SO I HAVE.
"YESTERDAY I GOT WORD THAT SOMEONE CALLING HIMSELF MULTIPLEX WAS PLANNING TO HIJACK A SHIPMENT OF HIGH-END ELECTRONICS IN SEATTLE.
"TURNED OUT THAT SOMEONE COULD TURN INTO A HALF DOZEN."

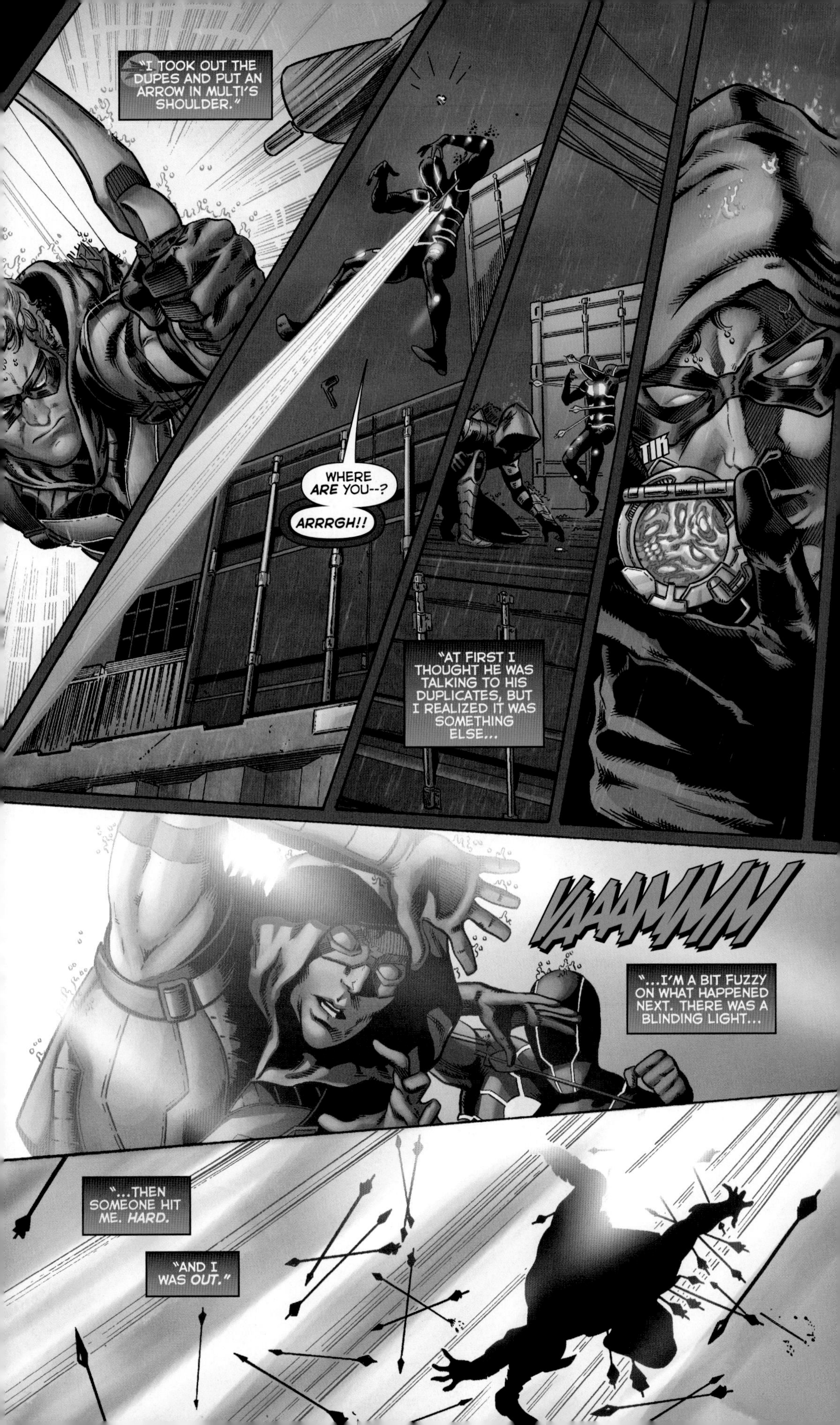
"I TOOK OUT THE DUPES AND PUT AN ARROW IN MULTI'S SHOULDER."
WHERE ARE YOU--?
ARRRGH!!
"AT FIRST I THOUGHT HE WAS TALKING TO HIS DUPLICATES, BUT I REALIZED IT WAS SOMETHING ELSE...
TIK
VAAMMM
"...I'M A BIT FUZZY ON WHAT HAPPENED NEXT. THERE WAS A BLINDING LIGHT...
"...THEN SOMEONE HIT ME. HARD.
"AND I WAS OUT."

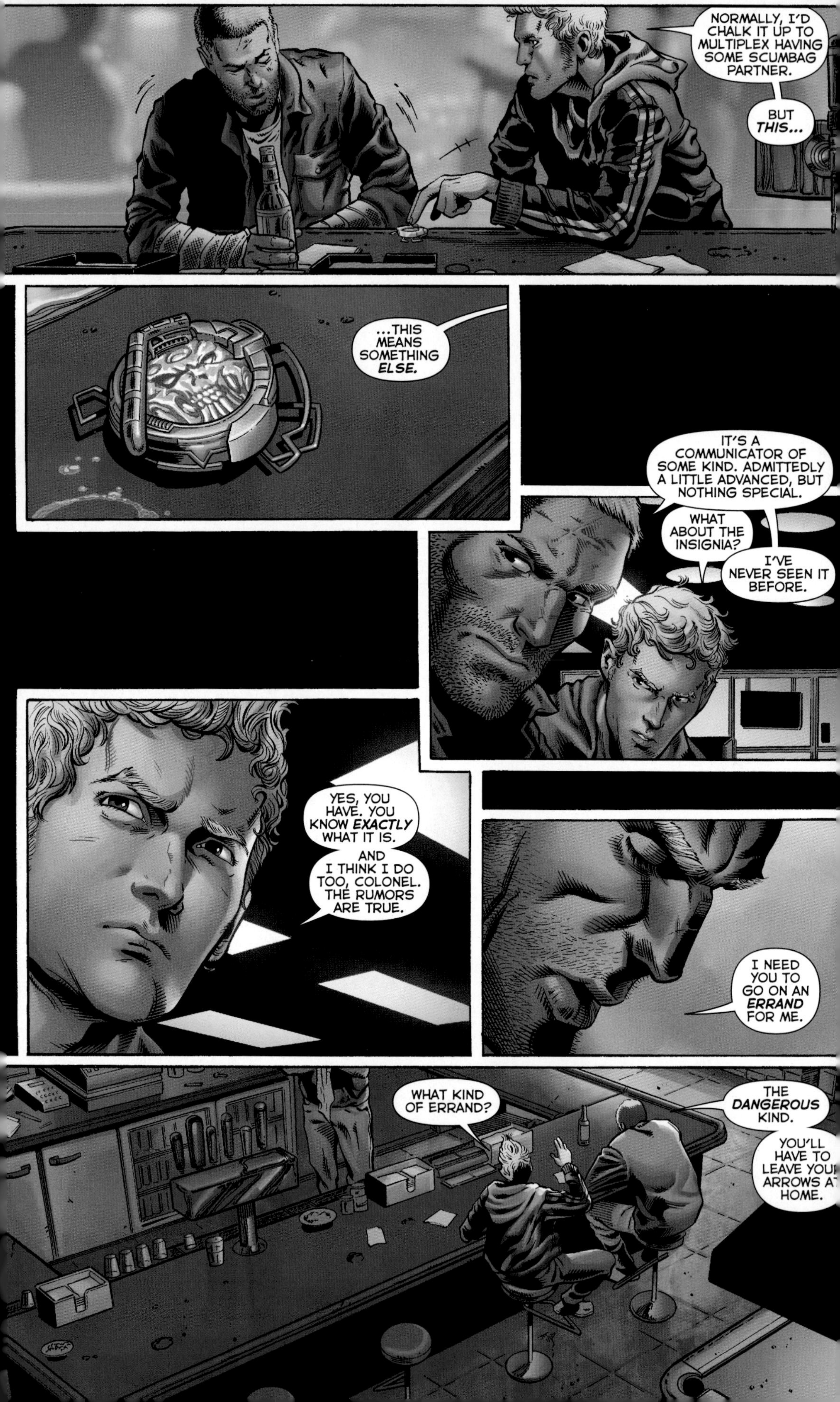
NORMALLY, I'D CHALK IT UP TO MULTIPLEX HAVING SOME SCUMBAG PARTNER.
BUT THIS...
...THIS MEANS SOMETHING ELSE.
IT'S A COMMUNICATOR OF SOME KIND. ADMITTEDLY A LITTLE ADVANCED, BUT NOTHING SPECIAL.
WHAT ABOUT THE INSIGNIA?
I'VE NEVER SEEN IT BEFORE.
YES, YOU HAVE. YOU KNOW EXACTLY WHAT IT IS.
AND I THINK I DO TOO, COLONEL. THE RUMORS ARE TRUE.
I NEED YOU TO GO ON AN ERRAND FOR ME.
WHAT KIND OF ERRAND?
THE DANGEROUS KIND.
YOU'LL HAVE TO LEAVE YOU ARROWS A HOME.

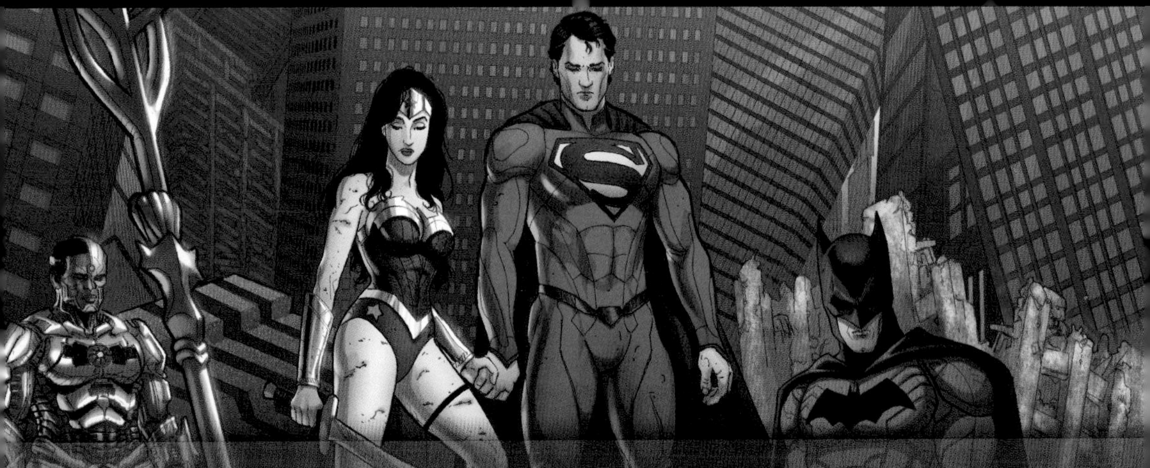

VARIANT COVER GALLERY

JUSTICE LEAGUE 13
By Alex Garner

JUSTICE LEAGUE 14
By Jason Fabok & Alex Sinclair

JUSTICE LEAGUE 15
By Jim Lee, Scott Williams & Alex Sinclair

AQUAMAN 15
By Jim Lee, Scott Williams & Alex Sinclair

JUSTICE LEAGUE 15
By Billy Tucci & Hi-Fi

JUSTICE LEAGUE 16
By Langdon Foss & Jose Villarrubia

JUSTICE LEAGUE 17
By Steve Skroce & Alex Sinclair

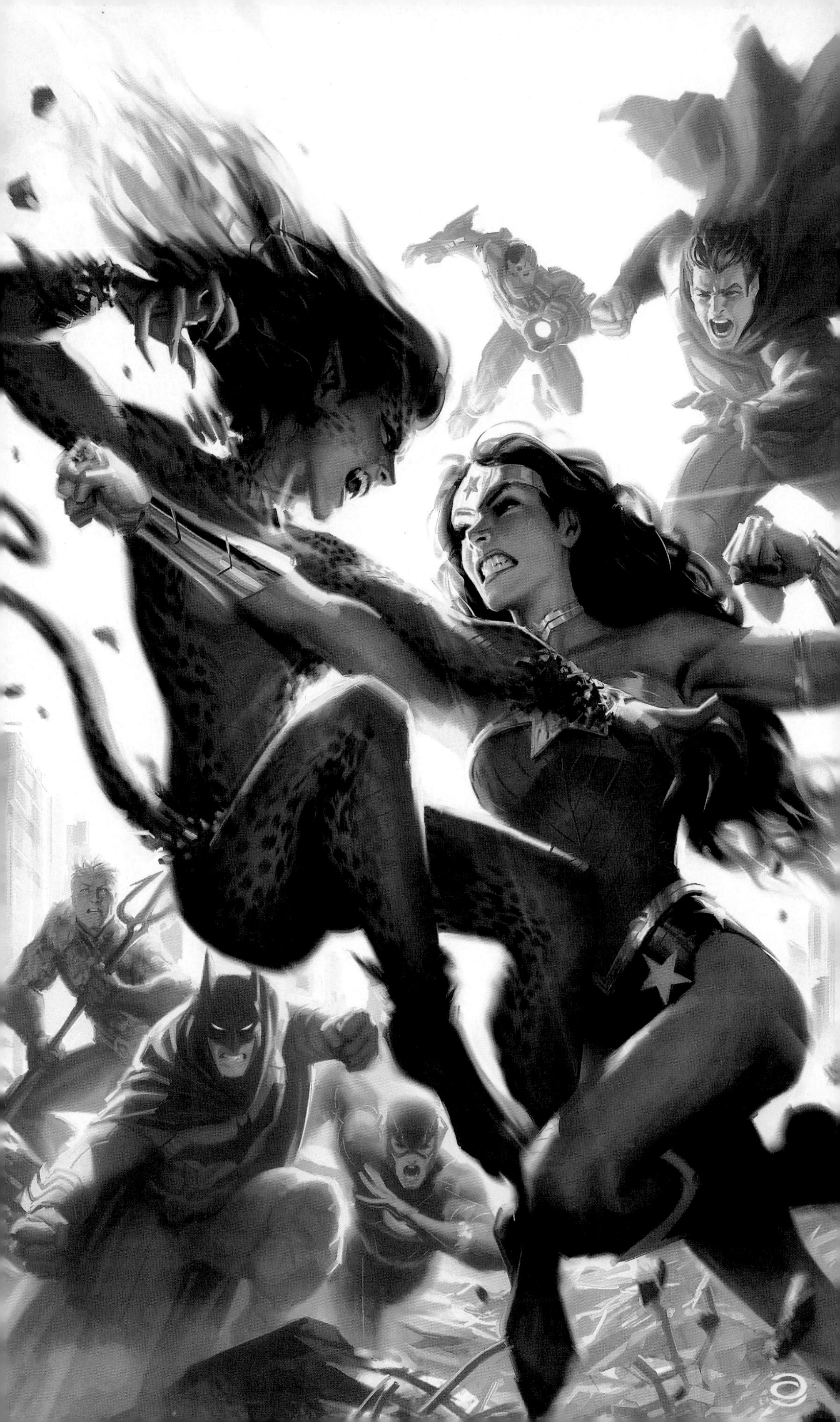

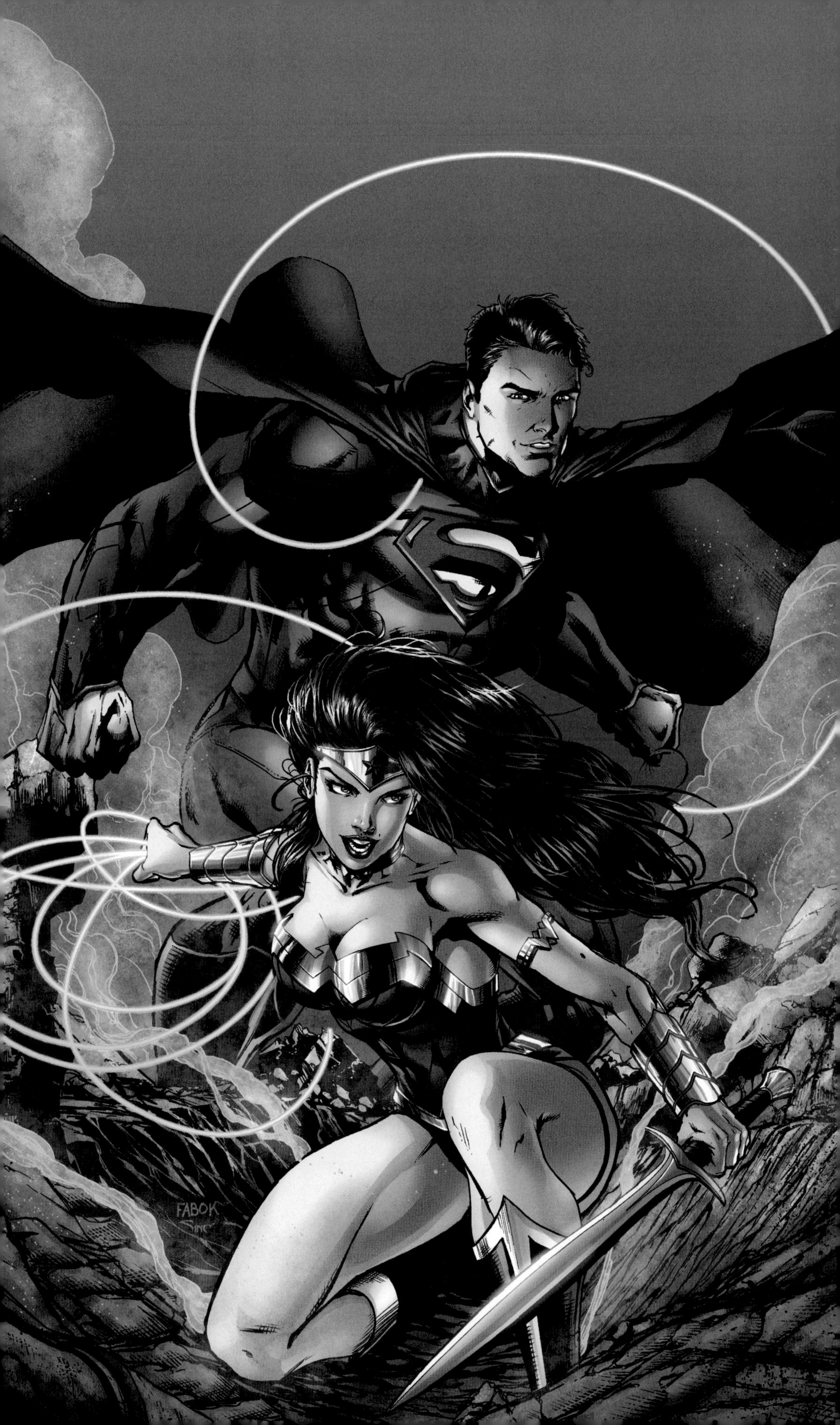
FABOK
SINC

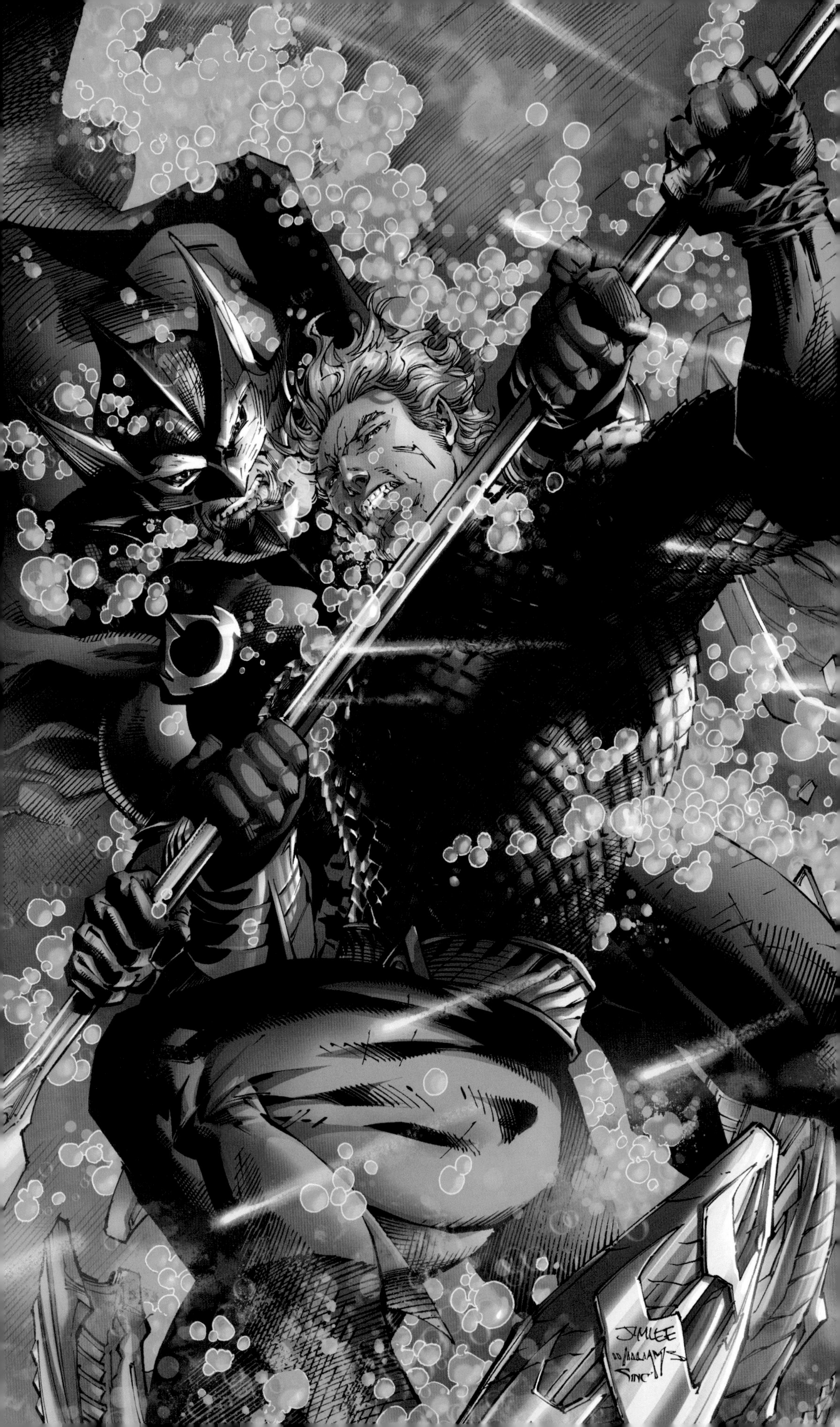
JIMLEE

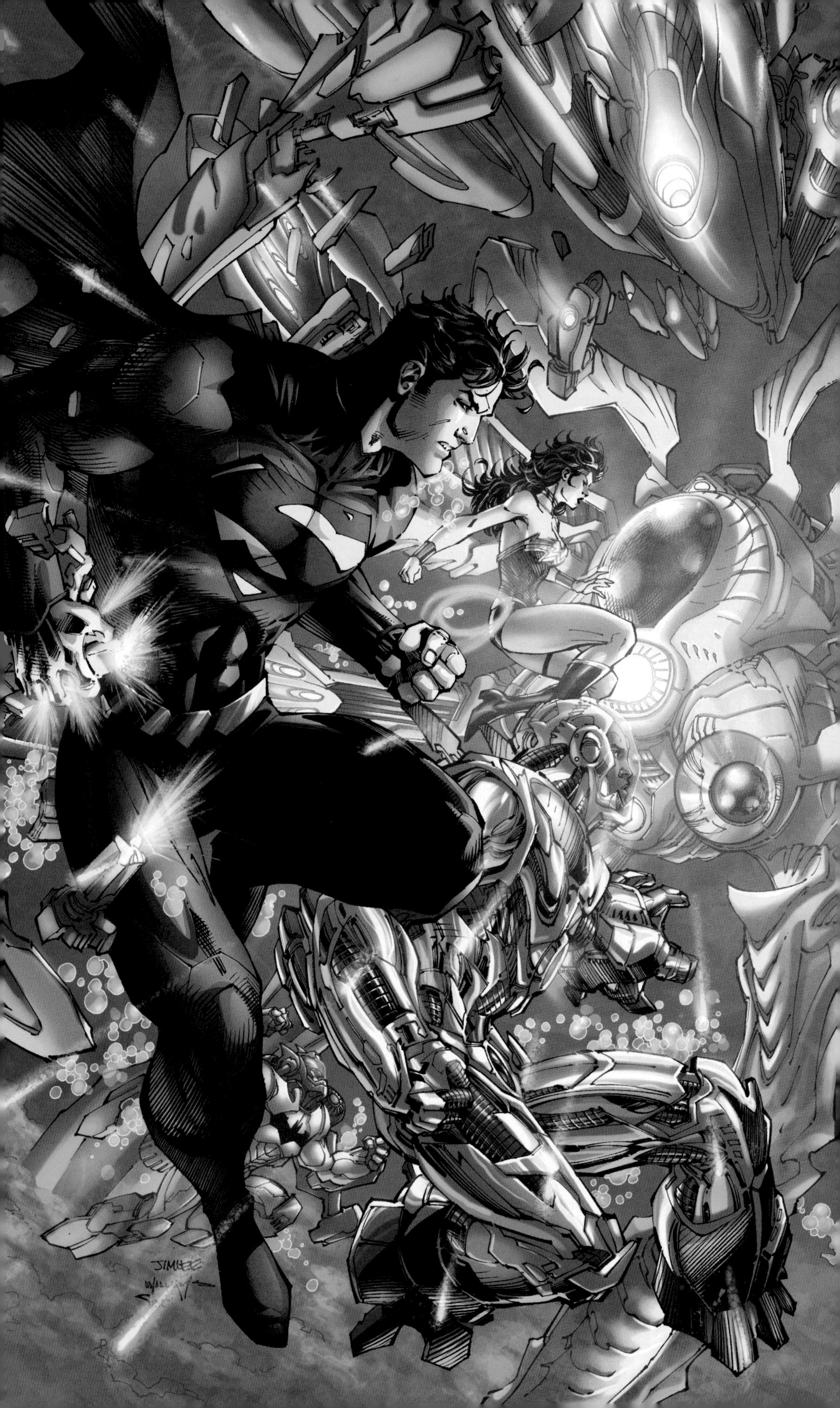

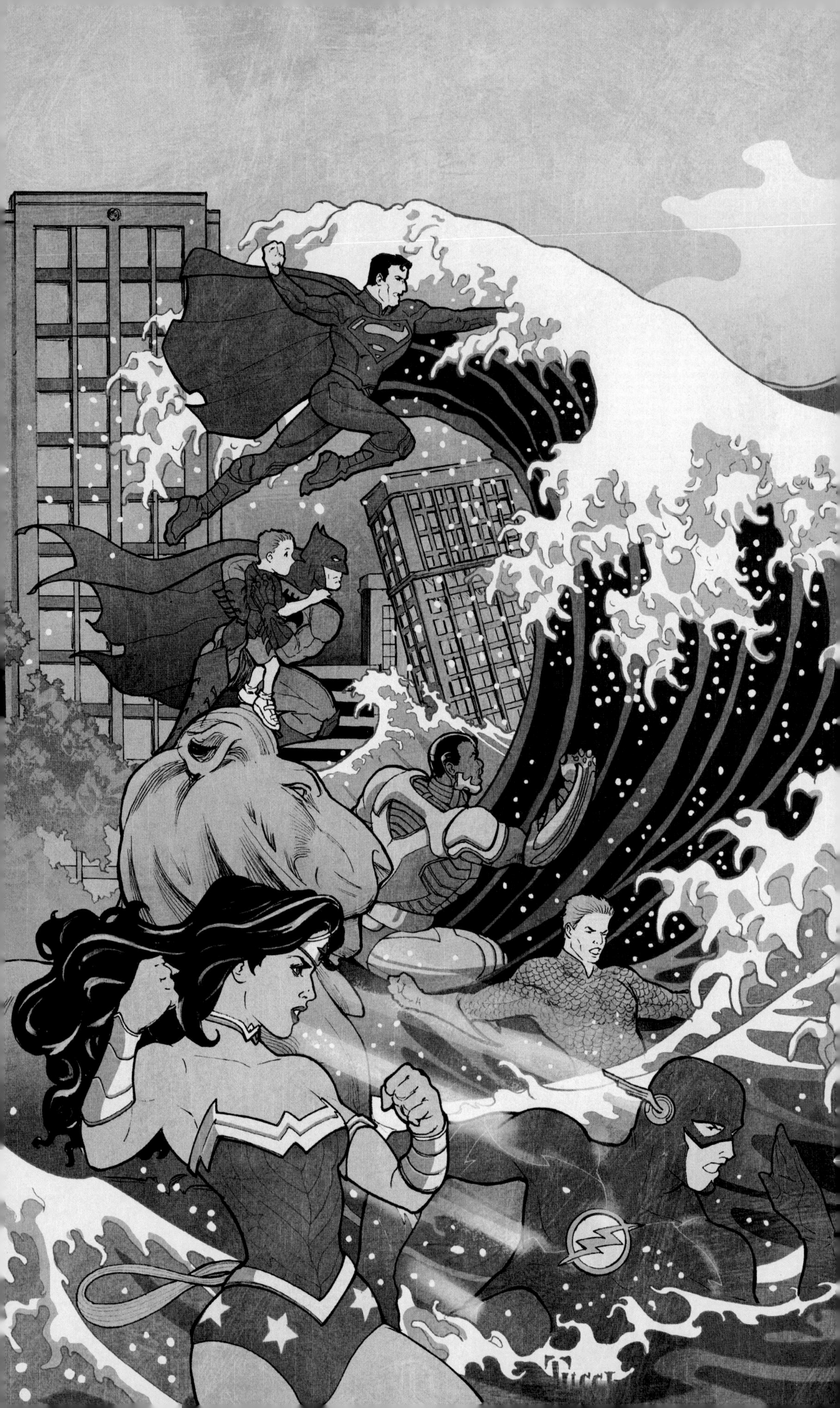

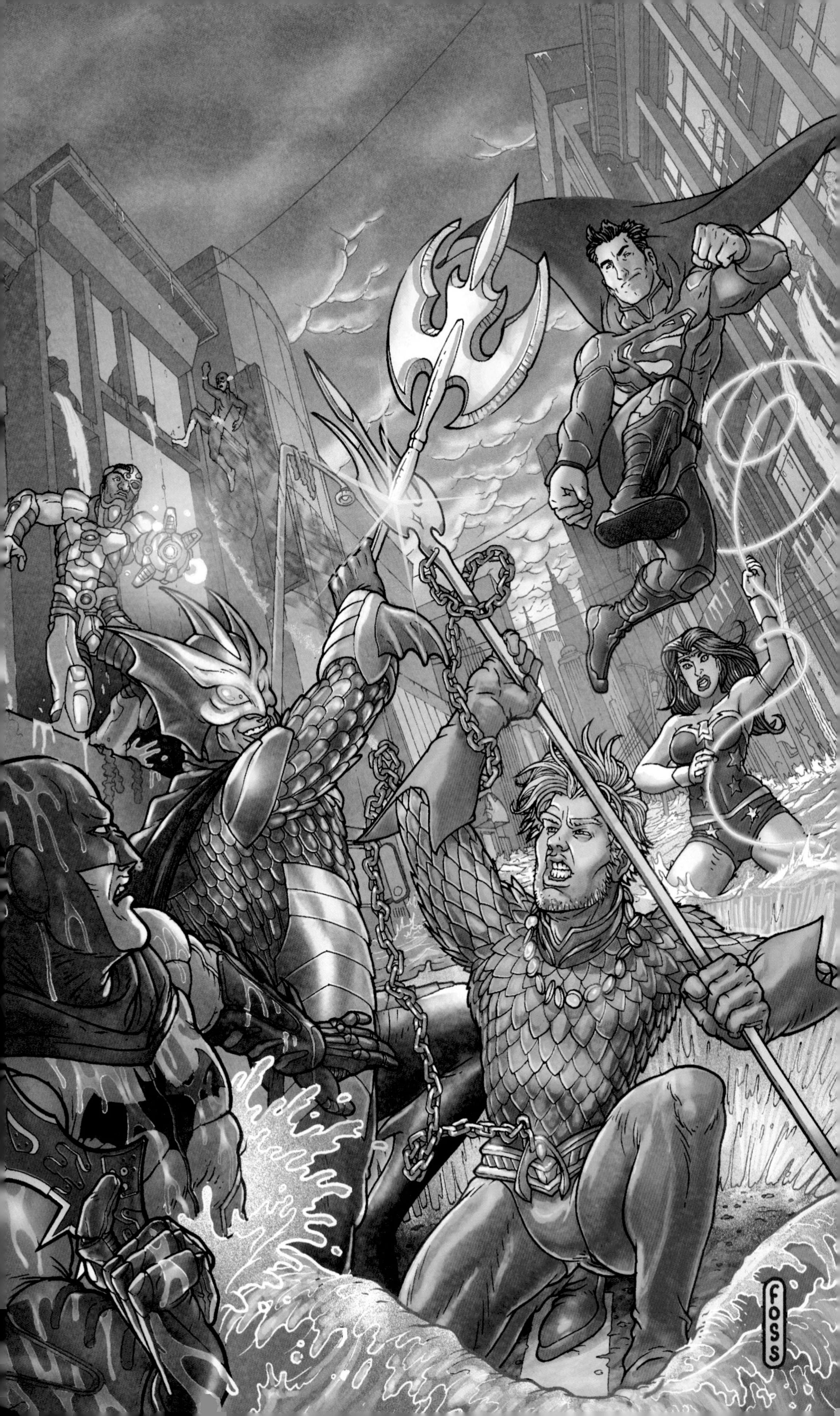
FOSS

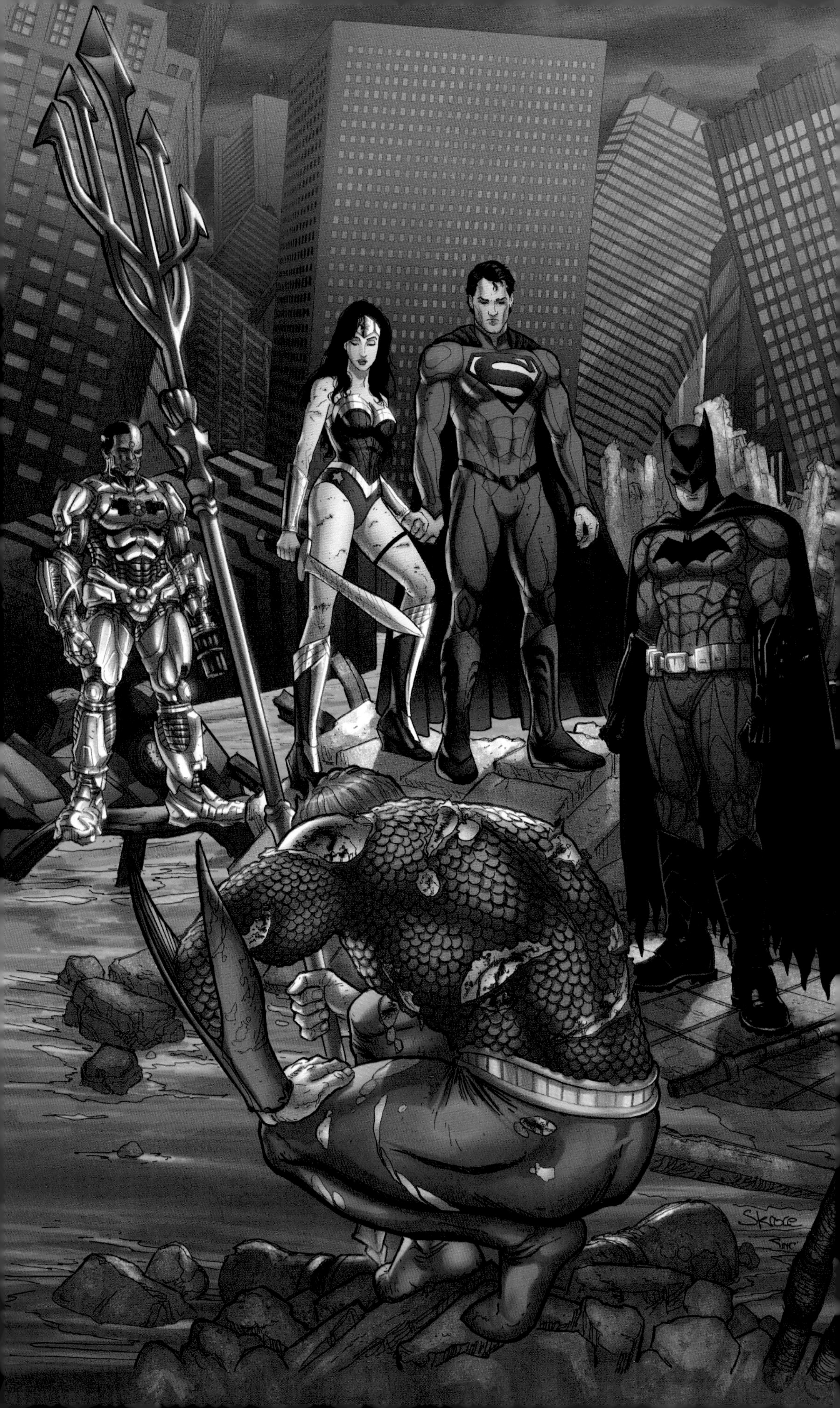

"Welcoming to new fans looking to get into superhero comics for the first time and old fans who gave up on the funny-books long ago."
—SCRIPPS HOWARD NEWS SERVICE

START AT THE BEGINNING!

JUSTICE LEAGUE VOLUME 1: ORIGIN

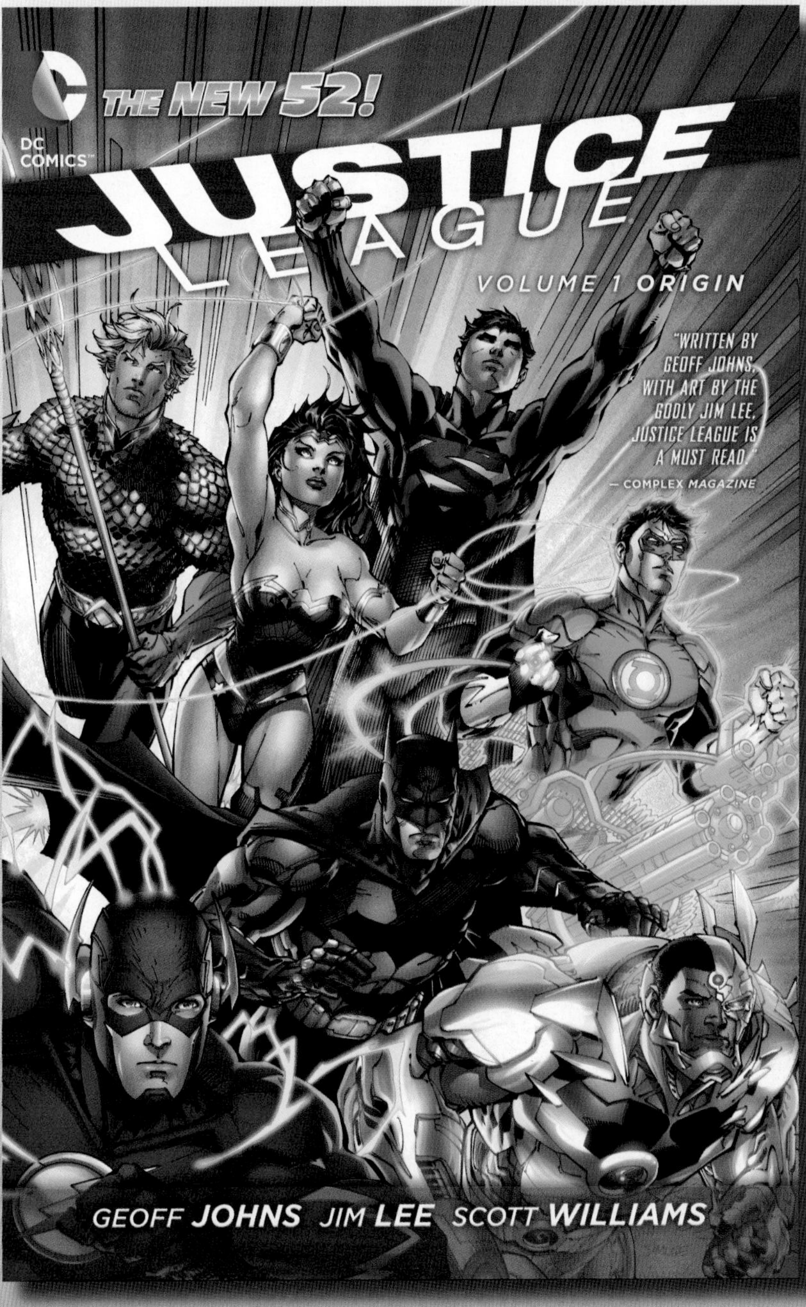
THE NEW 52!
DC COMICS
JUSTICE LEAGUE
VOLUME 1 ORIGIN
"WRITTEN BY GEOFF JOHNS, WITH ART BY THE GODLY JIM LEE, JUSTICE LEAGUE IS A MUST READ."
— COMPLEX MAGAZINE
GEOFF JOHNS JIM LEE SCOTT WILLIAMS

AQUAMAN VOLUME 1: THE TRENCH

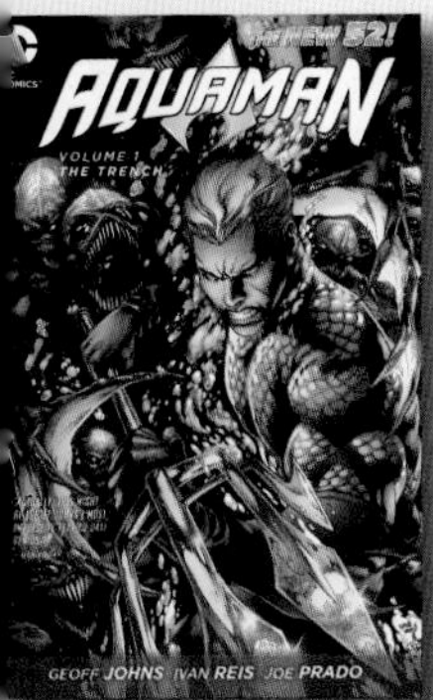
THE NEW 52!
AQUAMAN
VOLUME 1 THE TRENCH
GEOFF JOHNS IVAN REIS JOE PRADO

THE SAVAGE HAWKMAN VOLUME 1: DARKNESS RISING

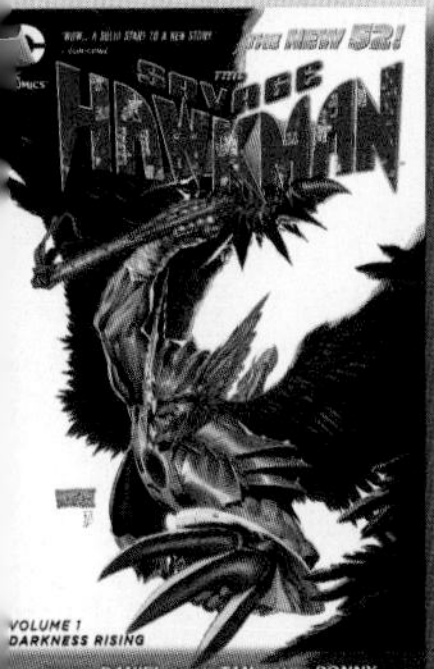
THE NEW 52!
THE SAVAGE HAWKMAN
VOLUME 1 DARKNESS RISING
TONY S. DANIEL PHILIP TAN JAMES BONNY

GREEN ARROW VOLUME 1: THE MIDAS TOUCH

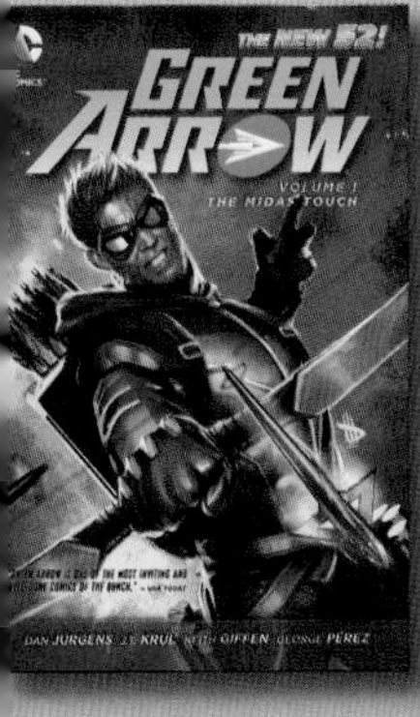
THE NEW 52!
GREEN ARROW
VOLUME 1 THE MIDAS TOUCH

DC COMICS™

START AT THE BEGINNING

WONDER WOMAN
VOLUME 1: BLOOD

**MR. TERRIFIC
VOLUME 1:
MIND GAMES**

**BLUE BEETLE
VOLUME 1:
METAMORPHOSIS**

**THE FURY OF FIRESTORM:
THE NUCLEAR MEN
VOLUME 1:
GOD PARTICLE**

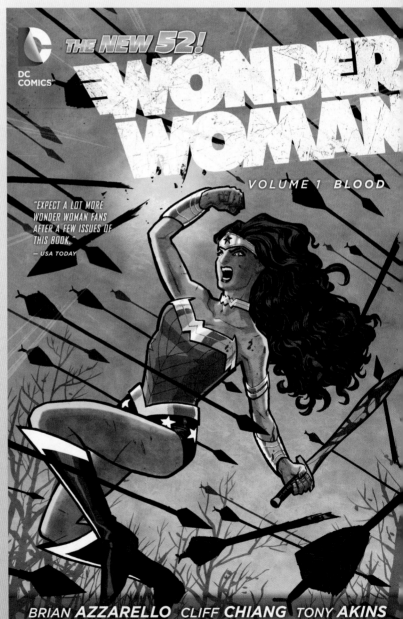

BRIAN **AZZARELLO** CLIFF **CHIANG** TONY **AKINS**

MICS™

START AT THE BEGINNING!

GREEN LANTERN
VOLUME 1: SINESTRO

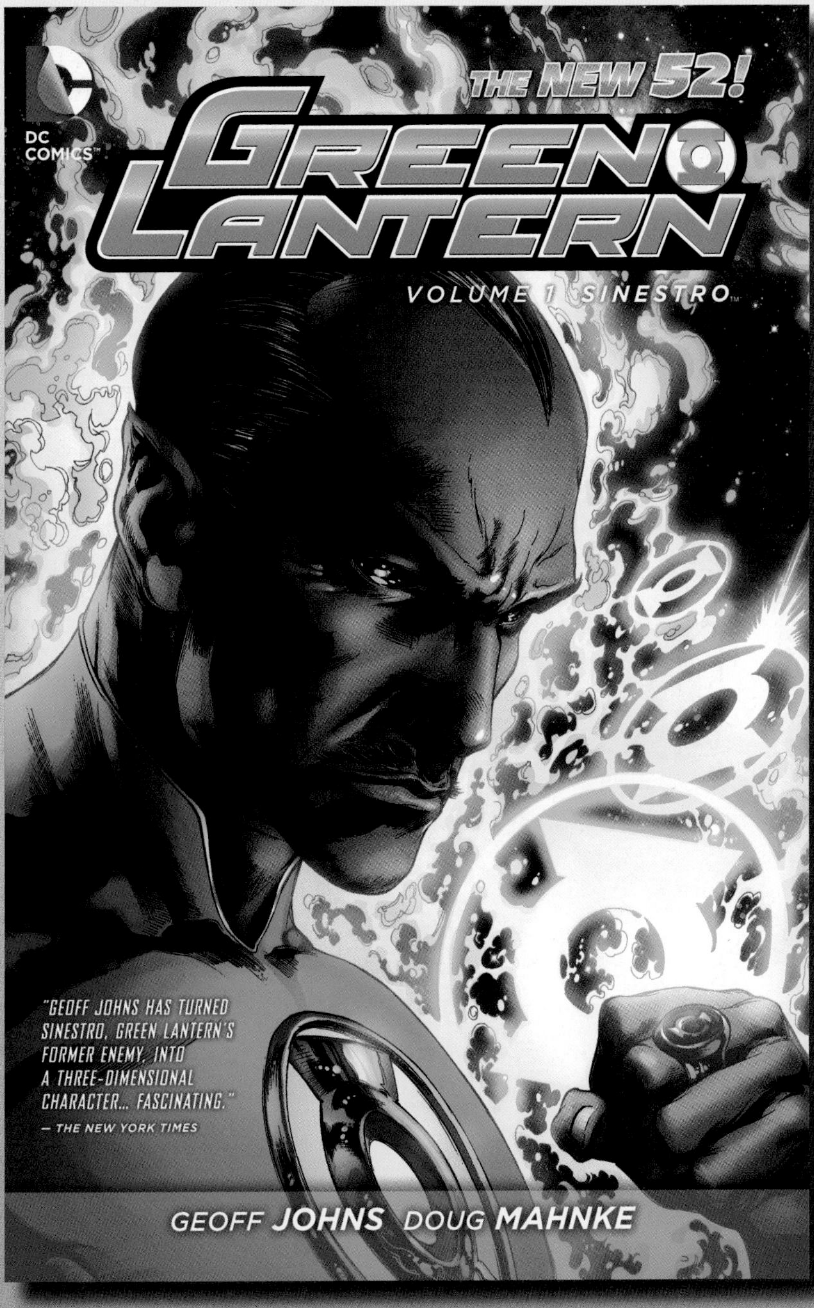

GREEN LANTERN CORPS VOLUME 1: FEARSOME

RED LANTERNS VOLUME 1: BLOOD AND RAGE

GREEN LANTERN: NEW GUARDIANS VOLUME 1: THE RING BEARER

THE NEW 52!

DC COMICS™

GREEN LANTERN

VOLUME 1: SINESTRO™

"GEOFF JOHNS HAS TURNED SINESTRO, GREEN LANTERN'S FORMER ENEMY, INTO A THREE-DIMENSIONAL CHARACTER... FASCINATING."
— THE NEW YORK TIMES

GEOFF JOHNS · DOUG MAHNKE

*"Flash fans should breathe a sig
of relief that the character is 100
definitely in the right hands*
—MTV GEE

START AT THE BEGINNING
THE FLAS
VOLUME 1: MOVE FORWARD

JUSTICE LEAGUE
INTERNATIONAL
VOLUME 1: THE
SIGNAL MASTERS

O.M.A.C.
VOLUME 1:
OMACTIVATE!

CAPTAIN ATOM
VOLUME 1:
EVOLUTION

FRANCIS **MANAPUL** BRIAN **BUCCELLATO**